MW00849817

THE SUBTLE ART OF
NOT GIVING A FUCK

The Subtle Art of Not Giving a Fuck

A Counterintuitive Approach to Living a Good Life

MARK MANSON

HARPER

An Imprint of HarperCollinsPublishers

HarperCollins books may be purchased for educational, business, or sales promotional use. For information, please email the Special Markets Department at SPsales@harpercollins.com.

First HarperOne hardcover published 2016.

FIRST EDITION

Designed by Joan Olson

Library of Congress Cataloging-in-Publication Data has been applied for.

ISBN 978–0–06–245771–4

23 24 25 26 27 LBC 76 75 74 73 72

Contents

Contents vii

THE SUBTLE ART OF NOT GIVING A FUCK

Don't Try

Charles Bukowski was an alcoholic, a womanizer, a chronic gambler, a lout, a cheapskate, a deadbeat, and on his worst days, a poet. He's probably the last person on earth you would ever look to for life advice or expect to see in any sort of self-help book.

Which is why he's the perfect place to start.

Bukowski wanted to be a writer. But for decades his work was rejected by almost every magazine, newspaper, journal, agent, and publisher he submitted to. His work was horrible, they said. Crude. Disgusting. Depraved. And as the stacks of rejection slips piled up, the weight of his failures pushed him deep into an alcohol-fueled depression that would follow him for most of his life.

Bukowski had a day job as a letter-filer at a post office. He got paid shit money and spent most of it on booze. He gambled away the rest at the racetrack. At night, he would drink alone and sometimes hammer out poetry on his beat-up old typewriter. Often, he'd wake up on the floor, having passed out the night before.

Thirty years went by like this, most of it a meaningless blur of alcohol, drugs, gambling, and prostitutes. Then, when Bukowski was fifty, after a lifetime of failure and self-loathing, an editor at a small independent publishing house took a strange interest in him. The editor couldn't offer Bukowski much money or much promise of sales. But he had a weird affection for the drunk loser, so he decided to take a chance on him. It was the first real shot Bukowski had ever gotten, and, he realized, probably the only one he would ever get. Bukowski wrote back to the editor: "I have one of two choices—stay in the post office and go crazy . . . or stay out here and play at writer and starve. I have decided to starve."

Upon signing the contract, Bukowski wrote his first novel in three weeks. It was called simply *Post Office.* In the dedication, he wrote, "Dedicated to nobody."

Bukowski would make it as a novelist and poet. He would go on and publish six novels and hundreds of po-ems, selling over two million copies of his books. His pop-ularity defied everyone's expectations, particularly his own.

Stories like Bukowski's are the bread and butter of our cultural narrative. Bukowski's life embodies the American Dream: a man fights for what he wants, never gives up, and eventually achieves his wildest dreams. It's practically a movie waiting to happen. We all look at stories like Bukowski's and say, "See? He never gave up. He never stopped trying. He always believed in himself. He persisted against all the odds and made something of himself!"

It is then strange that on Bukowski's tombstone, the epitaph reads: "Don't try."

See, despite the book sales and the fame, Bukowski was a loser. He knew it. And his success stemmed not from some determination to be a winner, but from the fact that he *knew* he was a loser, accepted it, and then wrote honestly about it. He never tried to be anything other than what he was. The genius in Bukowski's work was not in overcoming unbelievable odds or developing himself into a shining literary light. It was the opposite. It was his simple ability to be completely, unflinchingly honest with himself—especially the worst parts of himself—and to share his failings without hesitation or doubt.

This is the real story of Bukowski's success: his comfort with himself as a failure. Bukowski didn't give a fuck about success. Even after his fame, he still showed up to poetry readings hammered and verbally abused people in his audience. He still exposed himself in public and tried to sleep with every woman he could find. Fame and success didn't make him a better person. Nor was it by becoming a better person that he became famous and successful.

Self-improvement and success often occur together. But that doesn't necessarily mean they're the same thing.

Our culture today is obsessively focused on unrealistically positive expectations: Be happier. Be healthier. Be the best, better than the rest. Be smarter, faster, richer, sexier, more popular, more productive, more envied, and more admired. Be perfect and amazing and crap out twelve-karat-gold nuggets before breakfast each morning while kissing your selfie-ready spouse and two and a half kids goodbye. Then fly your helicopter to your wonderfully fulfilling job, where you spend your days doing incredibly meaningful work that's likely to save the planet one day.

But when you stop and really think about it, conventional life advice—all the positive and happy self-help stuff we hear all the time—is actually fixating on what you *lack*. It lasers in on *what you perceive your personal shortcomings and failures to already be,* and then emphasizes them for you. You learn about the best ways to make money *because* you feel you don't have enough money already. You stand in front of the mirror and repeat affirmations saying that you're beautiful *because* you feel as though you're not beautiful already. You follow dating and relationship advice *because* you feel that you're unlovable already. You try goofy visualization exercises about being more successful *because* you feel as though you aren't successful enough already.

Ironically, this fixation on the positive—on what's better, what's superior—only serves to remind us over and over again of what we are not, of what we lack, of what we should have been but failed to be. After all, no truly happy person feels the need to stand in front of a mirror and recite that she's happy. She just *is*.

There's a saying in Texas: "The smallest dog barks the loudest." A confident man doesn't feel a need to prove that he's confident. A rich woman doesn't feel a need to convince anybody that she's rich. Either you are or you are not. And if you're dreaming of something all the time, then you're reinforcing the same unconscious reality over and over: that you are *not that.*

Everyone and their TV commercial wants you to believe that the key to a good life is a nicer job, or a more rugged car, or a prettier girlfriend, or a hot tub with an inflatable pool for the kids. The world is constantly telling you that the path to a better life is more, more, more—buy more, own more, make more, fuck more, *be* more. You are constantly bombarded with messages to give a fuck about everything, all the time. Give a fuck about a new TV. Give a fuck about having a better vacation than your coworkers. Give a fuck about buying that new lawn ornament. Give a fuck about having the right kind of selfie stick.

Why? My guess: because giving a fuck about more stuff is good for business.

And while there's nothing wrong with good business, the problem is that giving too many fucks is bad for your mental health. It causes you to become overly attached to the superficial and fake, to dedicate your life to chasing a mirage of happiness and satisfaction. The key to a good life is not giving a fuck about more; it's giving a fuck about less, giving a fuck about only what is true and immediate and important.

The Feedback Loop from Hell

There's an insidious quirk to your brain that, if you let it, can drive you absolutely batty. Tell me if this sounds familiar to you:

You get anxious about confronting somebody in your life. That anxiety cripples you and you start wondering why you're so anxious. Now you're becoming *anxious about being anxious.* Oh no! Doubly anxious! Now you're anxious about your anxiety, which is causing *more* anxiety. Quick, where's the whiskey?

Or let's say you have an anger problem. You get pissed off at the stupidest, most inane stuff, and you have no idea why. And the fact that you get pissed off so easily starts to piss you off even more. And then, in your petty rage, you realize that being angry all the time makes you a shallow and mean person, and you hate this; you hate it so much that you get angry at yourself. Now look at you: you're angry at yourself getting angry about being angry. Fuck you, wall. Here, have a fist.

Or you're so worried about doing the right thing all the time that you become worried about how much you're worrying. Or you feel so guilty for every mistake you make that you begin to feel guilty about how guilty you're feeling. Or you get sad and alone so often that it makes you feel even more sad and alone just thinking about it.

Welcome to the Feedback Loop from Hell. Chances are you've engaged in it more than a few times. Maybe you're engaging in it right now: "God, I do the Feedback Loop all the time—I'm such a loser for doing it. I should stop. Oh my God, I feel like such a loser for calling myself a loser. I should stop calling myself a loser. Ah, fuck! I'm doing it again! See? I'm a loser! Argh!"

Calm down, amigo. Believe it or not, this is part of the

beauty of being human. Very few animals on earth have the ability to think cogent thoughts to begin with, but we humans have the luxury of being able to have thoughts *about* our thoughts. So I can think about watching Miley Cyrus videos on YouTube, and then immediately think about what a sicko I am for wanting to watch Miley Cyrus videos on YouTube. Ah, the miracle of consciousness!

Now here's the problem: Our society today, through the wonders of consumer culture and hey-look-my-life-is-cooler-than-yours social media, has bred a whole generation of people who believe that having these negative experiences—anxiety, fear, guilt, etc.—is totally not okay. I mean, if you look at your Facebook feed, everybody there is having a fucking grand old time. Look, eight people got married this week! And some sixteen-year-old on TV got a Ferrari for her birthday. And another kid just made two billion dollars inventing an app that automatically delivers you more toilet paper when you run out.

Meanwhile, you're stuck at home flossing your cat. And you can't help but think your life sucks even more than you thought.

The Feedback Loop from Hell has become a borderline epidemic, making many of us overly stressed, overly neurotic, and overly self-loathing.

Back in Grandpa's day, he would feel like shit and think to himself, "Gee whiz, I sure do feel like a cow turd today. But hey, I guess that's just life. Back to shoveling hay."

But now? Now if you feel like shit for even five minutes, you're bombarded with 350 images of people *totally happy and having amazing fucking lives,* and it's impossible to not feel like there's something wrong with you.

It's this last part that gets us into trouble. We feel bad about feeling bad. We feel guilty for feeling guilty. We get angry about getting angry. We get anxious about feeling anxious. *What is wrong with me?*

This is why not giving a fuck is so key. This is why it's going to save the world. And it's going to save it by accepting that the world is totally fucked and that's all right, because it's always been that way, and always will be.

By not giving a fuck that you feel bad, you short-circuit the Feedback Loop from Hell; you say to yourself, "I feel like shit, but who gives a fuck?" And then, as if sprinkled by magic fuck-giving fairy dust, you stop hating yourself for feeling so bad.

George Orwell said that to see what's in front of one's nose requires a constant struggle. Well, the solution to our stress and anxiety is right there in front of our noses, and we're too busy watching porn and advertisements for ab machines that don't work, wondering why we're not banging a hot blonde with a rocking six-pack, to notice.

We joke online about "first-world problems," but we really have become victims of our own success. Stress-related health issues, anxiety disorders, and cases of depression have skyrocketed over the past thirty years, despite the fact that everyone has a flat-screen TV and can have their groceries delivered. Our crisis is no longer material; it's existential, it's spiritual. We have so much fucking stuff and so many opportunities that we don't even know what to give a fuck about anymore.

Because there's an infinite amount of things we can now see or know, there are also an infinite number of ways we can discover that we don't measure up, that we're not good enough, that things aren't as great as they could be. And this rips us apart inside.

Because here's the thing that's wrong with all of the "How to Be Happy" shit that's been shared eight million times on Facebook in the past few years—here's what nobody realizes about all of this crap:

> **The desire for more positive experience is itself a negative experience. And, paradoxically, the acceptance of one's negative experience is itself a positive experience.**

This is a total mind-fuck. So I'll give you a minute to unpretzel your brain and maybe read that again: *Wanting positive experience is a negative experience; accepting negative experience is a positive experience.* It's what the philosopher Alan Watts used to refer to as "the backwards law"—the idea that the more you pursue feeling better all the time, the less satisfied you become, as pursuing something only reinforces the fact that you lack it in the first place. The more you desperately want to be rich, the more poor and unworthy you feel, regardless of how much money you actually make. The more you desperately want to be sexy and desired, the uglier you come to see yourself, regardless of your actual physical appearance. The more you desperately want to be happy and loved, the lonelier and more afraid you become, regardless of those who surround you. The more you want to be spiritually enlightened, the more self-centered and shallow you become in trying to get there.

It's like this one time I tripped on acid and it felt like the more I walked toward a house, the farther away the house got from me. And yes, I just used my LSD hallucinations to make a philosophical point about happiness. No fucks given.

As the existential philosopher Albert Camus said (and I'm pretty sure he wasn't on LSD at the time): "You will never be happy if you continue to search for what happiness consists of. You will never live if you are looking for the meaning of life."

Or put more simply:

Don't try.

Now, I know what you're saying: "Mark, this is making my nipples all hard, but what about the Camaro I've been saving up for? What about the beach body I've been starving myself for? After all, I paid a lot of money for that ab machine! What about the big house on the lake I've been dreaming of? If I stop giving a fuck about those things— well, then I'll never achieve *anything*. I don't want that to happen, do I?"

So glad you asked.

Ever notice that sometimes when you care *less* about something, you do better at it? Notice how it's often the person who is the least invested in the success of something that actually ends up achieving it? Notice how sometimes when you stop giving a fuck, everything seems to fall into place?

What's with that?

What's interesting about the backwards law is that it's called "backwards" for a reason: not giving a fuck works in reverse. If pursuing the positive *is* a negative, then pursuing the negative generates the positive. The pain you pursue in the gym results in better all-around health and energy. The failures in business are what lead to a better understanding of what's necessary to be successful. Being open with your insecurities paradoxically makes you more confident and charismatic around others. The pain of honest confrontation is what generates the greatest trust and respect in your relationships. Suffering through your fears and anxieties is what allows you to build courage and perseverance.

Seriously, I could keep going, but you get the point. *Everything worthwhile in life is won through surmounting the associated negative experience.* Any attempt to escape the negative, to avoid it or quash it or silence it, only backfires. The avoidance of suffering *is* a form of suffering. The avoidance of struggle *is* a struggle. The denial of failure *is* a failure. Hiding what is shameful *is* itself a form of shame.

Pain is an inextricable thread in the fabric of life, and to tear it out is not only impossible, but destructive: attempting to tear it out unravels everything else with it. To try to avoid pain is to give too many fucks about pain. In contrast, if you're able to not give a fuck about the pain, you become unstoppable.

In my life, I have given a fuck about many things. I have also *not* given a fuck about many things. And like the road not taken, it was the fucks not given that made all the difference.

Chances are you know somebody in your life who, at one time or another, did not give a fuck and then went on to accomplish amazing feats. Perhaps there was a time in your own life when you simply did not give a fuck and excelled to some extraordinary height. For myself, quitting my day job in finance after only six weeks to start an Internet business ranks pretty high up there in my own "didn't give a fuck" hall of fame. Same with deciding to sell most of my possessions and move to South America. Fucks given? None. Just went and did it.

These moments of non-fuckery are the moments that most define our lives. The major switch in careers; the spontaneous choice to drop out of college and join a rock band; the decision to finally dump that deadbeat boyfriend whom you caught wearing your pantyhose a few too many times.

To not give a fuck is to stare down life's most terrifying and difficult challenges and still take action.

While not giving a fuck may seem simple on the surface, it's a whole new bag of burritos under the hood. I don't even know what that sentence means, but I don't give a fuck. A bag of burritos sounds awesome, so let's just go with it.

Most of us struggle throughout our lives by giving too many fucks in situations where fucks do not deserve to be given. We give too many fucks about the rude gas station attendant who gave us our change in nickels. We give too many fucks when a show we liked was canceled on TV. We give too many fucks when our coworkers don't bother asking us about our awesome weekend.

Meanwhile, our credit cards are maxed out, our dog hates us, and Junior is snorting meth in the bathroom, yet we're getting pissed off about nickels and *Everybody Loves Raymond*.

Look, this is how it works. You're going to die one day. I know that's kind of obvious, but I just wanted to remind you in case you'd forgotten. You and everyone you know are going to be dead soon. And in the short amount of time between here and there, you have a limited amount of fucks to give. Very few, in fact. And if you go around giving a fuck about everything and everyone without conscious thought or choice—well, then you're going to get fucked.

There is a subtle art to not giving a fuck. And though the concept may sound ridiculous and I may sound like an asshole, what I'm talking about here is essentially learning how to focus and prioritize your thoughts effectively—how to pick and choose what matters to you and what does not matter to you based on finely honed personal values. This is incredibly difficult. It takes a lifetime of practice and discipline to achieve. And you will regularly fail. But it is perhaps the most worthy struggle one can undertake in one's life. It is perhaps the *only* struggle in one's life.

Because when you give too many fucks—when you give a fuck about everyone and everything—you will feel that you're perpetually entitled to be comfortable and happy at all times, that everything is supposed to be just exactly the fucking way *you* want it to be. This is a sickness. And it will eat you alive. You will see every adversity as an injustice, every challenge as a failure, every inconvenience as a personal slight, every disagreement as a betrayal. You will be confined to your own petty, skull-sized hell, burning with entitlement and bluster, running circles around your very own personal Feedback Loop from Hell, in constant motion yet arriving nowhere.

The Subtle Art of Not Giving a Fuck

When most people envision giving no fucks whatsoever, they imagine a kind of serene indifference to everything, a calm that weathers all storms. They imagine and aspire to be a person who is shaken by nothing and caves in to no one.

There's a name for a person who finds no emotion or meaning in anything: a psychopath. Why you would want to emulate a psychopath, I have no fucking clue.

So what *does* not giving a fuck mean? Let's look at three "subtleties" that should help clarify the matter.

> *Subtlety #1: Not giving a fuck does not mean being indifferent; it means being comfortable with being different.*

Let's be clear. There's absolutely nothing admirable or confident about indifference. People who are indifferent are lame and scared. They're couch potatoes and Internet trolls. In fact, indifferent people often attempt to be indifferent because in reality they give way too many fucks. They give a fuck about what everyone thinks of their hair, so they never bother washing or combing it. They give a fuck about what everyone thinks of their ideas, so they hide behind sarcasm and self-righteous snark. They're afraid to let anyone get close to them, so they imagine themselves as some special, unique snowflake who has problems that nobody else would ever understand.

Indifferent people are afraid of the world and the repercussions of their own choices. That's why they don't make any meaningful choices. They hide in a gray, emotionless pit of their own making, self-absorbed and self-pitying, perpetually distracting themselves from this unfortunate thing demanding their time and energy called life.

Because here's a sneaky truth about life. There's no such thing as not giving a fuck. *You must give a fuck about something.* It's part of our biology to always care about something and therefore to always give a fuck.

The question, then, is, *What* do we give a fuck about? What are we *choosing* to give a fuck about? And how can we not give a fuck about what ultimately does not matter?

My mother was recently screwed out of a large chunk of money by a close friend of hers. Had I been indifferent, I would have shrugged my shoulders, sipped my mocha, and downloaded another season of *The Wire*. Sorry, Mom.

But instead, I was indignant. I was pissed off. I said, "No, screw that, Mom. We're going to lawyer the fuck up and go after this asshole. Why? Because I don't give a fuck. I will ruin this guy's life if I have to."

This illustrates the first subtlety of not giving a fuck. When we say, "Damn, watch out, Mark Manson just don't give a fuck," we don't mean that Mark Manson doesn't care about *anything;* on the contrary, we mean that Mark Manson doesn't care about adversity in the face of his goals, he doesn't care about pissing some people off to do what he feels is right or important or noble. We mean that Mark Manson is the type of guy who would write about himself in third person just because he thought it was the right thing to do. He just doesn't give a fuck.

This is what is so admirable. No, not me, dumbass—the overcoming adversity stuff, the willingness to be different, an outcast, a pariah, all for the sake of one's own values. The willingness to stare failure in the face and shove your middle finger back at it. The people who don't give a fuck about adversity or failure or embarrassing themselves or shitting the bed a few times. The people who just laugh and then do what they believe in anyway. Because they know it's right. They know it's more important than they are, more important than their own feelings and their own pride and their own ego. They say, "Fuck it," not to everything in life, but rather to everything *unimportant* in life. They reserve their fucks for what truly matters. Friends. Family. Purpose. Burritos. And an occasional lawsuit or two. And because of that, because they reserve their fucks for only the big things that matter, people give a fuck about them in return.

Because here's another sneaky little truth about life. You can't be an important and life-changing presence for some people without also being a joke and an embarrassment to others. You just can't. Because there's no such thing as a lack of adversity. It doesn't exist. The old saying goes that no matter where you go, there you are. Well, the same is true for adversity and failure. No matter where you go, there's a five-hundred-pound load of shit waiting for you. And that's perfectly fine. The point isn't to get away from the shit. The point is to find the shit you enjoy dealing with.

Subtlety #2: To not give a fuck about adversity, you must first give a fuck about something more important than adversity.

Imagine you're at a grocery store, and you watch an elderly lady scream at the cashier, berating him for not accepting her thirty-cent coupon. Why does this lady give a fuck? It's just thirty cents.

I'll tell you why: That lady probably doesn't have anything better to do with her days than to sit at home cutting out coupons. She's old and lonely. Her kids are dickheads and never visit. She hasn't had sex in over thirty years. She can't fart without extreme lower-back pain. Her pension is on its last legs, and she's probably going to die in a diaper thinking she's in Candy Land.

So she snips coupons. That's all she's got. It's her and her damn coupons. It's all she can give a fuck about because there *is* nothing else to give a fuck about. And so when that pimply-faced seventeen-year-old cashier refuses to accept one of them, when he defends his cash register's purity the way knights used to defend maidens' virginity, you can bet Granny is going to erupt. Eighty years of fucks will rain down all at once, like a fiery hailstorm of "Back in my day" and "People used to show more respect" stories.

The problem with people who hand out fucks like ice cream at a goddamn summer camp is that they don't have anything more fuck-worthy to dedicate their fucks to.

If you find yourself consistently giving too many fucks about trivial shit that bothers you—your ex-boyfriend's new Facebook picture, how quickly the batteries die in the TV remote, missing out on yet another two-for-one sale on hand sanitizer—chances are you don't have much going on in your life to give a legitimate fuck about. And that's your real problem. Not the hand sanitizer. Not the TV remote.

I once heard an artist say that when a person has no problems, the mind automatically finds a way to invent some. I think what most people—especially educated, pampered middle-class white people—consider "life problems" are really just side effects of not having anything more important to worry about.

It then follows that finding something important and meaningful in your life is perhaps the most productive use of your time and energy. Because if you don't find that meaningful something, your fucks will be given to meaningless and frivolous causes.

Subtlety #3: Whether you realize it or not, you are always choosing what to give a fuck about.

People aren't just born not giving a fuck. In fact, we're born giving way too many fucks. Ever watch a kid cry his eyes out because his hat is the wrong shade of blue? Exactly. Fuck that kid.

When we're young, everything is new and exciting, and everything seems to matter so much. Therefore, we give tons of fucks. We give a fuck about everything and everyone—about what people are saying about us, about whether that cute boy/girl called us back or not, about whether our socks match or not, or what color our birthday balloon is.

As we get older, with the benefit of experience (and having seen so much time slip by), we begin to notice that most of these sorts of things have little lasting impact on our lives. Those people whose opinions we cared about so much before are no longer present in our lives. Rejections that were painful in the moment have actually worked out for the best. We realize how little attention people pay to the superficial details about us, and we choose not to obsess so much over them.

Essentially, we become more selective about the fucks we're willing to give. This is something called maturity. It's nice; you should try it sometime. Maturity is what happens when one learns to only give a fuck about what's truly fuck-worthy. As Bunk Moreland said to his partner Detective McNulty in *The Wire* (which, fuck you, I still downloaded): "That's what you get for giving a fuck when it wasn't your turn to give a fuck."

Then, as we grow older and enter middle age, something else begins to change. Our energy level drops. Our identity solidifies. We know who we are and we accept ourselves, including some of the parts we aren't thrilled about.

And, in a strange way, this is liberating. We no longer need to give a fuck about everything. Life is just what it is. We accept it, warts and all. We realize that we're never going to cure cancer or go to the moon or feel Jennifer Aniston's tits. And that's okay. Life goes on. We now reserve our ever-dwindling fucks for the most truly fuck-worthy parts of our lives: our families, our best friends, our golf swing. And, to our astonishment, *this is enough*. This simplification actually makes us really fucking happy on a consistent basis. And we start to think, Maybe that crazy alcoholic Bukowski was onto something. *Don't try.*

So Mark, What the Fuck Is the Point of This Book Anyway?

This book will help you think a little bit more clearly about what you're choosing to find important in life and what you're choosing to find unimportant.

I believe that today we're facing a psychological epidemic, one in which people no longer realize it's okay for things to suck sometimes. I know that sounds intellectually lazy on the surface, but I promise you, it's a life/death sort of issue.

Because when we believe that it's not okay for things to suck sometimes, then we unconsciously start blaming ourselves. We start to feel as though something is inherently wrong with us, which drives us to all sorts of overcompensation, like buying forty pairs of shoes or downing Xanax with a vodka chaser on a Tuesday night or shooting up a school bus full of kids.

This belief that it's not okay to be inadequate sometimes is the source of the growing Feedback Loop from Hell that is coming to dominate our culture.

The idea of not giving a fuck is a simple way of reorienting our expectations for life and choosing what is important and what is not. Developing this ability leads to something I like to think of as a kind of "practical enlightenment."

No, not that airy-fairy, eternal bliss, end-of-all-suffering, bullshitty kind of enlightenment. On the contrary, I see practical enlightenment as becoming comfortable with the idea that some suffering is always inevitable—that no matter what you do, life is comprised of failures, loss, regrets, and even death. Because once you become comfortable with all the shit that life throws at you (and it will throw a lot of shit, trust me), you become invincible in a sort of low-level spiritual way. After all, the only way to overcome pain is to first learn how to bear it.

This book doesn't give a fuck about alleviating your problems or your pain. And that is precisely why you will know it's being honest. This book is not some guide to greatness—it couldn't be, because greatness is merely an illusion in our minds, a made-up destination that we obligate ourselves to pursue, our own psychological Atlantis.

Instead, this book will turn your pain into a tool, your trauma into power, and your problems into slightly better problems. That is real progress. Think of it as a guide to suffering and how to do it better, more meaningfully, with more compassion and more humility. It's a book about moving lightly despite your heavy burdens, resting easier with your greatest fears, laughing at your tears as you cry them.

This book will not teach you how to gain or achieve, but rather how to lose and let go. It will teach you to take inventory of your life and scrub out all but the most important items. It will teach you to close your eyes and trust that you can fall backwards and still be okay. It will teach you to give fewer fucks. It will teach you to not try.

Happiness Is a Problem

About twenty-five hundred years ago, in the Himalayan foothills of present-day Nepal, there lived in a great palace a king who was going to have a son. For this son the king had a particularly grand idea: he would make the child's life perfect. The child would never know a moment of suffering—every need, every desire, would be accounted for at all times.

The king built high walls around the palace that prevented the prince from knowing the outside world. He spoiled the child, lavishing him with food and gifts, surrounding him with servants who catered to his every whim. And just as planned, the child grew up ignorant of the routine cruelties of human existence.

All of the prince's childhood went on like this. But despite the endless luxury and opulence, the prince became kind of a pissed-off young man. Soon, every experience felt empty and valueless. The problem was that no matter what his father gave him, it never seemed enough, never *meant* anything.

So late one night, the prince snuck out of the palace to see what was beyond its walls. He had a servant drive him through the local village, and what he saw horrified him.

For the first time in his life, the prince saw human suffering. He saw sick people, old people, homeless people, people in pain, even people dying.

The prince returned to the palace and found himself in a sort of existential crisis. Not knowing how to process what he'd seen, he got all emo about everything and complained a lot. And, as is so typical of young men, the prince ended up blaming his father for the very things his father had tried to do for him. It was the riches, the prince thought, that had made him so miserable, that had made life seem so meaningless. He decided to run away.

But the prince was more like his father than he knew. He had grand ideas too. He wouldn't just run away; he would give up his royalty, his family, and all of his possessions and live in the streets, sleeping in dirt like an animal. There he would starve himself, torture himself, and beg for scraps of food from strangers for the rest of his life.

The next night, the prince snuck out of the palace again, this time never to return. For years he lived as a bum, a discarded and forgotten remnant of society, the dog shit caked to the bottom of the social totem pole. And as planned, the prince suffered greatly. He suffered through disease, hunger, pain, loneliness, and decay. He confronted the brink of death itself, often limited to eating a single nut each day.

A few years went by. Then a few more. And then . . . nothing happened. The prince began to notice that this life of suffering wasn't all that it was cracked up to be. It wasn't bringing him the insight he had desired. It wasn't revealing any deeper mystery of the world or its ultimate purpose.

In fact, the prince came to know what the rest of us have always kind of known: that suffering totally sucks. And it's not necessarily that meaningful either. As with being rich, there is no value in suffering when it's done without purpose. And soon the prince came to the conclusion that his grand idea, like his father's, was in fact a fucking terrible idea and he should probably go do something else instead.

Totally confused, the prince cleaned himself up and went and found a big tree near a river. He decided that he would sit under that tree and not get up until he came up with another grand idea.

As the legend goes, the confused prince sat under that tree for forty-nine days. We won't delve into the biological viability of sitting in the same spot for forty-nine days, but let's just say that in that time the prince came to a number of profound realizations.

One of those realizations was this: that life itself is a form of suffering. The rich suffer because of their riches. The poor suffer because of their poverty. People without a family suffer because they have no family. People with a family suffer because of their family. People who pursue worldly pleasures suffer because of their worldly pleasures.

People who abstain from worldly pleasures suffer because of their abstention.

This isn't to say that all suffering is equal. Some suffering is certainly more painful than other suffering. But we all must suffer nonetheless.

Years later, the prince would build his own philosophy and share it with the world, and this would be its first and central tenet: that pain and loss are inevitable and we should let go of trying to resist them. The prince would later become known as the Buddha. And in case you haven't heard of him, he was kind of a big deal.

There is a premise that underlies a lot of our assumptions and beliefs. The premise is that happiness is algorithmic, that it can be worked for and earned and achieved as if it were getting accepted to law school or building a really complicated Lego set. If I achieve X, then I can be happy. If I look like Y, then I can be happy. If I can be with a person like Z, then I can be happy.

This premise, though, *is the problem.* Happiness is not a solvable equation. Dissatisfaction and unease are inherent parts of human nature and, as we'll see, necessary components to creating consistent happiness. The Buddha argued this from a theological and philosophical perspective. I will make the same argument in this chapter, but I will make it from a biological perspective, and with pandas.

The Misadventures of Disappointment Panda

If I could invent a superhero, I would invent one called Disappointment Panda. He'd wear a cheesy eye mask and a shirt (with a giant capital T on it) that was way too small for his big panda belly, and his superpower would be to tell people harsh truths about themselves that they needed to hear but didn't want to accept.

He would go door-to-door like a Bible salesman and ring doorbells and say things like, "Sure, making a lot of money makes you feel good, but it won't make your kids love you," or "If you have to ask yourself if you trust your wife, then you probably don't," or "What you consider 'friendship' is really just your constant attempts to impress people." Then he'd tell the homeowner to have a nice day and saunter on down to the next house.

It would be awesome. And sick. And sad. And uplifting. And necessary. After all, the greatest truths in life are usually the most unpleasant to hear.

Disappointment Panda would be the hero that none of us would want but all of us would need. He'd be the proverbial vegetables to our mental diet of junk food. He'd make our lives better despite making us feel worse. He'd make us stronger by tearing us down, brighten our future by showing us the darkness. Listening to him would be like watching a movie where the hero dies in the end: you love it even more despite making you feel horrible, because it feels real.

So while we're here, allow me to put on my Disappointment Panda mask and drop another unpleasant truth on you:

We suffer for the simple reason that suffering is biologically useful. It is nature's preferred agent for inspiring change. We have evolved to always live with a certain degree of dissatisfaction and insecurity, because it's the mildly dissatisfied and insecure creature that's going to do the most work to innovate and survive. We are wired to become dissatisfied with whatever we have and satisfied by only what we do not have. This constant dissatisfaction has kept our species fighting and striving, building and conquering. So no—our own pain and misery aren't a bug of human evolution; they're a feature.

Pain, in all of its forms, is our body's most effective means of spurring action. Take something as simple as stubbing your toe. If you're like me, when you stub your toe you scream enough four-letter words to make Pope Francis cry. You also probably blame some poor inanimate object for your suffering. "Stupid table," you say. Or maybe you even go so far as to question your entire interior design philosophy based on your throbbing foot: "What kind of idiot puts a table there anyway? Seriously?"

But I digress. That horrible stubbed-toe-induced pain, the one you and I and the pope hate so much, exists for an important reason. Physical pain is a product of our nervous system, a feedback mechanism to give us a sense of our own physical proportions—where we can and cannot move and what we can and cannot touch. When we exceed those limits, our nervous system duly punishes us to make sure that we pay attention and never do it again.

And this pain, as much as we hate it, *is* useful. Pain is what teaches us what to pay attention to when we're young or careless. It helps show us what's good for us versus what's bad for us. It helps us understand and adhere to our own limitations. It teaches us to not fuck around near hot stoves or stick metal objects into electrical sockets. Therefore, it's not always beneficial to avoid pain and seek pleasure, since pain can, at times, be life-or-death important to our well-being.

But pain is not merely physical. As anyone who has had to sit through the first *Star Wars* prequel can tell you, we humans are capable of experiencing acute psychological pain as well. In fact, research has found that our brains don't register much difference between physical pain and psychological pain. So when I tell you that my first girl-friend cheating on me and leaving me felt like having an ice pick slowly inserted into the center of my heart, that's because, well, it hurt so much I might as well have had an ice pick slowly inserted into the center of my heart.

Like physical pain, our psychological pain is an indication of something out of equilibrium, some limitation that has been exceeded. And like our physical pain, our psychological pain is not necessarily always bad or even undesirable. In some cases, experiencing emotional or psychological pain can be healthy or necessary. Just like stubbing our toe teaches us to walk into fewer tables, the emotional pain of rejection or failure teaches us how to avoid making the same mistakes in the future.

And this is what's so dangerous about a society that coddles itself more and more from the inevitable discomforts of life: we lose the benefits of experiencing healthy doses of pain, a loss that disconnects us from the reality of the world around us.

You may salivate at the thought of a problem-free life full of everlasting happiness and eternal compassion, but back here on earth the problems never cease. Seriously, problems don't end. Disappointment Panda just dropped by. We had margaritas, and he told me all about it: problems never fucking go away, he said—they just improve. Warren Buffett's got money problems; the drunk hobo down at Kwik-E Mart's got money problems. Buffett's just got *better* money problems than the hobo. All of life is like this.

"Life is essentially an endless series of problems, Mark," the panda told me. He sipped his drink and adjusted the little pink umbrella. "The solution to one problem is merely the creation of the next one."

A moment passed, and then I wondered where the fuck the talking panda came from. And while we're at it, who made these margaritas?

"Don't hope for a life without problems," the panda said. "There's no such thing. Instead, hope for a life full of good problems."

And with that, he set his glass down, adjusted his sombrero, and sauntered off into the sunset.

Happiness Comes from Solving Problems

Problems are a constant in life. When you solve your health problem by buying a gym membership, you create new problems, like having to get up early to get to the gym on time, sweating like a meth-head for thirty minutes on an elliptical, and then getting showered and changed for work so you don't stink up the whole office. When you solve your problem of not spending enough time with your partner by designating Wednesday night "date night," you generate new problems, such as figuring out what to do every Wednesday that you both won't hate, making sure you have enough money for nice dinners, rediscovering the chemistry and spark you two feel you've lost, and unraveling the logistics of fucking in a small bathtub filled with too many bubbles.

Problems never stop; they merely get exchanged and/or upgraded.

Happiness comes from solving problems. The keyword here is "solving." If you're avoiding your problems or feel like you don't have any problems, then you're going to make yourself miserable. If you feel like you have problems that you can't solve, you will likewise make yourself miserable. The secret sauce is in the *solving* of the problems, not in not having problems in the first place.

To be happy we need something to solve. Happiness is therefore a form of action; it's an activity, not something that is passively bestowed upon you, not something that you magically discover in a top-ten article on the Huffington Post or from any specific guru or teacher. It doesn't magically appear when you finally make enough money to add on that extra room to the house. You don't find it waiting for you in a place, an idea, a job—or even a book, for that matter.

Happiness is a constant work-in-progress, because solving problems is a constant work-in-progress—the solutions to today's problems will lay the foundation for tomorrow's problems, and so on. True happiness occurs only when you find the problems you enjoy having and enjoy solving.

Sometimes those problems are simple: eating good food, traveling to some new place, winning at the new video game you just bought. Other times those problems are abstract and complicated: fixing your relationship with your mother, finding a career you can feel good about, developing better friendships.

Whatever your problems are, the concept is the same: solve problems; be happy. Unfortunately, for many people, life doesn't feel that simple. That's because they fuck things up in at least one of two ways:

1. *Denial.* Some people deny that their problems exist in the first place. And because they deny reality, they must constantly delude or distract themselves from reality. This may make them feel good in the short term, but it leads to a life of insecurity, neuroticism, and emotional repression.

2. *Victim Mentality.* Some choose to believe that there is nothing they can do to solve their problems, even when they in fact could. Victims seek to blame others for their problems or blame outside circumstances. This may make them feel better in the short term, but it leads to a life of anger, helplessness, and despair.

People deny and blame others for their problems for the simple reason that it's easy and feels good, while solving problems is hard and often feels bad. Forms of blame and denial give us a quick high. They are a way to temporarily escape our problems, and that escape can provide us a quick rush that makes us feel better.

Highs come in many forms. Whether it's a substance like alcohol, the moral righteousness that comes from blaming others, or the thrill of some new risky adventure, highs are shallow and unproductive ways to go about one's life. Much of the self-help world is predicated on peddling highs to people rather than solving legitimate problems. Many self-help gurus teach you new forms of denial and pump you up with exercises that feel good in the short term, while ignoring the underlying issue. Remember, nobody who is actually happy has to stand in front of a mirror and tell himself that he's happy.

Highs also generate addiction. The more you rely on them to feel better about your underlying problems, the more you will seek them out. In this sense, almost anything can become addictive, depending on the motivation behind using it. We all have our chosen methods to numb the pain of our problems, and in moderate doses there is nothing wrong with this. But the longer we avoid and the longer we numb, the more painful it will be when we finally do confront our issues.

Emotions Are Overrated

Emotions evolved for one specific purpose: to help us live and reproduce a little bit better. That's it. They're feedback mechanisms telling us that something is either likely right or likely wrong for us—nothing more, nothing less.

Much as the pain of touching a hot stove teaches you not to touch it again, the sadness of being alone teaches you not to do the things that made you feel so alone again. Emotions are simply biological signals designed to nudge you in the direction of beneficial change.

Look, I don't mean to make light of your midlife crisis or the fact that your drunk dad stole your bike when you were eight years old and you still haven't gotten over it, but when it comes down to it, if you feel crappy it's because your brain is telling you that there's a problem that's unaddressed or unresolved. In other words, negative emotions are a *call to action*. When you feel them, it's because you're supposed to *do something*. Positive emotions, on the other hand, are rewards for taking the proper action. When you feel them, life seems simple and there is nothing else to do but enjoy it. Then, like everything else, the positive emotions go away, because more problems inevitably emerge.

Emotions are part of the equation of our lives, but not the *entire* equation. Just because something feels good doesn't mean it *is* good. Just because something feels bad doesn't mean it *is* bad. Emotions are merely signposts, *suggestions* that our neurobiology gives us, not commandments. Therefore, we shouldn't always trust our own emotions. In fact, I believe we should make a habit of questioning them.

Many people are taught to repress their emotions for various personal, social, or cultural reasons—particularly negative emotions. Sadly, to deny one's negative emotions is to deny many of the feedback mechanisms that help a person solve problems. As a result, many of these repressed individuals struggle to deal with problems throughout their lives. And if they can't solve problems, then they can't be happy. Remember, pain serves a purpose.

But then there are those people who overidentify with their emotions. Everything is justified for no other reason than they *felt* it. "Oh, I broke your windshield, but I was *really* mad; I couldn't help it." Or "I dropped out of school and moved to Alaska just because it *felt* right." Decision-making based on emotional intuition, without the aid of reason to keep it in line, pretty much always sucks. You know who bases their entire lives on their emotions? Three-year-old kids. And dogs. You know what else three-year-olds and dogs do? Shit on the carpet.

An obsession and overinvestment in emotion fails us for the simple reason that emotions never last. Whatever makes us happy today will no longer make us happy tomorrow, because our biology always needs something more. A fix-ation on happiness inevitably amounts to a never-ending pursuit of "something else"—a new house, a new relation-ship, another child, another pay raise. And despite all of our sweat and strain, we end up feeling eerily similar to how we started: inadequate.

Psychologists sometimes refer to this concept as the "hedonic treadmill": the idea that we're always working hard to change our life situation, but we actually never feel very different.

This is why our problems are recursive and unavoid-able. The person you marry is the person you fight with. The house you buy is the house you repair. The dream job you take is the job you stress over. Everything comes with an inherent sacrifice—whatever makes us feel good will also inevitably make us feel bad. What we gain is also what we lose. What creates our positive experiences will define our negative experiences.

This is a difficult pill to swallow. We *like* the idea that there's some form of ultimate happiness that can be attained. We *like* the idea that we can alleviate all of our suffering permanently. We *like* the idea that we can feel fulfilled and satisfied with our lives forever.

But we cannot.

Choose Your Struggle

If I ask you, "What do you want out of life?" and you say something like, "I want to be happy and have a great family and a job I like," your response is so common and expected that it doesn't really mean anything.

Everybody enjoys what feels good. Everyone wants to live a carefree, happy, and easy life, to fall in love and have amazing sex and relationships, to look perfect and make money and be popular and well-respected and admired and a total baller to the point that people part like the Red Sea when they walk into the room.

Everybody wants that. It's easy to want that.

A more interesting question, a question that most people never consider, is, "What *pain* do you want in your life? What are you willing to struggle for?" Because that seems to be a greater determinant of how our lives turn out.

For example, most people want to get the corner office and make a boatload of money—but not many people want to suffer through sixty-hour workweeks, long commutes, obnoxious paperwork, and arbitrary corporate hierarchies to escape the confines of an infinite cubicle hell.

Most people want to have great sex and an awesome relationship, but not everyone is willing to go through the tough conversations, the awkward silences, the hurt feelings, and the emotional psychodrama to get there. And so they settle. They settle and wonder, "What if?" for years and years, until the question morphs from "What if?" into "What else?" And when the lawyers go home and the alimony check is in the mail, they say, "What for?" If not for their lowered standards and expectations twenty years prior, then what for?

Because happiness requires struggle. It grows from problems. Joy doesn't just sprout out of the ground like daisies and rainbows. Real, serious, lifelong fulfillment and meaning have to be earned through the choosing and managing of our struggles. Whether you suffer from anxiety or loneliness or obsessive-compulsive disorder or a dickhead boss who ruins half of your waking hours every day, the solution lies in the acceptance and active engagement of that negative experience—not the avoidance of it, not the salvation from it.

People want an amazing physique. But you don't end up with one unless you legitimately appreciate the pain and physical stress that come with living inside a gym for hour upon hour, unless you love calculating and calibrating the food you eat, planning your life out in tiny plate–sized portions.

People want to start their own business. But you don't end up a successful entrepreneur unless you find a way to appreciate the risk, the uncertainty, the repeated failures, the insane hours devoted to something that may earn absolutely nothing.

People want a partner, a spouse. But you don't end up attracting someone amazing without appreciating the emotional turbulence that comes with weathering rejections, building the sexual tension that never gets released, and staring blankly at a phone that never rings. It's part of the game of love. You can't win if you don't play.

What determines your success isn't, "What do you want to enjoy?" The relevant question is, "What pain do you want to sustain?" The path to happiness is a path full of shitheaps and shame.

You have to choose something. You can't have a pain-free life. It can't all be roses and unicorns all the time. Pleasure is the easy question. And pretty much all of us have a similar answer.

The more interesting question is the pain. What is the pain that you want to sustain? That's the hard question that matters, the question that will actually get you somewhere. It's the question that can change a perspective, a life. It's what makes me, me, and you, you. It's what defines us and separates us and ultimately brings us together.

For most of my adolescence and young adulthood, I

fantasized about being a musician—a rock star, in particular. Any badass guitar song I heard, I would always close my eyes and envision myself up on stage, playing it to the screams of the crowd, people absolutely losing their minds to my sweet finger-noodling glory. This fantasy could keep me occupied for hours on end. For me, it was never a question of *if* I'd ever be up playing in front of screaming crowds, but *when*. I had it all planned out. I was simply biding my time before I could invest the proper amount of energy and effort into getting out there and making my mark. First I needed to finish school. Then I needed to make some extra money to buy gear. Then I needed to find enough free time to practice. Then I had to network and plan my first project. Then . . . and then nothing.

Despite my fantasizing about this for over half my lifetime, the reality never came to fruition. And it took me a long time and a lot of struggle to finally figure out why: *I didn't actually want it.*

I was in love with the result—the image of me on stage, people cheering, me rocking out, pouring my heart into what I was playing—but I wasn't in love with the process. And because of that, I failed at it. Repeatedly. Hell, I didn't even try hard enough to fail at it. I hardly tried at all. The daily drudgery of practicing, the logistics of finding a group and rehearsing, the pain of finding gigs and actually getting people to show up and give a shit, the broken strings, the blown tube amp, hauling forty pounds of gear to and from rehearsals with no car. It's a mountain of a dream and a mile-high climb to the top. And what it took me a long time to discover is that I didn't like to climb much. I just liked to imagine the summit.

The common cultural narratives would tell me that I somehow failed myself, that I'm a quitter or a loser, that I just didn't "have it," that I gave up on my dream and that maybe I let myself succumb to the pressures of society.

But the truth is far less interesting than any of these explanations. The truth is, I thought I wanted something, but it turns out I didn't. End of story.

I wanted the reward and not the struggle. I wanted the result and not the process. I was in love with not the fight but only the victory.

And life doesn't work that way.

Who you are is defined by what you're willing to struggle for. People who *enjoy* the struggles of a gym are the ones who run triathlons and have chiseled abs and can bench-press a small house. People who *enjoy* long workweeks and the politics of the corporate ladder are the ones who fly to the top of it. People who *enjoy* the stresses and uncertainties of the starving artist lifestyle are ultimately the ones who live it and make it.

This is not about willpower or grit. This is not another admonishment of "no pain, no gain." This is the most simple and basic component of life: our struggles determine our successes. Our problems birth our happiness, along with slightly better, slightly upgraded problems.

See: it's a never-ending upward spiral. And if you think at any point you're allowed to stop climbing, I'm afraid you're missing the point. Because the joy is in the climb itself.

CHAPTER

You Are Not Special

I once knew a guy; we'll call him Jimmy.

Jimmy always had various business ventures going. On any given day, if you asked him what he was doing, he'd rattle off the name of some firm he was consulting with, or he'd describe a promising medical app he was looking for angel investors to fund, or he'd talk about some charity event he was supposed to be the keynote speaker for, or how he had an idea for a more efficient type of gas pump that was going to make him billions. The guy was always rolling, always on, and if you gave him an inch of conversational daylight, he'd pulverize you about how world-spinning his work was, how brilliant his latest ideas were, and he'd name-drop so much it felt like you were talking to a tabloid reporter.

Jimmy was all positivity all the time. Always pushing

himself, always working an angle—a real go-getter, whatever the fuck that means.

The catch was that Jimmy was also a total deadbeat—all talk and no walk. Stoned a majority of the time, and spending as much money in bars and fine restaurants as he did on his "business ideas," Jimmy was a professional leech, living off his family's hard-won money by spinning them as well as everybody else in the city on false ideas of future tech glory. Sure, sometimes he'd put in some token effort, or pick up the phone and cold-call some bigwig and name-drop until he ran out of names, but nothing ever actually happened. None of these "ventures" ever blossomed into anything.

Yet the guy kept this up for years, living off girlfriends and more and more distant relatives well into his late twenties. And the most screwed-up part was that Jimmy *felt good about it*. He had a delusional level of self-confidence. People who laughed at him or hung up on him were, in his mind, "missing the opportunity of their lives." People who called him out on his bogus business ideas were "too ignorant and inexperienced" to understand his genius. People who pointed out his deadbeat lifestyle were "jealous"; they were "haters" who envied his success.

Jimmy did make some money, although it was usually through the sketchiest of means, like selling another person's business idea as his own, or finagling a loan from someone, or worse, talking someone into giving him equity in their start-up. He actually occasionally talked people into paying him to do some public speaking. (About what, I can't even imagine.)

The worst part was that Jimmy *believed* his own bullshit. His delusion was so bulletproof, it was honestly hard to get mad at him, it was actually kind of amazing.

Sometime in the 1960s, developing "high self-esteem"— having positive thoughts and feelings about oneself— became all the rage in psychology. Research found that people who *thought* highly about themselves generally performed better and caused fewer problems. Many researchers and policymakers at the time came to believe that raising a population's self-esteem could lead to some tangible social benefits: lower crime, better academic records, greater employment, lower budget deficits. As a result, beginning in the next decade, the 1970s, self-esteem practices began to be taught to parents, emphasized by therapists, politicians, and teachers, and instituted into educational policy. Grade inflation, for example, was implemented to make low-achieving kids feel better about their lack of achievement. Participation awards and bogus trophies were invented for any number of mundane and expected activities. Kids were given inane homework assignments, like writing down all the reasons why they thought they were special, or the five things they liked most about themselves. Pastors and ministers told their congregations that they were each uniquely special in God's eyes, and were destined to excel and not be average. Business and motivational seminars cropped up chanting the same paradoxical mantra: every single one of us can be exceptional and massively successful.

But it's a generation later and the data is in: we're *not* all exceptional. It turns out that merely feeling good about yourself doesn't really mean anything unless you have a *good reason* to feel good about yourself. It turns out that adversity and failure are actually useful and even necessary for developing strong-minded and successful adults. It turns out that teaching people to believe they're exceptional and to feel good about themselves no matter what doesn't lead to a population full of Bill Gateses and Martin Luther Kings. It leads to a population full of Jimmys.

Jimmy, the delusional start-up founder. Jimmy, who smoked pot every day and had no real marketable skills other than talking himself up and believing it. Jimmy, the type of guy who yelled at his business partner for being "immature," and then maxed out the company credit card at Le Bernardin trying to impress some Russian model. Jimmy, who was quickly running out of aunts and uncles who could loan him more money.

Yes, that confident, high-self-esteem Jimmy. The Jimmy who spent so much time talking about how good he was that he forgot to, you know, actually do something.

The problem with the self-esteem movement is that it measured self-esteem by how positively people felt about themselves. But a true and accurate measurement of one's self-worth is how people feel about the *negative* aspects of themselves. If a person like Jimmy feels absolutely fucking great 99.9 percent of the time, despite his life falling apart around him, then how can that be a valid metric for a successful and happy life?

Jimmy is entitled. That is, he feels as though he deserves good things without actually earning them. He believes he should be able to be rich without actually working for it. He believes he should be liked and well-connected without actually helping anyone. He believes he should have an amazing lifestyle without actually sacrificing anything.

People like Jimmy become so fixated on feeling good about themselves that they manage to delude themselves into believing that they *are* accomplishing great things even when they're not. They believe they're the brilliant presenter on stage when actually they're making a fool of themselves. They believe they're the successful start-up founder when, in fact, they've never had a successful venture. They call themselves life coaches and charge money to help others, even though they're only twenty-five years old and haven't actually accomplished anything substantial in their lives.

Entitled people exude a delusional degree of self-confidence. This confidence can be alluring to others, at least for a little while. In some instances, the entitled person's delusional level of confidence can become contagious and help the people around the entitled person feel more confident in themselves too. Despite all of Jimmy's shenanigans, I have to admit that it *was* fun hanging out with him sometimes. You felt indestructible around him.

But the problem with entitlement is that it makes people *need* to feel good about themselves all the time, even at the expense of those around them. And because entitled people always need to feel good about themselves, they end up spending most of their time thinking about themselves. After all, it takes a lot of energy and work to convince yourself that your shit doesn't stink, especially when you've actually been living in a toilet.

Once people have developed the thought pattern to constantly construe what happens around them as self-aggrandizing, it's extremely hard to break them out of it. Any attempt to reason with them is seen as simply another "threat" to their superiority by another person who "can't handle" how smart/talented/good-looking/successful they are.

Entitlement closes in upon itself in a kind of narcis-sistic bubble, distorting anything and everything in such a way as to reinforce itself. People who feel entitled view every occurrence in their life as either an affirmation of, or a threat to, their own greatness. If something good happens to them, it's because of some amazing feat they accomplished. If something bad happens to them, it's because somebody is jealous and trying to bring them down a notch. Entitlement is impervious. People who are entitled delude themselves into whatever feeds their sense of superiority. They keep their mental facade standing at all costs, even if it some-times requires being physically or emotionally abusive to those around them.

But entitlement is a failed strategy. It's just another high. It's *not* happiness.

The true measurement of self-worth is not how a per-son feels about her *positive* experiences, but rather how she feels about her *negative* experiences. A person like Jimmy hides from his problems by making up imagined successes for himself at every turn. And because he can't face his problems, no matter how good he feels about himself, he is weak.

A person who actually has a high self-worth is able to look at the negative parts of his character frankly—"Yes, sometimes I'm irresponsible with money," "Yes, sometimes I exaggerate my own successes," "Yes, I rely too much on others to support me and should be more self-reliant"— and then acts to improve upon them. But entitled people, because they are incapable of acknowledging their own problems openly and honestly, are incapable of improving their lives in any lasting or meaningful way. They are left chasing high after high and accumulate greater and greater levels of denial.

But eventually reality must hit, and the underlying problems will once again make themselves clear. It's just a question of when, and how painful it will be.

Things Fall Apart

I sat in my 9:00 A.M. biology class, arms cradling my head on my desk as I stared at the clock's second hand making laps, each tick syncopated with the teacher's dronings-on about chromosomes and mitosis. Like most thirteen-year-olds stuck in a stuffy, fluorescent classroom, I was bored.

A knock came on the door. Mr. Price, the school's assistant principal, stuck his head in. "Excuse me for interrupting. Mark, can you step outside with me for a moment? Oh, and bring your things with you."

Strange, I thought. Kids get sent to the principal, but the principal rarely gets sent to them. I gathered my things and stepped out.

The hallway was empty. Hundreds of beige lockers converged on the horizon. "Mark, can you take me to your locker, please?"

"Sure," I say, and slug myself down the hall, baggy jeans and moppy hair and oversized Pantera T-shirt and all.

We get to my locker. "Open it, please," Mr. Price says; so I do. He steps in front of me and gathers my coat, my gym bag, my backpack—all of the locker's contents, minus a few notebooks and pencils. He starts walking away. "Come with me, please," he says, without looking back. I start to get an uneasy feeling.

I follow him to his office, where he asks me to sit down. He closes the door and locks it. He goes over to the window and adjusts the blinds to block the view from outside. My palms begin to sweat. This is *not* a normal principal visit.

Mr. Price sits down and quietly rummages through my things, checking pockets, unzipping zippers, shaking out my gym clothes and placing them on the floor.

Without looking up at me, Mr. Price asks, "Do you know what I'm looking for, Mark?"

"No," I say.

"Drugs."

The word shocks me into nervous attention.

"D-d-drugs?" I stammer. "What kind?"

He looks at me sternly. "I don't know; what kind do you

have?" He opens one of my binders and checks the small pockets meant for pens.

My sweat blossoms like a fungal growth. It spreads from my palms to my arms and now my neck. My temples pulsate as blood floods my brain and face. Like most thirteen-year-olds freshly accused of possessing narcotics and bringing them to school, I want to run away and hide.

"I don't know what you're talking about," I protest, the words sounding far meeker than I'd like. I feel as if I should be sounding confident in myself right now. Or maybe not. Maybe I should be scared. Do liars sound more scared or confident? Because however they sound, I want to sound the opposite. Instead, my lack of confidence compounds, unconfidence about my sounding unconfident making me more unconfident. That fucking Feedback Loop from Hell.

"We'll see about that," he says, turning his attention to my backpack, which seemingly has one hundred pockets. Each is loaded with its own silly teen desiderata—colored pens, old notes passed in class, early-nineties CDs with cracked cases, dried-up markers, an old sketchpad with half its pages missing, dust and lint and crap accumulated during a maddeningly circuitous middle school existence.

My sweat must be pumping at the speed of light, because time extends itself and dilates such that what is mere seconds on that 9:00 A.M. second-period biology clock now feels like Paleolithic eons, and I'm growing up and dying every minute. Just me and Mr. Price and my bottomless backpack.

Somewhere around the Mesolithic Age, Mr. Price

finishes searching the backpack. Having found nothing, he seems flustered. He turns the pack upside down and lets all of my crap crash onto his office floor. He's now sweating as profusely as I am, except in place of my terror, there is his anger.

"No drugs today, eh?" He tries to sound casual.

"Nope." So do I.

He spreads my stuff out, separating each item and coagulating them into little piles beside my gym gear. My coat and backpack now lie empty and lifeless on his lap. He sighs and stares at the wall. Like most thirteen-year-olds locked in an office with a man angrily throwing their shit all over the floor, I want to cry.

Mr. Price scans the contents organized on the floor. Nothing illicit or illegal, no narcotics, not even anything against school policy. He sighs and then throws the coat and backpack on the floor too. He bends over and puts his elbows on his knees, making his face level with mine.

"Mark, I'm going to give you one last chance to be honest with me. If you are honest, this will turn out much better for you. If it turns out you're lying, then it's going to be much worse."

As if on cue, I gulp.

"Now tell me the truth," Mr. Price demands. "Did you bring drugs to school today?"

Fighting back tears, screams clawing at my throat, I stare my tormentor in the face and, in a pleading voice, dying to be relieved of its adolescent horrors, I say, "No, I don't have any drugs. I have no idea what you're talking about."

"Okay," he says, signaling surrender. "I guess you can collect your things and go."

He takes one last, longing gaze at my deflated backpack, lying like a broken promise there on his office floor. He casually puts one foot down on the pack, stomping lightly, a last-ditch effort. I anxiously wait for him to get up and leave so I can get on with my life and forget this whole nightmare.

But his foot stops on something. "What is this?" he asks, tapping with his foot.

"What is what?" I say.

"There's still something in here." He picks up the bag and starts feeling around the bottom of it. For me the room gets fuzzy; everything goes wobbly.

When I was young, I was smart. I was friendly. But I was also a shithead. I mean that in the most loving way possible. I was a rebellious, lying little shithead. Angry and full of resentment. When I was twelve, I hacked my house's security system with refrigerator magnets so I could sneak out undetected in the middle of the night. My friend and I would put his mom's car in neutral and push it into the street so we could drive around without waking her up. I would write papers about abortion because I knew my English teacher was a hardcore conservative Christian. Another friend and I stole cigarettes from his mom and sold them to kids out behind the school.

And I also cut a secret compartment into the bottom of my backpack to hide my marijuana.

That was the same hidden compartment Mr. Price found after stepping on the drugs I was hiding. I had been lying. And, as promised, Mr. Price didn't go easy on me. A few hours later, like most thirteen-year-olds handcuffed in the back of a police car, I thought my life was over.

And I was kind of right, in a way. My parents quarantined me at home. I was to have no friends for the foreseeable future. Having been expelled from school, I was to be homeschooled for the rest of the year. My mom made me get a haircut and threw out all of my Marilyn Manson and Metallica shirts (which, for an adolescent in 1998, was tantamount to being sentenced to death by lameness). My dad dragged me to his office with him in the mornings and made me file papers for hours on end. Once homeschooling was over, I was enrolled in a small, private Christian school, where—and this may not surprise you—I didn't exactly fit in.

And just when I had finally cleaned up my act and turned in my assignments and learned the value of good clerical responsibility, my parents decided to get divorced.

I tell you all of this only to point out that my adolescence sucked donkey balls. I lost all of my friends, my community, my legal rights, and my family within the span of about nine months. My therapist in my twenties would later call this "some real traumatic shit," and I would spend the next decade-and-change working on unraveling it and becoming less of a self-absorbed, entitled little prick.

The problem with my home life back then was not all of the horrible things that were said or done; rather, it was all of the horrible things that needed to be said and done but weren't. My family stonewalls the way Warren Buffett makes money or Jenna Jameson fucks: we're champions at it. The house could have been burning down around us and it would have been met with, "Oh no, everything's fine. A tad warm in here, perhaps—but really, everything's fine."

When my parents got divorced, there were no broken dishes, no slammed doors, no screaming arguments about who fucked whom. Once they had reassured my brother and me that it wasn't our fault, we had a Q&A session—yes, you read that right—about the logistics of the new living arrangements. Not a tear was shed. Not a voice was raised. The closest peek my brother and I got into our parents' unraveling emotional lives was hearing, "Nobody cheated on anybody." Oh, that's nice. It was a tad warm in the room, but really, everything was fine.

My parents are good people. I don't blame them for any of this (not anymore, at least). And I love them very much. They have their own stories and their own journeys and their own problems, just as all parents do. And just as all of *their* parents do, and so on. And like all parents, my parents, with the best of intentions, imparted some of their problems to me, as I probably will to my kids.

When "real traumatic shit" like this happens in our lives, we begin to unconsciously feel as though we have problems that we're incapable of ever solving. And this assumed inability to solve our problems causes us to feel miserable and helpless.

But it also causes something else to happen. If we have problems that are unsolvable, our unconscious figures that we're either uniquely special or uniquely defective in some way. That we're somehow unlike everyone else and that the rules must be different for us.

Put simply: we become entitled.

The pain from my adolescence led me down a road of entitlement that lasted through much of my early adulthood. Whereas Jimmy's entitlement played out in the business world, where he pretended to be a huge success, my entitlement played out in my relationships, particularly with women. My trauma had revolved around intimacy and acceptance, so I felt a constant need to overcompensate, to prove to myself that I was loved and accepted at all times. And as a result, I soon took to chasing women the same way a cocaine addict takes to a snowman made out of cocaine: I made sweet love to it, and then promptly suffocated myself in it.

I became a player—an immature, selfish, albeit sometimes charming player. And I strung up a long series of superficial and unhealthy relationships for the better part of a decade.

It wasn't so much the sex I craved, although the sex was fun. It was the validation. I was wanted; I was loved; for the first time since I could remember, I was *worthy*. My craving for validation quickly fed into a mental habit of self-aggrandizing and overindulgence. I felt entitled to say or do whatever I wanted, to break people's trust, to ignore people's feelings, and then justify it later with shitty, half-assed apologies.

While this period certainly had its moments of fun and excitement, and I met some wonderful women, my life was more or less a wreck the whole time. I was often unemployed, living on friends' couches or with my mom, drinking way more than I should have been, alienating a number of friends—and when I did meet a woman I really liked, my self-absorption quickly torpedoed everything.

The deeper the pain, the more helpless we feel against our problems, and the more entitlement we adopt to compensate for those problems. This entitlement plays out in one of two ways:

1. I'm awesome and the rest of you all suck, so I deserve special treatment.
2. I suck and the rest of you are all awesome, so I deserve special treatment.

Opposite mindset on the outside, but the same selfish creamy core in the middle. In fact, you will often see entitled people flip back and forth between the two. Either they're on top of the world or the world is on top of them, depending on the day of the week, or how well they're doing with their particular addiction at that moment.

Most people correctly identify a person like Jimmy as a raging narcissistic ass-hat. That's because he's pretty blatant in his delusionally high self-regard. What most people don't correctly identify as entitlement are those people who perpetually feel as though they're inferior and unworthy of the world.

Because construing everything in life so as to make yourself out to be constantly victimized requires just as much selfishness as the opposite. It takes just as much energy and delusional self-aggrandizement to maintain the belief that one has insurmountable problems as that one has no problems at all.

The truth is that there's no such thing as a personal problem. If you've got a problem, chances are millions of other people have had it in the past, have it now, and are going to have it in the future. Likely people you know too. That doesn't minimize the problem or mean that it shouldn't hurt. It doesn't mean you aren't legitimately a victim in some circumstances.

It just means that you're not special.

Often, it's this realization—that you and your problems are actually *not* privileged in their severity or pain—that is the first and most important step toward solving them.

But for some reason, it appears that more and more people, particularly young people, are forgetting this. Numerous professors and educators have noted a lack of emotional resilience and an excess of selfish demands in today's young people. It's not uncommon now for books to be removed from a class's curriculum for no other reason than that they made someone feel bad. Speakers and professors are shouted down and banned from campuses for infractions as simple as suggesting that maybe some Halloween costumes really aren't that offensive. School counselors note that more students than ever are exhibiting severe signs of emotional distress over what are otherwise run-of-the-mill daily college experiences, such as an argument with a roommate, or getting a low grade in a class.

It's strange that in an age when we are more connected than ever, entitlement seems to be at an all-time high. Something about recent technology seems to allow our insecurities to run amok like never before. The more freedom we're given to express ourselves, the more we want to be free of having to deal with anyone who may disagree with us or upset us. The more exposed we are to opposing viewpoints, the more we seem to get upset that those other viewpoints exist. The easier and more problem-free our lives become, the more we seem to feel entitled for them to get even better.

The benefits of the Internet and social media are unquestionably fantastic. In many ways, this is the best time in history to be alive. But perhaps these technologies are having some unintended social side effects. Perhaps these same technologies that have liberated and educated so many are simultaneously enabling people's sense of entitlement more than ever before.

The Tyranny of Exceptionalism

Most of us are pretty average at most things we do. Even if you're exceptional at one thing, chances are you're average or below average at most other things. That's just the nature of life. To become truly great at something, you have to dedicate shit-tons of time and energy to it. And because we all have limited time and energy, few of us ever become truly exceptional at more than one thing, if anything at all.

We can then say that it's a statistical improbability that any single person will be an extraordinary performer in all areas of life, or even in many areas of their life. Brilliant businesspeople are often fuckups in their personal lives. Extraordinary athletes are often shallow and as dumb as a lobotomized rock. Many celebrities are probably just as clueless about life as the people who gawk at them and follow their every move.

We're all, for the most part, pretty average people. But it's the extremes that get all of the publicity. We kind of know this already, but we rarely think and/or talk about it, and we certainly never discuss why this could be a problem.

Having the Internet, Google, Facebook, YouTube, and access to five hundred–plus channels of television is amazing. But our attention is limited. There's no way we can process the tidal waves of information flowing past us constantly. Therefore, the only zeroes and ones that break through and catch our attention are the truly exceptional pieces of information—those in the 99.999th percentile.

All day, every day, we are flooded with the truly extraordinary. The best of the best. The worst of the worst. The greatest physical feats. The funniest jokes. The most upsetting news. The scariest threats. Nonstop.

Our lives today are filled with information from the extremes of the bell curve of human experience, because in the media business that's what gets eyeballs, and eyeballs bring dollars. That's the bottom line. Yet the vast majority of life resides in the humdrum middle. The vast majority of life is *un*extraordinary, indeed quite average.

This flood of extreme information has conditioned us to believe that exceptionalism is the new normal. And because we're all quite average most of the time, the deluge of exceptional information drives us to feel pretty damn insecure and desperate, because clearly we are somehow not good enough. So more and more we feel the need to compensate through entitlement and addiction. We cope the only way we know how: either through self-aggrandizing or through other-aggrandizing.

Some of us do this by cooking up get-rich-quick schemes. Others do it by taking off across the world to save starving babies in Africa. Others do it by excelling in school and winning every award. Others do it by shooting up a school. Others do it by trying to have sex with anything that talks and breathes.

This ties in to the growing culture of entitlement that I talked about earlier. Millennials often get blamed for this cultural shift, but that's likely because millennials are the most plugged-in and visible generation. In fact, the tendency toward entitlement is apparent across all of society. And I believe it's linked to mass-media-driven exceptionalism.

The problem is that the pervasiveness of technology and mass marketing is screwing up a lot of people's expectations for themselves. The inundation of the exceptional makes people feel worse about themselves, makes them feel that they need to be more extreme, more radical, and more self-assured to get noticed or even matter.

When I was a young man, my insecurities around intimacy were exacerbated by all the ridiculous narratives of masculinity circulating throughout pop culture. And those same narratives are *still* circulating: to be a cool guy, you have to party like a rock star; to be respected, you have to be admired by women; sex is the most valuable thing a man can attain, and it's worth sacrificing anything (including your own dignity) to get it.

This constant stream of unrealistic media dogpiles onto our existing feelings of insecurity, by overexposing us to the unrealistic standards we fail to live up to. Not only do we feel subjected to unsolvable problems, but we feel like losers because a simple Google search shows us thousands of people without those same problems.

Technology has solved old economic problems by giving us new psychological problems. The Internet has not just open-sourced information; it has also open-sourced insecurity, self-doubt, and shame.

B-b-b-but, If I'm Not Going to Be Special or Extraordinary, What's the Point?

It has become an accepted part of our culture today to believe that we are *all* destined to do something truly extraordinary. Celebrities say it. Business tycoons say it. Politicians say it. Even Oprah says it (so it must be true). Each and every one of us can be extraordinary. We all *deserve* greatness.

The fact that this statement is inherently contradictory— after all, if *everyone* were extraordinary, then by definition *no one* would be extraordinary—is missed by most people. And instead of questioning what we actually deserve or don't deserve, we eat the message up and ask for more.

Being "average" has become the new standard of failure. The worst thing you can be is in the middle of the pack, the middle of the bell curve. When a culture's standard of success is to "be extraordinary," it then becomes better to be at the extreme low end of the bell curve than to be in the middle, because at least there you're still special and deserve attention. Many people choose this strategy: to prove to everyone that they are the most miserable, or the most oppressed, or the most victimized.

A lot of people are afraid to accept mediocrity because they believe that if they accept it, they'll never achieve anything, never improve, and that their life won't matter.

This sort of thinking is dangerous. Once you accept the premise that a life is worthwhile only if it is truly notable and great, then you basically accept the fact that most of the human population (including yourself) sucks and is worthless. And this mindset can quickly turn dangerous, to both yourself and others.

The rare people who do become truly exceptional at something do so not because they believe they're exceptional. On the contrary, they become amazing because they're obsessed with improvement. And that obsession with improvement stems from an unerring belief that they are, in fact, not that great at all. It's *anti*-entitlement. People who become great at something become great because they understand that they're not already great— they are mediocre, they are average—and that they could be so much better.

All of this "every person can be extraordinary and achieve greatness" stuff is basically just jerking off your ego. It's a message that tastes good going down, but in reality is nothing more than empty calories that make you emotionally fat and bloated, the proverbial Big Mac for your heart and your brain.

The ticket to emotional health, like that to physical health, comes from eating your veggies—that is, accepting the bland and mundane truths of life: truths such as "Your actions actually don't matter *that much* in the grand scheme of things" and "The vast majority of your life will be boring and not noteworthy, and that's okay." This vegetable course will taste bad at first. Very bad. You will avoid accepting it.

But once ingested, your body will wake up feeling more potent and more alive. After all, that constant pressure to be something amazing, to be the next big thing, will be lifted off your back. The stress and anxiety of always feeling inadequate and constantly needing to prove yourself will dissipate. And the knowledge and acceptance of your own mundane existence will actually free you to accomplish what you truly wish to accomplish, without judgment or lofty expectations.

You will have a growing appreciation for life's basic experiences: the pleasures of simple friendship, creating something, helping a person in need, reading a good book, laughing with someone you care about.

Sounds boring, doesn't it? That's because these things are ordinary. But maybe they're ordinary for a reason: because they are what *actually* matters.

4

The Value of Suffering

I n the closing months of 1944, after almost a decade of war, the tide was turning against Japan. Their economy was floundering, their military overstretched across half of Asia, and the territories they had won throughout the Pacific were now toppling like dominoes to U.S. forces. Defeat seemed inevitable.

On December 26, 1944, Second Lieutenant Hiroo Onoda of the Japanese Imperial Army was deployed to the small island of Lubang in the Philippines. His orders were to slow the United States' progress as much as possible, to stand and fight at all costs, and to never surrender. Both he and his commander knew it was essentially a suicide mission.

In February 1945, the Americans arrived on Lubang and took the island with overwhelming force. Within days, most of the Japanese soldiers had either surrendered or been killed, but Onoda and three of his men managed to hide in the jungle. From there, they began a guerrilla warfare campaign against the U.S. forces and the local population, attacking supply lines, shooting at stray soldiers, and interfering with the American forces in any way that they could.

That August, half a year later, the United States dropped atomic bombs on the cities of Hiroshima and Nagasaki. Japan surrendered, and the deadliest war in human history came to its dramatic conclusion.

However, thousands of Japanese soldiers were still scattered among the Pacific isles, and most, like Onoda, were hiding in the jungle, unaware that the war was over. These holdouts continued to fight and pillage as they had before. This was a real problem for rebuilding eastern Asia after the war, and the governments agreed something must be done.

The U.S. military, in conjunction with the Japanese government, dropped thousands of leaflets throughout the Pacific region, announcing that the war was over and it was time for everyone to go home. Onoda and his men, like many others, found and read these leaflets, but unlike most of the others, Onoda decided that they were fake, a trap set by the American forces to get the guerrilla fighters to show themselves. Onoda burned the leaflets, and he and his men stayed hidden and continued to fight.

Five years went by. The leaflets had stopped, and most of the American forces had long since gone home. The local population on Lubang attempted to return to their normal lives of farming and fishing. Yet there were Hiroo Onoda and his merry men, still shooting at the farmers, burning their crops, stealing their livestock, and murdering locals who wandered too far into the jungle. The Philippine government then took to drawing up new flyers and spreading them out across the jungle. Come out, they said. The war is over. You lost.

But these, too, were ignored.

In 1952, the Japanese government made one final effort to draw the last remaining soldiers out of hiding throughout the Pacific. This time, letters and pictures from the missing soldiers' families were air-dropped, along with a personal note from the emperor himself. Once again, Onoda refused to believe that the information was real. Once again, he believed the airdrop to be a trick by the Americans. Once again, he and his men stood and continued to fight.

Another few years went by and the Philippine locals, sick of being terrorized, finally armed themselves and began firing back. By 1959, one of Onoda's companions had surrendered, and another had been killed. Then, a decade later, Onoda's last companion, a man called Kozuka, was killed in a shootout with the local police while he was burning rice fields—*still* waging war against the local population a full quarter-century after the end of World War II!

Onoda, having now spent more than half of his life in the jungles of Lubang, was all alone.

In 1972, the news of Kozuka's death reached Japan and caused a stir. The Japanese people thought the last of the soldiers from the war had come home years earlier. The Japanese media began to wonder: if Kozuka had still been on Lubang until 1972, then perhaps Onoda himself, the last known Japanese holdout from World War II, might still be alive as well. That year, both the Japanese and Philippine governments sent search parties to look for the enigmatic second lieutenant, now part myth, part hero, and part ghost.

They found nothing.

As the months progressed, the story of Lieutenant Onoda morphed into something of an urban legend in Japan—the war hero who sounded too insane to actually exist. Many romanticized him. Others criticized him. Others thought he was the stuff of fairy tale, invented by those who still wanted to believe in a Japan that had disappeared long ago.

It was around this time that a young man named Norio Suzuki first heard of Onoda. Suzuki was an adventurer, an explorer, and a bit of a hippie. Born after the war ended, he had dropped out of school and spent four years hitchhiking his way across Asia, the Middle East, and Africa, sleeping on park benches, in stranger's cars, in jail cells, and under the stars. He volunteered on farms for food, and donated blood to pay for places to stay. He was a free spirit, and perhaps a little bit nuts.

In 1972, Suzuki needed another adventure. He had returned to Japan after his travels and found the strict cultural norms and social hierarchy to be stifling. He hated school. He couldn't hold down a job. He wanted to be back on the road, back on his own again.

For Suzuki, the legend of Hiroo Onoda came as the answer to his problems. It was a new and worthy adventure for him to pursue. Suzuki believed that *he* would be the one who would find Onoda. Sure, search parties conducted by the Japanese, Philippine, and American governments had not been able to find Onoda; local police forces had been scavenging the jungle for almost thirty years with no luck; thousands of leaflets had met with no response—but fuck it, this deadbeat, college-dropout hippie was going to be the one to find him.

Unarmed and untrained for any sort of reconnaissance or tactical warfare, Suzuki traveled to Lubang and began wandering around the jungle all by himself. His strategy: scream Onoda's name really loudly and tell him that the emperor was worried about him.

He found Onoda in four days.

Suzuki stayed with Onoda in the jungle for some time. Onoda had been alone by that point for over a year, and once found by Suzuki he welcomed the companionship and was desperate to learn what had been happening in the outside world from a Japanese source he could trust. The two men became sorta-kinda friends.

Suzuki asked Onoda why he had stayed and continued to fight. Onoda said it was simple: he had been given the order to "never surrender," so he stayed. For nearly thirty years he had simply been following an order. Onoda then asked Suzuki why a "hippie boy" like himself came looking for him. Suzuki said that he'd left Japan in search of three things: "Lieutenant Onoda, a panda bear, and the Abominable Snowman, in that order."

The two men had been brought together under the most

curious of circumstances: two well-intentioned adventurers chasing false visions of glory, like a real-life Japanese Don Quixote and Sancho Panza, stuck together in the damp recesses of a Philippine jungle, both imagining themselves heroes, despite both being alone with nothing, doing nothing. Onoda had already by then given up most of his life to a phantom war. Suzuki would give his up too. Having already found Hiroo Onoda and the panda bear, he would die a few years later in the Himalayas, still in search of the Abominable Snowman.

Humans often choose to dedicate large portions of their lives to seemingly useless or destructive causes. On the surface, these causes make no sense. It's hard to imagine how Onoda could have been happy on that island for those thirty years—living off insects and rodents, sleeping in the dirt, murdering civilians decade after decade. Or why Suzuki trekked off to his own death, with no money, no companions, and no purpose other than to chase an imaginary Yeti.

Yet, later in his life, Onoda said he regretted nothing. He claimed that he was proud of his choices and his time on Lubang. He said that it had been an honor to devote a sizable portion of his life in service to a nonexistent empire. Suzuki, had he survived, likely would have said something similar: that he was doing exactly what he was meant to do, that he regretted nothing.

These men both chose how they wished to suffer. Hiroo Onoda chose to suffer for loyalty to a dead empire. Suzuki chose to suffer for adventure, no matter how ill-advised. To both men, their suffering *meant* something; it fulfilled some greater cause. And because it meant something, they were able to endure it, or perhaps even enjoy it.

If suffering is inevitable, if our problems in life are un-avoidable, then the question we should be asking is not "How do I stop suffering?" but "*Why* am I suffering—for what purpose?"

Hiroo Onoda returned to Japan in 1974 and became a kind of celebrity in his home country. He was shuttled around from talk show to radio station; politicians clam-ored to shake his hand; he published a book and was even offered a large sum of money by the government.

But what he found when he returned to Japan horrified him: a consumerist, capitalist, superficial culture that had lost all of the traditions of honor and sacrifice upon which his generation had been raised.

Onoda tried to use his sudden celebrity to espouse the values of Old Japan, but he was tone-deaf to this new so-ciety. He was seen more as a showpiece than as a serious cultural thinker—a Japanese man who had emerged from a time capsule for all to marvel at, like a relic in a museum.

And in the irony of ironies, Onoda became far more depressed than he'd ever been in the jungle for all those years. At least in the jungle his life had stood for some-thing; it had meant something. That had made his suffer-ing endurable, indeed even a little bit desirable. But back in Japan, in what he considered to be a vacuous nation full of hippies and loose women in Western clothing, he was confronted with the unavoidable truth: that his fighting had meant nothing. The Japan he had lived and fought for no longer existed. And the weight of this realization pierced him in a way that no bullet ever had. Because his suffering had meant nothing, it suddenly became realized and true: thirty years wasted.

And so, in 1980, Onoda packed up and moved to Brazil, where he remained until he died.

The Self-Awareness Onion

Self-awareness is like an onion. There are multiple layers to it, and the more you peel them back, the more likely you're going to start crying at inappropriate times.

Let's say the first layer of the self-awareness onion is a simple understanding of one's emotions. "This is when I feel happy." "This makes me feel sad." "This gives me hope."

Unfortunately, there are many people who suck at even this most basic level of self-awareness. I know because I'm one of them. My wife and I sometimes have a fun back-and-forth that goes something like this:

> HER. What's wrong?
> ME. Nothing's wrong. Nothing at all.
> HER. No, something's wrong. Tell me.
> ME. I'm fine. Really.
> HER. Are you sure? You look upset.
> ME, *with nervous laughter.* Really? No, I'm okay,
>   seriously.

[*Thirty minutes later . . .*]

ME. . . . And that's why I'm so fucking pissed off! He just acts as if I don't exist half the time.

We all have emotional blind spots. Often they have to do with the emotions that we were taught were inappropriate growing up. It takes years of practice and effort to get good at identifying blind spots in ourselves and then expressing the affected emotions appropriately. But this task is hugely important, and worth the effort.

The second layer of the self-awareness onion is an ability to ask *why* we feel certain emotions.

These *why* questions are difficult and often take months or even years to answer consistently and accurately. Most people need to go to some sort of therapist just to hear these questions asked for the first time. Such questions are important because they illuminate what we consider success or failure. Why do you feel angry? Is it because you failed to achieve some goal? Why do you feel lethargic and uninspired? Is it because you don't think you're good enough?

This layer of questioning helps us understand the root cause of the emotions that overwhelm us. Once we understand that root cause, we can ideally do something to change it.

But there's another, even deeper level of the self-awareness onion. And that one is full of fucking tears. The third level is our personal values: *Why* do I consider this to be success/failure? How am I choosing to measure myself? By what standard am I judging myself and everyone around me?

This level, which takes constant questioning and effort, is incredibly difficult to reach. But it's the most important, because our values determine the nature of our problems, and the nature of our problems determines the quality of our lives.

Values underlie everything we are and do. If what we value is unhelpful, if what we consider success/failure is poorly chosen, then everything based upon those values— the thoughts, the emotions, the day-to-day feelings—will all be out of whack. Everything we think and feel about a situation ultimately comes back to how valuable we perceive it to be.

Most people are horrible at answering these *why* questions accurately, and this prevents them from achieving a deeper knowledge of their own values. Sure, they may *say* they value honesty and a true friend, but then they turn around and lie about you behind your back to make themselves feel better. People may perceive that they feel lonely. But when they ask themselves *why* they feel lonely, they tend to come up with a way to blame others—everyone else is mean, or no one is cool or smart enough to understand them—and thus they further avoid their problem instead of seeking to solve it.

For many people this passes as self-awareness. And yet, if they were able to go deeper and look at their underlying values, they would see that their original analysis was based on avoiding responsibility for their own problem, rather than accurately identifying the problem. They would see that their decisions were based on chasing highs, not generating true happiness.

Most self-help gurus ignore this deeper level of self-awareness as well. They take people who are miserable because they want to be rich, and then give them all sorts of advice on how to make more money, all the while ignoring important values-based questions: *Why* do they feel such a need to be rich in the first place? How are they choosing to measure success/failure for themselves? Is it not perhaps some particular value that's the root cause of their unhappiness, and not the fact that they don't drive a Bentley yet?

Much of the advice out there operates at a shallow level of simply trying to make people feel good in the short term, while the real long-term problems never get solved. People's perceptions and feelings may change, but the underlying values, and the metrics by which those values are assessed, stay the same. This is not real progress. This is just another way to achieve more highs.

Honest self-questioning is difficult. It requires asking yourself simple questions that are uncomfortable to answer. In fact, in my experience, the more uncomfortable the answer, the more likely it is to be true.

Take a moment and think of something that's really bugging you. Now ask yourself *why* it bugs you. Chances are the answer will involve a failure of some sort. Then take that failure and ask why it seems "true" to you. What if that failure wasn't really a failure? What if you've been looking at it the wrong way?

A recent example from my own life:

"It bugs me that my brother doesn't return my texts or
    emails."
Why?
"Because it feels like he doesn't give a shit about me."
Why does this seem true?
"Because if he wanted to have a relationship with me,
    he would take ten seconds out of his day to interact
    with me."
*Why does his lack of relationship with you feel like a
    failure?*
"Because we're brothers; we're supposed to have a good
    relationship!"

Two things are operating here: a value that I hold dear,
and a metric that I use to assess progress toward that value.
My value: brothers are supposed to have a good relationship
with one another. My metric: being in contact by phone or
email—this is how I measure my success as a brother. By
holding on to this metric, I make myself feel like a failure,
which occasionally ruins my Saturday mornings.

We could dig even deeper, by repeating the process:

Why are brothers supposed to have a good relationship?
"Because they're family, and family are supposed to be
    close!"
Why does that seem true?

"Because your family is supposed to matter to you
    more than anyone else!"
Why does that seem true?
"Because being close with your family is 'normal' and
    'healthy,' and I don't have that."

In this exchange I'm clear about my underlying value—
having a good relationship with my brother—but I'm still
struggling with my metric. I've given it another name, "close-
ness," but the metric hasn't really changed: I'm still judging
myself as a brother based on frequency of contact—and
comparing myself, using that metric, against other people I
know. Everyone else (or so it seems) has a close relationship
with their family members, and I don't. So obviously there
must be something wrong with me.

But what if I'm choosing a poor metric for myself and
my life? What else could be true that I'm not considering?
Well, perhaps I don't need to be *close* to my brother to have
that good relationship that I *value*. Perhaps there just needs
to be some mutual respect (which there is). Or maybe mutual trust is what to look for (and it's there). Perhaps *these*
metrics would be better assessments of brotherhood than
how many text messages he and I exchange.

This clearly makes sense; it feels true for me. But it still
fucking hurts that my brother and I aren't close. And there's
no positive way to spin it. There's no secret way to glorify
myself through this knowledge. Sometimes brothers—even
brothers who love each other—don't have close relationships,

and that's fine. It is hard to accept at first, but that's fine. What is objectively true about your situation is not as important as how you come to see the situation, how you choose to measure it and value it. Problems may be inevitable, but the *meaning* of each problem is not. We get to control what our problems mean based on how we choose to think about them, the standard by which we choose to measure them.

Rock Star Problems

In 1983, a talented young guitarist was kicked out of his band in the worst possible way. The band had just been signed to a record deal, and they were about to record their first album. But a couple days before recording began, the band showed the guitarist the door—no warning, no discussion, no dramatic blowout; they literally woke him up one day by handing him a bus ticket home.

As he sat on the bus back to Los Angeles from New York, the guitarist kept asking himself: How did this happen? What did I do wrong? What will I do now? Record contracts didn't exactly fall out of the sky, especially for raucous, upstart metal bands. Had he missed his one and only shot?

But by the time the bus hit L.A., the guitarist had gotten over his self-pity and had vowed to start a new band. He decided that this new band would be so successful that his old band would forever regret their decision. He would become so famous that they would be subjected to decades of seeing him on TV, hearing him on the radio, seeing posters of him in the streets and pictures of him in magazines. They'd be flipping burgers somewhere, loading vans from their shitty club gigs, fat and drunk with their ugly wives, and he'd be rocking out in front of stadium crowds live on television. He'd bathe in the tears of his betrayers, each tear wiped dry by a crisp, clean hundred-dollar bill.

And so the guitarist worked as if possessed by a musical demon. He spent months recruiting the best musicians he could find—far better musicians than his previous band-mates. He wrote dozens of songs and practiced religiously. His seething anger fueled his ambition; revenge became his muse. Within a couple years, his new band had signed a record deal of their own, and a year after that, their first record would go gold.

The guitarist's name was Dave Mustaine, and the new band he formed was the legendary heavy-metal band Megadeth. Megadeth would go on to sell over 25 million al-bums and tour the world many times over. Today, Mustaine is considered one of the most brilliant and influential mu-sicians in the history of heavy-metal music.

Unfortunately, the band he was kicked out of was Metallica, which has sold over 180 million albums world-wide. Metallica is considered by many to be one of the greatest rock bands of all time.

And because of this, in a rare intimate interview in 2003, a tearful Mustaine admitted that he couldn't help but *still* consider himself a failure. Despite all that he had accom-plished, in his mind he would always be the guy who got kicked out of Metallica.

We're apes. We think we're all sophisticated with our toaster ovens and designer footwear, but we're just a bunch of finely ornamented apes. And because we are apes, we instinctually measure ourselves against others and vie for status. The question is not *whether* we evaluate ourselves against others; rather, the question is *by what standard* do we measure ourselves?

Dave Mustaine, whether he realized it or not, chose to measure himself by whether he was more successful and popular than Metallica. The experience of getting thrown out of his former band was so painful for him that he adopted "success relative to Metallica" as the metric by which to measure himself and his music career.

Despite taking a horrible event in his life and making something positive out of it, as Mustaine did with Megadeth, his choice to hold on to Metallica's success as his life-defining metric continued to hurt him decades later. Despite all the money and the fans and the accolades, he still considered himself a failure.

Now, you and I may look at Dave Mustaine's situation and laugh. Here's this guy with millions of dollars, hundreds of thousands of adoring fans, a career doing the thing he loves best, and *still* he's getting all weepy-eyed that his rock star buddies from twenty years ago are way more famous than he is.

This is because you and I have different values than Mustaine does, and we measure ourselves by different metrics. Our metrics are probably more like "I don't want to work a job for a boss I hate," or "I'd like to earn enough money to send my kid to a good school," or "I'd be happy to not wake up in a drainage ditch." And by these metrics,

Mustaine is wildly, unimaginably successful. But by *his* metric, "Be more popular and successful than Metallica," he's a failure.

Our values determine the metrics by which we measure ourselves and everyone else. Onoda's value of loyalty to the Japanese empire is what sustained him on Lubang for almost thirty years. But this same value is also what made him miserable upon his return to Japan. Mustaine's metric of being better than Metallica likely helped him launch an incredibly successful music career. But that same metric later tortured him in spite of his success.

If you want to change how you see your problems, you have to change what you value and/or how you measure failure/success.

As an example, let's look at another musician who got kicked out of another band. His story eerily echoes that of Dave Mustaine, although it happened two decades earlier.

It was 1962 and there was a buzz around an up-and-coming band from Liverpool, England. This band had funny haircuts and an even funnier name, but their music was undeniably good, and the record industry was finally taking notice.

There was John, the lead singer and songwriter; Paul, the boyish-faced romantic bass player; George, the rebellious lead guitar player. And then there was the drummer.

He was considered the best-looking of the bunch—the girls all went wild for him, and it was his face that began to appear in the magazines first. He was the most professional member of the group too. He didn't do drugs. He had a steady girlfriend. There were even a few people in suits and ties who thought *he* should be the face of the band, not John or Paul.

His name was Pete Best. And in 1962, after landing their first record contract, the other three members of the Beatles quietly got together and asked their manager, Brian Epstein, to fire him. Epstein agonized over the decision. He liked Pete, so he put it off, hoping the other three guys would change their minds.

Months later, a mere three days before the recording of the first record began, Epstein finally called Best to his office. There, the manager unceremoniously told him to piss off and find another band. He gave no reason, no explanation, no condolences—just told him that the other guys wanted him out of the group, so, uh, best of luck.

As a replacement, the band brought in some oddball named Ringo Starr. Ringo was older and had a big, funny nose. Ringo agreed to get the same ugly haircut as John, Paul, and George, and insisted on writing songs about octopuses and submarines. The other guys said, Sure, fuck it, why not?

Within six months of Best's firing, Beatlemania had erupted, making John, Paul, George, and ~~Pete~~ Ringo arguably four of the most famous faces on the entire planet.

Meanwhile, Best understandably fell into a deep depression and spent a lot of time doing what any Englishman will do if you give him a reason to: drink.

The rest of the sixties were not kind to Pete Best. By 1965, he had sued two of the Beatles for slander, and all of his other musical projects had failed horribly. In 1968, he attempted suicide, only to be talked out of it by his mother. His life was a wreck.

Best didn't have the same redemptive story Dave Mustaine did. He never became a global superstar or made millions of dollars. Yet, in many ways, Best ended up better off than Mustaine. In an interview in 1994, Best said, "I'm happier than I would have been with the Beatles."

What the hell?

Best explained that the circumstances of his getting kicked out of the Beatles ultimately led him to meet his wife. And then his marriage led him to having children. His values changed. He began to measure his life differently. Fame and glory would have been nice, sure—but he decided that what he already had was more important: a big and loving family, a stable marriage, a simple life. He even still got to play drums, touring Europe and recording albums well into the 2000s. So what was really lost? Just a lot of attention and adulation, whereas what was gained meant so much more to him.

These stories suggest that some values and metrics are better than others. Some lead to good problems that are easily and regularly solved. Others lead to bad problems that are not easily and regularly solved.

Shitty Values

There are a handful of common values that create really poor problems for people—problems that can hardly be solved. So let's go over some of them quickly:

1. *Pleasure.* Pleasure is great, but it's a horrible value to prioritize your life around. Ask any drug addict how his pursuit of pleasure turned out. Ask an adulterer who shattered her family and lost her children whether pleasure ultimately made her happy. Ask a man who almost ate himself to death how pleasure helped him solve his problems.

   Pleasure is a false god. Research shows that people who focus their energy on superficial pleasures end up more anxious, more emotionally unstable, and more depressed. Pleasure is the most superficial form of life satisfaction and therefore the easiest to obtain and the easiest to lose.

   And yet, pleasure is what's marketed to us, twenty-four/seven. It's what we fixate on. It's what we use to numb and distract ourselves. But pleasure, while necessary in life (in certain doses), isn't, by itself, sufficient.

   Pleasure is not the cause of happiness; rather, it is the effect. If you get the other stuff right (the other values and metrics), then pleasure will naturally occur as a by-product.

2. *Material Success.* Many people measure their self-worth based on how much money they make or what kind of car they drive or whether their front lawn is greener and prettier than the next-door neighbor's.

   Research shows that once one is able to provide for basic physical needs (food, shelter, and so on), the correlation between happiness and worldly success quickly approaches zero. So if you're starving and living on the street in the middle of India, an extra ten thousand dollars a year would affect your happiness a lot. But if you're sitting pretty in the middle class in a developed country, an extra ten thousand dollars per year won't affect anything much—meaning that you're killing yourself working overtime and weekends for basically nothing.

The other issue with overvaluing material success is the danger of prioritizing it over other values, such as honesty, nonviolence, and compassion. When people measure themselves not by their behavior, but by the status symbols they're able to collect, then not only are they shallow, but they're probably assholes as well.

3. *Always Being Right.* Our brains are inefficient machines. We consistently make poor assumptions, misjudge probabilities, misremember facts, give in to cognitive biases, and make decisions based on our emotional whims. As humans, we're wrong pretty much constantly, so if your metric for life success is to be right—well, you're going to have a difficult time rationalizing all of the bullshit to yourself.

The fact is, people who base their self-worth on being right about everything prevent themselves from learning from their mistakes. They lack the ability to take on new perspectives and empathize with others. They close themselves off to new and important information.

It's far more helpful to assume that you're ignorant and don't know a whole lot. This keeps you unattached to superstitious or poorly informed beliefs and promotes a constant state of learning and growth.

4. *Staying Positive.* Then there are those who measure their lives by the ability to be positive about, well, pretty much everything. Lost your job? Great! That's an opportunity to explore your passions. Husband cheated on you with your sister? Well, at least you're learning what you really mean to the people around you. Child dying of throat cancer? At least you don't have to pay for college anymore!

While there is something to be said for "staying on the sunny side of life," the truth is, sometimes life sucks, and the healthiest thing you can do is admit it.

Denying negative emotions leads to experiencing deeper and more prolonged negative emotions and to emotional dysfunction. Constant positivity is a form of avoidance, not a valid solution to life's problems—problems which, by the way, if you're choosing the right values and metrics, should be invigorating you and motivating you.

It's simple, really: things go wrong, people upset us, accidents happen. These things make us feel like shit. And that's fine. Negative emotions are a necessary component of emotional health. To deny that negativity is to *perpetuate* problems rather than solve them.

The trick with negative emotions is to 1) express them in a socially acceptable and healthy manner and 2) express them in a way that aligns with your values. Simple example: A value of mine is nonviolence. Therefore, when I get mad at somebody, I express that anger, but I also make a point of not punching them in the face. Radical idea, I know. But the anger is not the problem.

Anger is natural. Anger is a part of life. Anger is arguably quite healthy in many situations. (Remember, emotions are just feedback.)

See, it's the punching people in the face that's the problem. Not the anger. The anger is merely the messenger for my fist in your face. Don't blame the messenger. Blame my fist (or your face).

When we force ourselves to stay positive at all times, we deny the existence of our life's problems. And when we deny our problems, we rob ourselves of the chance to solve them and generate happiness. Problems add a sense of meaning and importance to our life. Thus to duck our problems is to lead a meaningless (even if supposedly pleasant) existence.

In the long run, completing a marathon makes us happier than eating a chocolate cake. Raising a child makes us happier than beating a video game. Starting a small business with friends while struggling to make ends meet makes us happier than buying a new computer. These activities are stressful, arduous, and often unpleasant. They also require withstanding problem after problem. Yet they are some of the most meaningful moments and joyous things we'll ever do. They involve pain, struggle, even anger and despair—yet once they're accomplished, we look back and get all misty-eyed telling our grandkids about them.

As Freud once said, "One day, in retrospect, the years of struggle will strike you as the most beautiful."

This is why these values—pleasure, material success, always being right, staying positive—are poor ideals for a person's life. Some of the greatest moments of one's life are *not* pleasant, *not* successful, *not* known, and *not* positive.

The point is to nail down some good values and metrics, and pleasure and success will naturally emerge as a result. These things are side effects of good values. By themselves, they are empty highs.

Defining Good and Bad Values

Good values are 1) reality-based, 2) socially constructive, and 3) immediate and controllable.

Bad values are 1) superstitious, 2) socially destructive, and 3) not immediate or controllable.

Honesty is a good value because it's something you have complete control over, it reflects reality, and it benefits others (even if it's sometimes unpleasant). Popularity, on the other hand, is a bad value. If that's your value, and if your metric is being the most popular guy/girl at the dance party, much of what happens will be out of your control: you don't know who else will be at the event, and you probably won't know who half those people are. Second, the value/metric isn't based on reality: you may *feel* popular or unpopular, when in fact you have no fucking clue what anybody else really thinks about you. (Side Note: As a rule, people who are terrified of what others think about them are actually terrified of all the shitty things they think about themselves being reflected back at them.)

Some examples of good, healthy values: honesty,

innovation, vulnerability, standing up for oneself, standing up for others, self-respect, curiosity, charity, humility, creativity.

Some examples of bad, unhealthy values: dominance through manipulation or violence, indiscriminate fucking, feeling good all the time, always being the center of attention, not being alone, being liked by everybody, being rich for the sake of being rich, sacrificing small animals to the pagan gods.

You'll notice that good, healthy values are achieved internally. Something like creativity or humility can be experienced right now. You simply have to orient your mind in a certain way to experience it. These values are immediate and controllable and engage you with the world as it is rather than how you wish it were.

Bad values are generally reliant on external events—flying in a private jet, being told you're right all the time, owning a house in the Bahamas, eating a cannoli while getting blown by three strippers. Bad values, while sometimes fun or pleasurable, lie outside of your control and often require socially destructive or superstitious means to achieve.

Values are about prioritization. *Everybody* would love a good cannoli or a house in the Bahamas. The question is your priorities. What are the values that you prioritize above everything else, and that therefore influence your decision-making more than anything else?

Hiroo Onoda's highest value was complete loyalty and service to the Japanese empire. This value, in case you couldn't tell from reading about him, stank worse than a rotten sushi roll. It created really shitty problems for Hiroo—namely, he got stuck on a remote island where he lived off bugs and worms for thirty years. Oh, and he felt compelled to murder innocent civilians too. So despite the fact that Hiroo saw himself as a success, and despite the fact he lived up to his metrics, I think we can all agree that his life really sucked—none of us would trade shoes with him given the opportunity, nor would we commend his actions.

Dave Mustaine achieved great fame and glory and felt like a failure anyway. This is because he'd adopted a crappy value based on some arbitrary comparison to the success of others. This value gave him awful problems such as, "I need to sell 150 million more records; *then* everything will be great," and "My next tour needs to be nothing but stadiums"—problems he thought he needed to solve in order to be happy. It's no surprise that he wasn't.

On the contrary, Pete Best pulled a switcheroo. Despite being depressed and distraught by getting kicked out of the Beatles, as he grew older he learned to reprioritize what he cared about and was able to measure his life in a new light. Because of this, Best grew into a happy and healthy old man, with an easy life and great family—things that, ironically, the four Beatles would spend decades struggling to achieve or maintain.

When we have poor values—that is, poor standards we set for ourselves and others—we are essentially giving fucks about the things that don't matter, things that in fact make our life worse. But when we choose better values, we are able to divert our fucks to something better—toward things that matter, things that improve the state of our well-being and that generate happiness, pleasure, and success as side effects.

This, in a nutshell, is what "self-improvement" is really about: prioritizing better values, choosing better things to give a fuck about. Because when you give better fucks, you get better problems. And when you get better problems, you get a better life.

The rest of this book is dedicated to five counterintuitive values that I believe are the most beneficial values one can adopt. All follow the "backwards law" we talked about earlier, in that they're "negative." All require *confronting* deeper problems rather than avoiding them through highs. These five values are both unconventional and uncomfortable. But, to me, they are life-changing.

The first, which we'll look at in the next chapter, is a radical form of responsibility: taking responsibility for everything that occurs in your life, regardless of who's at fault. The second is uncertainty: the acknowledgement of your own ignorance and the cultivation of constant doubt in your own beliefs. The next is failure: the willingness to discover your own flaws and mistakes so that they may be improved upon. The fourth is rejection: the ability to both say and hear no, thus clearly defining what you will and will not accept in your life. The final value is the contemplation of one's own mortality; this one is crucial, because paying vigilant attention to one's own death is perhaps the only thing capable of helping us keep all our other values in proper perspective.

CHAPTER

5

You Are Always Choosing

Imagine that somebody puts a gun to your head and tells you that you have to run 26.2 miles in under five hours, or else he'll kill you and your entire family.

That would suck.

Now imagine that you bought nice shoes and running gear, trained religiously for months, and completed your first marathon with all of your closest family and friends cheering you on at the finish line.

That could potentially be one of the proudest moments of your life.

Exact same 26.2 miles. Exact same person running them. Exact same pain coursing through your exact same legs. But when you chose it freely and prepared for it, it was a glorious and important milestone in your life. When it was forced upon you against your will, it was one of the most terrifying and painful experiences of your life.

Often the only difference between a problem being painful or being powerful is a sense that we *chose* it, and that we are responsible for it.

If you're miserable in your current situation, chances are it's because you feel like some part of it is outside your control—that there's a problem you have no ability to solve, a problem that was somehow thrust upon you without your choosing.

When we feel that we're choosing our problems, we feel empowered. When we feel that our problems are being forced upon us against our will, we feel victimized and miserable.

The Choice

William James had problems. Really bad problems.

Although born into a wealthy and prominent family, from birth James suffered life-threatening health issues: an eye problem that left him temporarily blinded as a child; a terrible stomach condition that caused excessive vomiting and forced him to adopt an obscure and highly sensitive diet; trouble with his hearing; back spasms so bad that for days at a time he often couldn't sit or stand upright.

Due to his health problems, James spent most of his time at home. He didn't have many friends, and he wasn't particularly good at school. Instead, he passed the days painting. That was the only thing he liked and the only thing he felt particularly good at.

Unfortunately, nobody else thought he was good at it. When he grew to adulthood, nobody bought his work. And as the years dragged on, his father (a wealthy businessman) began ridiculing him for his laziness and his lack of talent.

Meanwhile, his younger brother, Henry James, went on to become a world-renowned novelist; his sister, Alice James, made a good living as a writer as well. William was the family oddball, the black sheep.

In a desperate attempt to salvage the young man's future, James's father used his business connections to get him admitted into Harvard Medical School. It was his last chance, his father told him. If he screwed this up, there was no hope for him.

But James never felt at home or at peace at Harvard. Medicine never appealed to him. He spent the whole time feeling like a fake and a fraud. After all, if he couldn't overcome his own problems, how could he ever hope to have the energy to help others with theirs? After touring a psychiatric facility one day, James mused in his diary that he felt he had more in common with the patients than with the doctors.

A few years went by and, again to his father's disapproval, James dropped out of medical school. But rather than deal with the brunt of his father's wrath, he decided to get away: he signed up to join an anthropological expedition to the Amazon rain forest.

This was in the 1860s, so transcontinental travel was difficult and dangerous. If you ever played the computer game *Oregon Trail* when you were a kid, it was kind of like that, with the dysentery and drowning oxen and everything.

Anyway, James made it all the way to the Amazon, where the real adventure was to begin. Surprisingly, his fragile health held up that whole way. But once he finally made it, on the first day of the expedition, he promptly contracted smallpox and nearly died in the jungle.

Then his back spasms returned, painful to the point of making James unable to walk. By this time, he was emaciated and starved from the smallpox, immobilized by his bad back, and left alone in the middle of South America (the rest of the expedition having gone on without him) with no clear way to get home—a journey that would take months and likely kill him anyway.

But somehow he eventually made it back to New England, where he was greeted by an (even more) disappointed father. By this point the young man wasn't so young anymore—nearly thirty years old, still unemployed, a failure at everything he had attempted, with a body that routinely betrayed him and wasn't likely to ever get better. Despite all the advantages and opportunities he'd been given in life, everything had fallen apart. The only constants in his life seemed to be suffering and disappointment. James fell into a deep depression and began making plans to take his own life.

But one night, while reading lectures by the philosopher Charles Peirce, James decided to conduct a little experiment. In his diary, he wrote that he would spend one year believing that he was 100 percent responsible for everything that occurred in his life, no matter what. During this period, he would do everything in his power to change his circumstances, no matter the likelihood of failure. If nothing improved in that year, then it would be apparent that he was truly powerless to the circumstances around him, and then he would take his own life.

The punch line? William James went on to become the father of American psychology. His work has been translated into a bazillion languages, and he's regarded as one of the most influential intellectuals/philosophers/psychologists of his generation. He would go on to teach at Harvard and would tour much of the United States and Europe giving lectures. He would marry and have five children (one of whom, Henry, would become a famous biographer and win a Pulitzer Prize). James would later refer to his little experiment as his "rebirth," and would credit it with *everything* that he later accomplished in his life.

There is a simple realization from which all personal improvement and growth emerges. This is the realization that we, individually, are responsible for everything in our lives, no matter the external circumstances.

We don't always control what happens to us. But we *always* control how we interpret what happens to us, as well as how we respond.

Whether we consciously recognize it or not, we are always responsible for our experiences. It's impossible not to be. Choosing to *not* consciously interpret events in our lives is still an interpretation of the events of our lives. Choosing to *not* respond to the events in our lives is still a response to the events in our lives. Even if you get run over by a clown car and pissed on by a busload of schoolchildren, it's still *your responsibility* to interpret the meaning of the event and choose a response.

Whether we like it or not, we are *always* taking an active role in what's occurring to and within us. We are always interpreting the meaning of every moment and every occurrence. We are always choosing the values by which we live and the metrics by which we measure everything that happens to us. Often the same event can be good or bad, depending on the metric we choose to use.

The point is, we are *always* choosing, whether we recognize it or not. Always.

It comes back to how, in reality, there is no such thing as not giving a single fuck. It's impossible. We must all give a fuck about something. To not give a fuck about *anything* is still to give a fuck about *something*.

The real question is, What are we choosing to give a fuck about? What values are we choosing to base our actions on? What metrics are we choosing to use to measure our life? And are those *good* choices—good values and good metrics?

The Responsibility/Fault Fallacy

Years ago, when I was much younger and stupider, I wrote a blog post, and at the end of it I said something like, "And as a great philosopher once said: 'With great power comes great responsibility.'" It sounded nice and authoritative. I couldn't remember who had said it, and my Google search had turned up nothing, but I stuck it in there anyway. It fit the post nicely.

About ten minutes later, the first comment came in: "I think the 'great philosopher' you're referring to is Uncle Ben from the movie *Spider-Man*."

As another great philosopher once said, "Doh!"

"With great power comes great responsibility." The last words of Uncle Ben before a thief whom Peter Parker let get away murders him on a sidewalk full of people for absolutely no explicable reason. *That* great philosopher.

Still, we've all heard the quote. It gets repeated a lot—usually ironically and after about seven beers. It's one of those perfect quotes that sound really intelligent, and yet it's basically just telling you what you already know, even if you've never quite thought about the matter before.

"With great power comes great responsibility."

It is true. But there's a better version of this quote, a version that actually *is* profound, and all you have to do is switch the nouns around: "With great responsibility comes great power."

The more we choose to accept responsibility in our lives, the more power we will exercise over our lives. Accepting responsibility for our problems is thus the first step to solving them.

I once knew a man who was convinced that the reason no woman would date him was because he was too short. He was educated, interesting, and good-looking—a good catch, in principle—but he was absolutely convinced that women found him too short to date.

And because *he* felt that he was too short, he didn't often go out and try to meet women. The few times he did, he would hone in on the smallest behaviors from any woman he talked with that could possibly indicate he wasn't attractive enough for her and then convince himself that she didn't like him, even if she really did. As you can imagine, his dating life sucked.

What he didn't realize was that *he* had chosen the value that was hurting him: height. Women, he assumed, are attracted only to height. He was screwed, no matter what he did.

This choice of value was disempowering. It gave this man a really crappy problem: not being tall enough in a world meant (in his view) for tall people. There are far better values that he could have adopted in his dating life. "I want to date only women who like me for who I am" might have been a nice place to start—a metric that assesses the values of honesty and acceptance. But he did not choose these values. He likely wasn't even aware that he *was* choosing his value (or *could* do so). Even though he didn't realize it, he was responsible for his own problems.

Despite that responsibility, he went on complaining: "But I don't have a choice," he would tell the bartender. "There's nothing I can do! Women are superficial and vain and will never like me!" Yes, it's *every single woman's fault* for not liking a self-pitying, shallow guy with shitty values. Obviously.

A lot of people hesitate to take responsibility for their problems because they believe that to be *responsible* for your problems is to also be *at fault* for your problems.

Responsibility and fault often appear together in our

culture. But they're not the same thing. If I hit you with my car, I am both at fault and likely legally responsible to compensate you in some way. Even if hitting you with my car was an accident, I am still responsible. This is the way fault works in our society: if you fuck up, you're on the hook for making it right. And it should be that way.

But there are also problems that we *aren't* at fault for, yet we are still responsible for them.

For example, if you woke up one day and there was a newborn baby on your doorstep, it would not be your *fault* that the baby had been put there, but the baby would now be your *responsibility*. You would have to choose what to do. And whatever you ended up choosing (keeping it, getting rid of it, ignoring it, feeding it to a pit bull), there would be problems associated with your choice—and you would be responsible for those as well.

Judges don't get to choose their cases. When a case goes to court, the judge assigned to it did not commit the crime, was not a witness to the crime, and was not affected by the crime, but he or she is still *responsible* for the crime. The judge must then choose the consequences; he or she must identify the metric against which the crime will be measured and make sure that the chosen metric is carried out.

We are responsible for experiences that aren't our fault all the time. This is part of life.

Here's one way to think about the distinction between the two concepts. Fault is past tense. Responsibility is present tense. Fault results from choices that have already been made. Responsibility results from the choices you're

currently making, every second of every day. You are choosing to read this. You are choosing to think about the concepts. You are choosing to accept or reject the concepts. It
may be *my* fault that you think my ideas are lame, but *you*
are responsible for coming to your own conclusions. It's not
your fault that I chose to write this sentence, but you are still
responsible for choosing to read it (or not).

There's a difference between blaming someone else for
your situation and that person's actually being responsible for your situation. Nobody else is ever responsible for
your situation but you. Many people may be to blame for
your unhappiness, but nobody is ever *responsible* for your
unhappiness but you. This is because *you* always get to
choose how you see things, how you react to things, how
you value things. You always get to choose the metric by
which to measure your experiences.

My first girlfriend dumped me in spectacular fashion.
She was cheating on me with her teacher. It was awesome.
And by awesome, I mean it felt like getting punched in the
stomach about 253 times. To make things worse, when I
confronted her about it, she promptly left me for him.
Three years together, down the toilet just like that.

I was miserable for months afterward. That was to be
expected. But I also held her responsible for my misery.
Which, take it from me, didn't get me very far. It just made
the misery worse.

See, I couldn't control her. No matter how many times
I called her, or screamed at her, or begged her to take me
back, or made surprise visits to her place, or did other

creepy and irrational ex-boyfriend things, I could never control her emotions or her actions. Ultimately, while she was *to blame* for how I felt, she was never *responsible* for how I felt. I was.

At some point, after enough tears and alcohol, my thinking began to shift and I began to understand that although she had done something horrible to me and she could be blamed for that, it was now my own responsibility to make myself happy again. She was never going to pop up and fix things for me. I had to fix them for myself.

When I took that approach, a few things happened. First, I began to improve myself. I started exercising and spending more time with my friends (whom I had been neglecting). I started deliberately meeting new people. I took a big study-abroad trip and did some volunteer work. And slowly, I started to feel better.

I still resented my ex for what she had done. But at least now I was taking responsibility for my own emotions. And by doing so, I was choosing better values—values aimed at taking care of myself, learning to feel better about myself, rather than aimed at getting her to fix what she'd broken.

(By the way, this whole "holding her responsible for my emotions" thing is probably part of why she left in the first place. More on that in a couple chapters.)

Then, about a year later, something funny began to happen. As I looked back on our relationship, I started to notice problems I had never noticed before, problems that *I* was to blame for and that *I* could have done something to solve. I realized that it was likely that I hadn't been a great boyfriend, and that people don't just magically cheat on somebody they've been with unless they are unhappy for some reason.

I'm not saying that this excused what my ex did—not at all. But recognizing my mistakes helped me to realize that I perhaps hadn't been the innocent victim I'd believed myself to be. That I had a role to play in enabling the shitty relationship to continue for as long as it did. After all, people who date each other tend to have similar values. And if I dated someone with shitty values for that long, what did that say about me and my values? I learned the hard way that if the people in your relationships are selfish and doing hurtful things, it's likely you are too, you just don't realize it.

In hindsight, I was able to look back and see warning signs of my ex-girlfriend's character, signs I had chosen to ignore or brush off when I was with her. *That* was my fault. I could look back and see that I hadn't exactly been the Boyfriend of the Year to her either. In fact, I had often been cold and arrogant toward her; other times I took her for granted and blew her off and hurt her. *These* things were my fault too.

Did my mistakes justify her mistake? No. But still, I took on the responsibility of never making those same mistakes again, and never overlooking the same signs again, to help guarantee that I will never suffer the same consequences again. I took on the responsibility of striving to make my future relationships with women that much better. And I'm happy to report that I have. No more cheating girl-friends leaving me, no more 253 stomach punches. I took responsibility for my problems and improved upon them. I took responsibility for my role in that unhealthy relationship and improved upon it with later relationships.

And you know what? My ex leaving me, while one of the most painful experiences I've ever had, was also one of the most important and influential experiences of my life. I credit it with inspiring a significant amount of personal growth. I learned more from that single problem than dozens of my successes combined.

We all love to take responsibility for success and happiness. Hell, we often *fight over* who gets to be responsible for success and happiness. But taking responsibility for our problems is far more important, because that's where the real learning comes from. That's where the real-life improvement comes from. To simply blame others is only to hurt yourself.

Responding to Tragedy

But what about really awful events? A lot of people can get on board with taking responsibility for work-related problems and maybe watching too much TV when they should really be playing with their kids or being productive. But when it comes to horrible tragedies, they pull the emergency cord on the responsibility train and get off when it stops. Some things just feel too painful for them to own up to.

But think about it: the intensity of the event doesn't change the underlying truth. If you get robbed, say, you're obviously not at fault for being robbed. No one would ever choose to go through that. But as with the baby on your doorstep, you are immediately thrust into responsibility for a life-and-death situation. Do you fight back? Do you panic? Do you freeze up? Do you tell the police? Do you try to forget it and pretend it never happened? These are all choices and reactions you're responsible for making or rejecting. You didn't choose the robbery, but it's still your responsibility to manage the emotional and psychological (and legal) fallout of the experience.

In 2008, the Taliban took control of the Swat Valley, a remote part of northeastern Pakistan. They quickly implemented their Muslim extremist agenda. No television. No films. No women outside the house without a male escort. No girls attending school.

By 2009, an eleven-year-old Pakistani girl named Malala Yousafzai had begun to speak out against the school ban. She continued to attend her local school, risking both her and her father's lives; she also attended conferences in nearby cities. She wrote online, "How dare the Taliban take away my right for education?"

In 2012, at the age of fourteen, she was shot in the face as she rode the bus home from school one day. A masked Taliban soldier armed with a rifle boarded the bus and asked, "Who is Malala? Tell me, or I will shoot everyone here." Malala identified herself (an amazing choice in and of itself), and the man shot her in the head in front of all the other passengers.

Malala went into a coma and almost died. The Taliban

stated publicly that if she somehow survived the attempt, they would kill both her and her father.

Today, Malala is still alive. She still speaks out against violence and oppression toward women in Muslim countries, now as a best-selling author. In 2014 she received the Nobel Peace Prize for her efforts. It would seem that being shot in the face only gave her a larger audience and more courage than before. It would have been easy for her to lie down and say, "I can't do anything," or "I have no choice." That, ironically, would still have been her choice. But she chose the opposite.

A few years ago, I had written about some of the ideas in this chapter on my blog, and a man left a comment. He said that I was shallow and superficial, adding that I had no real understanding of life's problems or human responsibility. He said that his son had recently died in a car accident. He accused me of not knowing what true pain was and said that I was an asshole for suggesting that he himself was responsible for the pain he felt over his son's death.

This man had obviously suffered pain much greater than most people ever have to confront in their lives. He didn't choose for his son to die, nor was it his fault that his son died. The responsibility for coping with that loss was given to him even though it was clearly and understandably unwanted. But despite all that, he was still responsible for his own emotions, beliefs, and actions. How he reacted to his son's death was his own choice. Pain of one sort or another is inevitable for all of us, but we get to choose what it means to and for us. Even in claiming that he had *no* choice in the matter and simply wanted his son back, he was making a choice—one of many ways he could have chosen to use that pain.

Of course, I didn't say any of this to him. I was too busy being horrified and thinking that yes, perhaps I was way in over my head and had no idea what the fuck I was talking about. That's a hazard that comes with my line of work. A problem that I chose. And a problem that I was responsible for dealing with.

At first, I felt awful. But then, after a few minutes, I began to get angry. His objections had little to do with what I was actually saying, I told myself. And what the hell? Just because I don't have a kid who died doesn't mean I haven't experienced terrible pain myself.

But then I actually applied my own advice. I chose my problem. I could get mad at this man and argue with him, try to "outpain" him with my own pain, which would just make us both look stupid and insensitive. Or I could choose a better problem, working on practicing patience, understanding my readers better, and keeping that man in mind every time I wrote about pain and trauma from then on. And that's what I've tried to do.

I replied simply that I was sorry for his loss and left it at that. What else can you say?

Genetics and the Hand We're Dealt

In 2013, the BBC rounded up half a dozen teenagers with obsessive-compulsive disorder (OCD) and followed them as they attended intensive therapies to help them overcome their unwanted thoughts and repetitive behaviors.

There was Imogen, a seventeen-year-old girl who had a compulsive need to tap every surface she walked past; if she failed to do so, she was flooded with horrible thoughts of her family dying. There was Josh, who needed to do everything with both sides of his body—shake a person's hand with both his right and his left hand, eat his food with each hand, step through a doorway with both feet, and so on. If he didn't "equalize" his two sides, he suffered from severe panic attacks. And then there was Jack, a classic germophobe who refused to leave his house without wearing gloves, boiled all his water before drinking it, and refused to eat food not cleaned and prepared himself.

OCD is a terrible neurological and genetic disorder that cannot be cured. At best, it can be managed. And, as we'll see, managing the disorder comes down to managing one's values.

The first thing the psychiatrists on this project do is tell the kids that they're to accept the imperfections of their compulsive desires. What that means, as one example, is that when Imogen becomes flooded with horrible thoughts of her family dying, she is to accept that her family may actually die and that there's nothing she can do about it; simply put, she is told that what happens to her is not her fault. Josh is forced to accept that over the long term, "equalizing" all of his behaviors to make them symmetrical is actually destroying his life more than occasional panic attacks would. And Jack is reminded that no matter what he does, germs are always present and always infecting him.

The goal is to get the kids to recognize that their values are not rational—that in fact their values are not even theirs, but rather are the disorder's—and that by fulfilling these irrational values they are actually harming their ability to function in life.

The next step is to encourage the kids to choose a value that is more important than their OCD value and to focus on that. For Josh, it's the possibility of not having to hide his disorder from his friends and family all the time, the prospect of having a normal, functioning social life. For Imogen, it's the idea of taking control over her own thoughts and feelings and being happy again. And for Jack, it's the ability to leave his house for long periods of time without suffering traumatic episodes.

With these new values held front and center in their minds, the teenagers set out on intensive desensitization exercises that force them to live out their new values. Panic attacks ensue; tears are shed; Jack punches an array of inanimate objects and then immediately washes his hands. But by the end of the documentary, major progress has been made. Imogen no longer needs to tap every surface she comes across. She says, "There are still monsters in the back of my mind, and there probably always will be, but they're getting quieter now." Josh is able to go periods of twenty-five to thirty minutes without "equalizing" his behaviors between both sides of his body. And Jack, who makes perhaps the most improvement, is actually able to go out to restaurants and drink out of bottles and glasses without washing them first. Jack sums up well what he learned: "I didn't choose this life; I didn't choose this horrible, horrible condition. But I get to choose how to live with it; I *have to* choose how to live with it."

A lot of people treat being born with a disadvantage, whether OCD or small stature or something very different, as though they were screwed out of something highly valuable. They feel that there's nothing they can do about it, so they avoid responsibility for their situation. They figure, "I didn't choose my crappy genetics, so it's not my fault if things go wrong."

And it's true, it's not their fault.

But it's still their responsibility.

Back in college, I had a bit of a delusional fantasy of becoming a professional poker player. I won money and everything, and it was fun, but after almost a year of serious play, I quit. The lifestyle of staying up all night staring at a computer screen, winning thousands of dollars one day and then losing most of it the next, wasn't for me, and it wasn't exactly the most healthy or emotionally stable means of earning a living. But my time playing poker had a surprisingly profound influence on the way I see life.

The beauty of poker is that while luck is always involved, luck doesn't dictate the long-term results of the game. A person can get dealt terrible cards and beat someone who was dealt great cards. Sure, the person who gets dealt great cards has a higher likelihood of winning the hand, but ultimately the winner is determined by—yup, you guessed it—the *choices* each player makes through-out play.

I see life in the same terms. We all get dealt cards. Some of us get better cards than others. And while it's easy to get hung up on our cards, and feel we got screwed over, the real game lies in the choices we make with those cards, the risks we decide to take, and the consequences we choose to live with. People who consistently make the best choices in the situations they're given are the ones who eventually come out ahead in poker, just as in life. And it's not necessarily the people with the best cards.

There are those who suffer psychologically and emotion-ally from neurological and/or genetic deficiencies. But this changes nothing. Sure, they inherited a bad hand and are not to blame. No more than the short guy wanting to get a date is to blame for being short. Or the person who got robbed is to blame for being robbed. But it's still their responsibility. Whether they choose to seek psychiatric treatment, under-go therapy, or do nothing, the choice is ultimately theirs to make. There are those who suffer through bad childhoods. There are those who are abused and violated and screwed over, physically, emotionally, financially. They are not to blame for their problems and their hindrances, but they are still responsible—*always* responsible—to move on despite their problems and to make the best choices they can, given their circumstances.

And let's be honest here. If you were to add up *all* of the people who have some psychiatric disorder, struggle with depression or suicidal thoughts, have been subjected to neglect or abuse, have dealt with tragedy or the death of a loved one, and have survived serious health issues, accidents, or trauma—if you were to round up *all of those people* and put them in the room, well, you'd probably have to round up everyone, because nobody makes it through life without collecting a few scars on the way out.

Sure, some people get saddled with worse problems than others. And some people are legitimately victimized in horrible ways. But as much as this may upset us or disturb us, it ultimately changes nothing about the responsibility equation of our individual situation.

Victimhood Chic

The responsibility/fault fallacy allows people to pass off the responsibility for solving their problems to others. This ability to alleviate responsibility through blame gives people a temporary high and a feeling of moral righteousness.

Unfortunately, one side effect of the Internet and social media is that it's become easier than ever to push responsibility—for even the tiniest of infractions—onto some other group or person. In fact, this kind of public blame/shame game has become popular; in certain crowds it's even seen as "cool." The public sharing of "injustices" garners far more attention and emotional outpouring than most other events on social media, rewarding people who are able to perpetually feel victimized with ever-growing amounts of attention and sympathy.

"Victimhood chic" is in style on both the right and the left today, among both the rich and the poor. In fact, this may be the first time in human history that every single demographic group has felt unfairly victimized simultaneously. And they're all riding the highs of the moral indignation that comes along with it.

Right now, *anyone* who is offended about *anything*—whether it's the fact that a book about racism was assigned in a university class, or that Christmas trees were banned at the local mall, or the fact that taxes were raised half a percent on investment funds—feels as though they're being oppressed in some way and therefore deserve to be outraged and to have a certain amount of attention.

The current media environment both encourages and perpetuates these reactions because, after all, it's good for business. The writer and media commentator Ryan Holiday refers to this as "outrage porn": rather than report on real stories and real issues, the media find it much easier (and more profitable) to find something mildly offensive, broadcast it to a wide audience, generate outrage, and then broadcast that outrage back across the population in a way that outrages yet another part of the population. This triggers a kind of echo of bullshit pinging back and forth between two imaginary sides, meanwhile distracting everyone from real societal problems. It's no wonder we're more politically polarized than ever before.

The biggest problem with victimhood chic is that it sucks attention away from *actual* victims. It's like the boy who cried wolf. The more people there are who proclaim themselves victims over tiny infractions, the harder it becomes to see who the real victims actually are.

People get addicted to feeling offended all the time because it gives them a high; being self-righteous and morally superior feels *good*. As political cartoonist Tim Kreider put it in a *New York Times* op-ed: "Outrage is like a lot of other things that feel good but over time devour us from the inside out. And it's even more insidious than most vices because we don't even consciously acknowledge that it's a pleasure."

But part of living in a democracy and a free society is that we all have to deal with views and people we don't necessarily like. That's simply the price we pay—you could even say it's the whole point of the system. And it seems more and more people are forgetting that.

We should pick our battles carefully, while simultaneously attempting to empathize a bit with the so-called enemy. We should approach the news and media with a healthy dose of skepticism and avoid painting those who disagree with us with a broad brush. We should prioritize values of being honest, fostering transparency, and welcoming doubt over the values of being right, feeling good, and getting revenge. These "democratic" values are harder to maintain amidst the constant noise of a networked world. But we must accept the responsibility and nurture them regardless. The future stability of our political systems may depend on it.

There Is No "How"

A lot of people might hear all of this and then say something like, "Okay, but how? I get that my values suck and that I avoid responsibility for all of my problems and that I'm an entitled little shit who thinks the world should revolve around me and every inconvenience I experience—but *how* do I change?"

And to this I say, in my best Yoda impersonation: "Do, or do not; there is no 'how.'"

You are *already choosing,* in every moment of every day, what to give a fuck about, so change is as simple as choosing to give a fuck about something else.

It really *is* that simple. It's just not easy.

It's not easy because you're going to feel like a loser, a fraud, a dumbass at first. You're going to be nervous. You're going to freak out. You may get pissed off at your wife or your friends or your father in the process. These are all side effects of changing your values, of changing the fucks you're giving. But they are inevitable.

It's simple but really, really hard.

Let's look at some of these side effects. You're going to feel uncertain; I guarantee it. "Should I really give this up? Is this the right thing to do?" Giving up a value you've depended on for years is going to feel disorienting, as if you don't really know right from wrong anymore. This is hard, but it's normal.

Next, you'll feel like a failure. You've spent half your life measuring yourself by that old value, so when you change your priorities, change your metrics, and stop behaving in the same way, you'll fail to meet that old, trusted metric and thus immediately feel like some sort of fraud or nobody. This is also normal and also uncomfortable.

And certainly you will weather rejections. Many of the relationships in your life were built around the values you've been keeping, so the moment you change those values—the moment you decide that studying is more important than partying, that getting married and having a family is more important than rampant sex, that working a job you believe in is more important than money—your turnaround will reverberate out through your relationships, and many of them will blow up in your face. This too is normal and this too will be uncomfortable.

These are necessary, though painful, side effects of choosing to place your fucks elsewhere, in a place far more important and more worthy of your energies. As you reassess your values, you will be met with internal and external resistance along the way. More than anything, you will feel uncertain; you will wonder if what you're doing is wrong.

But as we'll see, this is a good thing.

CHAPTER

You're Wrong About Everything (But So Am I)

Five hundred years ago cartographers believed that California was an island. Doctors believed that slicing a person's arm open (or causing bleeding anywhere) could cure disease. Scientists believed that fire was made out of something called phlogiston. Women believed that rubbing dog urine on their face had anti-aging benefits. Astronomers believed that the sun revolved around the earth.

When I was a little boy, I used to think "mediocre" was a kind of vegetable that I didn't want to eat. I thought my brother had found a secret passageway in my grandmother's house because he could get outside without having to leave the bathroom (spoiler alert: there was a window). I also thought that when my friend and his family visited

"Washington, B.C.," they had somehow traveled back in time to when the dinosaurs lived, because after all, "B.C." was a long time ago.

As a teenager, I told everybody that I didn't care about anything, when the truth was I cared about way too much. Other people ruled my world without my even knowing. I thought happiness was a destiny and not a choice. I thought love was something that just happened, not something that you worked for. I thought being "cool" had to be practiced and learned from others, rather than invented for oneself.

When I was with my first girlfriend, I thought we would be together forever. And then, when that relationship ended, I thought I'd never feel the same way about a woman again. And then when I felt the same way about a woman again, I thought that love sometimes just wasn't enough. And then I realized that each individual gets to *decide* what is "enough," and that love can be whatever we let it be.

Every step of the way I was wrong. About everything. Throughout my life, I've been flat-out wrong about myself, others, society, culture, the world, the universe—everything.

And I hope that will continue to be the case for the rest of my life.

Just as Present Mark can look back on Past Mark's every flaw and mistake, one day Future Mark will look back on Present Mark's assumptions (including the contents of this book) and notice similar flaws. And that will be a good thing. Because that will mean I have grown.

There's a famous Michael Jordan quote about him failing over and over and over again, and that's why he succeeded.

Well, I'm always wrong about everything, over and over and over again, and that's why my life improves.

Growth is an endlessly *iterative* process. When we learn something new, we don't go from "wrong" to "right." Rather, we go from wrong to slightly less wrong. And when we learn something additional, we go from slightly less wrong to slightly less wrong than that, and then to even less wrong than that, and so on. We are always in the process of approaching truth and perfection without actually ever reaching truth or perfection.

We shouldn't seek to find the ultimate "right" answer for ourselves, but rather, we should seek to chip away at the ways that we're wrong today so that we can be a little less wrong tomorrow.

When viewed from this perspective, personal growth can actually be quite scientific. Our values are our hypotheses: this behavior is good and important; that other behavior is not. Our actions are the experiments; the resulting emotions and thought patterns are our data.

There is no correct dogma or perfect ideology. There is only what your experience has shown you to be right *for you*—and even then, that experience is probably somewhat wrong too. And because you and I and everybody else all have differing needs and personal histories and life circumstances, we will all inevitably come to differing "correct" answers about what our lives mean and how they should be lived. My correct answer involves traveling alone for years on end, living in obscure places, and laughing at my own farts. Or at least that was the correct answer up until recently. That answer will change and evolve, because I change and evolve; and as I grow older and more experienced, I chip away at how wrong I am, becoming less and less wrong every day.

Many people become so obsessed with being "right" about their life that they never end up actually *living* it.

A certain woman is single and lonely and wants a partner, but she never gets out of the house and does anything about it. A certain man works his ass off and believes he deserves a promotion, but he never explicitly says that to his boss.

They're told that they're afraid of failure, of rejection, of someone saying no.

But that's not it. Sure, rejection hurts. Failure sucks. But there are particular certainties that we hold on to—certainties that we're afraid to question or let go of, values that have given our lives meaning over the years. That woman doesn't get out there and date because she would be forced to confront her beliefs about her own desirability. That man doesn't ask for the promotion because he would have to confront his beliefs about what his skills are actually worth.

It's easier to sit in a painful certainty that nobody would find you attractive, that nobody appreciates your talents, than to actually *test* those beliefs and find out for sure.

Beliefs of this sort—that I'm not attractive enough, so why bother; or that my boss is an asshole, so why bother—are designed to give us moderate comfort now by mortgaging greater happiness and success later on. They're terrible long-term strategies, yet we cling to them because we assume we're right, because we assume we already know what's supposed to happen. In other words, we assume we know how the story ends.

Certainty is the enemy of growth. Nothing is for certain until it has already happened—and even then, it's still debatable. That's why accepting the inevitable imperfections of our values is necessary for any growth to take place.

Instead of striving for certainty, we should be in constant search of doubt: doubt about our own beliefs, doubt about our own feelings, doubt about what the future may hold for us unless we get out there and create it for ourselves. Instead of looking to be right all the time, we should be looking for how we're wrong all the time. Because we are.

Being wrong opens us up to the possibility of change. Being wrong brings the opportunity for growth. It means not cutting your arm open to cure a cold or splashing dog piss on your face to look young again. It means not thinking "mediocre" is a vegetable, and not being afraid to care about things.

Because here's something that's weird but true: we don't *actually* know what a positive or negative experience is. Some of the most difficult and stressful moments of our lives also end up being the most formative and motivating. Some of the best and most gratifying experiences of our lives are also the most distracting and demotivating. Don't trust your conception of positive/negative experiences. All that we know for certain is what hurts in the moment and what doesn't. And that's not worth much.

Just as we look back in horror at the lives of people five hundred years ago, I imagine people five hundred years from now will laugh at us and our certainties today. They will laugh at how we let our money and our jobs define our lives. They will laugh at how we were afraid to show appreciation for those who matter to us most, yet heaped praise on public figures who didn't deserve anything. They will laugh at our rituals and superstitions, our worries and our wars; they will gawk at our cruelty. They will study our art and argue over our history. They will understand truths about us of which none of us are yet aware.

And they, too, will be wrong. Just less wrong than we were.

Architects of Our Own Beliefs

Try this. Take a random person and put them in a room with some buttons to push. Then tell them that if they do something specific—some undefined something that they have to figure out—a light will flash on indicating that they've won a point. Then tell them to see how many points they can earn within a thirty-minute period.

When psychologists have done this, what happens is what you might expect. People sit down and start mashing buttons at random until eventually the light comes on to tell them they got a point. Logically, they then try repeating whatever they were doing to get more points. Except now the light's not coming on. So they start experimenting with more complicated sequences—press this button three times, then this button once, then wait five seconds, and—*ding!* Another point. But eventually *that* stops work-ing. Perhaps it doesn't have to do with buttons at all, they think. Perhaps it has to do with how I'm sitting. Or what I'm touching. Maybe it has to do with my feet. *Ding!* Another point. Yeah, maybe it's my feet *and then* I press another but-ton. *Ding!*

Generally, within ten to fifteen minutes each person has figured out the specific sequence of behaviors required to net more points. It's usually something weird like stand-ing on one foot or memorizing a long sequence of buttons pressed in a specific amount of time while facing a certain direction.

But here's the funny part: the points really are random. There's no sequence; there's no pattern. Just a light that keeps coming on with a ding, and people doing cartwheels thinking that what they're doing is giving them points.

Sadism aside, the point of the experiment is to show how quickly the human mind is capable of coming up with and believing in a bunch of bullshit that isn't real. And it turns out, we're all really good at it. Every person leaves that room convinced that he or she nailed the experiment and won the game. They all believe that they discovered the "perfect" sequence of buttons that earned them their points. But the methods they come up with are as unique as the individu-als themselves. One man came up with a long sequence of button-pushing that made no sense to anyone but himself. One girl came to believe that she had to tap the ceiling a certain number of times to get points. When she left the room she was exhausted from jumping up and down.

Our brains are meaning machines. What we understand as "meaning" is generated by the associations our brain makes between two or more experiences. We press a button, then we see a light go on; we assume the button *caused* the light to go on. This, at its core, is the basis of meaning. Button, light; light, button. We see a chair. We note that it's gray. Our brain then draws the association between the color (gray) and the object (chair) and forms meaning: "The chair is gray."

Our minds are constantly whirring, generating more and more associations to help us understand and control the environment around us. Everything about our experiences, both external and internal, generates new associations and connections within our minds. Everything from the words on this page, to the grammatical concepts you use to decipher them, to the dirty thoughts your mind wanders into when my writing becomes boring or repetitive—each of these thoughts, impulses, and perceptions is composed of thousands upon thousands of neural connections, firing in conjunction, alighting your mind in a blaze of knowledge and understanding.

But there are two problems. First, the brain is imperfect. We mistake things we see and hear. We forget things or misinterpret events quite easily.

Second, once we create meaning for ourselves, our brains are designed to hold on to that meaning. We are biased toward the meaning our mind has made, and we don't want to let go of it. Even if we see evidence that contradicts the meaning we created, we often ignore it and keep on believing anyway.

The comedian Emo Philips once said, "I used to think the human brain was the most wonderful organ in my body. Then I realized who was telling me this." The unfortunate fact is, most of what we come to "know" and believe is the product of the innate inaccuracies and biases present in our brains. Many or even most of our values are products of events that are not representative of the world at large, or are the result of a totally misconceived past.

The result of all this? Most of our beliefs are wrong. Or, to be more exact, *all* beliefs are wrong—some are just less wrong than others. The human mind is a jumble of inaccuracy. And while this may make you uncomfortable, it's an incredibly important concept to accept, as we'll see.

The Dangers of Pure Certainty

Erin sits across from me at the sushi restaurant and tries to explain why she doesn't believe in death. It's been almost three hours, and she's eaten exactly four cucumber rolls and drunk an entire bottle of sake by herself. (In fact, she's about halfway through bottle number two now.) It's four o'clock on a Tuesday afternoon.

I didn't invite her here. She found out where I was via the Internet and flew out to come find me.

Again.

She's done this before. You see, Erin is convinced that she can cure death, but she's also convinced that she needs my help to do it. But not my help in like a business sense. If she just needed some PR advice or something, that would be one thing. No, it's more than that: she needs me to be her boyfriend. Why? After three hours of questioning and a bottle and a half of sake, it still isn't clear.

My fiancée was with us in the restaurant, by the way. Erin thought it important that she be included in the discussion; Erin wanted her to know that she was "willing to share" me and that my girlfriend (now wife) "shouldn't feel threatened" by her.

I met Erin at a self-help seminar in 2008. She seemed like a nice enough person. A little bit on the woo-woo, New Agey side of things, but she was a lawyer and had gone to an Ivy League school, and was clearly smart. And she laughed at my jokes and thought I was cute—so, of course, knowing me, I slept with her.

A month later, she invited me to uproot across the country and move in with her. This struck me as somewhat of a red flag, and so I tried to break things off with her. She responded by saying that she would kill herself if I refused to be with her. Okay, so make that two red flags. I promptly blocked her from my email and all my devices.

This would slow her down but not stop her.

Years before I met her, Erin had gotten into a car accident and nearly died. Actually, she *had* medically "died" for a few moments—all brain activity had stopped—but she had somehow miraculously been revived. When she "came back," she claimed everything had changed. She became a very spiritual person. She became interested in, and started believing in, energy healing and angels and universal consciousness and tarot cards. She also believed that she had become a healer and an empath and that she could see the future. And for whatever reason, upon meeting me, she decided that she and I were destined to save the world together. To "cure death," as she put it.

After I'd blocked her, she began to create new email addresses, sometimes sending me as many as a dozen angry emails in a single day. She created fake Facebook and Twitter accounts that she used to harass me as well as people close to me. She created a website identical to mine and wrote dozens of articles claiming that I was her ex-boyfriend and that I had lied to her and cheated her, that I had promised to marry her and that she and I belonged together. When I contacted her to take the site down, she said that she would take it down only if I flew to California to be with her. This was her idea of a compromise.

And through all of this, her justification was the same: I was destined to be with her, that God had preordained it, that she literally woke up in the middle of the night to the voices of angels commanding that "our special relationship" was to be the harbinger of a new age of permanent peace on earth. (Yes, she really told me this.)

By the time we were sitting in that sushi restaurant together, there had been thousands of emails. Whether I responded or didn't respond, replied respectfully or replied angrily, nothing ever changed. Her mind never changed; her beliefs never budged. This had gone on for over seven years by then (and counting).

And so it was, in that small sushi restaurant, with Erin guzzling sake and babbling for hours about how she'd cured her cat's kidney stones with energy tapping, that something occurred to me:

Erin is a self-improvement junkie. She spends tens of thousands of dollars on books and seminars and courses. And the craziest part of all this is that Erin embodies all the lessons she's learned to a T. She has her dream. She stays persistent with it. She visualizes and takes action and weathers the rejections and failures and gets up and tries again. She's relentlessly positive. She thinks pretty damn highly of herself. I mean, she claims to heal cats the same way Jesus healed Lazarus—come the fuck on.

And yet her values are so fucked that none of this matters. The fact that she does everything "right" doesn't make *her* right.

There is a certainty in her that refuses to relinquish itself. She has even told me this in so many words: that she knows her fixation is completely irrational and unhealthy and is making both her and me unhappy. But for some reason it feels so right to her that she can't ignore it and she can't stop.

In the mid-1990s, psychologist Roy Baumeister began researching the concept of evil. Basically, he looked at people who do bad things and at why they do them.

At the time it was assumed that people did bad things because they felt horrible about themselves—that is, they had low self-esteem. One of Baumeister's first surprising findings was that this was often not true. In fact, it was usually the opposite. Some of the worst criminals felt pretty damn good about themselves. And it was this feeling good about themselves in spite of the reality around them that gave them the sense of justification for hurting and disrespecting others.

For individuals to feel justified in doing horrible things to other people, they must feel an unwavering certainty in their own righteousness, in their own beliefs and deservedness. Racists do racist things because they're certain about their genetic superiority. Religious fanatics blow themselves up and murder dozens of people because they're certain of their place in heaven as martyrs. Men rape and abuse women out of their certainty that they're entitled to women's bodies.

Evil people never believe that *they* are evil; rather, they believe that everyone else is evil.

In controversial experiments, now simply known as the Stanford Prison Experiment, organized by the psychologist Philip Zimbardo, researchers told "normal" people that they were to punish other volunteers for breaking various rules. And punish them they did, sometimes escalating the punishment to the point of physical abuse. Almost none of the punishers objected or asked for explanation. On the contrary, many of them seemed to relish the certainty of the moral righteousness bestowed upon them by the experiments.

The problem here is that not only is certainty unattainable, but the pursuit of certainty often breeds more (and worse) insecurity.

Many people have an unshakable certainty in their ability

at their job or in the amount of salary they *should* be making. But that certainty makes them feel worse, not better. They see others getting promoted over them, and they feel slighted. They feel unappreciated and underacknowledged.

Even a behavior as simple as sneaking a peek at your boyfriend's text messages or asking a friend what people are saying about you is driven by insecurity and that aching desire to be certain.

You can check your boyfriend's text messages and find nothing, but that's rarely the end of it; then you may start wondering if he has a second phone. You can feel slighted and stepped over at work to explain why you missed out on a promotion, but then that causes you to distrust your coworkers and second-guess everything they say to you (and how you think they feel about you), which in turn makes you even less likely to get promoted. You can keep pursuing that special someone you're "supposed" to be with, but with each rebuffed advance and each lonely night, you only begin to question more and more what you're doing wrong.

And it's in these moments of insecurity, of deep despair, that we become susceptible to an insidious entitlement: believing that we *deserve* to cheat a little to get our way, that other people *deserve* to be punished, that we *deserve* to take what we want, and sometimes violently.

It's the backwards law again: the more you try to be certain about something, the more uncertain and insecure you will feel.

But the converse is true as well: the more you embrace

being uncertain and not knowing, the more comfortable you will feel in knowing what you don't know.

Uncertainty removes our judgments of others; it pre-empts the unnecessary stereotyping and biases that we otherwise feel when we see somebody on TV, in the office, or on the street. Uncertainty also relieves us of our judgment of ourselves. We don't know if we're lovable or not; we don't know how attractive we are; we don't know how successful we could potentially become. The only way to achieve these things is to remain uncertain of them and be open to finding them out through experience.

Uncertainty is the root of all progress and all growth. As the old adage goes, the man who believes he knows everything learns nothing. We cannot learn anything without first not knowing something. The more we admit we do not know, the more opportunities we gain to learn.

Our values are imperfect and incomplete, and to assume that they are perfect and complete is to put us in a dangerously dogmatic mindset that breeds entitlement and avoids responsibility. The only way to solve our problems is to first admit that our actions and beliefs up to this point have been wrong and are not working.

This openness to being wrong *must exist* for any real change or growth to take place.

Before we can look at our values and prioritizations and change them into better, healthier ones, we must first become *uncertain* of our current values. We must intellectually strip them away, see their faults and biases, see how they don't fit in with much of the rest of the world, to stare our own ignorance in the face and concede, because our own ignorance is greater than us all.

Manson's Law of Avoidance

Chances are you've heard some form of Parkinson's law: "Work expands so as to fill up the time available for its completion."

You've also undoubtedly heard of Murphy's law: "Whatever can go wrong will go wrong."

Well, next time you're at a swanky cocktail party and you want to impress somebody, try dropping Manson's law of avoidance on them:

> The more something threatens your identity, the more you will avoid it.

That means the more something threatens to change how you view yourself, how successful/unsuccessful you believe yourself to be, how well you see yourself living up to your values, the more you will avoid ever getting around to doing it.

There's a certain comfort that comes with knowing how you fit in the world. Anything that shakes up that comfort—even if it could potentially make your life better—is inherently scary.

Manson's law applies to both good and bad things in life. Making a million dollars could threaten your identity just as much as losing all your money; becoming a famous rock star could threaten your identity just as much as losing your job. This is why people are often so afraid of success—for the exact same reason they're afraid of failure: it threatens who they believe themselves to be.

You avoid writing that screenplay you've always dreamed of because doing so would call into question your identity as a practical insurance adjuster. You avoid talking to your husband about being more adventurous in the bedroom because that conversation would challenge your identity as a good, moral woman. You avoid telling your friend that you don't want to see him anymore because ending the friendship would conflict with your identity as a nice, forgiving person.

These are good, important opportunities that we consistently pass up because they threaten to change how we view and feel about ourselves. They threaten the values that we've chosen and have learned to live up to.

I had a friend who, for the longest time, talked about putting his artwork online and trying to make a go of it as a professional (or at least semiprofessional) artist. He talked about it for years; he saved up money; he even built a few different websites and uploaded his portfolio.

But he never launched. There was always some reason: the resolution on his work wasn't good enough, or he had just painted something better, or he wasn't in a position to dedicate enough time to it yet.

Years passed and he never did give up his "real job." Why? Because despite dreaming about making a living through his art, the real potential of becoming An Artist Nobody Likes was far, far scarier than remaining An Artist Nobody's

Heard Of. At least he was comfortable with and used to being An Artist Nobody's Heard Of.

I had another friend who was a party guy, always going out drinking and chasing girls. After years of living the "high life," he found himself terribly lonely, depressed, and unhealthy. He wanted to give up his party lifestyle. He spoke with a fierce jealousy of those of us who were in relationships and more "settled down" than he was. Yet he never changed. For years he went on, empty night after empty night, bottle after bottle. Always some excuse. Always some reason he couldn't slow down.

Giving up that lifestyle threatened his identity too much. The Party Guy was all he knew how to be. To give that up would be like committing psychological hara-kiri.

We all have values for ourselves. We protect these values. We try to live up to them and we justify them and maintain them. Even if we don't mean to, that's how our brain is wired. As noted before, we're unfairly biased toward what we already know, what we believe to be certain. If I believe I'm a nice guy, I'll avoid situations that could potentially contradict that belief. If I believe I'm an awesome cook, I'll seek out opportunities to prove that to myself over and over again. The belief always takes precedence. Until we change how we view ourselves, what we believe we are and are not, we cannot overcome our avoidance and anxiety. We cannot change.

In this way, "knowing yourself" or "finding yourself" can be dangerous. It can cement you into a strict role and saddle you with unnecessary expectations. It can close you off to inner potential and outer opportunities.

I say *don't* find yourself. I say *never* know who you are. Because that's what keeps you striving and discovering. And it forces you to remain humble in your judgments and accepting of the differences in others.

Kill Yourself

Buddhism argues that your idea of who "you" are is an arbitrary mental construction and that you should let go of the idea that "you" exist at all; that the arbitrary metrics by which you define yourself actually trap you, and thus you're better off letting go of everything. In a sense, you could say that Buddhism encourages you to not give a fuck.

It sounds wonky, but there are some psychological benefits to this approach to life. When we let go of the stories we tell about ourselves, to ourselves, we free ourselves up to actually act (and fail) and grow.

When someone admits to herself, "You know, maybe I'm not good at relationships," then she is suddenly free to act and end her bad marriage. She has no identity to protect by staying in a miserable, crappy marriage just to prove something to herself.

When the student admits to himself, "You know, maybe I'm not a rebel; maybe I'm just scared," then he's free to be ambitious again. He has no reason to feel threatened by pursuing his academic dreams and maybe failing.

When the insurance adjuster admits to himself, "You

know, maybe there's nothing unique or special about my dreams or my job," then he's free to give that screenplay an honest go and see what happens.

I have both some good news and some bad news for you: *there is little that is unique or special about your problems.* That's why letting go is so liberating.

There's a kind of self-absorption that comes with fear based on an irrational certainty. When you assume that your plane is the one that's going to crash, or that your project idea is the stupid one everyone is going to laugh at, or that you're the one everyone is going to choose to mock or ignore, you're implicitly telling yourself, "I'm the exception; I'm unlike everybody else; I'm different and special."

This is narcissism, pure and simple. You feel as though *your* problems deserve to be treated differently, that *your* problems have some unique math to them that doesn't obey the laws of the physical universe.

My recommendation: *don't* be special; *don't* be unique. Redefine your metrics in mundane and broad ways. Choose to measure yourself not as a rising star or an undiscovered genius. Choose to measure yourself not as some horrible victim or dismal failure. Instead, measure yourself by more mundane identities: a student, a partner, a friend, a creator.

The narrower and rarer the identity you choose for yourself, the more everything will seem to threaten you. For that reason, define yourself in the simplest and most ordinary ways possible.

This often means giving up some grandiose ideas about

yourself: that you're uniquely intelligent, or spectacularly talented, or intimidatingly attractive, or especially victimized in ways other people could never imagine. This means giving up your sense of entitlement and your belief that you're somehow owed something by this world. This means giving up the supply of emotional highs that you've been sustaining yourself on for years. Like a junkie giving up the needle, you're going to go through withdrawal when you start giving these things up. But you'll come out the other side so much better.

How to Be a Little Less Certain of Yourself

Questioning ourselves and doubting our own thoughts and beliefs is one of the hardest skills to develop. But it can be done. Here are some questions that will help you breed a little more uncertainty in your life.

Question #1: What if I'm wrong?

A friend of mine recently got engaged to be married. The guy who proposed to her is pretty solid. He doesn't drink. He doesn't hit her or mistreat her. He's friendly and has a good job.

But since the engagement, my friend's brother has been admonishing her nonstop about her immature life choices, warning her that she's going to hurt herself with this guy, that she's making a mistake, that she's being irresponsible. And whenever my friend asks her brother, "What is your problem? Why does this bother you so much?" he acts as though there *is* no problem, that nothing about the engagement bothers him, that he's just trying to be helpful and look out for his little sister.

But it's clear that something *does* bother him. Perhaps it's his own insecurities about getting married. Perhaps it's a sibling rivalry thing. Perhaps it's jealousy. Perhaps he's just so caught up in his own victimhood that he doesn't know how to show happiness for others without trying to make them feel miserable first.

As a general rule, we're all the world's worst observers of ourselves. When we're angry, or jealous, or upset, we're oftentimes the last ones to figure it out. And the only way to figure it out is to put cracks in our armor of certainty by consistently questioning how wrong we might be about ourselves.

"Am I jealous—and if I am, then why?" "Am I angry?" "Is she right, and I'm just protecting my ego?"

Questions like these need to become a mental habit. In many cases, the simple act of asking ourselves such questions generates the humility and compassion needed to resolve a lot of our issues.

But it's important to note that just because you ask yourself if you have the wrong idea doesn't necessarily mean that you do. If your husband beats the crap out of you for burning the pot roast and you ask yourself if you're wrong to believe he's mistreating you—well, sometimes you're right. The goal is merely to ask the question and entertain the thought at the moment, not to hate yourself.

It's worth remembering that for any change to happen

in your life, *you must be wrong about something*. If you're sitting there, miserable day after day, then that means you're *already wrong* about something major in your life, and until you're able to question yourself to find it, nothing will change.

Question #2: What would it mean if I were wrong?

Many people are able to ask themselves if they're wrong, but few are able to go the extra step and admit what it would *mean* if they were wrong. That's because the potential meaning behind our wrongness is often painful. Not only does it call into question our values, but it forces us to consider what a different, contradictory value could potentially look and feel like.

Aristotle wrote, "It is the mark of an educated mind to be able to entertain a thought without accepting it." Being able to look at and evaluate different values without necessarily adopting them is perhaps *the* central skill required in changing one's own life in a meaningful way.

As for my friend's brother, his question to himself should be, "What would it mean if I were wrong about my sister's wedding?" Often the answer to such a question is pretty straightforward (and some form of "I'm being a selfish/insecure/narcissistic asshole"). If he *is* wrong, and his sister's engagement is fine and healthy and happy, there's really no way to explain his own behavior other than through his own insecurities and fucked-up values. He assumes that he knows what's best for his sister and that she can't make major life decisions for herself; he assumes that he has the right and responsibility to make decisions for her; he is certain that he's right and everyone else must be wrong.

Even once uncovered, whether in my friend's brother or in ourselves, that sort of entitlement is hard to admit. It hurts. That's why few people ask the difficult questions. But probing questions are necessary in order to get at the core problems that are motivating his, and our, dickish behavior.

Question #3: Would being wrong create a better or a worse problem than my current problem, for both myself and others?

This is the litmus test for determining whether we've got some pretty solid values going on, or we're totally neurotic fuckwads taking our fucks out on everyone, including ourselves.

The goal here is to look at which *problem* is better. Because after all, as Disappointment Panda said, life's problems are endless.

My friend's brother, what are his options?

A. Continue causing drama and friction within the family, complicating what should otherwise be a happy moment, and damage the trust and respect he has with his sister, all because he has a hunch (some might call it an intuition) that this guy is bad for her.

B. Mistrust his own ability to determine what's right or wrong for his sister's life and remain humble, trust her ability to make her own decisions, and even if he doesn't, live with the results out of his love and respect for her.

Most people choose option A. That's because option A is the easier path. It requires little thought, no second-guessing, and zero tolerance of decisions other people make that you don't like.

It also creates the most misery for everyone involved.

It's option B that sustains healthy and happy relationships built on trust and respect. It's option B that forces people to remain humble and admit ignorance. It's option B that allows people to grow beyond their insecurities and recognize situations where they're being impulsive or unfair or selfish.

But option B is hard and painful, so most people don't choose it.

My friend's brother, in protesting her engagement, entered into an imaginary battle with himself. Sure, he believed he was trying to protect his sister, but as we've seen, beliefs are arbitrary; worse yet, they're often made up after the fact to justify whatever values and metrics we've chosen for ourselves. The truth is, he would rather fuck up his relationship with his sister than consider that he might be wrong—even though the latter could help him to grow out of the insecurities that made him wrong in the first place.

I try to live with few rules, but one that I've adopted over the years is this: if it's down to me being screwed up, or everybody else being screwed up, it is far, far, far more likely that I'm the one who's screwed up. I have learned this from experience. I have been the asshole acting out based on my own insecurities and flawed certainties more times than I can count. It's not pretty.

That's not to say there aren't certain ways in which most people are screwed up. And that's not to say that there aren't times when you'll be more right than most other people.

That's simply reality: if it feels like it's you versus the world, chances are it's really just you versus yourself.

7

Failure Is the Way Forward

I really mean it when I say it: I was fortunate.

I graduated college in 2007, just in time for the financial collapse and Great Recession, and attempted to enter the worst job market in more than eighty years.

Around the same time, I found out that the person who was subletting one of the rooms in my apartment hadn't paid any rent for three months. When confronted about this, she cried and then disappeared, leaving my other roommate and me to cover everything. Goodbye, savings. I spent the next six months living on a friend's couch, stringing together odd jobs and trying to stay in as little debt as possible while looking for a "real job."

I say I was fortunate because I entered the adult world already a failure. I started out at rock bottom. That's basically everybody's biggest fear later on in life, when confronted with starting a new business or changing careers or quitting an awful job, and I got to experience it right out of the gates. Things could only get better.

So yeah, lucky. When you're sleeping on a smelly futon and have to count coins to figure out whether you can afford McDonald's this week and you've sent out twenty résumés without hearing a single word back, then starting a blog and a stupid Internet business doesn't sound like such a scary idea. If every project I started failed, if every post I wrote went unread, I'd only be back exactly where I started. So why not try?

Failure itself is a relative concept. If my metric had been to become an anarcho-communist revolutionary, then my complete failure to make any money between 2007 and 2008 would have been a raving success. But if, like most people, my metric had been to simply find a first serious job that could pay some bills right out of school, I was a dismal failure.

I grew up in a wealthy family. Money was never a problem. On the contrary, I grew up in a wealthy family where money was more often used to avoid problems than solve them. I was again fortunate, because this taught me at an early age that making money, by itself, was a lousy metric for myself. You could make plenty of money and be miserable, just as you could be broke and be pretty happy. Therefore, why use money as a means to measure my self-worth?

Instead, my value was something else. It was freedom, autonomy. The idea of being an entrepreneur had always appealed to me because I hated being told what to do and preferred to do things my way. The idea of working on the Internet appealed to me because I could do it from anywhere and work whenever I wanted.

I asked myself a simple question: "Would I rather make decent money and work a job I hated, or play at Internet entrepreneur and be broke for a while?" The answer was immediate and clear for me: the latter. I then asked myself, "If I try this thing and fail in a few years and have to go get a job anyway, will I have really lost anything?" The answer was no. Instead of a broke and unemployed twenty-two-year-old with no experience, I'd be a broke and unemployed twenty-five-year-old with no experience. Who cares?

With this value, to *not* pursue my own projects became the failure—not a lack of money, not sleeping on friends' and family's couches (which I continued to do for most of the next two years), and not an empty résumé.

The Failure/Success Paradox

When Pablo Picasso was an old man, he was sitting in a café in Spain, doodling on a used napkin. He was nonchalant about the whole thing, drawing whatever amused him in that moment—kind of the same way teenage boys draw penises on bathroom stalls—except this was Picasso, so his bathroom-stall penises were more like cubist/impressionist awesomeness laced on top of faint coffee stains.

Anyway, some woman sitting near him was looking on in awe. After a few moments, Picasso finished his coffee and crumpled up the napkin to throw away as he left.

The woman stopped him. "Wait," she said. "Can I have that napkin you were just drawing on? I'll pay you for it."

"Sure," Picasso replied. "Twenty thousand dollars."

The woman's head jolted back as if he had just flung a brick at her. "What? It took you like two minutes to draw that."

"No, ma'am," Picasso said. "It took me over sixty years to draw this." He stuffed the napkin in his pocket and walked out of the café.

Improvement at anything is based on thousands of tiny failures, and the magnitude of your success is based on how many times you've failed at something. If someone is better than you at something, then it's likely because she has failed at it more than you have. If someone is worse than you, it's likely because he hasn't been through all of the painful learning experiences you have.

If you think about a young child trying to learn to walk, that child will fall down and hurt itself hundreds of times. But at no point does that child ever stop and think, "Oh, I guess walking just isn't for me. I'm not good at it."

Avoiding failure is something we learn at some later point in life. I'm sure a lot of it comes from our education system, which judges rigorously based on performance and punishes those who don't do well. Another large share of it comes from overbearing or critical parents who don't let their kids screw up on their own often enough, and instead punish them for trying anything new or not preordained. And then we have all the mass media that constantly expose us to stellar success after success, while not showing us the thousands of hours of dull practice and tedium that were required to achieve that success.

At some point, most of us reach a place where we're afraid to fail, where we instinctively avoid failure and stick only to what is placed in front of us or only what we're already good at.

This confines us and stifles us. We can be truly successful only at something we're willing to fail at. If we're unwilling to fail, then we're unwilling to succeed.

A lot of this fear of failure comes from having chosen shitty values. For instance, if I measure myself by the standard "Make everyone I meet like me," I will be anxious, because failure is 100 percent defined by the actions of others, not by my own actions. I am not in control; thus my self-worth is at the mercy of judgments by others.

Whereas if I instead adopt the metric "Improve my social life," I can live up to my value of "good relations with others" regardless of how other people respond to me. My self-worth is based on my own behaviors and happiness.

Shitty values, as we saw in chapter 4, involve tangible external goals outside of our control. The pursuit of these goals causes great anxiety. And even if we manage to achieve them, they leave us feeling empty and lifeless, because once they're achieved there are no more problems to solve.

Better values, as we saw, are process-oriented. Something like "Express myself honestly to others," a metric for the value "honesty," is never completely finished; it's a problem that must continuously be reengaged. Every new conversation, every new relationship, brings new challenges and opportunities for honest expression. The value is an ongoing, lifelong process that defies completion.

If your metric for the value "success by worldly standards" is "Buy a house and a nice car," and you spend twenty years working your ass off to achieve it, once it's achieved the metric has nothing left to give you. Then say hello to your midlife crisis, because the problem that drove you your entire adult life was just taken away from you. There are no other opportunities to keep growing and improving, and yet it's growth that generates happiness, not a long list of arbitrary achievements.

In this sense, goals, as they are conventionally defined— graduate from college, buy a lake house, lose fifteen pounds—are limited in the amount of happiness they can produce in our lives. They may be helpful when pursuing quick, short-term benefits, but as guides for the overall trajectory of our life, they suck.

Picasso remained prolific his entire life. He lived into his nineties and continued to produce art up until his final years. Had his metric been "Become famous" or "Make a buttload of money in the art world" or "Paint one thousand pictures," he would have stagnated at some point along the way. He would have been overcome by anxiety or self-doubt. He likely wouldn't have improved and innovated his craft in the ways he did decade after decade.

The reason for Picasso's success is exactly the same reason why, as an old man, he was happy to scribble drawings on a napkin alone in a café. His underlying value was simple and humble. And it was endless. It was the value "honest expression." And this is what made that napkin so valuable.

Pain Is Part of the Process

In the 1950s, a Polish psychologist named Kazimierz Dabrowski studied World War II survivors and how they'd coped with traumatic experiences in the war. This was Poland, so things had been pretty gruesome. These people had experienced or witnessed mass starvation, bombings that turned cities to rubble, the Holocaust, the torture of prisoners of war, and the rape and/or murder of family members, if not by the Nazis, then a few years later by the Soviets.

As Dabrowski studied the survivors, he noticed something both surprising and amazing. A sizable percentage of them believed that the wartime experiences they'd suffered, although painful and indeed traumatic, had actually caused them to become better, more responsible, and yes, even happier people. Many described their lives before the war as if they'd been different people then: ungrateful for and unappreciative of their loved ones, lazy and consumed by petty problems, entitled to all they'd been given. After the war they felt more confident, more sure of themselves, more grateful, and unfazed by life's trivialities and petty annoyances.

Obviously, their experiences had been horrific, and these survivors weren't happy about having had to experience them. Many of them still suffered from the emotional scars the lashings of war had left on them. But some of them had managed to leverage those scars to transform themselves in positive and powerful ways.

And they aren't alone in that reversal. For many of us, our proudest achievements come in the face of the greatest adversity. Our pain often makes us stronger, more resilient, more grounded. Many cancer survivors, for example, report feeling stronger and more grateful after winning their battle to survive. Many military personnel report a mental resilience gained from withstanding the dangerous environments of being in a war zone.

Dabrowski argued that fear and anxiety and sadness are not necessarily always undesirable or unhelpful states of mind; rather, they are often representative of the necessary pain of psychological growth. And to deny that pain is to deny our own potential. Just as one must suffer physical pain to build stronger bone and muscle, one must suffer emotional pain to develop greater emotional resilience, a stronger sense of self, increased compassion, and a generally happier life.

Our most radical changes in perspective often happen at the tail end of our worst moments. It's only when we feel intense pain that we're willing to look at our values and question why they seem to be failing us. We *need* some sort of existential crisis to take an objective look at how we've been deriving meaning in our life, and then consider changing course.

You could call it "hitting bottom" or "having an existential crisis." I prefer to call it "weathering the shitstorm." Choose what suits you.

And perhaps you're in that kind of place right now. Perhaps you're coming out of the most significant challenge of your life and are bewildered because everything you previously thought to be true and normal and good has turned out to be the opposite.

That's good—that's the beginning. I can't stress this enough, but *pain is part of the process*. It's important to *feel* it. Because if you just chase after highs to cover up the pain, if you continue to indulge in entitlement and delusional positive thinking, if you continue to overindulge in various substances or activities, then you'll never generate the requisite motivation to actually change.

When I was young, any time my family got a new VCR or stereo, I would press every button, plug and unplug every cord and cable, just to see what everything did. With time, I learned how the whole system worked. And because I knew how it all worked, I was often the only person in the house who used the stuff.

As is the case for many millennial children, my parents looked on as if I were some sort of prodigy. To them, the fact that I could program the VCR without looking at the instruction manual made me the Second Coming of Tesla.

It's easy to look back at my parents' generation and chuckle at their technophobia. But the further I get into adulthood, the more I realize that we all have areas of our lives where we're like my parents with the new VCR: we sit and stare and shake our heads and say, "But *how*?" When really, it's as simple as just doing it.

I get emails from people asking questions like this all the

time. And for many years, I never knew what to say to them.

There's the girl whose parents are immigrants and saved for their whole lives to put her through med school. But now she's in med school and she hates it; she doesn't want to spend her life as a doctor, so she wants to drop out more than anything. Yet she feels stuck. So stuck, in fact, that she ends up emailing a stranger on the Internet (me) and asking him a silly and obvious question like, "How do I drop out of med school?"

Or the college guy who has a crush on his tutor. So he agonizes over every sign, every laugh, every smile, every diversion into small talk, and emails me a twenty-eight-page novella that concludes with the question, "How do I ask her out?" Or the single mother whose now-adult kids have finished school and are loafing around on her couch, eating her food, spending her money, not respecting her space or her desire for privacy. She wants them to move on with their lives. She wants to move on with *her* life. Yet she's scared to death of pushing her children away, scared to the point of asking, "How do I ask them to move out?"

These are VCR questions. From the outside, the answer is simple: just shut up and do it.

But from the inside, from the perspective of each of these people, these questions feel impossibly complex and opaque—existential riddles wrapped in enigmas packed in a KFC bucket full of Rubik's Cubes.

VCR questions are funny because the answer appears difficult to anyone who has them and appears easy to anyone who does not.

The problem here is pain. Filling out the appropriate paperwork to drop out of med school is a straightforward and obvious action; breaking your parents' hearts is not. Asking a tutor out on a date is as simple as saying the words; risking intense embarrassment and rejection feels far more complicated. Asking someone to move out of your house is a clear decision; feeling as if you're abandoning your own children is not.

I struggled with social anxiety throughout much of my adolescence and young adult life. I spent most of my days distracting myself with video games and most of my nights either drinking or smoking away my uneasiness. For many years, the thought of speaking to a stranger—especially if that stranger happened to be particularly attractive/interesting/popular/smart—felt impossible to me. I walked around in a daze for years, asking myself dumb VCR questions:

"How? How do you just walk up and talk to a person? How can somebody *do* that?"

I had all sorts of screwed-up beliefs about this, like that you weren't allowed to speak to someone unless you had some practical reason to, or that women would think I was a creepy rapist if I so much as said, "Hello."

The problem was that my emotions defined my reality. Because it *felt* like people didn't want to talk to me, I came to *believe* that people didn't want to talk to me. And thus, my VCR question: "How do you just walk up and talk to a person?"

Because I failed to separate what I *felt* from what *was,* I was incapable of stepping outside myself and seeing the world for what it was: a simple place where two people can walk up to each other at any time and speak.

Many people, when they feel some form of pain or anger or sadness, drop everything and attend to numbing out whatever they're feeling. Their goal is to get back to "feeling good" again as quickly as possible, even if that means substances or deluding themselves or returning to their shitty values.

Learn to sustain the pain you've chosen. When you choose a new value, you are choosing to introduce a new form of pain into your life. Relish it. Savor it. Welcome it with open arms. Then act *despite* it.

I won't lie: this is going to feel impossibly hard at first. But you can start simple. You're going to feel as though you don't know what to do. But we've discussed this: you don't know *anything*. Even when you think you do, you really don't know what the fuck you're doing. So really, what is there to lose?

Life is about not knowing and then doing something anyway. *All* of life is like this. It never changes. Even when you're happy. Even when you're farting fairy dust. Even when you win the lottery and buy a small fleet of Jet Skis, you still won't know what the hell you're doing. Don't ever forget that. And don't ever be afraid of that.

The "Do Something" Principle

In 2008, after holding down a day job for all of six weeks, I gave up on the whole job thing to pursue an online business.

At the time, I had absolutely no clue what I was doing, but I figured if I was going to be broke and miserable, I might as well be while working on my own terms. And at that time, all I seemed to really care about was chasing girls. So fuck it, I decided to start a blog about my crazy dating life.

That first morning that I woke up self-employed, terror quickly consumed me. I found myself sitting with my laptop and realized, for the first time, that I was entirely responsible for *all* of my own decisions, as well as the consequences of those decisions. I was responsible for teaching myself web design, Internet marketing, search engine optimization, and other esoteric topics. It was all on my shoulders now. And so I did what any twenty-four-year-old who'd just quit his job and had no idea what he was doing would do: I downloaded some computer games and avoided work like it was the Ebola virus.

As the weeks went on and my bank account turned from black to red, it was clear that I needed to come up with some sort of strategy to get myself to put in the twelve- or fourteen-hour days that were necessary to get a new business off the ground. And that plan came from an unexpected place.

When I was in high school, my math teacher Mr. Packwood used to say, "If you're stuck on a problem, don't sit there and think about it; just start working on it. Even if you don't know what you're doing, the simple act of working on it will eventually cause the right ideas to show up in your head."

During that early self-employment period, when I struggled every day, completely clueless about what to do and terrified of the results (or lack thereof), Mr. Packwood's advice started beckoning me from the recesses of my mind. I heard it like a mantra:

> Don't just sit there. *Do* something. The answers will follow.

In the course of applying Mr. Packwood's advice, I learned a powerful lesson about motivation. It took about eight years for this lesson to sink in, but what I discovered, over those long, grueling months of bombed product launches, laughable advice columns, uncomfortable nights on friends' couches, overdrawn bank accounts, and hundreds of thousands of words written (most of them unread), was perhaps the most important thing I've ever learned in my life:

> Action isn't just the effect of motivation; it's also the cause of it.

Most of us commit to action only if we feel a certain level of motivation. And we feel motivation only when we feel enough emotional inspiration. We assume that these steps occur in a sort of chain reaction, like this:

> Emotional inspiration → Motivation → Desirable action

If you want to accomplish something but don't feel motivated or inspired, then you assume you're just screwed. There's nothing you can do about it. It's not until a major emotional life event occurs that you can generate enough motivation to actually get off the couch and do something.

The thing about motivation is that it's not only a three-part chain, but an endless loop:

Inspiration → Motivation → Action → Inspiration → Motivation → Action → Etc.

Your actions create further emotional reactions and inspirations and move on to motivate your future actions. Taking advantage of this knowledge, we can actually reorient our mindset in the following way:

Action → Inspiration → Motivation

If you lack the motivation to make an important change in your life, *do something*—anything, really—and then harness the reaction to that action as a way to begin motivating yourself.

I call this the "do something" principle. After using it myself to build my business, I began teaching it to readers who came to me perplexed by their own VCR questions: "How do I apply for a job?" or "How do I tell this guy I want to be his girlfriend?" and the like.

During the first couple years I worked for myself, entire weeks would go by without my accomplishing much, for no other reason than that I was anxious and stressed about what I had to do, and it was too easy to put everything off. I quickly learned, though, that forcing myself to do *something*, even the most menial of tasks, quickly made the larger tasks seem much easier. If I had to redesign an entire website, I'd force myself to sit down and would say, "Okay, I'll just design the header right now." But after the header was done, I'd find myself moving on to other parts of the site. And before I knew it, I'd be energized and engaged in the project.

The author Tim Ferriss relates a story he once heard about a novelist who had written over seventy novels. Someone asked the novelist how he was able to write so consistently and remain inspired and motivated. He replied, "Two hundred crappy words per day, that's it." The idea was that if he forced himself to write two hundred crappy words, more often than not the act of writing would inspire him; and before he knew it, he'd have thousands of words down on the page.

If we follow the "do something" principle, failure *feels* unimportant. When the standard of success becomes merely acting—when *any* result is regarded as progress and important, when inspiration is seen as a reward rather than a prerequisite—we propel ourselves ahead. We feel free to fail, and that failure moves us forward.

The "do something" principle not only helps us overcome procrastination, but it's also the process by which we adopt new values. If you're in the midst of an existential shitstorm and everything feels meaningless—if all the ways you used to measure yourself have come up short and you have no idea what's next, if you know that you've been hurting yourself chasing false dreams, or if you know that there's some better metric you should be measuring yourself with but you don't know how—the answer is the same:

Do something.

That "something" can be the smallest viable action toward something else. It can be *anything*.

Recognize that you've been an entitled prick in all of your relationships and want to start developing more compassion for others? Do something. Start simple. Make it a goal to listen to someone's problem and give some of your time to helping that person. Just do it once. Or promise yourself that you will assume that *you* are the root of your problems next time you get upset. Just try on the idea and see how it feels.

That's often all that's necessary to get the snowball rolling, the action needed to inspire the motivation to keep going. You can become your own source of inspiration. You can become your own source of motivation. Action is always within reach. And with simply *doing something* as your only metric for success—well, then even failure pushes you forward.

CHAPTER

8

The Importance of Saying No

n 2009, I gathered up all my possessions, sold them or put them into storage, left my apartment, and set off for Latin America. By this time my little dating advice blog was getting some traffic and I was actually making a modest amount of money selling PDFs and courses online. I planned on spending much of the next few years living abroad, experiencing new cultures, and taking advantage of the lower cost of living in a number of developing countries in Asia and Latin America to build my business further. It was the digital nomad dream and as a twenty-five-year-old adventure-seeker, it was exactly what I wanted out of life.

But as sexy and heroic as my plan sounded, not all of the values driving me to this nomadic lifestyle were healthy ones. Sure, I had some admirable values going on—a thirst to see the world, a curiosity for people and culture, some old-fashioned adventure-seeking. But there also existed a faint outline of shame underlying everything else. At the time I was hardly aware of it, but if I was completely honest with myself, I knew there was a screwed-up value lurking there, somewhere beneath the surface. I couldn't see it, but in quiet moments when I was completely honest with myself, I could feel it.

Along with the entitlement of my early twenties, the "real traumatic shit" of my teenage years had left me with a nice bundle of commitment issues. I had spent the past few years overcompensating for the inadequacy and social anxiety of my teenager years, and as a result I felt like I could meet anybody I wanted, be friends with anybody I wanted, love anybody I wanted, have sex with anybody I wanted— so why would I ever commit to a single person, or even a single social group, a single city or country or culture? If I *could* experience everything equally, then I *should* experience them all equally, right?

Armed with this grandiose sense of connectivity to the world, I bounced back and forth across countries and oceans in a game of global hopscotch that lasted over five years. I visited fifty-five countries, made dozens of friends, and found myself in the arms of a number of lovers—all of whom were quickly replaced and some of whom were already forgotten by the next flight to the next country.

It was a strange life, replete with fantastic, horizon-breaching experiences as well as superficial highs designed to numb my underlying pain. It seemed both so profound yet so meaningless at the same time, and still does. Some of my greatest life lessons and character-defining moments came on the road during this period. But some of the biggest wastes of my time and energy came during this period as well.

Now I live in New York. I have a house and furniture and an electric bill and a wife. None of it is particularly glamorous or exciting. And I like it that way. Because after all the years of excitement, the biggest lesson I took from my adventuring was this: absolute freedom, by itself, means nothing.

Freedom grants the opportunity for greater meaning, but by itself there is nothing necessarily meaningful about it. Ultimately, the only way to achieve meaning and a sense of importance in one's life is through a rejection of alternatives, a *narrowing* of freedom, a choice of commitment to one place, one belief, or (gulp) one person.

This realization came to me slowly over the course of my years traveling. As with most excesses in life, you have to drown yourself in them to realize that they don't make you happy. Such was traveling with me. As I drowned in my fifty-third, fifty-fourth, fifty-fifth country, I began to understand that while all of my experiences were exciting and great, few of them would have any lasting significance. Whereas my friends back home were settling down into marriages, buying houses, and giving their time to interesting companies or political causes, I was floundering from one high to the next.

In 2011, I traveled to Saint Petersburg, Russia. The food sucked. The weather sucked. (Snow in May? Are you fucking kidding me?) My apartment sucked. Nothing worked. Everything was overpriced. The people were rude and smelled funny. Nobody smiled and everyone drank too much. Yet, I loved it. It was one of my favorite trips.

There's a bluntness to Russian culture that generally rubs Westerners the wrong way. Gone are the fake niceties and verbal webs of politeness. You don't smile at strangers or pretend to like anything you don't. In Russia, if something is stupid, you say it's stupid. If someone is being an asshole, you tell him he's being an asshole. If you really like someone and are having a great time, you tell her that you like her and are having a great time. It doesn't matter if this person is your friend, a stranger, or someone you met five minutes ago on the street.

The first week I found all of this really uncomfortable. I went on a coffee date with a Russian girl, and within three minutes of sitting down she looked at me funny and told me that what I'd just said was stupid. I nearly choked on my drink. There was nothing combative about the way she said it; it was spoken as if it were some mundane fact—like the quality of the weather that day, or her shoe size—but I was still shocked. After all, in the West such outspokenness is seen as highly offensive, especially from someone you just met. But it went on like this with everyone. Everyone came across as rude all the time, and as a result, my Western-coddled mind felt attacked on all sides. Nagging insecurities began to surface in situations where they hadn't existed in years.

But as the weeks wore on, I got used to the Russian

frankness, much as I did the midnight sunsets and the vodka that went down like ice water. And then I started appreciating it for what it really was: unadulterated expression. Honesty in the truest sense of the word. Communication with no conditions, no strings attached, no ulterior motive, no sales job, no desperate attempt to be liked.

Somehow, after years of travel, it was in perhaps the most un-American of places where I first experienced a particular flavor of freedom: the ability to say whatever I thought or felt, without fear of repercussion. It was a strange form of liberation *through* accepting rejection. And as someone who had been starved of this kind of blunt expression most of his life—first by an emotionally repressed family life, then later by a meticulously constructed false display of confidence—I got drunk on it like, well, like it was the finest damn vodka I'd ever had. The month I spent in Saint Petersburg went by in a blur, and by the end I didn't want to leave.

Travel is a fantastic self-development tool, because it extricates you from the values of your culture and shows you that another society can live with entirely different values and still function and not hate themselves. This exposure to different cultural values and metrics then forces you to reexamine what seems obvious in your own life and to consider that perhaps it's not necessarily the best way to live. In this case, Russia had me reexamining the bullshitty, fake-nice communication that is so common in Anglo culture, and asking myself if this wasn't somehow making us more insecure around each other and worse at intimacy.

I remember discussing this dynamic with my Russian teacher one day, and he had an interesting theory. Having lived under communism for so many generations, with little to no economic opportunity and caged by a culture of fear, Russian society found the most valuable currency to be trust. And to build trust you have to be honest. That means when things suck, you say so openly and without apology. People's displays of unpleasant honesty were rewarded for the simple fact that they were necessary for survival—you had to know whom you could rely on and whom you couldn't, and you needed to know quickly.

But, in the "free" West, my Russian teacher continued, there existed an abundance of economic opportunity—so much economic opportunity that it became far more valuable to present yourself in a certain way, even if it was false, than to actually *be* that way. Trust lost its value. Appearances and salesmanship became more advantageous forms of expression. Knowing a lot of people superficially was more beneficial than knowing a few people closely.

This is why it became the norm in Western cultures to smile and say polite things even when you don't feel like it, to tell little white lies and agree with someone whom you don't actually agree with. This is why people learn to pretend to be friends with people they don't actually like, to buy things they don't actually want. The economic system promotes such deception.

The downside of this is that you never know, in the West, if you can completely trust the person you're talking to. Sometimes this is the case even among good friends or family members. There is such pressure in the West to be likable that people often reconfigure their entire personality depending on the person they're dealing with.

Rejection Makes Your Life Better

As an extension of our positivity/consumer culture, many of us have been "indoctrinated" with the belief that we should try to be as inherently accepting and affirmative as possible. This is a cornerstone of many of the so-called positive thinking books: open yourself up to opportunities, be accepting, say yes to everything and everyone, and so on.

But we *need* to reject something. Otherwise, we stand for nothing. If nothing is better or more desirable than anything else, then we are empty and our life is meaningless. We are without values and therefore live our life without any purpose.

The avoidance of rejection (both giving and receiving it) is often sold to us as a way to make ourselves feel better. But avoiding rejection gives us short-term pleasure by making us rudderless and directionless in the long term.

To truly appreciate something, you must confine yourself to it. There's a certain level of joy and meaning that you reach in life only when you've spent decades investing in a single relationship, a single craft, a single career. And you cannot achieve those decades of investment without rejecting the alternatives.

The act of choosing a value for yourself requires rejecting alternative values. If I choose to make my marriage the most important part of my life, that means I'm (probably) choosing *not* to make cocaine-fueled hooker orgies an important part of my life. If I'm choosing to judge myself based on my ability to have open and accepting friendships, that means I'm rejecting trashing my friends behind their backs. These are all healthy decisions, yet they require rejection at every turn.

The point is this: we all must give a fuck about *something,* in order to *value* something. And to value something, we must reject what is *not* that something. To value X, we must reject non-X.

That rejection is an inherent and necessary part of maintaining our values, and therefore our identity. We are defined by what we choose to reject. And if we reject nothing (perhaps in fear of being rejected by something ourselves), we essentially have no identity at all.

The desire to avoid rejection at all costs, to avoid confrontation and conflict, the desire to attempt to accept everything equally and to make everything cohere and harmonize, is a deep and subtle form of entitlement. Entitled people, because they feel as though they *deserve* to feel great all the time, avoid rejecting anything because doing so might make them or someone else feel bad. And because they refuse to reject anything, they live a valueless, pleasure-driven, and self-absorbed life. All they give a fuck about is sustaining the high a little bit longer, to avoid the inevitable failures of their life, to pretend the suffering away.

Rejection is an important and crucial life skill. Nobody wants to be stuck in a relationship that isn't making them happy. Nobody wants to be stuck in a business doing work they hate and don't believe in. Nobody wants to feel that they can't say what they really mean.

Yet people choose these things. All the time.

Honesty is a natural human craving. But part of having honesty in our lives is becoming comfortable with saying and hearing the word "no." In this way, rejection actually makes our relationships better and our emotional lives healthier.

Boundaries

Once upon a time, there were two youngsters, a boy and a girl. Their families hated each other. But the boy snuck into a party hosted by the girl's family because he was kind of a dick. The girl sees the boy, and angels sing so sweetly to her lady-parts that she instantly falls in love with him. Just like that. And so he sneaks into her garden and they decide to get married *the next freaking day*, because, you know, that's totally practical, especially when your parents want to murder each other. Jump ahead a few days. Their families find out about the marriage and throw a shit-fit. Mercutio dies. The girl is so upset that she drinks a potion that will put her to sleep for two days. But, unfortunately, the young couple hasn't learned the ins and outs of good marital communication yet, and the young girl totally forgets to mention something about it to her new husband. The young man therefore mistakes his new wife's self-induced coma for suicide. He then totally loses his marbles and *he* commits suicide, thinking he's going to be with her in the afterlife or some shit. But then she wakes up from her two-day coma, only to learn that her new husband has committed suicide, so *she* has the exact same idea and kills herself too. The end.

Romeo and Juliet is synonymous with "romance" in our culture today. It is seen as *the* love story in English-speaking culture, an emotional ideal to live up to. Yet when you really get down to what happens in the story, these kids are absolutely out of their fucking minds. And they just killed themselves to prove it!

It's suspected by many scholars that Shakespeare wrote *Romeo and Juliet* not to celebrate romance, but rather to satirize it, to show how absolutely nutty it was. He didn't mean for the play to be a glorification of love. In fact, he meant it to be the opposite: a big flashing neon sign blinking KEEP OUT, with police tape around it saying DO NOT CROSS.

For most of human history, romantic love was not celebrated as it is now. In fact, up until the mid-nineteenth century or so, love was seen as an unnecessary and potentially dangerous psychological impediment to the more important things in life—you know, like farming well and/or marrying a guy with a lot of sheep. Young people were often forcibly steered clear of their romantic passions in favor of practical economic marriages that would yield stability for both them and their families.

But today, we all get brain boners for this kind of batshit crazy love. It dominates our culture. And the more dramatic, the better. Whether it's Ben Affleck working to destroy an asteroid to save the earth for the girl he loves, or Mel Gibson murdering hundreds of Englishmen and fantasizing about his raped and murdered wife while being tortured to death, or that Elven chick giving up her immortality to be with Aragorn in *Lord of the Rings,* or stupid romantic comedies where Jimmy Fallon forgoes his Red Sox playoff tickets because Drew Barrymore has, like, *needs* or something.

If this sort of romantic love were cocaine, then as a culture we'd all be like Tony Montana in *Scarface:* burying our faces in a fucking mountain of it, screaming, "Say hello to my lee-tle friend!"

The problem is that we're finding out that romantic love *is* kind of like cocaine. Like, frighteningly similar to cocaine. Like, stimulates the exact same parts of your brain as cocaine. Like, gets you high and makes you feel good for a while but also creates as many problems as it solves, as does cocaine.

Most elements of romantic love that we pursue—the dramatic and dizzyingly emotional displays of affection, the topsy-turvy ups and downs—aren't healthy, genuine displays of love. In fact, they're often just another form of entitlement playing out through people's relationships.

I know: that makes me sound like such a downer. Seriously, what kind of guy shits on romantic love? But hear me out.

The truth is, there are healthy forms of love and unhealthy forms of love. Unhealthy love is based on two people trying to escape their problems through their emotions for each other—in other words, they're using each other as an escape. Healthy love is based on two people acknowledging and addressing their own problems with each other's support.

The difference between a healthy and an unhealthy relationship comes down to two things: 1) how well each person in the relationship accepts responsibility, and 2) the willingness of each person to both reject and be rejected by their partner.

Anywhere there is an unhealthy or toxic relationship, there will be a poor and porous sense of responsibility on both sides, and there will be an inability to give and/or receive rejection. Wherever there is a healthy and loving relationship, there will be clear boundaries between the two people and their values, and there will be an open avenue of giving and receiving rejection when necessary.

By "boundaries" I mean the delineation between two people's responsibilities for their own problems. People in a healthy relationship with strong boundaries will take responsibility for their own values and problems and not take responsibility for their partner's values and problems. People in a toxic relationship with poor or no boundaries will regularly avoid responsibility for their own problems and/or take responsibility for their partner's problems.

What do poor boundaries look like? Here are some examples:

> "*You can't go out with your friends without me. You know how jealous I get. You have to stay home with me.*"
> "*My coworkers are idiots; they always make me late to*

meetings because I have to tell them how to do their jobs."

"I can't believe you made me feel so stupid in front of my own sister. Never disagree with me in front of her again!"

"I'd love to take that job in Milwaukee, but my mother would never forgive me for moving so far away."

"I can date you, but can you not tell my friend Cindy? She gets really insecure when I have a boyfriend and she doesn't."

In each scenario, the person is either taking responsibility for problems/emotions that are not theirs, or demanding that someone else take responsibility for their problems/emotions.

In general, entitled people fall into one of two traps in their relationships. Either they expect other people to take responsibility for *their* problems: *"I wanted a nice relaxing weekend at home. You should have known that and canceled your plans."* Or they take on too much responsibility for other people's problems: *"She just lost her job again, but it's probably my fault because I wasn't as supportive of her as I could have been. I'm going to help her rewrite her résumé tomorrow."*

Entitled people adopt these strategies in their relationships, as with everything, to help avoid accepting responsibility for their own problems. As a result, their relationships are fragile and fake, products of avoiding inner pain rather than embracing a genuine appreciation and adoration of their partner.

This goes not just for romantic relationships, by the way, but also for family relationships and friendships. An overbearing mother may take responsibility for every problem in her children's lives. Her own entitlement then encourages an entitlement in her children, as they grow up to believe other people should always be responsible for their problems.

(This is why the problems in your romantic relationships always eerily resemble the problems in your parents' relationship.)

When you have murky areas of responsibility for your emotions and actions—areas where it's unclear who is responsible for what, whose fault is what, why you're doing what you're doing—you never develop strong values for yourself. Your only value *becomes* making your partner happy. Or your only value *becomes* your partner making you happy.

This is self-defeating, of course. And relationships characterized by such murkiness usually go down like the *Hindenburg,* with all the drama and fireworks.

People can't solve your problems for you. And they shouldn't try, because that won't make you happy. You can't solve other people's problems for them either, because that likewise won't make them happy. The mark of an unhealthy relationship is two people who try to solve each other's problems in order to feel good about themselves. Rather, a healthy relationship is when two people solve their own problems in order to feel good about each other.

The setting of proper boundaries doesn't mean you can't help or support your partner or be helped and supported yourself. You both should support each other. But only because you *choose* to support and be supported. Not because you feel obligated or entitled.

Entitled people who blame others for their own emotions and actions do so because they believe that if they constantly paint themselves as victims, eventually someone will come along and save them, and they will receive the love they've always wanted.

Entitled people who take the blame for other people's emotions and actions do so because they believe that if they "fix" their partner and save him or her, they will receive the love and appreciation they've always wanted.

These are the yin and yang of any toxic relationship: the victim and the saver, the person who starts fires because it makes her feel important and the person who puts out fires because it makes him feel important.

These two types of people are drawn strongly to one another, and they usually end up together. Their pathologies match one another perfectly. Often they've grown up with parents who each exhibit one of these traits as well. So their model for a "happy" relationship is one based on entitlement and poor boundaries.

Sadly, they both fail in meeting the other's actual needs. In fact, their pattern of overblaming and overaccepting blame perpetuates the entitlement and shitty self-worth that have been keeping them from getting their emotional needs met in the first place. The victim creates more and more problems to solve—not because additional real problems exist, but because it gets her the attention and affection she craves. The saver solves and solves—not because she actually cares about the problems, but because she believes she must fix others' problems in order to deserve attention and affection for herself. In both cases, the intentions are selfish and conditional and therefore self-sabotaging, and genuine love is rarely experienced.

The victim, if he really loved the saver, would say, "Look, this is my problem; you don't have to fix it for me. Just support me while I fix it myself." That would *actually* be a demonstration of love: taking responsibility for your own problems and not holding your partner responsible for them.

If the saver really wanted to save the victim, the saver would say, "Look, you're blaming others for your own problems; deal with this yourself." And in a sick way, that would *actually* be a demonstration of love: helping someone solve their own problems.

Instead, victims and savers both use each other to achieve emotional highs. It's like an addiction they fulfill in one another. Ironically, when presented with emotionally healthy people to date, they usually feel bored or lack "chemistry" with them. They pass on emotionally healthy, secure individuals because the secure partner's solid boundaries don't feel "exciting" enough to stimulate the constant highs necessary in the entitled person.

For victims, the hardest thing to do in the world is to hold themselves accountable for their problems. They've spent their whole life believing that others are responsible for their fate. That first step of taking responsibility for themselves is often terrifying.

For savers, the hardest thing to do in the world is to stop taking responsibility for other people's problems. They've spent their whole life feeling valued and loved only when they're saving somebody else—so letting go of this need is terrifying to them as well.

If you make a sacrifice for someone you care about, it needs to be because you want to, not because you feel obligated or because you fear the consequences of not doing so. If your partner is going to make a sacrifice for you, it needs to be because he or she genuinely wants to, not because you've manipulated the sacrifice through anger or guilt. Acts of love are valid only if they're performed without conditions or expectations.

It can be difficult for people to recognize the difference between doing something out of obligation and doing it voluntarily. So here's a litmus test: ask yourself, "If I refused, how would the relationship change?" Similarly, ask, "If my partner refused something I wanted, how would the relationship change?"

If the answer is that a refusal would cause a blowout of drama and broken china plates, then that's a bad sign for your relationship. It suggests that your relationship is conditional—based on superficial benefits received from one another, rather than on unconditional acceptance of each other (along with each other's problems).

People with strong boundaries are not afraid of a temper tantrum, an argument, or getting hurt. People with weak boundaries are terrified of those things and will constantly mold their own behavior to fit the highs and lows of their relational emotional roller coaster.

People with strong boundaries understand that it's unreasonable to expect two people to accommodate each other 100 percent and fulfill every need the other has. People with strong boundaries understand that they may hurt someone's feelings sometimes, but ultimately they can't determine how other people feel. People with strong boundaries understand that a healthy relationship is not about controlling one another's emotions, but rather about each partner supporting the other in their individual growth and in solving their own problems.

It's not about giving a fuck about everything your partner gives a fuck about; it's about giving a fuck about your partner regardless of the fucks he or she gives. That's unconditional love, baby.

How to Build Trust

My wife is one of those women who spend a lot of time in front of the mirror. She loves to look amazing, and I love for her to look amazing too (obviously).

Nights before we go out, she comes out of the bathroom after an hour-long makeup/hair/clothes/whatever-women-do-in-there session and asks me how she looks. She's usually gorgeous. Every once in a while, though, she looks bad. Maybe she tried to do something new with her hair, or decided to wear a pair of boots that some flamboyant fashion designer from Milan thought were avant-garde. Whatever the reason—it just doesn't work.

When I tell her this, she usually gets pissed off. As she marches back into the closet or the bathroom to redo everything and make us thirty minutes late, she spouts a bunch of four-letter words and sometimes even slings a few of them in my direction.

Men stereotypically lie in this situation to make their girlfriends/wives happy. But I don't. Why? Because honesty in my relationship is more important to me than feeling good all the time. The last person I should ever have to censor myself with is the woman I love.

Fortunately, I'm married to a woman who agrees and is willing to hear my uncensored thoughts. She calls me out on my bullshit too, of course, which is one of the most important traits she offers me as a partner. Sure, my ego gets bruised sometimes, and I bitch and complain and try to argue, but a few hours later I come sulking back and admit that she was right. And holy crap she makes me a better person, even though I hate hearing it at the time.

When our highest priority is to always make ourselves feel good, or to always make our partner feel good, then nobody ends up feeling good. And our relationship falls apart without our even knowing it.

Without conflict, there can be no trust. Conflict exists

to show us who is there for us unconditionally and who is just there for the benefits. No one trusts a yes-man. If Disappointment Panda were here, he'd tell you that the pain in our relationship is necessary to cement our trust in each other and produce greater intimacy.

For a relationship to be healthy, both people must be willing and able to both say no and hear no. Without that negation, without that occasional rejection, boundaries break down and one person's problems and values come to dominate the other's. Conflict is not only normal, then; it's *absolutely necessary* for the maintenance of a healthy relationship. If two people who are close are not able to hash out their differences openly and vocally, then the relationship is based on manipulation and misrepresentation, and it will slowly become toxic.

Trust is the most important ingredient in any relationship, for the simple reason that without trust, the relationship doesn't actually *mean* anything. A person could tell you that she loves you, wants to be with you, would give up everything for you, but if you don't trust her, you get no benefit from those statements. You don't feel loved until you trust that the love being expressed toward you comes without any special conditions or baggage attached to it.

This is what's so destructive about cheating. It's not about the sex. It's about the trust that has been destroyed as a result of the sex. Without trust, the relationship can no longer function. So it's either rebuild the trust or say your goodbyes.

I often get emails from people who have been cheated

on by their significant other but want to stay with that partner and are wondering how they can trust him or her again. Without trust, they tell me, the relationship has begun to feel like a burden, like a threat that must be monitored and questioned rather than enjoyed.

The problem here is that most people who get caught cheating apologize and give the "It will never happen again" spiel and that's that, as if penises fell into various orifices completely by accident. Many cheatees accept this response at face value, and don't question the values and fucks given by their partner (pun totally intended); they don't ask themselves whether those values and fucks make their partner a good person to stay with. They're so concerned with holding on to their relationship that they fail to recognize that it's become a black hole consuming their self-respect.

If people cheat, it's because something other than the relationship is more important to them. It may be power over others. It may be validation through sex. It may be giving in to their own impulses. Whatever it is, it's clear that the cheater's values are not aligned in a way to support a healthy relationship. And if the cheater doesn't admit this or come to terms with it, if he just gives the old "I don't know what I was thinking; I was stressed out and drunk and she was there" response, then he lacks the serious self-awareness necessary to solve any relationship problems.

What needs to happen is that cheaters have to start peeling away at their self-awareness onion and figure out what fucked-up values caused them to break the trust of the relationship (and whether they actually still value the relationship). They need to be able to say, "You know what: I am selfish. I care about myself more than the relationship; to be honest, I don't really respect the relationship much at all." If cheaters can't express their shitty values, and show that those values have been overridden, then there's no reason to believe that they can be trusted. And if they can't be trusted, then the relationship is not going to get better or change.

The other factor in regaining trust after it's been broken is a practical one: a track record. If someone breaks your trust, words are nice; but you then need to see a consistent track record of improved behavior. Only then can you begin trusting that the cheater's values are now aligned properly and the person really will change.

Unfortunately, building a track record for trust takes time—certainly a lot more time than it takes to break trust. And during that trust-building period, things are likely to be pretty shitty. So both people in the relationship must be conscious of the struggle they're choosing to undertake.

I use the example of cheating in a romantic relationship, but this process applies to a breach in any relationship. When trust is destroyed, it can be rebuilt only if the following two steps happen: 1) the trust-breaker admits the true values that caused the breach and owns up to them, and 2) the trust-breaker builds a solid track record of improved behavior over time. Without the first step, there should be no attempt at reconciliation in the first place.

Trust is like a china plate. If you break it once, with some care and attention you can put it back together again. But if you break it again, it splits into even more pieces and it takes far longer to piece together again. If you break it more and more times, eventually it shatters to the point where it's impossible to restore. There are too many broken pieces, and too much dust.

Freedom Through Commitment

Consumer culture is very good at making us want more, more, more. Underneath all the hype and marketing is the implication that more is always better. I bought into this idea for years. Make more money, visit more countries, have more experiences, be with more women.

But more is not always better. In fact, the opposite is true. We are actually often happier with less. When we're overloaded with opportunities and options, we suffer from what psychologists refer to as the paradox of choice. Basically, the more options we're given, the less satisfied we become with whatever we choose, because we're aware of all the other options we're potentially forfeiting.

So if you have a choice between two places to live and pick one, you'll likely feel confident and comfortable that you made the right choice. You'll be satisfied with your decision.

But if you have a choice among twenty-eight places to live and pick one, the paradox of choice says that you'll likely spend years agonizing, doubting, and second-guessing yourself, wondering if you really made the "right" choice, and if you're truly maximizing your own happiness. And this anxiety, this desire for certainty and perfection and success, will make you unhappy.

So what do we do? Well, if you're like I used to be, you avoid choosing anything at all. You aim to keep your options open as long as possible. You avoid commitment.

But while investing deeply in one person, one place, one job, one activity might deny us the breadth of experience we'd like, pursuing a breadth of experience denies us the opportunity to experience the rewards of depth of experience. There are some experiences that you can have *only* when you've lived in the same place for five years, when you've been with the same person for over a decade, when you've been working on the same skill or craft for half your lifetime. Now that I'm in my thirties, I can finally recognize that commitment, in its own way, offers a wealth of opportunity and experiences that would otherwise never be available to me, no matter where I went or what I did.

When you're pursuing a wide breadth of experience, there are diminishing returns to each new adventure, each new person or thing. When you've never left your home country, the first country you visit inspires a massive perspective shift, because you have such a narrow experience base to draw on. But when you've been to twenty countries, the twenty-first adds little. And when you've been to fifty, the fifty-first adds even less.

The same goes for material possessions, money, hobbies, jobs, friends, and romantic/sexual partners—all the lame superficial values people choose for themselves. The older you get, the more experienced you get, the less significantly each new experience affects you. The first time I drank at a party was exciting. The hundredth time was fun. The five hundredth time felt like a normal weekend. And the thousandth time felt boring and unimportant.

The big story for me personally over the past few years has been my ability to open myself up to commitment. I've chosen to reject all but the very best people and experiences and values in my life. I shut down all my business projects and decided to focus on writing full-time. Since then, my website has become more popular than I'd ever imagined possible. I've committed to one woman for the long haul and, to my surprise, have found this more rewarding than any of the flings, trysts, and one-night stands I had in the past. I've committed to a single geographic location and doubled down on the handful of my significant, genuine, healthy friendships.

And what I've discovered is something entirely counterintuitive: that there is a freedom and liberation in commitment. I've found *increased* opportunity and upside in rejecting alternatives and distractions in favor of what I've chosen to let truly matter to me.

Commitment gives you freedom because you're no longer distracted by the unimportant and frivolous. Commitment gives you freedom because it hones your attention and focus, directing them toward what is most efficient at making you healthy and happy. Commitment makes decision-making easier and removes any fear of missing out; knowing that what you already have is good enough, why would you ever stress about chasing more, more, more again? Commitment allows you to focus intently on a few highly important goals and achieve a greater degree of success than you otherwise would.

In this way, the rejection of alternatives liberates us—rejection of what does not align with our most important values, with our chosen metrics, rejection of the constant pursuit of breadth without depth.

Yes, breadth of experience is likely necessary and desirable when you're young—after all, you have to go out there and discover what seems worth investing yourself in. But depth is where the gold is buried. And you have to stay committed to something and go deep to dig it up. That's true in relationships, in a career, in building a great lifestyle—in everything.

... And Then You Die

S eek the truth for yourself, and I will meet you there."
That was the last thing Josh ever said to me. He said
it ironically, attempting to sound deep while simultaneously making fun of people who attempt to sound deep.
He was drunk and high. And he was a good friend.

The most transformational moment of my life occurred
when I was nineteen years old. My friend Josh had taken me
to a party on a lake just north of Dallas, Texas. There were
condos on a hill and below the hill was a pool, and below
the pool was a cliff overlooking the lake. It was a small cliff,
maybe thirty feet high—certainly high enough to give you
a second thought about jumping, but low enough that with
the right combination of alcohol and peer pressure that second thought could easily vanish.

Shortly after arriving at the party, Josh and I sat in the

pool together, drinking beers and talking as young angsty males do. We talked about drinking and bands and girls and all of the cool stuff Josh had done that summer since dropping out of music school. We talked about playing in a band together and moving to New York City—an impossible dream at the time.

We were just kids.

"Is it okay to jump off that?" I asked after a while, nodding toward the cliff over the lake.

"Yeah," Josh said, "people do it all the time here."

"Are you going to do it?"

He shrugged. "Maybe. We'll see."

Later in the evening, Josh and I got separated. I had become distracted by a pretty Asian girl who liked video games, which to me, as a teenage nerd, was akin to winning the lottery. She had no interest in me, but she was friendly and happy to let me talk, so I talked. After a few beers, I gathered enough courage to ask her to go up to the house with me to get some food. She said sure.

As we walked up the hill, we bumped into Josh coming down. I asked him if he wanted food, but he declined. I asked him where I could find him later on. He smiled and said, "Seek the truth for yourself, and I will meet you there!"

I nodded and made a serious face. "Okay, I'll see you there," I replied, as if everyone knew exactly where the truth was and how to get to it.

Josh laughed and walked down the hill toward the cliff. I laughed and continued up the hill toward the house.

I don't remember how long I was inside. I just remember

that when the girl and I came out again, everyone was gone and there were sirens. The pool was empty. People were running down the hill toward the shoreline below the cliff. There were others already down by the water. I could make out a couple guys swimming around. It was dark and hard to see. The music droned on, but nobody listened.

Still not putting two-and-two together, I hurried down to the shoreline, gnawing on my sandwich, curious as to what everyone was looking at. Halfway down, the pretty Asian girl said to me, "I think something terrible has happened."

When I got to the bottom of the hill, I asked someone where Josh was. No one looked at me or acknowledged me. Everyone stared at the water. I asked again, and a girl started crying uncontrollably.

That's when I put two-and-two together.

It took scuba divers three hours to find Josh's body at the bottom of the lake. The autopsy would later say that his legs had cramped up due to dehydration from the alcohol, as well as to the impact of the jump from the cliff. It was dark out when he went in, the water layered on the night, black on black. No one could see where his screams for help were coming from. Just the splashes. Just the sounds. His parents later told me that he was a terrible swimmer. I'd had no idea.

It took me twelve hours to let myself cry. I was in my car, driving back home to Austin the next morning. I called my dad and told him that I was still near Dallas and that I was going to miss work. (I'd been working for him that summer.) He asked, "Why; what happened? Is everything

all right?" And that's when it all came out: the waterworks.
The wails and the screams and the snot. I pulled the car over
to the side of the road and clutched the phone and cried the
way a little boy cries to his father.

I went into a deep depression that summer. I thought
I'd been depressed before, but this was a whole new level of
meaninglessness—sadness so deep that it physically hurt.
People would come by and try to cheer me up, and I would
sit there and hear them say all the right things and do all the
right things; and I would tell them thank you and how nice
it was of them to come over, and I would fake a smile and
lie and say that it was getting better, but underneath I just
felt nothing.

I dreamed about Josh for a few months after that.
Dreams where he and I would have full-blown conversations about life and death, as well as about random, point-
less things. Up until that point in my life, I had been a pretty
typical middle-class stoner kid: lazy, irresponsible, socially
anxious, and deeply insecure. Josh, in many ways, had been
a person I looked up to. He was older, more confident, more
experienced, and more accepting of and open to the world
around him. In one of my last dreams of Josh, I was sitting
in a Jacuzzi with him (yeah, I know, weird), and I said something like, "I'm really sorry you died." He laughed. I don't
remember exactly what his words were, but he said something like, "Why do you care that I'm dead when you're still
so afraid to live?" I woke up crying.

It was sitting on my mom's couch that summer, staring
into the so-called abyss, seeing the endless and incomp-

rehensible nothingness where Josh's friendship used to be, when I came to the startling realization that if there really is no reason to do anything, then there is also no reason to *not* do anything; that in the face of the inevitability of death, there is no reason to ever give in to one's fear or embarrassment or shame, since it's all just a bunch of nothing anyway; and that by spending the majority of my short life avoiding what was painful and uncomfortable, I had essentially been avoiding being alive at all.

That summer, I gave up the weed and the cigarettes and the video games. I gave up my silly rock star fantasies and dropped out of music school and signed up for college courses. I started going to the gym and lost a bunch of weight. I made new friends. I got my first girlfriend. For the first time in my life I actually studied for classes, gaining me the startling realization that I could make good grades if only I gave a shit. The next summer, I challenged myself to read fifty nonfiction books in fifty days, and then did it. The following year, I transferred to an excellent university on the other side of the country, where I excelled for the first time, both academically and socially.

Josh's death marks the clearest before/after point I can identify in my life. Pre-tragedy, I was inhibited, unambitious, forever obsessed and confined by what I imagined the world might be thinking of me. Post-tragedy, I morphed into a new person: responsible, curious, hardworking. I still had my insecurities and my baggage—as we always do—but now I gave a fuck about something more important than my insecurities and my baggage.

And that made all the difference. Oddly, it was someone else's death that gave me permission to finally live. And perhaps the worst moment of my life was also the most transformational.

Death scares us. And because it scares us, we avoid thinking about it, talking about it, sometimes even acknowledging it, even when it's happening to someone close to us.

Yet, in a bizarre, backwards way, death is the light by which the shadow of all of life's meaning is measured. Without death, everything would feel inconsequential, all experience arbitrary, all metrics and values suddenly zero.

Something Beyond Our Selves

Ernest Becker was an academic outcast. In 1960, he got his Ph.D. in anthropology; his doctoral research compared the unlikely and unconventional practices of Zen Buddhism and psychoanalysis. At the time, Zen was seen as something for hippies and drug addicts, and Freudian psychoanalysis was considered a quack form of psychology left over from the Stone Age.

In his first job as an assistant professor, Becker quickly fell into a crowd that denounced the practice of psychiatry as a form of fascism. They saw the practice as an unscientific form of oppression against the weak and helpless.

The problem was that Becker's boss was a psychiatrist. So it was kind of like walking into your first job and proudly comparing your boss to Hitler.

As you can imagine, he was fired.

So Becker took his radical ideas somewhere that they

might be accepted: Berkeley, California. But this, too, didn't last long.

Because it wasn't just his anti-establishment tendencies that got Becker into trouble; it was his odd teaching methods as well. He would use Shakespeare to teach psychology, psychology textbooks to teach anthropology, and anthropological data to teach sociology. He'd dress up as King Lear and do mock sword fights in class and go on long political rants that had little to do with the lesson plan. His students adored him. The other faculty loathed him. Less than a year later, he was fired again.

Becker then landed at San Francisco State University, where he actually kept his job for more than a year. But when student protests erupted over the Vietnam War, the university called in the National Guard and things got violent. When Becker sided with the students and publicly condemned the actions of the dean (again, his boss being Hitleresque and everything), he was, once again, promptly fired.

Becker changed jobs four times in six years. And before he could get fired from the fifth, he got colon cancer. The prognosis was grim. He spent the next few years bedridden and had little hope of surviving. So Becker decided to write a book. This book would be about death.

Becker died in 1974. His book *The Denial of Death*, would win the Pulitzer Prize and become one of the most influential intellectual works of the twentieth century, shaking up the fields of psychology and anthropology, while making profound philosophical claims that are still influential today.

The Denial of Death essentially makes two points:

1. Humans are unique in that we're the only animals that can conceptualize and think about ourselves abstractly. Dogs don't sit around and worry about their career. Cats don't think about their past mistakes or wonder what would have happened if they'd done something differently. Monkeys don't argue over future possibilities, just as fish don't sit around wondering if other fish would like them more if they had longer fins.

   As humans, we're blessed with the ability to imagine ourselves in hypothetical situations, to contemplate both the past and the future, to imagine other realities or situations where things might be different. And it's because of this unique mental ability, Becker says, that we all, at some point, become aware of the inevitability of our own death. Because we're able to conceptualize alternate versions of reality, we are also the only animal capable of imagining a reality without ourselves in it.

   This realization causes what Becker calls "death terror," a deep existential anxiety that underlies *everything* we think or do.

2. Becker's second point starts with the premise that we essentially have two "selves." The first self is the physical self—the one that eats, sleeps, snores, and poops. The second self is our conceptual self—our identity, or how we see ourselves.

   Becker's argument is this: We are all aware on some

level that our physical self will eventually die, that this death is inevitable, and that its inevitability—on some unconscious level—scares the shit out of us. Therefore, in order to compensate for our fear of the inevitable loss of our physical self, we try to construct a conceptual self that will live forever. This is why people try so hard to put their names on buildings, on statues, on spines of books. It's why we feel compelled to spend so much time giving ourselves to others, especially to children, in the hopes that our influence—our conceptual self—will last way beyond our physical self. That we will be remembered and revered and idolized long after our physical self ceases to exist.

Becker called such efforts our "immortality projects," projects that allow our conceptual self to live on way past the point of our physical death. All of human civilization, he says, is basically a result of immortality projects: the cities and governments and structures and authorities in place today were all immortality projects of men and women who came before us. They are the remnants of conceptual selves that ceased to die. Names like Jesus, Muhammad, Napoleon, and Shakespeare are just as powerful today as when those men lived, if not more so. And that's the whole point. Whether it be through mastering an art form, conquering a new land, gaining great riches, or simply having a large and loving family that will live on for generations, *all the meaning in our life is shaped by this innate desire to never truly die.*

Religion, politics, sports, art, and technological innovation are the result of people's immortality projects. Becker argues that wars and revolutions and mass murder occur when one group of people's immortality projects rub up against another group's. Centuries of oppression and the bloodshed of millions have been justified as the defense of one group's immortality project against another's.

But, when our immortality projects fail, when the meaning is lost, when the prospect of our conceptual self outliving our physical self no longer seems possible or likely, death terror—that horrible, depressing anxiety—creeps back into our mind. Trauma can cause this, as can shame and social ridicule. As can, as Becker points out, mental illness.

If you haven't figured it out yet, our immortality projects are our values. They are the barometers of meaning and worth in our life. And when our values fail, so do we, psychologically speaking. What Becker is saying, in essence, is that we're all driven by fear to give way too many fucks about something, because giving a fuck about something is the only thing that distracts us from the reality and inevitability of our own death. And to truly not give a single fuck is to achieve a quasi-spiritual state of embracing the impermanence of one's own existence. In that state, one is far less likely to get caught up in various forms of entitlement.

Becker later came to a startling realization on his deathbed: that people's immortality projects were actually the problem, not the solution; that rather than attempting to implement, often through lethal force, their conceptual self across the world, people should question their conceptual self and become more comfortable with the reality of their own death. Becker called this "the bitter antidote," and struggled with reconciling it himself as he stared down his own demise. While death is bad, it is inevitable. Therefore, we should not avoid this realization, but rather come to terms with it as best we can. Because once we become comfortable with the fact of our own death—the root terror, the underlying anxiety motivating all of life's frivolous ambitions—we can then choose our values more freely, unrestrained by the illogical quest for immortality, and freed from dangerous dogmatic views.

The Sunny Side of Death

I step from rock to rock, climbing steadily, leg muscles stretching and aching. In that trancelike state that comes from slow, repetitive physical exertion, I'm nearing the top. The sky gets wide and deep. I'm alone now. My friends are far below me, taking pictures of the ocean.

Finally, I climb over a small boulder and the view opens up. I can see from here to the infinite horizon. It feels as though I'm staring at the edge of the earth, where water meets the sky, blue on blue. The wind screams across my skin. I look up. It's bright. It's beautiful.

I'm at South Africa's Cape of Good Hope, once thought to be the southern tip of Africa and the southernmost point in the world. It's a tumultuous place, a place full of storms and treacherous waters. A place that's seen centuries of trade and commerce and human endeavor. A place, ironically, of lost hopes.

There is a saying in Portuguese: *Ele dobra o Cabo da Boa Esperança.* It means, "He's rounding the Cape of Good Hope." Ironically, it means that the person's life is in its final phase, that he's incapable of accomplishing anything more.

I step across the rocks toward the blue, allowing its vastness to engulf my field of vision. I'm sweating yet cold. Excited yet nervous. *Is this it?*

The wind is slapping my ears. I hear nothing, but I see the edge: where the rock meets oblivion. I stop and stand for a moment, several yards away. I can see the ocean below, lapping and frothing against cliffs stretching out for miles to either side. The tides are furious against the impenetrable walls. Straight ahead, it's a sheer drop of at least fifty yards to the water below.

To my right, tourists are dotted across the landscape below, snapping photos and aggregating themselves into antlike formations. To my left is Asia. In front of me is the sky and behind me is everything I've ever hoped for and brought with me.

What if this is it? What if this is all there is?

I look around. I'm alone. I take my first step toward the edge of the cliff.

The human body seems to come equipped with a natural radar for death-inducing situations. For example, the moment you get within about ten feet of a cliff edge, minus guardrail, a certain tension digs into your body. Your back stiffens. Your skin ripples. Your eyes become hyperfocused on every detail of your environment. Your feet feel as though they're made of rock. It's as if there were a big, invisible magnet gently pulling your body back to safety.

But I fight the magnet. I drag the feet made of rock closer to the edge.

At five feet away, your mind joins the party. You can now see not only the edge of the cliff, but *down* the cliff face itself, which induces all sorts of unwanted visualizations of tripping and falling and tumbling to a splashy death. It's really fucking far, your mind reminds you. Like, *really* fucking far. *Dude, what are you doing? Stop moving. Stop it.*

I tell my mind to shut up, and keep inching forward.

At three feet, your body goes into full-scale red alert. You are now within an errant shoelace-trip of your life ending. It feels as though a hefty gust of wind could send you sailing off into that blue-bisected eternity. Your legs shake. As do your hands. As does your voice, in case you need to remind yourself you're not about to plummet to your death.

The three-foot distance is most people's absolute limit. It's just close enough to lean forward and catch a glimpse of the bottom, but still far enough to feel as though you're not at any real risk of killing yourself. Standing that close to the edge of a cliff, even one as beautiful and mesmerizing as the Cape of Good Hope, induces a heady sense of vertigo, and threatens to regurgitate any recent meal.

Is this it? Is this all there is? Do I already know everything I will ever know?

I take another microstep, then another. Two feet now. My forward leg vibrates as I put the weight of my body on it. I shuffle on. Against the magnet. Against my mind. Against all my better instincts for survival.

One foot now. I'm now looking straight down the cliff face. I feel a sudden urge to cry. My body instinctively crouches, protecting itself against something imagined and inexplicable. The wind comes in hailstorms. The thoughts come in right hooks.

At one foot you feel like you're floating. Anything but looking straight down feels as though you're part of the sky itself. You actually kind of expect to fall at this point.

I crouch there for a moment, catching my breath, collecting my thoughts. I force myself to stare down at the water hitting the rocks below me. Then I look again to my right, at the little ants milling about the signage below me, snapping photos, chasing tour buses, on the off chance that somebody somehow sees me. This desire for attention is wholly irrational. But so is all of this. It's impossible to make me out up here, of course. And even if it weren't, there's nothing that those distant people could say or do.

All I hear is the wind.

Is this it?

My body shudders, the fear becoming euphoric and blinding. I focus my mind and clear my thoughts in a kind of meditation. Nothing makes you present and mindful like being mere inches away from your own death. I straighten up and look out again, and find myself smiling. I remind myself that it's all right to die.

This willing and even exuberant interfacing with one's own mortality has ancient roots. The Stoics of ancient Greece and Rome implored people to keep death in mind at all times, in order to appreciate life more and remain humble in the face of its adversities. In various forms of Buddhism, the practice of meditation is often taught as a means of preparing oneself for death while still remaining alive. Dissolving one's ego into an expansive nothingness—achieving the enlightened state of nirvana—is seen as a trial run of letting oneself cross to the other side. Even Mark Twain, that hairy goofball who came in and left on Halley's Comet, said, "The fear of death follows from the fear of life. A man who lives fully is prepared to die at any time."

Back on the cliff, I bend down, slightly leaning back. I put my hands on the ground behind me and gently lower myself onto my butt. I then gradually slide one leg over the edge of the cliff. There's a small rock jutting out of the cliff side. I rest my foot on it. Then I slide my other foot off the edge and put it on the same small rock. I sit there a moment, leaning back on my palms, wind ruffling my hair. The anxiety is bearable now, as long as I stay focused on the horizon.

Then I sit up straight and look down the cliff again. Fear shoots back up through my spine, electrifying my limbs and laser-focusing my mind on the exact coordinates of every inch of my body. The fear is stifling at times. But each time it stifles me, I empty my thoughts, focus my attention on the bottom of the cliff below me, force myself to gaze at my potential doom, and then to simply acknowledge its existence.

I was now sitting on the edge of the world, at the southern-most tip of hope, the gateway to the east. The feeling was exhilarating. I can feel the adrenaline pumping through my body. Being so still, so conscious, never felt so thrilling. I listen to the wind and watch the ocean and look out upon the ends of the earth—and then I laugh with the light, all that it touches being good.

Confronting the reality of our own mortality is important because it obliterates all the crappy, fragile, superficial values in life. While most people whittle their days chasing another buck, or a little bit more fame and attention, or a little bit more assurance that they're right or loved, death confronts all of us with a far more painful and important question: What is your legacy?

How will the world be different and better when you're gone? What mark will you have made? What influence will you have caused? They say that a butterfly flapping its wings in Africa can cause a hurricane in Florida; well, what hurricanes will you leave in your wake?

As Becker pointed out, this is arguably the *only* truly important question in our life. Yet we avoid thinking about it. One, because it's hard. Two, because it's scary. Three, because we have no fucking clue what we're doing.

And when we avoid this question, we let trivial and hateful values hijack our brains and take control of our desires and ambitions. Without acknowledging the ever-present gaze of death, the superficial will appear important, and the important will appear superficial. Death is the only thing we can know with any certainty. And as such, it must be the compass by which we orient all of our other values and decisions. It is the correct answer to all of the questions we should ask but never do. The only way to be comfortable with death is to understand and see yourself as something bigger than yourself; to choose values that stretch beyond serving yourself, that are simple and immediate and controllable and tolerant of the chaotic world around you. This is the basic root of all happiness. Whether you're listening to Aristotle or the psychologists at Harvard or Jesus Christ or the goddamn Beatles, they all say that happiness comes from the same thing: caring about something greater than yourself, believing that you are a contributing component in some much larger entity, that your life is but a mere side process of some great unintelligible production. This feeling is what people go to church for; it's what they fight in wars for; it's what they raise families and save pensions and build bridges and invent cell phones for: this fleeting sense of being part of something greater and more unknowable than themselves.

And entitlement strips this away from us. The gravity of entitlement sucks all attention inward, toward ourselves, causing us to feel as though *we* are at the center of all of the problems in the universe, that *we* are the one suffering all of the injustices, that *we* are the one who deserves greatness over all others.

As alluring as it is, entitlement isolates us. Our curiosity and excitement for the world turns in upon itself and reflects our own biases and projections onto every person we meet and every event we experience. This feels sexy and enticing and may feel good for a while and sells a lot of tickets, but it's spiritual poison.

It's these dynamics that plague us now. We are so materially well off, yet so psychologically tormented in so many low-level and shallow ways. People relinquish all responsibility, demanding that society cater to *their* feelings and sensibilities. People hold on to arbitrary certainties and try to enforce them on others, often violently, in the name of some made-up righteous cause. People, high on a sense of false superiority, fall into inaction and lethargy for fear of trying something worthwhile and failing at it.

The pampering of the modern mind has resulted in a population that feels deserving of something without earning that something, a population that feels they have a right to something without sacrificing for it. People declare themselves experts, entrepreneurs, inventors, innovators, mavericks, and coaches without any real-life experience. And they do this not because they actually think they *are* greater than everybody else; they do it because they feel that they *need to be great* to be accepted in a world that broadcasts only the extraordinary.

Our culture today confuses great attention and great success, assuming them to be the same thing. But they are not.

You *are* great. Already. Whether you realize it or not. Whether anybody else realizes it or not. And it's not because you launched an iPhone app, or finished school a year early, or bought yourself a sweet-ass boat. These things do not define greatness.

You are already great because in the face of endless confusion and certain death, you continue to choose what to give a fuck about and what not to. This mere fact, this simple optioning for your own values in life, already makes you beautiful, already makes you successful, and already makes you loved. Even if you don't realize it. Even if you're sleeping in a gutter and starving.

You too are going to die, and that's because you too were fortunate enough to have lived. You may not feel this. But go stand on a cliff sometime, and maybe you will.

Bukowski once wrote, "We're all going to die, all of us. What a circus! That alone should make us love each other, but it doesn't. We are terrorized and flattened by life's trivialities; we are eaten up by nothing."

Looking back on that night, out by that lake, when I watched my friend Josh's body getting fished out of the lake by paramedics. I remember staring into the black Texas night and watching my ego slowly dissolve into it. Josh's death taught me much more than I initially realized. Yes, it helped me to seize the day, to take responsibility for my choices, and to pursue my dreams with less shame and inhibition.

But these were side effects of a deeper, more primary lesson. And the primary lesson was this: there is nothing to be afraid of. Ever. And reminding myself of my own death repeatedly over the years—whether it be through meditation, through reading philosophy, or through doing crazy shit like standing on a cliff in South Africa—is the only thing that has helped me hold this realization front and center in my mind. This acceptance of my death, this understanding of my own fragility, has made everything easier—untangling my addictions, identifying and confronting my own entitlement, accepting responsibility for my own problems—suffering through my fears and uncertainties, accepting my failures and embracing rejections—it has all been made lighter by the thought of my own death. The more I peer into the darkness, the brighter life gets, the quieter the world becomes, and the less unconscious resistance I feel to, well, anything.

I sit there on the Cape for a few minutes, taking in everything. When I finally decide to get up, I put my hands behind me and scoot back. Then, slowly, I stand. I check the ground around me—making sure there's no errant rock ready to sabotage me. Having recognized that I am safe, I begin to walk back to reality—five feet, ten feet—my body restoring itself with each step. My feet become lighter. I let life's magnet draw me in.

As I step back over some rocks, back to the main path, I look up to see a man staring at me. I stop and make eye contact with him.

"Um. I saw you sitting on the edge over there," he says. His accent is Australian. The word "there" rolls out of his mouth awkwardly. He points toward Antarctica.

"Yeah. The view is gorgeous, isn't it?" I am smiling. He is not. He has a serious look on his face.

I brush my hands off on my shorts, my body still buzzing from my surrender. There's an awkward silence.

The Aussie stands for a moment, perplexed, still looking at me, clearly thinking of what to say next. After a moment, he carefully pieces the words together.

"Is everything okay? How are you feeling?"

I pause for a moment, still smiling. "Alive. Very alive."

His skepticism breaks and reveals a smile in its place. He gives a slight nod and heads down the trail. I stand above, taking in the view, waiting for my friends to arrive on the peak.

ACKNOWLEDGMENTS

This book began as a big, messy thing and required more than just my own hands to chisel something comprehensible out of it.

First and foremost, thank you to my brilliant and beautiful wife, Fernanda, who never hesitates to say no to me when I need to hear it most. Not only do you make me a better person, but your unconditional love and constant feedback during the writing process were indispensable.

To my parents, for putting up with my shit all these years and continuing to love me anyway. In many ways, I don't feel as though I fully became an adult until I understood many of the concepts in this book. In that sense, it's been a joy to get to know you as an adult these past few years. And to my brother as well: I never doubt the existence of mutual love and respect between us, even if I sometimes get butthurt that you don't text me back.

To Philip Kemper and Drew Birnie—two big brains that conspire to make my brain appear much larger than it actually is. Your hard work and brilliance continue to floor me.

To Michael Covell, for being my intellectual stress test, especially when it comes to understanding psychological research, and for always challenging me on my assumptions. To my editor, Luke Dempsey, for mercilessly tightening the screws on my writing, and for possibly having an even fouler mouth than I do. To my agent, Mollie Glick, for helping me define the vision for the book and pushing it much farther into the world than I ever expected to see it go. To Taylor Pearson, Dan Andrews, and Jodi Ettenberg, for their support during this process; you three kept me both accountable and sane, which are the only two things every writer needs.

And finally, to the millions of people who, for whatever reason, decided to read a potty-mouthed asshole from Boston writing about life on his blog. The flood of emails I've received from those of you willing to open up the most intimate corners of your life to me, a complete stranger, both humbles me and inspires me. At this point in my life, I've spent thousands of hours reading and studying these subjects. But you all continue to be my true education. Thank you.

EVERY
THING
IS
F*CKED

Also by MARK MANSON

The Subtle Art of Not Giving a Fuck

EVERY THING IS F*CKED

A BOOK ABOUT HOPE

MARK MANSON

HARPER

An Imprint of HarperCollinsPublishers

HarperCollins books may be purchased for educational, business, or sales
promotional use. For information, please email the Special Markets Department at SPsales@harpercollins.com.

FIRST EDITION

Designed by Leah Carlson-Stanisic

Library of Congress Cataloging-in-Publication Data has been applied for.

ISBN 978-0-06-288843-3
ISBN 978-0-06-288846-4 (International Edition)

24 25 26 27 28 LBC 12 11 10 9 8

For Fernanda, of course

Contents

Part I:

HOPE

The Uncomfortable Truth

On a small plot of land in the monotonous countryside of central Europe, amid the warehouses of a former military barracks, a nexus of geographically concentrated evil would arise, denser and darker than anything the world had ever seen. Over the span of four years, more than 1.3 million people would be systematically sorted, enslaved, tortured, and murdered here, and it would all happen in an area slightly larger than Central Park in Manhattan. And no one would do anything to stop it.

Except for one man.

It is the stuff of fairy tales and comic books: a hero marches headlong into the fiery jaws of hell to confront some great manifestation of evil. The odds are impossible. The rationale is laughable. Yet our fantastical hero never hesitates, never flinches. He stands tall and slays the dragon, crushes the demon invaders, saves the planet and maybe even a princess or two.

And for a brief time, there is hope.

But this is not a story of hope. This is a story of everything being completely and utterly fucked. Fucked in proportions and on scales that today, with the comfort of our free Wi-Fi and oversize Snuggie blankets, you and I can hardly imagine.

Witold Pilecki was already a war hero before he decided to sneak into Auschwitz. As a young man, Pilecki had been a decorated officer in the Polish-Soviet War of 1918. He had kicked the

Communists in the nuts before most people even knew what a pinko Commie bastard was. After the war, Pilecki moved to the Polish countryside, married a schoolteacher, and had two kids. He enjoyed riding horses and wearing fancy hats and smoking cigars. Life was simple and good.

Then that whole Hitler thing happened, and before Poland could get both its boots on, the Nazis had already Blitzkrieged through half the country. Poland lost its entire territory in a little more than a month. It wasn't exactly a fair fight: while the Nazis invaded in the west, the Soviets invaded in the east. It was like being stuck between a rock and a hard place—except the rock was a megalomaniacal mass murderer trying to conquer the world and the hard place was rampant, senseless genocide. I'm still not sure which was which.

Early on, the Soviets were actually far crueler than the Nazis. They had done this shit before, you know—the whole "overthrow a government and enslave a population to your faulty ideology" thing. The Nazis were still somewhat imperialist virgins (which, when you look at pictures of Hitler's mustache, isn't hard to imagine). In those first months of the war, it's estimated that the Soviets rounded up over a million Polish citizens and sent them east. Think about that for a second. A million people, in a matter of months, just gone. Some didn't stop until they hit the gulags in Siberia; others were found in mass graves decades later. Many are still unaccounted for to this day.

Pilecki fought in those battles—against both the Germans and the Soviets. And after their defeat, he and fellow Polish officers started an underground resistance group in Warsaw. They called themselves the Secret Polish Army.

In the spring of 1940, the Secret Polish Army got wind of the fact that the Germans were building a massive prison complex outside some backwater town in the southern part of the country. The Germans named this new prison complex Auschwitz. By the summer of 1940, thousands of military officers and leading Polish nationals were disappearing from western Poland. Fears arose among the resistance that the same mass incarceration that had occurred in the east with the Soviets was now on the menu in the west. Pilecki and his crew suspected that Auschwitz, a prison the size of a small town, was likely involved in the disappearances and that it might already house thousands of former Polish soldiers.

That's when Pilecki volunteered to sneak into Auschwitz. Initially, it was a rescue mission—he would allow himself to get arrested, and once there, he would organize with other Polish soldiers, coordinate a mutiny, and break out of the prison camp.

It was a mission so suicidal that he might as well have asked his commander permission to drink a bucket of bleach. His superiors thought he was crazy, and told him as much.

But, as the weeks went by, the problem only grew worse: thousands of elite Poles were disappearing, and Auschwitz was still a huge blind spot in the Allied intelligence network. The Allies had no idea what was going on there and little chance of finding out. Eventually, Pilecki's commanders relented. One evening, at a routine checkpoint in Warsaw, Pilecki let himself be arrested by the SS for violating curfew. And soon, he was on his way to Auschwitz, the only man known ever to have voluntarily entered a Nazi concentration camp.

Once he got there, he saw that the reality of Auschwitz was far worse than anyone had suspected. Prisoners were routinely shot in roll call lineups for transgressions as minor as fidgeting or not standing up straight. The manual labor was grueling and endless. Men were literally worked to death, often performing tasks that were useless or meant nothing. The first month Pilecki was there, a full third of the men in his barracks died of exhaustion or pneumonia or were shot. Regardless, by the end of the 1940, Pilecki, the comic book superhero motherfucker, had still somehow set up an espionage operation.

Oh, Pilecki—you titan, you champion, flying above the abyss—how did you manage to create an intelligence network by embedding messages in laundry baskets? How did you build your own transistor radio out of spare parts and stolen batteries, *MacGyver*-style, and then successfully transmit plans for an attack on the prison camp to the Secret Polish Army in Warsaw? How did you create smuggling rings to bring in food, medicine, and clothing for prisoners, saving countless lives and delivering hope to the remotest desert of the human heart? What did this world do to deserve you?

Over the course of two years, Pilecki built an entire resistance unit within Auschwitz. There was a chain of command, with ranks and officers; a logistics network; and lines of communication to the outside world. And all this went undiscovered by the SS guards for almost two years. Pilecki's ultimate aim was to foment a full-scale revolt within the camp. With help and coordination from the outside, he believed he could stoke a prison break, overrun the undermanned SS guards, and release tens of thousands of highly trained Polish guerrilla fighters into the wild. He sent his plans and reports to Warsaw. For months, he waited. For months, he survived.

But then came the Jews. First, in buses. Then, packed in train cars. Soon, they were arriving by the tens of thousands, an undulating current of people floating in an ocean of death and despair. Stripped of all family possessions and dignity, they filed mechanically into the newly renovated "shower" barracks, where they were gassed and their bodies burned.

Pilecki's reports to the outside became frantic. They're murdering tens of thousands of people here each day. Mostly Jews. The death toll could potentially be in the millions. He pleaded with the Secret Polish Army to liberate the camp at once. He said if you can't liberate the camp, then at least bomb it. For God's sake, at least destroy the gas chambers. At least.

The Secret Polish Army received his messages but figured he was exaggerating. In the farthest reaches of their minds, nothing could be that fucked. Nothing.

Pilecki was the first person ever to alert the world to the Holocaust. His intelligence was forwarded through the various resistance groups around Poland, then on to the Polish government-in-exile in the United Kingdom, who then passed his reports to the Allied Command in London. The information eventually even made its way to Eisenhower and Churchill.

They, too, figured Pilecki had to be exaggerating.

In 1943, Pilecki realized that his plans of a mutiny and prison break were never going to happen: The Secret Polish Army wasn't coming. The Americans and British weren't coming. And in all likelihood, it was the Soviets who were coming—and they would be worse. Pilecki decided that remaining inside the camp was too risky. It was time to escape.

He made it look easy, of course. First, he faked illness and got himself admitted to the camp's hospital. From there, he lied to the doctors about what work group he was supposed to return to, saying he had the night shift at the bakery, which was on the edge of camp, near the river. When the doctors discharged him, he headed to the bakery, where he proceeded to "work" until 2:00 a.m., when the last batch of bread finished baking. From there, it was just a matter of cutting the telephone wire, silently prying open the back door, changing into stolen civilian clothes without the SS guards noticing, sprinting to the river a mile away while being shot at, and then navigating his way back to civilization via the stars.

Today, much in our world appears to be fucked. Not Nazi Holocaust–level fucked (not even close), but still, pretty fucked nonetheless.

Stories such as Pilecki's inspire us. They give us hope. They make us say, "Well, damn, things were *way* worse then, and *that* guy transcended it all. What have *I* done lately?"—which, in this couch-potato-pundit era of tweetstorms and outrage porn is probably what we should be asking ourselves. When we zoom out and get perspective, we realize that while heroes like Pilecki save the world, we swat at gnats and complain that the AC isn't high enough.

Pilecki's story is the single most heroic thing I've ever come across in my life. Because heroism isn't just bravery or guts or shrewd maneuvering. These things are common and are often used in unheroic ways. No, being heroic is the ability to conjure hope where there is none. To strike a match to light up the void. To show us a possibility for a better world—not a better world we *want* to exist, but a better world we didn't know *could* exist. To take a situation where everything seems to be absolutely fucked and still somehow make it good.

Bravery is common. Resilience is common. But heroism has a philosophical component to it. There's some great "Why?" that heroes bring to the table—some incredible cause or belief that goes unshaken, no matter what. And *this* is why, as a culture, we are so desperate for a hero today: not because things are necessarily so bad, but because we've lost the clear "Why?" that drove previous generations.

We are a culture in need not of peace or prosperity or new hood ornaments for our electric cars. We have all that. We are a culture in need of something far more precarious. We are a culture and a people in need of hope.

After witnessing years of war, torture, death, and genocide, Pilecki never lost hope. Despite losing his country, his family, his friends, and nearly his own life, he never lost hope. Even after the war, while enduring Soviet domination, he never lost the hope of a free and independent Poland. He never lost the hope of a quiet and happy life for his children. He never lost the hope of being able to save a few more lives, of helping a few more people.

After the war, Pilecki returned to Warsaw and continued spying, this time on the Communist Party, which had just come to power there. Again, he would be the first person to notify the West of an ongoing evil, in this case that the Soviets had infiltrated the Polish government and rigged its elections. He would also be the first to document the Soviet atrocities committed in the east during the war.

This time, though, he was discovered. He was warned that he was about to be arrested, and he had a chance to flee to Italy. Yet, Pilecki declined—he would rather stay and die Polish than run and live as something he didn't recognize. A free and independent Poland, by then, was his only source of hope. Without it, he was nothing.

And thus, his hope would also be his undoing. The Communists captured Pilecki in 1947, and they didn't go easy on him. He was tortured for almost a year, so harshly and consistently that he told his wife that "Auschwitz was just a trifle" by comparison.

Still, he never cooperated with his interrogators.

Eventually, realizing they could get no information from him, the Communists decided to make an example of him. In 1948, they held a show trial and charged Pilecki with everything from falsifying documents and violating curfew to engaging in espionage and treason. A month later, he was found guilty and sentenced to death. On the final day of the trial, Pilecki was allowed to speak. He stated that his allegiance had always been to Poland and its people, that he had never harmed or betrayed any Polish citizen, and that he regretted nothing. He concluded his statement with "I have tried to live my life such that in the hour of my death I would feel joy rather than fear."

And if that's not the most hardcore thing you've ever heard, then I want some of what you're having.

How May I Help You?

If I worked at Starbucks, instead of writing people's names on their coffee cup, I'd write the following:

> One day, you and everyone you love will die. And beyond a small group of people for an extremely brief period of time, little of what you say or do will ever matter. This is the Uncomfortable Truth of life. And everything you think or do is but an elaborate avoidance of it. We are inconsequential cosmic dust, bumping and milling about on a tiny blue speck. We imagine our own importance. We invent our purpose—we are nothing.
>
> Enjoy your fucking coffee.

I'd have to write it in really tiny lettering, of course. And it'd take a while to write, meaning the line of morning rush-hour customers would be backed out the door. Not exactly stellar customer service, either. This is probably just one of the reasons why I'm not employable.

But seriously, how could you tell someone, in good conscience, to "have a nice day" while knowing that all their thoughts and motivations stem from a never-ending need to avoid the inherent meaninglessness of human existence?

Because, in the infinite expanse of space/time, the universe does not care whether your mother's hip replacement goes well, or your kids attend college, or your boss thinks you made a bitching spreadsheet. It doesn't care if the Democrats or the Republicans win the presidential election. It doesn't care if a celebrity gets caught doing cocaine while furiously masturbating in an airport bathroom (again). It doesn't care if the forests burn or the ice melts or the waters rise or the air simmers or we all get vaporized by a superior alien race.

You care.

You care, and you desperately convince yourself that because you care, it all must have some great cosmic meaning behind it.

You care because, deep down, you need to feel that sense of importance in order to avoid the Uncomfortable Truth, to avoid the incomprehensibility of your existence, to avoid being crushed by the weight of your own material insignificance. And you—like me, like everyone—then project that imagined sense of importance onto the world around you because it gives you hope.

Is it too early to have this conversation? Here, have another coffee. I even made a winky-smiley face with the steamed milk. Isn't it cute? I'll wait while you Instagram it.

Okay, where were we? Oh yeah! The incomprehensibility of your existence—right. Now, you might be thinking, "Well, Mark, I believe we're all here for a reason, and nothing is a coincidence, and everyone matters because all our actions affect *somebody*, and even if we can help one person, then it's still worth it, right?"

Now, aren't you just as cute as a button!

See, that's your hope talking. That's a story your mind spins to make it worth waking up in the morning: *something* needs to matter because without something mattering, then there's no reason to go on living. And some form of simple altruism or a reduction in suffering is always our mind's go-to for making it feel like it's worth doing anything.

Our psyche needs hope to survive the way a fish needs water. Hope is the fuel for our mental engine. It's the butter on our biscuit. It's a lot of really cheesy metaphors. Without hope, your whole mental apparatus will stall out or starve. If we don't believe there's any hope that the future will be better than the present, that our lives will improve in some way, then we spiritually die. After all, if there's no hope of things ever being better, then why live—why do anything?

Here's what a lot of people don't get: the opposite of happiness is not anger or sadness.[1] If you're angry or sad, that means you still give a fuck about something. That means something still matters. That means you still have hope.[2]

No, the opposite of happiness is hopelessness, an endless gray horizon of resignation and indifference.[3] It's the belief that everything is fucked, so why do anything at all?

Hopelessness is a cold and bleak nihilism, a sense that there is no point, so fuck it—why not run with scissors or sleep with your boss's wife or shoot up a school? It is the Uncomfortable Truth, a silent realization that in the face of infinity, everything we could possibly care about quickly approaches zero.

Hopelessness is the root of anxiety, mental illness, and depression. It is the source of all misery and the cause of all addiction.

This is not an overstatement.⁴ Chronic anxiety is a crisis of hope. It is the fear of a failed future. Depression is a crisis of hope. It is the belief in a meaningless future. Delusion, addiction, obsession—these are all the mind's desperate and compulsive attempts at generating hope one neurotic tic or obsessive craving at a time.⁵

The avoidance of hopelessness—that is, the construction of hope—then becomes our mind's primary project. All meaning, everything we understand about ourselves and the world, is constructed for the purpose of maintaining hope. Therefore, hope is the only thing any of us willingly dies for. Hope is what we believe to be greater than ourselves. Without it, we believe we are nothing.

When I was in college, my grandfather died. For a few years afterward, I had this intense feeling that I must live in such a way as to make him proud. This *felt* reasonable and obvious on some deep level, but it wasn't. In fact, it made no logical sense at all. I hadn't had a close relationship with my grandfather. We'd never talked on the phone. We hadn't corresponded. I didn't even see him the last five years or so that he was alive.

Not to mention: he was dead. How did my "living to make him proud" affect anything?

His death caused me to brush up against that Uncomfortable Truth. So, my mind got to work, looking to build hope out of the situation in order to sustain me, to keep any nihilism at bay. My mind decided that because my grandfather was now deprived of his ability to hope and aspire in his own life, it was important for me to carry on hope and aspiration in his honor. This was my mind's bite-size piece of faith, my own personal mini-religion of purpose.

And it worked! For a short while, his death infused otherwise banal and empty experiences with import and meaning. And that meaning gave me hope. You've probably felt something similar when someone close to you passed away. It's a common feeling. You tell yourself you'll live in a way that will make your loved one proud. You tell yourself you will use *your* life to celebrate *his*. You tell yourself that this is an important and good thing.

And that "good thing" is what sustains us in these moments of existential terror. I walked around imagining that my grandfather was following me, like a really nosy ghost, constantly looking over my shoulder. This man whom I barely knew when he was alive was now somehow extremely concerned with how I did on my calculus exam. It was totally irrational.

Our psyches construct little narratives like this whenever they face adversity, these before/after stories we invent for ourselves. And we must keep these hope narratives alive, all the time, even if they become unreasonable or destructive, as they are the only stabilizing force protecting our minds from the Uncomfortable Truth.

These hope narratives are then what give our lives a sense of purpose. Not only do they imply that there *is* something better in the future, but also that it's actually possible to go out and achieve that something. When people prattle on about needing to find their "life's purpose," what they really mean is that it's no longer clear to them what matters, what is a worthy use of their limited time here on earth[6]—in short, what to hope for. They are struggling to see what the before/after of their lives should be.

That's the hard part: finding that before/after for yourself. It's difficult because there's no way ever to know for sure if you've got it right. This is why a lot of people flock to religion, because religions acknowledge this permanent state of unknowing and demand faith in the face of it. This is also probably partly why religious people suffer from depression and commit suicide in far fewer numbers than nonreligious people: that practiced faith protects them from the Uncomfortable Truth.[7]

But your hope narratives don't need to be religious. They can be anything. This book is *my* little source of hope. It gives me purpose; it gives me meaning. And the narrative that I've constructed around that hope is that I believe this book might help some people, that it might make both my life and the world a little bit better.

Do I know that for sure? No. But it's my little before/after story, and I'm sticking to it. It gets me up in the morning and gets me excited about my life. And not only is that not a bad thing, it's the *only* thing.

For some people, the before/after story is raising their kids well. For others, it's saving the environment. For others, it's making a bunch of money and having a big-ass boat. For others, it's simply trying to improve their golf swing.

Whether we realize it or not, we all have these narratives we've elected to buy into for whatever reason. It doesn't matter if the way you get to hope is via religious faith or evidence-based theory or an intuition or a well-reasoned argument—they all produce the same result: you have some belief that (a) there is potential for growth or improvement or salvation in the future, and (b) there are ways we can navigate ourselves to get there. That's it. Day after day, year after year, our lives are made up of the endless overlapping of these hope narratives. They are the psychological carrot at the end of the stick.

If this all sounds nihilistic, please, don't get the wrong idea. This book is not an argument for nihilism. It is one *against* nihilism—both the nihilism within us and the growing sense of nihilism that seems to emerge with the modern world.[8] And to successfully argue against nihilism, you must start at nihilism. You must start at the Uncomfortable Truth. From there, you must slowly build a convincing case for hope. And not just any hope, but a sustainable, benevolent form of hope. A hope that can bring us together rather than tear us apart. A hope that is robust and powerful, yet still grounded in reason and reality. A hope that can carry us to the end of our days with a sense of gratitude and satisfaction.

This is not easy to do (obviously). And in the twenty-first century, it's arguably more difficult than ever. Nihilism and the pure indulgence of desire that accompanies it are gripping the modern world. It is power for the sake of power. Success for the sake of success. Pleasure for the sake of pleasure. Nihilism acknowledges no broader "Why?" It adheres to no great truth or cause. It's a simple "Because it feels good." And this, as we'll see, is what is making everything seem so bad.

The Paradox of Progress

We live in an interesting time in that, materially, things are arguably better than they have ever been before, yet we all seem to be losing our minds thinking the world is one giant toilet bowl about to be flushed. An irrational sense of hopelessness is spreading across the rich, developed world. It's a paradox of progress: the better things get, the more anxious and desperate we all seem to feel.[9]

In recent years, writers such as Steven Pinker and Hans Rosling have been making the case that we're wrong to feel so pessimistic, that things are, in fact, the best they've ever been and likely going to get even better.[10] Both men have filled long, heavy books with many charts and graphs that start at one corner and always seem somehow to end up in the opposite corner.[11] Both men have explained, at length, the biases and incorrect assumptions we all carry that cause us to feel that things are much worse than they are. Progress, they argue, has continued, uninterrupted, throughout modern history. People are more educated and literate than ever before.[12] Violence has trended down for decades, possibly centuries.[13] Racism, sexism, discrimination, and violence against women are at their lowest points in recorded history.[14] We have more rights than ever before.[15] Half the planet has access to the internet.[16] Extreme poverty is at an all-time low worldwide.[17] Wars are smaller and less frequent than at any other time in recorded history.[18] Children are dying less, and people are living longer.[19] There's more wealth than ever before.[20] We've, like, cured a bunch of diseases and stuff.[21]

And they're right. It's important to know these facts. But reading these books is also kind of like listening to your Uncle Larry prattle on about how much worse things were when he was your age. Even though he's right, it doesn't necessarily make you feel any better about *your* problems.

Because, for all the good news being published today, here are some other surprising statistics: in the United States, symptoms of depression and anxiety are on an eighty-year upswing among young people and a twenty-year upswing among the adult population.[22] Not only are people experiencing depression in greater numbers, but they're experiencing it at earlier ages, with each generation.[23] Since 1985, men and women have reported lower levels of life satisfaction.[24] Part of that is probably because stress levels have risen over the past thirty years.[25] Drug overdoses have recently hit an all-time high as the opioid crisis has wrecked much of the United States and Canada.[26] Across the U.S. population, feelings of loneliness and social isolation are up. Nearly half of all Americans now report feeling isolated, left out, or alone in their lives.[27] Social trust is also not only down across the developed world but plummeting, meaning fewer people than ever trust their government, the media, or one another.[28] In the 1980s, when researchers asked survey participants how many people they had discussed important personal matters with over the previous six months, the most common answer was "three." By 2006, the most common answer was "zero."[29]

Meanwhile, the environment is completely fucked. Nutjobs either have access to nuclear weapons or are a hop, skip, and a jump away from getting them. Extremism across the world continues to grow—in all forms, on both the right and the left, both religious and secular. Conspiracy theorists, citizen militias, survivalists, and "preppers" (as in, prepping for Armageddon) are all becoming more popular subcultures, to the point where they are borderline mainstream.

Basically, we are the safest and most prosperous humans in the history of the world, yet we are feeling more hopeless than ever before. The better things get, the more we seem to despair. It's the paradox of progress. And perhaps it can be summed up in one startling fact: the wealthier and safer the place you live, the more likely you are to commit suicide.[30]

The incredible progress made in health, safety, and material wealth over the past few hundred years is not to be denied. But these are statistics about the past, not the future. And that's where hope inevitably must be found: in our visions of the future.

Because hope is not based on statistics. Hope doesn't care about the downward trend of gun-related deaths or car accident fatalities. It doesn't care that there wasn't a commercial plane crash last year or that literacy hit an all-time high in Mongolia (well, unless you're Mongolian).[31]

Hope doesn't care about the problems that have already been

solved. Hope cares only about the problems that still need to be solved. Because the better the world gets, the more we have to lose. And the more we have to lose, the less we feel we have to hope for.

To build and maintain hope, we need three things: a sense of control, a belief in the value of something, and a community.[32] "Control" means we feel as though we're in control of our own life, that we can affect our fate. "Values" means we find something important enough to work toward, something better, that's worth striving for. And "community" means we are part of a group that values the same things we do and is working toward achieving those things. Without a community, we feel isolated, and our values cease to mean anything. Without values, nothing appears worth pursuing. And without control, we feel powerless to pursue anything. Lose any of the three, and you lose the other two. Lose any of the three, and you lose hope.

For us to understand why we're suffering through such a crisis of hope today, we need to understand the mechanics of hope, how it is generated and maintained. The next three chapters will look at how we develop these three areas of our lives: our sense of control (chapter 2), our values (chapter 3), and our communities (chapter 4).

We will then return to the original question: what is happening in our world that is causing us to feel worse despite everything consistently getting better?

And the answer might surprise you.

CHAPTER 2

Self-Control Is an Illusion

It all started with a headache.[1]

"Elliot" was a successful man, an executive at a successful company. He was well liked by his coworkers and neighbors. He could be charming and disarmingly funny. He was a husband and a father and a friend and took sweet-ass beach vacations.

Except he had headaches, regularly. And these weren't your typical, pop-an-Advil kind of headaches. These were mind-crunching, corkscrewing headaches, like a wrecking ball banging against the back of your eye sockets.

Elliot took medicine. He took naps. He tried to de-stress and chill out and hang loose and brush it off and suck it up. Yet, the headaches continued. In fact, they only got worse. Soon, they became so severe that Elliot couldn't sleep at night or work during the day.

Finally, he went to a doctor. The doctor did doctor things and ran doctor tests and received the doctor results and told Elliot the bad news: he had a brain tumor, right there on his frontal lobe. Right there. See it? That gray blotch, in the front. And man, is it a big one. Size of a baseball, I reckon.

The surgeon cut the tumor out, and Elliot went home. He went back to work. He went back to his family and friends. Everything seemed fine and normal.

Then things went horribly wrong.

Elliot's work performance suffered. Tasks that were once a breeze to him now required mountains of concentration and effort. Simple decisions, such as whether to use a blue pen or a black pen, would consume him for hours. He would make basic errors and leave them unfixed for weeks. He became a scheduling black hole, missing meetings and deadlines as if they were an insult to the fabric of space/time itself.

At first, his coworkers felt bad and covered for him. After all, the guy had just had a tumor the size of a small fruit basket cut out of his head. But then the covering became too much for them, and Elliot's excuses too unreasonable. You skipped an investor's meeting to buy a new stapler, Elliot? Really? What were you thinking?[2]

After months of the botched meetings and the bullshit, the truth was undeniable: Elliot had lost something more than a tumor in the surgery, and as far as his colleagues were concerned, that something was a shitload of company money. So, Elliot was fired.

Meanwhile, his home life wasn't faring much better. Imagine if you took a deadbeat dad, stuffed him inside a couch potato, lightly glazed it with *Family Feud* reruns, and baked it at 350°F for twenty-four hours a day. That was Elliot's new life. He missed his son's Little League games. He skipped a parent-teacher conference to watch a James Bond marathon on TV. He forgot that his wife generally preferred it if he spoke to her more than once a week.

Fights erupted in Elliot's marriage along new and unexpected fault lines—except, they couldn't really be considered fights. Fights require that two people give a shit. And while his wife breathed fire, Elliot had trouble following the plot. Instead of acting with urgency to change or to patch things up, to show that he loved and cared for these people who were his own, he remained isolated and indifferent. It was as though he were living in another area code, one never quite reachable from anywhere on earth.

Eventually, his wife couldn't take it anymore. Elliot had lost something else besides that tumor, she yelled. And that something was called his goddamn heart. She divorced him and took the kids. And Elliot was alone.

Dejected and confused, Elliot began looking for ways to restart his career. He got sucked into some bad business ventures. A scam artist conned him out of much of his savings. A predatory woman seduced him, convinced him to elope, and then divorced him a year later, making off with half his assets. He loafed around town, settling in increasingly cheaper and shittier apartments until, after a few years, he was effectively homeless. His brother took him in and began supporting him. Friends and family looked on aghast while, over a few short years, a man they had once admired essentially threw his life away. No one could make sense of it. It was undeniable that something in Elliot had changed; that those debilitating headaches had caused more than pain.

The question was, what had changed?

Elliot's brother chaperoned him from one doctor's visit to the next. "He's not himself," the brother would say. "He has a problem. He seems fine, but he's not. I promise."

The doctors did their doctor things and received their doctor results, and unfortunately, they said that Elliot was perfectly normal—or, at least, he fit *their* definition of normal; above average, even. His CAT scans looked fine. His IQ was still high. His reasoning was solid. His memory was great. He could discuss, at length, the repercussions and consequences of his poor choices. He could converse on a wide range of subjects with humor and charm. His psychiatrist said Elliot wasn't depressed. On the contrary, he had high self-esteem, and no signs of chronic anxiety or stress—he exhibited almost Zen-like calm in the eye of a hurricane caused by his own negligence.

His brother couldn't accept this. Something *was* wrong. Something *was* missing in him.

Finally, in desperation, Elliot was referred to a famous neuroscientist named Antonio Damasio.

Initially, Antonio Damasio did the same things the other doctors had done: he gave Elliot a bunch of cognitive tests. Memory, reflexes, intelligence, personality, spatial relations, moral reasoning—everything checked out. Elliot passed with flying colors.

Then, Damasio did something to Elliot no other doctor had thought to do: he talked to him—like, *really* talked to him. He wanted to know everything: every mistake, every error, every regret. How had he lost his job, his family, his house, his savings? Take me through each decision, explain the thought process (or, in this case, the lack of a thought process).

Elliot could explain, at length, *what* decisions he'd made, but he couldn't explain the *why* of those decisions. He could recount facts and sequences of events with perfect fluidity and even a certain dramatic flair, but when asked to analyze his decision making—why did he decide that buying a new stapler was more important than meeting with an investor, why did he decide that James Bond was more interesting than his kids?—he was at a loss. He had no answers. And not only that, he wasn't even upset about having no answers. In fact, he didn't care.

This was a man who had lost *everything* due to his own poor choices and mistakes, who had exhibited *no self-control* whatsoever, and who was completely aware of the disaster his life had become, and yet he apparently showed no remorse, no self-loathing, not even a little bit of embarrassment. Many people have been driven to suicide for less than what Elliot had endured. Yet there he was, not only comfortable with his own misfortune but *indifferent* to it.

That's when Damasio had a brilliant realization: the psychological tests Elliot had undergone were designed to measure his ability to *think*, but none of the tests was designed to measure his ability to *feel*. Every doctor had been so concerned about Elliot's reasoning abilities that no one had stopped to consider that it was Elliot's *capacity for emotion* that had been damaged. And even if they had realized it, there was no standardized way of measuring that damage.

One day, one of Damasio's colleagues printed up a bunch of grotesque and disturbing pictures. There were burn victims, gruesome murder scenes, war-torn cities, and starving children. He then showed Elliot the photos, one by one.

Elliot was completely indifferent. He felt nothing. And the fact that he didn't care was so shocking that even he had to comment on how fucked up it was. He admitted that he knew for sure that these images would have disturbed him in the past, that his heart would have welled up with empathy and horror, that he would have turned away in disgust. But now? As he sat there, staring at the darkest corruptions of the human experience, Elliot felt nothing.

And this, Damasio discovered, was the problem: while Elliot's knowledge and reasoning were left intact, the tumor and/or the surgery to remove it had debilitated his ability to empathize and feel. His inner world no longer possessed lightness and darkness but was instead an endless gray miasma. Attending his daughter's piano recital evoked in him all the vibrancy and joyful fatherly pride of buying a new pair of socks. Losing a million dollars felt exactly the same to him as pumping gas, laundering his sheets, or watching *Family Feud*. He had become a walking, talking indifference machine. And without that ability to make value judgments, to determine better from worse, no matter how intelligent he was, Elliot had lost his self-control.[3]

But this raised a huge question: if Elliot's cognitive abilities (his intelligence, his memory, his attention) were all in perfect shape, why couldn't he make effective decisions anymore?

This stumped Damasio and his colleagues. We've all wished at times that we couldn't feel emotion, because our emotions often drive us to do stupid shit we later regret. For centuries, psychologists and philosophers assumed that dampening or suppressing our emotions was the solution to all life's problems. Yet, here was a man stripped of his emotions and empathy entirely, someone who had nothing but his intelligence and reasoning, and his life had quickly degenerated into a total clusterfuck. His case went against all the common wisdom about rational decision making and self-control.

But there was a second, equally perplexing question: If Elliot was still as smart as a whip and could reason his way through problems presented to him, why did his work performance fall off a cliff? Why did his productivity morph into a raging dumpster fire? Why did he essentially abandon his family knowing full well the negative consequences? Even if you don't give a shit about your wife or your job anymore, you should be able to *reason* that it's still important to maintain them, right? I mean, that's what sociopaths eventually figure out. So, why couldn't Elliot? Really, how hard is it to show up to a Little League game every once in a while? Somehow, by losing his ability to feel, Elliot had also lost his ability to make decisions. He'd lost the ability to control his own life.

We've all had the experience of knowing what we *should* do yet failing to do it. We've all put off important tasks, ignored people we care about, and failed to act in our own self-interest. And usually when we fail to do the things we should, we assume it's because we can't sufficiently control our emotions. We're too undisciplined or we lack knowledge.

Yet Elliot's case called all this into question. It called into question the very idea of self-control, the idea that we can logically force ourselves to do things that are good for us despite our impulses and emotions.

To generate hope in our lives, we must first feel as though we have control over our lives. We must feel as though we're following through on what we know is good and right; that we're chasing after "something better." Yet many of us struggle with the inability to control ourselves. Elliot's case would be one of the breakthroughs to understanding why this occurs. This man, poor, isolated and alone; this man staring at photos of broken bodies and earthquake rubble that could easily have been metaphors for his life; this man who had lost everything, absolutely everything, and still cracked a smile to tell about it—this man would be the key to revolutionizing our understanding of the human mind, how we make decisions, and how much self-control we actually have.

The Classic Assumption

Once, when asked about his drinking, the musician Tom Waits famously muttered, "I'd rather have a bottle in front of me than a frontal lobotomy." He appeared to be hammered when he said it. Oh, and he was on national television.[4]

The frontal lobotomy is a form of brain surgery wherein a hole is drilled into your skull through your nose and then the frontal lobe is gently sliced with an icepick.[5] The procedure was invented in 1935 by a neurologist named António Egas Moniz.[6] Egas Moniz discovered that if you took people with extreme anxiety, suicidal depression, or other mental health issues (aka crises of hope) and maimed their brain in just the right way, they'd chill the fuck out.

Egas Moniz believed that the lobotomy, once perfected, could cure all mental illness, and he marketed it to the world as such. By end of the 1940s, the procedure was a hit, being performed on tens of thousands of patients all over the world. Egas Moniz would even win a Nobel Prize for his discovery.

But by the 1950s, people began to notice that—and this might sound crazy—drilling a hole through somebody's face and scraping their brain the same way you clean ice off your windshield can produce a few negative side effects. And by "a few negative side effects," I mean the patients became goddamn potatoes. While often "curing" patients of their extreme emotional afflictions, the procedure also left them with an inability to focus, make decisions, have careers, make long-term plans, or think abstractly about themselves. Essentially, they became mindlessly satisfied zombies. They became Elliots.

The Soviet Union, of all places, was the first country to outlaw the lobotomy. The Soviets declared the procedure "contrary to human principles" and claimed that it "turned an insane person into an idiot."[7] This was sort of a wake-up call to the rest of the world, because let's face it, when Joseph Stalin is lecturing you about ethics and human decency, you know you've fucked up.

After that, the rest of the world began, slowly, to ban the practice, and by the 1960s, pretty much everyone hated it. The last lobotomy would be performed in the United States in 1967, and the patient would die. Ten years later, a drunken Tom Waits muttered his famous line on television, and the rest, as they say, is history.

Tom Waits was a blistering alcoholic who spent most of the 1970s trying to keep his eyes open and remember where he last left his cigarettes.[8] He also found time to write and record seven brilliant albums in this period. He was both prolific and profound, winning awards and selling millions of records that were celebrated worldwide. He was one of those rare artists whose insight into the human condition could be startling.

Waits's quip about the lobotomy makes us laugh, but there's a hidden wisdom to it: that he'd rather have the problem of passion with the bottle than have no passion at all; that it's better to find hope in lowly places than to find none; that without our unruly impulses, we are nothing.

There's pretty much always been a tacit assumption that our emotions cause all our problems, and that our reason must swoop in to clean up the mess. This line of thinking goes all the way back to Socrates, who declared reason the root of all virtue.[9] At the beginning of the Enlightenment, Descartes argued that our reason was separate from our animalistic desires and that it had to learn to control those desires.[10] Kant sort of said the same thing.[11] Freud, too, except there were a lot of penises involved.[12] And when Egas Moniz lobotomized his first patient in 1935, I'm sure he thought he had just discovered a way to do what, for more than two thousand years, philosophers had declared needed to be done: to grant reason dominion over the unruly passions, to help humanity finally exercise some damn control over itself.

This assumption (that we must use our rational mind to dominate our emotions) has trickled down through the centuries and continues to define much of our culture today. Let's call it the "Classic Assumption." The Classic Assumption says that if a person is undisciplined, unruly, or malicious, it's because he lacks the ability to subjugate his feelings, that he is weak-willed or just plain fucked up. The Classic Assumption sees passion and emotion as flaws, errors within the human psyche that must be overcome and fixed within the self.

Today, we usually judge people based on the Classic Assumption. Obese people are ridiculed and shamed because their obesity is seen as a failure of self-control. They *know* they should be thin, yet they continue to eat. Why? Something must be wrong with them, we assume. Smokers: same deal. Drug addicts receive the same treatment, of course, but often with the extra stigma of being defined as criminals.

Depressed and suicidal people are subjected to the Classic Assumption in a way that's dangerous, being told that their inability to create hope and meaning in their lives is their own damn fault, that maybe, if they just tried a little harder, hanging themselves by the necktie wouldn't sound so appealing.

We see succumbing to our emotional impulses as a moral failing. We see a lack of self-control as a sign of a deficient character. Conversely, we celebrate people who beat their emotions into submission. We get collective hard-ons for athletes and businessmen and leaders who are ruthless and robotic in their efficiency. If a CEO sleeps under his desk and doesn't see his kids for six weeks at a time—fuck yeah, that's determination! See? Anyone can be successful!

Clearly, it's not hard to see how the Classic Assumption can lead to some damaging . . . er, assumptions. If the Classic Assumption is true, then we *should* be able to exhibit self-control, prevent emotional outbursts and crimes of passion, and stave off addiction and indulgences through mental effort alone. And any failure to do so reflects something inherently faulty or damaged within us.

This is why we often develop the false belief that we need to change who we are. Because if we can't achieve our goals, if we can't lose the weight or get the promotion or learn the skill, then that signifies some internal deficiency. Therefore, in order to maintain hope, we decide we must *change ourselves*, become somebody totally new and different. This desire to change ourselves then refills us with hope. The "old me" couldn't shake that terrible smoking habit, but the "new me" will. And we're off to the races again.

The constant desire to change yourself then becomes its own sort of addiction: each cycle of "changing yourself" results in similar failures of self-control, therefore making you feel as though you need to "change yourself" all over again. Each cycle refuels you with the hope you're looking for. Meanwhile, the Classic Assumption, the root of the problem, is never addressed or questioned, let alone thrown out.

Like a bad case of acne, a whole industry has sprouted up over the past couple of centuries around this "change yourself" idea. This industry is replete with false promises and clues to the secrets of happiness, success, and self-control. Yet all the industry does is reinforce the same impulses that drive people to feel inadequate in the first place.[13]

The truth is that the human mind is far more complex than any "secret." And you can't simply change yourself; nor, I would argue, should you always feel you must.

We cling to this narrative about self-control because the belief that we're in complete control of ourselves is a major source of hope. We *want* to believe that changing ourselves is as simple as knowing what to change. We *want* to believe that the ability to do something is as simple as deciding to do it and mustering enough willpower to get there. We *want* to believe ourselves to be the masters of our own destiny, capable of anything we can dream.

This is what made Damasio's discovery with "Elliot" such a

big deal: it showed that the Classic Assumption is wrong. If the Classic Assumption were true, if life were as simple as learning to control one's emotions and make decisions based on reason, then Elliot should have been an unstoppable badass, tirelessly industrious, and a ruthless decision maker. Similarly, if the Classic Assumption were true, lobotomies should be all the rage. We'd all be saving up for them as if they were boob jobs.

But lobotomies *don't* work, and Elliot's life was ruined.

The fact is that we require more than willpower to achieve self-control. It turns out that our emotions are instrumental in our decision making and our actions. We just don't always realize it.

You Have Two Brains, and They're Really Bad at Talking to Each Other

Let's pretend your mind is a car. Let's call it the "Consciousness Car." Your Consciousness Car is driving along the road of life, and there are intersections, on-ramps, and off-ramps. These roads and intersections represent the decisions you must make as you drive, and they will determine your destination.

Now, there are two travelers in your Consciousness Car: a Thinking Brain and a Feeling Brain.[14] The Thinking Brain represents your conscious thoughts, your ability to make calculations, and your ability to reason through various options and express ideas through language. Your Feeling Brain represents your emotions, impulses, intuition, and instincts. While your Thinking Brain is calculating payment schedules on your credit card statement, your Feeling Brain wants to sell everything and run away to Tahiti.

Each of your two brains has its strengths and weaknesses. The Thinking Brain is conscientious, accurate, and impartial. It is methodical and rational, but it is also slow. It requires a lot of effort and energy, and like a muscle, it must be built up over time and can become fatigued if overexerted.[15] The Feeling Brain, however, arrives at its conclusions quickly and effortlessly. The problem is that it is often inaccurate and irrational. The Feeling Brain is also a bit of a drama queen and has a bad habit of overreacting.

When we think of ourselves and our decision making, we generally assume that the Thinking Brain is driving our Consciousness Car and the Feeling Brain is sitting in the passenger seat shouting out where it wants to go. We're driving along, accomplishing our goals and figuring out how to get home, when that damn Feeling Brain sees something shiny or sexy or fun-looking and yanks the steering wheel in another direction, thus causing us to careen into oncoming traffic, harming other people's Consciousness Cars as well as our own.

This is the Classic Assumption, the belief that our reason is ultimately in control of our life and that we must train our emotions to sit the fuck down and shut up while the adult is driving. We then applaud this kidnapping and abuse of our emotions by congratulating ourselves on our self-control.

But our Consciousness Car doesn't work that way. When his tumor was removed, Elliot's Feeling Brain got thrown out of his moving mental vehicle, and nothing got better for him. In fact, his Consciousness Car stalled out. Lobotomy patients had their Feeling Brains tied up and thrown in the car's trunk, and that merely caused them to become sedated and lazy, unable to get out of bed or even dress themselves much of the time.

Meanwhile, Tom Waits was pretty much all Feeling Brain all the time, and he got paid copious amounts of money to be drunk on television talk shows. So, there's that.

Here's the truth: the Feeling Brain is driving our Consciousness Car. And I don't care how scientific you think you are or how many letters you have after your name, you're one of us, bucko. You're a crazy Feeling Brain–piloted meat robot just like the rest of us. Keep your bodily fluids to yourself, please.

The Feeling Brain drives our Consciousness Car because, ultimately, *we are moved to action only by emotion.* That's because action *is* emotion.[16] Emotion is the biological hydraulic system that pushes our bodies into movement. Fear is not this magical thing your brain invents. No, it happens in our bodies. It's the tightening of your stomach, the tensing of your muscles, the release of adrenaline, the overwhelming desire for space and emptiness around your body. While the Thinking Brain exists solely within the synaptic arrangements inside your skull, the Feeling Brain is the wisdom and stupidity of the entire body. Anger pushes your body to move. Anxiety pulls it into retreat. Joy lights up the facial muscles, while sadness attempts to shade your existence from view. Emotion inspires action, and action inspires emotion. The two are inseparable.

This leads to the simplest and most obvious answer to the timeless question, why don't we do things we know we should do?

Because we don't *feel* like it.

Every problem of self-control is not a problem of information or discipline or reason but, rather, of *emotion.* Self-control is an emotional problem; laziness is an emotional problem; procrastination is an emotional problem; underachievement is an emotional problem; impulsiveness is an emotional problem.

This sucks. Because emotional problems are much harder to deal with than logical ones. There are equations to help you calculate the monthly payments on your car loan. There are no equations to help you end a bad relationship.

And as you've probably figured out by now, intellectually understanding how to change your behavior doesn't change your behavior. (Trust me, I've read like twelve books on nutrition and am still chomping on a burrito as I write this.) We *know* we should stop smoking cigarettes or stop eating sugar or stop talking shit about our friends behind their backs, but we still do it. And it's not because we don't know better; it's because we don't *feel* better.

Emotional problems are irrational, meaning they cannot be reasoned with. And this brings us to even worse news: emotional problems can only have emotional solutions. It's all up to the Feeling Brain. And if you've seen how most people's Feeling Brains drive, that's pretty fucking scary.

Meanwhile, while all this is going on, the Thinking Brain is sitting in the passenger seat imagining itself to be totally in control of the situation. If the Feeling Brain is our driver, then the Thinking Brain is the navigator. It has stacks of maps to reality that it has drawn and accumulated throughout life. It knows how to double back and find alternate routes to the same destination. It knows where the bad turns are and where to find the shortcuts. It correctly sees itself as the intelligent, rational brain, and it believes that this somehow privileges it to be in control of the Consciousness Car. But, alas, it doesn't. As Daniel Kahneman once put it, the Thinking Brain is "the supporting character who imagines herself to be the hero."[17]

Even if sometimes they can't stand each other, our two brains need each other. The Feeling Brain generates the emotions that cause us to move into action, and the Thinking Brain suggests where to direct that action. The keyword here is *suggests*. While the Thinking Brain is not able to control the Feeling Brain, it is able to *influence* it, sometimes to a great degree. The Thinking Brain can convince the Feeling Brain to pursue a new road to a better future, to pull a U-turn when it has made a mistake, or to consider new routes or territories once ignored. But the Feeling Brain is stubborn, and if it wants to go in one direction, it will drive that way no matter how many facts or data the Thinking Brain provides. Moral psychologist Jonathan Haidt compares the two brains to an elephant and its rider: the rider can gently steer and pull the elephant in a particular direction, but ultimately the elephant is going to go where it wants to go.[18]

The Clown Car

The Feeling Brain, as great as it is, has its dark side. In the Consciousness Car, your Feeling Brain is like a verbally abusive boyfriend who refuses to pull over and ask for directions—he *hates* being told where to go and he will absolutely make you fucking miserable if you question his driving.

In order to avoid these psychological kerfuffles, and to maintain a sense of hope, the Thinking Brain develops a tendency to draw maps explaining or justifying where the Feeling Brain has already decided it wants to go. If the Feeling Brain wants ice cream, instead of contradicting it with facts about processed sugar and excess calories, your Thinking Brain decides, "You know what, I worked hard today. I *deserve* some ice cream," and your Feeling Brain responds with a sense of ease and satisfaction. If your Feeling Brain decides that your partner is an asshole and you've done nothing wrong, your Thinking Brain's immediate reaction will be to recall instances when you, in fact, were a beacon of patience and humility while your partner was secretly conspiring to ruin your life.

In this way, the two brains develop a really unhealthy relationship that might resemble your mom and dad on road trips when you were a kid. The Thinking Brain makes shit up that the Feeling Brain wants to hear. And in return, the Feeling Brain promises not to career off the side of the road, killing everyone.

It's incredibly easy to let your Thinking Brain fall into the trap of merely drawing the maps the Feeling Brain wants to follow. This is called the "self-serving bias," and it's the basis for pretty much everything awful about humanity.

Usually, the self-serving bias simply makes you prejudiced and a little bit self-centered. You assume that what *feels* right *is* right. You make snap judgments about people, places, groups, and ideas, many of which are unfair or even a little bit bigoted.

But in its extreme form, the self-serving bias can become outright delusion, causing you to believe in a reality that is not there, smudging memories and exaggerating facts, all in the service of the Feeling Brain's never-ending cravings. If the Thinking Brain is weak and/or uneducated, or if the Feeling Brain is riled up, the Thinking Brain will succumb to the Feeling Brain's fiery whims and dangerous driving. It will lose the ability to think for itself or to contradict the Feeling Brain's conclusions.

This effectively turns your Consciousness Car into a Clown Car, with big, springy red wheels and circus music playing over a loudspeaker wherever you go.[19] Your Consciousness Car becomes a Clown Car when your Thinking Brain has completely capitulated to your Feeling Brain, when your life's pursuits are determined purely by self-gratification, when truth warps into a cartoon of self-serving assumptions, when all beliefs and principles are lost in a sea of nihilism.

The Clown Car invariably drives toward addiction, narcissism, and compulsion. People whose minds are Clown Cars are easily manipulated by whatever person or group makes them feel good consistently—whether it is a religious leader, politician, self-help guru, or sinister internet forum. A Clown Car will gladly steamroll other Consciousness Cars (i.e., other people) with its big, red rubbery tires because its Thinking Brain will justify this by saying they deserved it—they were evil, inferior, or part of some made-up problem.

Some Clown Cars merely drive toward fun—they're all about drinking and fucking and partying. Others drive toward power. These are the most dangerous Clown Cars, as their Thinking Brains set to work justifying their abuse and subjugation of others through intellectual-sounding theories about economics, politics, race, genetics, gender, biology, history, and so on. A Clown Car will sometimes pursue hate, too, because hate brings its own odd satisfaction and self-assurance. Such a mind is prone to self-righteous anger, as having an external target reassures it of its own moral superiority. Inevitably, it drives toward the destruction of others because it is only through the destruction and subjugation of the outer world that its endless inner impulses can be satisfied.

It's hard to pull someone out of the Clown Car once they're in it. In the Clown Car, the Thinking Brain has been bullied and abused by the Feeling Brain for so long that it develops a sort of Stockholm syndrome—it can't imagine a life beyond pleasing and justifying the Feeling Brain. It can't fathom contradicting the Feeling Brain or challenging it on where it's going, and it resents you for suggesting that it should. With the Clown Car, there's no independent thought and no ability to measure contradiction or switch beliefs or opinions. In a sense, the person with a Clown Car mind ceases to have an individual identity at all.

This is why cultish leaders always start by encouraging people to shut off their Thinking Brains as much as possible. Initially, this *feels* profound to people because the Thinking Brain is often correcting the Feeling Brain, showing it where it took a wrong turn. So, silencing the Thinking Brain will feel extremely good for a short period. And people are always mistaking what *feels* good for what *is* good.

The metaphorical Clown Car is what inspired ancient philosophers to warn against the overindulgence and worship of feelings.[20] It was the fear of the Clown Car that inspired the Greeks
and Romans to teach of the virtues and, later, the Christian Church
to push a message of abstinence and self-denial.[21] Both classical
philosophers and the Church had seen the destruction wrought by
narcissistic and megalomaniacal men in power. And they all believed that the only way to manage the Feeling Brain was to deprive
it, to give it as little oxygen as possible, thus preventing it from
exploding and destroying the world around it. This thinking gave
birth to the Classic Assumption: that the only way to be a good person is through dominance of the Thinking Brain over the Feeling
Brain, the championing of reason over emotion, duty over desire.

For most of human history, people have been brutal, superstitious, and uneducated. People in the Middle Ages used to torture
cats for sport and take their kids to watch the local burglar get his
nuts chopped off in the town square.[22] People were sadistic, impulsive fuckers. For most of history, the world has not been a pleasant place to live, and that was largely because everyone's Feeling
Brains were running amok.[23] The Classic Assumption was often
the only thing that stood between civilization and total anarchy.

Then something happened in the last couple of hundred years.
People built trains and cars and invented central heating and stuff.
Economic prosperity outran human impulses. People were no
longer worried about not being able to eat or about being killed for
insulting the king. Life was more comfortable and easier. People
now had a ton of free time to sit and think and worry about all
sorts of existential shit that they had never considered before.

As a result, several movements arose in the late twentieth century championing the Feeling Brain.[24] And indeed, liberating
the Feeling Brain from the Thinking Brain's suppression was in-

credibly therapeutic for millions of people (and continues to be so today).

The problem was that people began to go too far the other way. They went from recognizing and honoring their feelings to the other extreme of believing that their feelings *were the only thing that mattered*. This has been particularly true for white, middle-class yuppies who were raised under the Classic Assumption, grew up miserable, and then got in touch with their Feeling Brains at a much later age. Because these people never had any real problems in their lives other than feeling bad, they erroneously came to believe that feelings were all that mattered and that the Thinking Brain's maps were merely inconvenient distractions from those feelings. Many of these people called this shutting off of their Thinking Brains in favor of their Feeling Brains "spiritual growth," and convinced themselves that being self-absorbed twats brought them closer to enlightenment,[25] when, really, they were indulging the old Feeling Brain. It was the same old Clown Car with a new, spiritual-looking paint job.[26]

The overindulgence of emotion leads to a crisis of hope, but so does the repression of emotion.[27]

The person who denies his Feeling Brain numbs himself to the world around him. By rejecting his emotions, he rejects making value judgments, that is, deciding that one thing is better than another. As a result, he becomes indifferent to life and the results of his decisions. He struggles to engage with others. His relationships suffer. And eventually, his chronic indifference leads him to an unpleasant visit with the Uncomfortable Truth. After all, if nothing is more or less important, then there's no reason to do anything. And if there's no reason to do anything, then why live at all?

Meanwhile, the person who denies his Thinking Brain becomes impulsive and selfish, warping reality to conform to his whims and fancies, which are then never satiated. His crisis of hope is that no matter how much he eats, drinks, dominates, or fucks, it will never be enough—it will never matter enough, it will never feel significant enough. He will be on a perpetual treadmill of desperation, always running, though never moving. And if at any point he stops, the Uncomfortable Truth immediately catches up to him.

I know. I'm being dramatic again. But I have to be, Thinking Brain. Otherwise, the Feeling Brain will get bored and close this book. Ever wonder why a page-turner is a page-turner? It's not *you* turning those pages, idiot; it's your Feeling Brain. It's the anticipation and suspense; the joy of discovery and the satisfaction of resolution. Good writing is writing that is able to speak to and stimulate both brains at the same time.

And this is the whole problem: speaking to both brains, integrating our brains into a cooperative, coordinated, unified whole. Because if self-control is an illusion of the Thinking Brain's overblown self-regard, then it's self-acceptance that will save us—accepting our emotions and working with them rather than against them. But to develop that self-acceptance, we have to do some work, Thinking Brain. Let's talk. Meet me in the next section.

An Open Letter to Your Thinking Brain

Hey, Thinking Brain.

How are things? How's the family? How'd that tax situation work out?

Oh, wait. Never mind. I forgot—I don't fucking care.

Look, I know there's something the Feeling Brain is screwing up for you. Maybe it's an important relationship. Maybe it's causing you to make embarrassing phone calls at 3:00 a.m. Maybe it's constantly medicating itself with substances it probably shouldn't be using. I know there's something you wish you could control about yourself but can't. And I imagine, at times, this problem causes you to lose hope.

But listen, Thinking Brain, those things you hate so much about your Feeling Brain—the cravings, the impulses, the horrible decision making? You need to find a way to empathize with them. Because that's the only language the Feeling Brain really understands: empathy. The Feeling Brain is a sensitive creature; it's made out of your damn feelings, after all. I wish it weren't true. I wish you could just show it a spreadsheet to make it understand—you know, like *we* understand. But you can't.

Instead of bombarding the Feeling Brain with *facts* and *reason*, start by asking how it's feeling. Say something like "Hey, Feeling Brain, how do you feel about going to the gym today?" or "How do you feel about changing careers?" or "How do you feel about selling everything and moving to Tahiti?"

The Feeling Brain won't respond with words. No, the Feeling Brain is too quick for words. Instead, it will respond with feelings. Yeah, I know that's obvious, but sometimes you're kind of a dumbass, Thinking Brain.

The Feeling Brain might respond with a feeling of laziness or a feeling of anxiety. There might even be multiple emotions, a little bit of excitement with a pinch of anger thrown into the mix. Whatever it is, you, as the Thinking Brain (aka, the responsible one in this cranium), need to remain nonjudgmental in the face of whatever feelings arise. Feeling lazy? That's okay; we all feel lazy sometimes. Feeling self-loathing? Perhaps that's an invitation to take the conversation further. The gym can wait.

It's important to let the Feeling Brain air out all its icky, twisted feelings. Just get them out into the open where they can breathe, because the more they breathe, the weaker their grip is on the steering wheel of your Consciousness Car.[28]

Then, once you feel you've reached a point of understanding with your Feeling Brain, it's time to appeal to it in a way it understands: through feelings. Maybe think about all the benefits of some desired new behavior. Maybe mention all the sexy, shiny, fun things at the desired destination. Maybe remind the Feeling Brain how good it feels to have exercised, how great it will feel to look good in a bathing suit this summer, how much you respect yourself when you've followed through on your goals, how happy you are when you live by your values, when you act as an example to the ones you love.

Basically, you need to bargain with your Feeling Brain the way you'd bargain with a Moroccan rug seller: it needs to believe it's getting a good deal, or else there'll just be a lot of hand waving and shouting with no result. Maybe you agree to do something the Feeling Brain likes, as long as it does something it doesn't like. Watch your favorite TV show, but only at the gym while you're on the treadmill. Go out with friends, but only if you've paid your bills for the month.[29]

Start easy. Remember, the Feeling Brain is highly sensitive, and completely unreasonable.

When you offer something easy with an emotional benefit (e.g., feeling good after a workout; pursuing a career that feels significant; being admired and respected by your kids), the Feeling Brain will respond with another emotion, either positive or negative. If the emotion is positive, the Feeling Brain will be willing to drive a little bit in that direction—but only a little bit! Remember: feelings never last. That's why you start small. Just put on your gym shoes today, Feeling Brain. That's all. Let's just see what happens.[30]

If the Feeling Brain's response is negative, you simply acknowledge that negative emotion and offer another compromise. See how the Feeling Brain responds. Then rinse and repeat.

But whatever you do, *do not fight* the Feeling Brain. That just makes things worse. For one, you won't win, ever. The Feeling Brain is always driving. Second, fighting with the Feeling Brain about feeling bad will only cause the Feeling Brain to feel even worse. So, why would you do that? You were supposed to be the smart one, Thinking Brain.

This dialogue with your Feeling Brain will continue back and forth like this, on and off, for days, weeks, or maybe even months. Hell, years. This dialogue between the brains takes practice. For some, the practice will be recognizing what emotion the Feeling Brain is putting out there. Some people's Thinking Brains have ignored their Feeling Brains for so long that it takes them a while to learn how to listen again.

Others will have the opposite problem: They will have to train their Thinking Brain to speak up, force it to propose an independent thought (a new direction) that's separate from the Feeling Brain's feelings. They will have to ask themselves, what if my Feeling Brain is wrong to feel this way? and then consider the alternatives. This will be difficult for them at first. But the more this dialogue occurs, the more the two brains will begin to listen to each other. The Feeling Brain will start giving off different emotions, and the Thinking Brain will have a better understanding of how to help the Feeling Brain navigate the road of life.

This is what's referred to in psychology as "emotional regulation," and it's basically learning how to put a bunch of fucking guardrails and One Way signs along your road of life to keep your Feeling Brain from careening off a cliff.[31] It's hard work, but it's arguably the *only* work.

Because you don't get to control your feelings, Thinking Brain. Self-control is an illusion. It's an illusion that occurs when both brains are aligned and pursuing the same course of action. It's an illusion designed to give people hope. And when the Thinking Brain isn't aligned with the Feeling Brain, people feel powerless, and the world around them begins to feel hopeless. The only way you consistently nail that illusion is by consistently communicating and aligning the brains around the same values. It's a skill, much the same as playing water polo or juggling knives is a skill. It takes work. And there will be failures along the way. You might slice your arm open and bleed everywhere. But that's just the cost of admission.

But here's what you do have, Thinking Brain. You may not have self-control, but you do have *meaning* control. This is your superpower. This is your gift. You get to control the *meaning* of your impulses and feelings. You get to decipher them however you see fit. You get to draw the map. And this is incredibly powerful, because it's the meaning that we ascribe to our feelings that can often alter how the Feeling Brain reacts to them.

And this is how you produce hope. This is how you produce a sense that the future can be fruitful and pleasant: by interpreting the shit the Feeling Brain slings at you in a profound and useful way. Instead of justifying and enslaving yourself to the impulses, challenge them and analyze them. Change their character and their shape.

This is basically what good therapy is, of course. Self-acceptance and emotional intelligence and all that. Actually, this whole "teach your Thinking Brain to decipher and cooperate with your Feeling Brain instead of judging him and thinking he's an evil piece of shit" is the basis for CBT (cognitive behavioral therapy) and ACT (acceptance and commitment therapy) and a lot of other fun acronyms that clinical psychologists invented to make our lives better.

Our crises of hope often start with a basic sense that we do not have control over ourselves or our destiny. We feel victims to the world around us or, worse, to our own minds. We fight our Feeling Brain, trying to beat it into submission. Or we do the opposite and follow it mindlessly. We ridicule ourselves and hide from the world because of the Classic Assumption. And in many ways, the affluence and connectivity of the modern world only make the pain of the illusion of self-control that much worse.

But this is your mission, Thinking Brain, should you choose to accept it: Engage the Feeling Brain on its own terms. Create an environment that can bring about the Feeling Brain's best impulses and intuition, rather than its worst. Accept and work *with*, rather than against, whatever the Feeling Brain spews at you.

Everything else (all the judgments and assumptions and self-aggrandizement) is an illusion. It was always an illusion. You don't have control, Thinking Brain. You never did, and you never will. Yet, you needn't lose hope.

Antonio Damasio ended up writing a celebrated book called *Descartes' Error* about his experiences with "Elliot," and much of his other research. In it, he argues that the same way the Thinking Brain produces a logical, factual form of knowledge, the Feeling Brain develops its own type of value-laden knowledge.[32] The Thinking Brain makes associations among facts, data, and observations. Similarly, the Feeling Brain makes value judgments based on those same facts, data, and observations. The Feeling Brain decides what is good and what is bad; what is desirable and what is undesirable; and most important, what we *deserve* and what we *don't deserve*.

The Thinking Brain is objective and factual. The Feeling Brain is subjective and relative. And no matter what we do, we can never translate one form of knowledge into the other.[33] This is the *real* problem of hope. It's rare that we don't understand *intellectually* how to cut back on carbs, or wake up earlier, or stop smoking. It's that somewhere inside our Feeling Brain, we have decided that we don't *deserve* to do those things, that we are unworthy of doing them. And that's why we feel so bad about them.

This feeling of unworthiness is usually the result of some bad shit happening to us at some point. We suffer through some terrible stuff, and our Feeling Brain decides that we *deserved* those bad experiences. Therefore, it sets out, despite the Thinking Brain's better knowledge, to repeat and reexperience that suffering.

This is the fundamental problem of self-control. This is the fundamental problem of hope—not an uneducated Thinking Brain, but an uneducated Feeling Brain, a Feeling Brain that has adopted and accepted poor value judgments about itself and the world. And this is the real work of anything that even resembles psychological healing: getting our values straight with ourselves so that we can get our values straight with the world.

Put another way, the problem isn't that we don't know how *not* to get punched in the face. The problem is that, at some point, likely a long time ago, we got punched in face, and instead of punching back, we decided we deserved it.

CHAPTER 3

Newton's Laws of Emotion

The first time Isaac Newton got hit in the face, he was standing in a field. His uncle had been explaining to him why wheat should be planted in diagonal rows, but Isaac wasn't listening. He was gazing into the sun, wondering what the light was made of.

He was seven years old.[1]

His uncle backhanded him so hard across his left cheek that Isaac's sense of self temporarily broke upon the ground on which his body fell. He lost any feeling of personal cohesion. And as the parts of his psyche put themselves back together, some secret piece of himself remained in the dirt, left behind in a place from which it would never be recovered.

Isaac's father had died before he was born, and his mother soon abandoned her son to marry some old rich guy the next village over. As a result, Isaac spent his formative years being shuffled among uncles, cousins, and grandparents. No one particularly wanted him. Few knew what to do with him. He was a burden. Love came difficultly, and usually not at all.

Isaac's uncle was an uneducated drunk, but he did know how to count hedges and rows in fields. It was his one intellectual skill, and because of this, he did it probably more often than he needed to. Isaac often tagged along to these row-counting sessions because it was the only time his uncle ever paid attention to him.

And like water in a desert, any attention the boy got he desperately soaked in.

As it turned out, the boy was a kind of prodigy. By age eight, he could project the amount of feed required to sustain the sheep and pigs for the following season. By nine, he could rattle off the top of his head calculations for hectares of wheat, barley, and potatoes.

By age ten, Isaac had decided that farming was stupid and instead turned his attention to calculating the exact trajectory of the sun throughout the seasons. His uncle didn't care about the exact trajectory of the sun because it wouldn't put food on the table—at least not directly—so, again, he hit Isaac.

School didn't make things any better. Isaac was pale and scrawny and absentminded. He lacked social skills. He was into nerdy shit like sundials, Cartesian planes, and determining whether the moon was actually a sphere. While the other kids played cricket or chased one another through the woods, Isaac stood staring for hours into local streams, wondering how the eyeball was capable of seeing light.

Isaac Newton's early life was one hit after another. And with each blow, his Feeling Brain learned to *feel* an immutable truth: that there must be something inherently *wrong* with him. Why else would his parents have abandoned him? Why else would his peers ridicule him? What other explanation for his near-constant solitude? While his Thinking Brain occupied itself drawing fanciful graphs and charting the lunar eclipses, his Feeling Brain silently internalized the knowledge that there was something fundamentally broken about this small English boy from Lincolnshire.

One day, he wrote in his school notebook, "I am a little fellow. Pale and weak. There is no room for me. Not in the house or in the bottom of hell. What can I do? What am I good for? I cannot but weep."[2]

Up until this point, everything you've read about Newton is true—or at least highly plausible. But let's pretend for a moment that there's a parallel universe. And let's say that in this parallel universe there is another Isaac Newton, much like our own. He still comes from a broken and abusive family. He still lives a life of angry isolation. He still prodigiously measures and calculates everything he encounters.

But let's say that instead of obsessively measuring and calculating the external, natural world, this Parallel Universe Newton decides to obsessively measure and calculate the internal, psychological world, the world of the human mind and heart.

This isn't a huge leap of the imagination, as the victims of abuse are often the keenest observers of human nature. For you and me, people-watching may be something fun to do on a random Sunday in the park. But for the abused, it's a survival skill. For them, violence might erupt at any moment, therefore, they develop a keen Spidey sense to protect themselves. A lilt in someone's voice, the rise of an eyebrow, the depth of a sigh—anything can set off their internal alarm.

So, let's imagine this Parallel Universe Newton, this "Emo Newton," turned his obsession toward the people around him. He kept notebooks, cataloging all the observable behaviors of his peers and family. He scribbled relentlessly, documenting every action, every word. He filled hundreds of pages with inane observations of the kind of stuff people don't even realize they do. Emo Newton hoped that if measurement could be used to predict and control the natural world, the shapes and configurations of the sun and moon and stars, then it should also be able to predict and control the internal, emotional world.

And through his observations, Emo Newton realized something painful that we all kind of know, but that few of us ever want to admit: that people are liars, all of us. We lie constantly and habitually.[3] We lie about important things and trifling things. And we usually don't lie out of malice—rather, we lie to others because we're in such a habit of lying to ourselves.[4]

Isaac noted that light refracted through people's hearts in ways that they themselves did not seem to see; that people said they loved those whom they appeared to hate; professed to believe one thing while doing another; imagined themselves righteous while committing acts of the grandest dishonesty and cruelty. Yet, in their own minds, they somehow believed their actions to be consistent and true.

Isaac decided that no one could be trusted. Ever. He calculated that his pain was inversely proportional to the distance squared he put between himself and the world. Therefore, he kept to himself, staying in no one's orbit, spinning out and away from the gravitational tug of any other human heart. He had no friends; nor, he decided, did he want any. He concluded that the world was a bleak, wretched place and that the only value to his pathetic life was his ability to document and calculate that wretchedness.

For all his surliness, Isaac certainly didn't lack ambition. He wanted to know the trajectory of men's hearts, the velocity of their pain. He wished to know the force of their values and the mass of their hopes. And most important, he wanted to understand the relationships among all these elements.

He decided to write Newton's Three Laws of Emotion.[5]

For Every Action, There Is an Equal and Opposite Emotional Reaction

Imagine that I punch you in the face. No reason. No justification. Just pure violence.

Your instinctual reaction might be to retaliate in some way. Maybe it'd be physical: you'd punch me back. Maybe it'd be verbal: you'd call me a bunch of four-letter words. Or maybe your retaliation would be social: you'd call the police or some other authority and have me punished for assaulting you.

Regardless of your response, you would feel a rush of negative emotion directed toward me. And rightly so—clearly, I'm an awful person. After all, the idea that I get to cause you pain with no justification, without your *deserving* pain, generates a sense of injustice between us. A kind of *moral gap* opens between us: the sense that one of us is inherently righteous, and the other is an inferior piece of shit.[6]

Pain causes moral gaps. And it's not just between people. If a dog bites you, your instinct is to punish it. If you stub your toe on a coffee table, what do you do? You yell at the damn coffee table. If your home is washed away in a flood, you are overcome with grief and become furious at God, the universe, life itself.

These are moral gaps. They are a sense that something wrong has just happened and you (or someone else) *deserve* to be made whole again. Wherever there is pain, there is always an inherent sense of superiority/inferiority. And there's always pain.

When confronted with moral gaps, we develop overwhelming emotions toward *equalization*, or a return to moral equality. These desires for equalization take the form of a sense of *deserving*. Because I punched you, you feel I *deserve* to be punched back or punished in some way. This feeling (of my deserving pain) will cause you to have strong emotions about me (most likely anger). You will also have strong emotions around the feeling that you *didn't deserve* to be punched, that you did no wrong, and that you *deserve* better treatment from me and everyone else around you. These feelings might take the form of sadness, self-pity, or confusion.

This whole sense of "deserving" something is a value judgment we make in the face of a moral gap. We decide that something is better than something else; that one person is more righteous or just than another; that one event is less desirable than another. Moral gaps are where our values are born.

Now, let's pretend I apologize to you for punching you. I say, "Hey, reader, that was totally unfair and, wow, I was way out of line. That will never, ever happen again. And as a symbol of my overwhelming regret and guilt—here, I baked you a cake. Oh, and here's a hundred bucks. Enjoy."

Let's also pretend that this is somehow satisfying to you. You accept my apology and my cake and the hundred dollars and genuinely feel that everything is fine. We've now "equalized." The moral gap that was between us is gone. I've "made up" for it. You might even say we're even—neither of us is a better or worse person than the other, neither of us deserves better or worse treatment than the other any longer. We're operating on the same moral plane.

Equalizing like this restores hope. It means that there's nothing necessarily wrong with you or wrong with the world. That you can go about your day with a sense of self-control, a hundred bucks, and a sweet-ass cake.

Now let's imagine another scenario. This time, instead of punching you, let's say I buy you a house.

Yes, reader, I just bought you a fucking house.

This will open up another moral gap between us. But instead of an overwhelming feeling of wanting to equalize the pain I've caused you, you will instead experience an overwhelming feeling of wanting to equalize the joy I've created. You might hug me, say "thank you" a hundred times, give me a gift in return, or promise to babysit my cat from now until eternity.

Or, if you're particularly well mannered (and have some self-control), you may even *attempt to refuse* my offer to buy you a house because you recognize that it will open up a moral gap that you will never be able to surmount. You may acknowledge this by saying to me, "Thank you, but absolutely not. There's no way for me ever to *repay* you."

As with the negative moral gap, with the positive moral gap you will feel indebted to me, that you "owe me" something, that I deserve something good or that you need to "make it up" to me somehow. You will have intense feelings of gratitude and appreciation in my presence. You might even shed a tear of joy. (Aw, reader!)

It's our natural psychological inclination to equalize across moral gaps, to reciprocate actions: positive for positive; negative for negative. The forces that impel us to fill those gaps are our emotions. In this sense, every *action* demands an equal and opposite emotional *reaction*. This is Newton's First Law of Emotion.

Newton's First Law is constantly dictating the flow of our lives because it is the algorithm by which our Feeling Brain interprets the world.[7] If a movie causes more pain than it relieves, you become bored, or perhaps even angry. (Maybe you even attempt to equalize by demanding your money back.) If your mother forgets your birthday, maybe you equalize by ignoring her for the next six months. Or, if you're more mature, you communicate your disappointment to her.[8] If your favorite sports team loses in a horrible way, you will feel compelled to attend fewer games, or to cheer for them less. If you discover you have a talent for drawing, the admiration and satisfaction you derive from your competence will inspire you to invest time, energy, emotion, and money into the craft.[9] If your country elects a bozo whom you can't stand, you will feel a disconnect with your nation and government and even other citizens. You will also feel as though you are owed something in return for putting up with terrible policies.

Equalization is present in every experience because *the drive to equalize is emotion itself.* Sadness is a feeling of powerlessness to make up for a perceived loss. Anger is the desire to equalize through force and aggression. Happiness is feeling liberated from pain, while guilt is the feeling that you deserve some pain that never arrived.[10]

This desire for equalization underlies our sense of justice. It's been codified throughout the ages into rules and laws, such as the Babylonian king Hammurabi's classic "an eye for an eye, and a tooth for a tooth," or the biblical Golden Rule, "Do unto others what you would have done unto you." In evolutionary biology, it's known as "reciprocal altruism,"[11] and in game theory, it's called a "tit for tat" strategy.[12]

Newton's First Law generates our sense of morality. It underlies our perceptions of fairness. It is the bedrock of every human culture. And . . .

It is the operating system of the Feeling Brain.

While our Thinking Brain creates factual knowledge around observation and logic, the Feeling Brain creates our values around our experiences of pain. Experiences that *cause* us pain create a moral gap within our minds, and our Feeling Brain deems those experiences inferior and undesirable. Experiences that *relieve* pain create a moral gap in the opposite direction, and our Feeling Brain deems those experiences superior and desirable.

One way to think about it is that the Thinking Brain makes lateral connections between events (sameness, contrasts, cause/effect, etc.), while the Feeling Brain makes hierarchical connections (better/worse, more desirable/less desirable, morally superior/morally inferior).[13] Our Thinking Brain thinks horizontally (how are these things *related?*), while our Feeling Brain thinks vertically (which of these things is *better/worse?*). Our Thinking Brain decides how things *are*, and our Feeling Brain decides how things *ought to be*.

When we have experiences, our Feeling Brain creates a sort of *value hierarchy* for them.[14] It's as though we have a massive bookshelf in our subconscious where the best and most important experiences in life (with family, friends, burritos) are on the top shelf and the least desirable experiences (death, taxes, indigestion) are on the bottom. Our Feeling Brain then makes its decisions by simply pursuing experiences on the highest shelf possible.

Both brains have access to the value hierarchy. While the Feeling Brain determines what shelf something is on, the Thinking Brain is able to point out how certain experiences are connected and to suggest how the value hierarchy should be reorganized. This is essentially what "growth" is: reprioritizing one's value hierarchy in an optimal way.[15]

For example, I once had a friend who was probably the hardest partier I'd ever known. She would stay out all night and then go straight to work from the party in the morning, with zero hours of sleep. She thought it lame to wake up early or stay home on a Friday night. Her value hierarchy went something like this:

- Really awesome DJs
- Really good drugs
- Work
- Sleep

One could predict her behavior solely from this hierarchy. She'd rather work than sleep. She'd rather party and get fucked up than work. And *everything* was about the music.

Then she did one of those volunteer abroad things, where young people spend a couple of months working with orphans in a Third World country and—well, that changed everything. The experience was so emotionally powerful that it completely rearranged her value hierarchy. Her hierarchy now looked something like this:

- Saving children from unnecessary suffering
- Work
- Sleep
- Parties

And suddenly, as if by magic, the parties stopped being fun. Why? Because they interfered with her new top value: helping suffering kids. She switched careers and was all about work now. She stayed in most nights. She didn't drink or do drugs. She slept well—after all, she needed tons of energy to save the world.

Her party friends looked at her and pitied her; they judged her by their values, which were her old values. Poor party girl has to go to bed and get up for work every morning. Poor party girl can't stay out doing MDMA every weekend.

But here's the funny thing about value hierarchies: when they change, you don't actually lose anything. It's not that my friend decided to start giving up the parties for her career, it's that the parties stopped being fun. That's because "fun" is the product of our value hierarchies. When we stop valuing something, it ceases to be fun or interesting to us. Therefore, there is no sense of loss, no sense of missing out when we stop doing it. On the contrary, we look back and wonder how we ever spent so much time caring about such a silly, trivial thing, why we wasted so much energy on issues and causes that didn't matter. These pangs of regret or embarrassment are good; they signify growth. They are the product of our achieving our hopes.

Our Self-Worth Equals the Sum of Our Emotions Over Time

Let's return to the punching example, except this time, let's pretend I exist within this magical force field that prevents any consequences from ever befalling me. You can't punch me back. You can't say anything to me. You can't even say anything to anyone else about me. I am impervious—an all-seeing, all-powerful, evil ass-face.

Newton's First Law of Emotion states that when someone (or something) causes us pain, a moral gap opens up and our Feeling Brain summons up icky emotions to motivate us to equalize.

But what if that equalization never comes? What if someone (or something) makes us feel awful, yet we are incapable of ever retaliating or reconciling? What if we feel powerless to do anything to equalize or "make things right?" What if my force field is just too powerful for you?

When moral gaps persist for a long enough time, they normalize.[16] They become our default expectation. They lodge themselves into our value hierarchy. If someone hits us and we're never able to hit him back, eventually our Feeling Brain will come to a startling conclusion:

We deserve to be hit.

After all, if we didn't deserve it, we would have been able to equalize, right? The fact that we could not equalize means that there must be something inherently inferior about us, and/or something inherently superior about the person who hit us.

This, too, is part of our hope response. Because if equalization seems impossible, our Feeling Brain comes up with the next best thing: giving in, accepting defeat, judging itself to be inferior and of low value. When someone harms us, our immediate reaction is usually "He is shit, and I am righteous." But if we're not able to equalize and act on that righteousness, our Feeling Brain will believe the only alternative explanation: "I am shit, and *he* is righteous."[17]

This surrender to persisting moral gaps is a fundamental part of our Feeling Brain's nature. And it is Newton's Second Law of Emotion: How we come to value everything in life relative to ourselves is the sum of our emotions over time.

This surrender to and acceptance of ourselves as inherently inferior is often referred to as shame or low self-worth. Call it what you want, the result is the same: Life kicks you around a little bit, and you feel powerless to stop it. Therefore, your Feeling Brain concludes that you must deserve it.

Of course, the reverse moral gap must be true as well. If we're given a bunch of stuff without earning it (participation trophies and grade inflation and gold medals for coming in ninth place), we (falsely) come to believe ourselves inherently superior to what we actually are. We therefore develop a deluded version of *high self-worth*, or, as it's more commonly known, being an asshole.

Self-worth is contextual. If you were bullied for your geeky glasses and funny nose as a child, your Feeling Brain will "know" that you're a dweeb, even if you grow up to be a flaming sexpot of hotness. People who are raised in strict religious environments and are punished harshly for their sexual impulses often grow up with their Feeling Brain "knowing" that sex is wrong, even though their Thinking Brain has long worked out that sex is natural and totally awesome.

High and low self-worth appear different on the surface, but they are two sides of the same counterfeit coin. Because whether you feel as though you're better than the rest of the world or worse than the rest of the world, the same thing is true: you're imagining yourself as something special, something separate from the world.

A person who believes he deserves special treatment because of how great he is isn't so different from someone who believes she deserves special treatment because of how shitty she is. Both are narcissistic. Both think they're special. Both think the world should make exceptions and cater to their values and feelings over others'.

Narcissists will oscillate between feelings of superiority and inferiority.[18] Either everyone loves them or everyone hates them. Everything is amazing, or everything is fucked. An event was either the best moment of their lives or traumatizing. With the narcissist, there's no in-between, because to recognize the nuanced, indecipherable reality before him would require that he relinquish his privileged view that he is somehow special. Mostly, narcissists are unbearable to be around. They make everything about them and demand that people around them do the same.

You'll see this high/low-self-worth switcheroo everywhere if you keep an eye out for it: mass murderers, dictators, whiny kids, your obnoxious aunt who ruins Christmas every year. Hitler preached that the world treated Germany so poorly after World War I only because it was afraid of German superiority.[19] And in California more recently, one disturbed gunman justified trying to shoot up a sorority house with the fact that while women hooked up with "inferior" men he was forced to remain a virgin.[20]

You can even find it within yourself, if you're being honest. The more insecure you are about something, the more you'll fly back and forth between delusional feelings of superiority ("I'm the best!") and delusional feelings of inferiority ("I'm garbage!")

Self-worth is an illusion.[21] It's a psychological construct that our Feeling Brain spins in order to predict what will help it and what will hurt it. Ultimately, we must feel *something* about ourselves in order to feel something about the world, and without those feelings, it's impossible for us to find hope.

We all possess some degree of narcissism. It's inevitable, as everything we ever know or experience has happened to us or been learned by us. The nature of our consciousness dictates that everything happen *through us*. It's only natural, then, that our immediate assumption is that we are at the center of everything—because we *are* at the center of everything *we* experience.[22]

We all overestimate our skills and intentions and underestimate the skills and intentions of others. Most people believe that they are of above-average intelligence and have an above-average ability at most things, especially when they are not and do not.[23] We all tend to believe that we're more honest and ethical than we actually are.[24] We will each, given the chance, delude ourselves into believing that what's good for us is also good for everyone else.[25] When we screw up, we tend to assume it was some happy accident.[26] But when someone else screws up, we immediately rush to judge that person's character.[27]

Persistent low-level narcissism is natural, but it's also likely at the root of many of our sociopolitical problems. This is not a right-wing or a left-wing problem. This is not an older generation or younger generation problem. This is not an Eastern or Western problem.

This is a human problem.

Every institution will decay and corrupt itself. Each person, given more power and fewer restraints, will predictably bend that power to suit himself. Every individual will blind herself to her own flaws while seeking out the glaring flaws of others.

Welcome to Earth. Enjoy your stay.

Our Feeling Brains warp reality in such a way so that we believe that our problems and pain are somehow special and unique in the world, despite all evidence to the contrary. Human beings require this level of built-in narcissism because narcissism is our last line of defense against the Uncomfortable Truth. Because, let's be real: People suck, and life is exceedingly difficult and unpredictable. Most of us are winging it as we go, if not completely lost. And if we didn't have some false belief in our own superiority (or inferiority), a deluded belief that we're extraordinary at *something*, we'd line up to swan-dive off the nearest bridge. Without a little bit of that narcissistic delusion, without that perpetual lie we tell ourselves about our specialness, we'd likely give up hope.

But our inherent narcissism comes at a cost. Whether you believe you're the best in the world or the worst in the world, one thing is also true: you are separate from the world.

And it's this separateness that ultimately perpetuates unnecessary suffering.[28]

Your Identity Will Stay Your Identity Until a New Experience Acts Against It

Here's a common sob story. Boy cheats on girl. Girl is heartbroken. Girl despairs. Boy leaves girl, and girl's pain lingers for years afterward. Girl feels like shit about herself. And in order for her Feeling Brain to maintain hope, her Thinking Brain must pick one of two explanations. She can believe either that (a) all boys are shit or (b) she is shit.[29]

Well, shit. Neither of those is a good option.

But she decides to go with option (a), "all boys are shit," because, after all, she still has to live with herself. This choice isn't made consciously, mind you. It just kind of happens.[30]

Jump ahead a few years. Girl meets another boy. This boy isn't shit. In fact, this boy is the opposite of shit. He's pretty rad. And sweet. And cares. Like, really, truly cares.

But girl is in a conundrum. How can this boy be real? How can he be true? After all, she *knows* that all boys are shit. It's true. It must be true; she has the emotional scars to prove it.

Sadly, the realization that this boy is not shit is too painful for girl's Feeling Brain to handle, so she convinces herself that he is, indeed, shit. She nitpicks his tiniest flaws. She notices every errant word, every misplaced gesture, every awkward touch. She zeroes in on his most insignificant mistakes until they stand bright in her mind like a flashing strobe light screaming, "Run away! Save yourself!"

So, she does. She runs. And she runs in the most horrible of ways. She leaves him for another boy. After all, all boys are shit. So, what's trading one piece of shit for another? It means nothing.

Boy is heartbroken. Boy despairs. The pain lingers for years and morphs into shame. And this shame puts the boy in a tough position. Because now his Thinking Brain must make a choice: either (a) all girls are shit or (b) he is shit.

Our values aren't just collections of feelings. Our values are stories.

When our Feeling Brain feels something, our Thinking Brain sets to work constructing a narrative to *explain* that something. Losing your job doesn't just suck; you've constructed an entire narrative around it: Your asshole boss wronged you after years of loyalty! You gave yourself to that company! And what did you get in return?

Our narratives are sticky, clinging to our minds and hanging onto our identities like tight, wet clothes. We carry them around with us and define ourselves by them. We trade narratives with others, looking for people whose narratives match our own. We call these people friends, allies, good people. And those who carry narratives that contradict our own? We call them evil.

Our narratives about ourselves and the world are fundamentally about (a) something or someone's value and (b) whether that something/someone deserves that value. All narratives are constructed in this way:

Bad thing happens to person/thing, and he/she/it doesn't deserve it.

Good thing happens to person/thing, and he/she/it doesn't
   deserve it.
Good thing happens to person/thing, and he/she/it
   deserves it.
Bad thing happens to person/thing, and he/she/it
   deserves it.

Every book, myth, fable, history—all human meaning that's
communicated and remembered is merely the daisy-chaining of
these little value-laden narratives, one after the other, from now
until eternity.[31]

These narratives we invent for ourselves around what's important and what's not, what is deserving and what is not—these
stories stick with us and define us, they determine how we fit
ourselves into the world and with each other. They determine how
we feel about ourselves—whether we deserve a good life or not,
whether we deserve to be loved or not, whether we deserve success or not—and they define what we know and understand about
ourselves.

This network of value-based narratives is our *identity*. When
you think to yourself, I'm a pretty bad-ass boat captain, har-de-
har, that is a narrative you've constructed to define yourself and to
know yourself. It's a component of your walking, talking self that
you introduce to others and plaster all over your Facebook page.
You captain boats, and you do it damn well, and therefore you
deserve good things.

But here's the funny thing: when you adopt these little narratives as your identity, you protect them and react emotionally
to them as though they were an inherent part of you. The same
way that getting punched will cause a violent emotional reaction,

someone coming up and saying you're a shitty boat captain will produce a similarly negative emotional reaction, because we react to protect the metaphysical body just as we protect the physical.

Our identities snowball through our lives, accumulating more and more values and meaning as they tumble along. You are close with your mom growing up, and that relationship brings you hope, so you construct a story in your mind that comes to partly define you, just as your thick hair or your brown eyes or your creepy toenails define you. Your mom is a huge part of your life. Your mom is an amazing woman. You owe everything to your mom . . . and other shit people say at the Academy Awards. You then protect that piece of your identity as if it were a part of you. Someone comes along and talks shit about your mom, and you absolutely lose your mind and start breaking things.

Then *that experience* creates a new narrative and new value in your mind. You, you decide, have anger issues . . . especially around your mother. And now *that* becomes an inherent part of your identity.

And on and on it goes.

The longer we've held a value, the deeper inside the snowball it is and the more fundamental it is to how we see ourselves and how we see the world. Like interest on a bank loan, our values compound over time, growing stronger and coloring future experiences. It's not just the bullying from when you were in grade school that fucks you up. It's the bullying *plus* all the self-loathing and narcissism you brought to decades worth of future relationships, causing them all to fail, that adds up over time.

Psychologists don't know much for certain,[32] but one thing they definitely *do* know is that childhood trauma fucks us up.[33] This "snowball effect" of early values is why our childhood experiences, both good and bad, have long-lasting effects on our identities and generate the fundamental values that go on to define much of our lives. Your early experiences become your core values, and if your core values are fucked up, they create a domino effect of suckage that extends through the years, infecting experiences large and small with their toxicity.

When we're young, we have tiny and fragile identities. We've experienced little. We're completely dependent on our caretakers for everything, and inevitably, they're going to mess it up. Neglect or harm can cause extreme emotional reactions, resulting in large moral gaps that are never equalized. Dad walks out, and your three-year-old Feeling Brain decides that you were never lovable in the first place. Mom abandons you for some rich new husband, and you decide that intimacy doesn't exist, that no one can ever be trusted.

No wonder Newton was such a cranky loner.[34]

And the worst thing is, the longer we've held onto these narratives, the less aware we are that we have them. They become the background noise of our thoughts, the interior decoration of our minds. Despite being arbitrary and completely made up, they seem not only natural but inevitable.[35]

The values we pick up throughout our lives crystallize and form a sediment on top of our personality.[36] The only way to change our values is to have experiences *contrary* to our values. And any attempt to break free from those values through new or contrary experiences will inevitably be met with pain and discomfort.[37] This is why there is no such thing as change without pain, no growth without discomfort. It's why it is impossible to become someone new without first grieving the loss of who you used to be.

Because when we lose our values, we grieve the death of those defining narratives as though we've lost a part of ourselves—because we *have* lost a part of ourselves. We grieve the same way we would grieve the loss of a loved one, the loss of a job, a house, a community, a spiritual belief, or a friendship. These are all defining, fundamental parts of you. And when they are torn away from you, the hope they offered your life is also torn away, leaving you exposed, once again, to the Uncomfortable Truth.

There are two ways to heal yourself—that is, to replace old, faulty values with better, healthier values. The first is to reexamine the experiences of your past and rewrite the narratives around them. Wait, did he punch me because *I'm* an awful person; or is *he* the awful person?

Reexamining the narratives of our lives allows us to have a do-over, to decide: you know, maybe I wasn't such a great boat captain after all, and that's fine. Often, with time, we realize that what we used to believe was important about the world actually isn't. Other times, we *extend* the story to get a clearer view of our self-worth—oh, she left me because some asshole left *her* and she felt ashamed and unworthy around intimacy—and suddenly, that breakup is easier to swallow.

The other way to change your values is to begin writing the narratives of your future self, to envision what life *would* be like if you had certain values or possessed a certain identity. By visualizing the future we want for ourselves, we allow our Feeling Brain to try on those values for size, to see what they feel like before we make the final purchase. Eventually, once we've done this enough, the Feeling Brain becomes accustomed to the new values and starts to believe them.

This sort of "future projection" is usually taught in the worst of ways. "Imagine you're fucking rich and own a fleet of yachts! Then it will come true!"[38]

Sadly, that kind of visualization is not replacing a current unhealthy value (materialism) with a better one. It's just masturbating to your current value. Real change would entail fantasizing what *not wanting yachts in the first place* would feel like.

Fruitful visualization should be a little bit uncomfortable. It should challenge you and be difficult to fathom. If it's not, then it means that nothing is changing.

The Feeling Brain doesn't know the difference between past, present, and future; that's the Thinking Brain's domain.[39] And one of the strategies our Thinking Brain uses to nudge the Feeling Brain into the correct lane of life is asking "what if" questions: What if you hated boats and instead spent your time helping disabled kids? What if you didn't have to prove anything to the people in your life for them to like you? What if people's unavailability has more to do with them than it does with you?

Other times, you can just tell your Feeling Brain stories that might or might not be true but that *feel* true. Jocko Willink, former Navy SEAL and author, writes in his book *Discipline Equals Freedom: Field Manual* that he wakes up at four thirty every morning because he imagines his enemy is somewhere out there in the world.[40] He doesn't know where, but he assumes that his enemy wants to kill him. And he realizes that if he's awake before his enemy, that gives him an advantage. Willink developed this narrative for himself while serving in the Iraq War, where there were actual enemies who *did* want to kill him. But he has maintained that narrative since returning to civilian life.

Objectively, the narrative Willink creates for himself makes no fucking sense. Enemy? Where? But figuratively, emotionally, it is incredibly powerful. Willink's Feeling Brain still buys into it, and it still gets Willink up every damn morning before some of us are done drinking from the night before. *That* is the illusion of self-control.

Without these narratives—without developing a clear vision of the future we desire, of the values we want to adopt, of the identities we want to shed or step into—we are forever doomed to repeat the failures of our past pain. The stories of our past define our identity. The stories of our future define our hopes. And our ability to step into those narratives and live them, to make them reality, is what gives our lives meaning.

Emotional Gravity

Emo Newton sat alone in his childhood bedroom. It was dark outside. He didn't know how long he had been awake, what time it was, or what day it was. He had been alone and working for weeks now. Food that his family had left for him sat uneaten by the door, rotting.

He took out a blank piece of paper and drew a large circle on it. He then marked points along the edges of the circle and, with dotted lines, indicated the pull of each dot toward the center. Beneath this, he wrote, "There is an emotional gravity to our values: we attract those into our orbit who value the same things we do, and instinctively repel, as if by reverse magnetism, those whose values are contrary to our own.[41] These attractions form large orbits of like-minded people around the same principle. Each falls along the same path, circling and revolving around the same cherished thing."

He then drew another circle, adjacent to the first. The two circles' edges nearly touched. From there, he drew lines of tension between the edges of each circle, the places where the gravity pulled in both directions, disrupting the perfect symmetry of each orbit. He then wrote:

"Large swaths of people coalesce together, forming tribes and communities based on the similar evaluations of their emotional histories. You, sir, may value science. I, too, value science. Therefore, there is an emotional magnetism between us. Our values attract one another and cause us to fall perpetually into each other's orbit, in a metaphysical dance of friendship. Our values align, and our cause becomes one!

"But! Let's say that one gentleman sees value in Puritanism and another in Anglicanism. They are inhabitants of two closely related yet different gravities. This causes each to disrupt the other's orbit, cause tension within the value hierarchies, challenge the other's identity, and thus generate negative emotions that will push them apart and put their causes at odds.

"This emotional gravity, I declare, is the fundamental organization of all human conflict and endeavor."

At this, Isaac took out another page and drew a series of circles of differing sizes. "The stronger we hold a value," he wrote, "that is, the stronger we determine something as superior or inferior than all else, the stronger its gravity, the tighter its orbit, and the more difficult it is for outside forces to disrupt its path and purpose.[42]

"Our strongest values therefore demand either the affinity or the antipathy of others—the more people there are who share some value, the more those people begin to congeal and organize themselves into a single, coherent body around that value: scientists with scientists, clergy with clergy. People who love the same thing love each other. People who hate the same thing also love each other. And people who love or hate different things hate each other. All human systems eventually reach equilibrium by clustering and conforming into constellations of mutually shared value systems—people come together, altering and modifying their own personal narratives until their narratives are one and the same, and the personal identity thus becomes the group identity.

"Now, you may be saying, 'But, my good man, Newton! Don't most people value the same things? Don't most people simply want a bit of bread and a safe place to sleep at night?' And to that, I say you are correct, my friend!

"All peoples are more the same than they are different. We all mostly want the same things out of life. But those slight differences generate emotion, and emotion generates a sense of importance. Therefore, we come to perceive our differences as disproportionately more important than our similarities. And this is the true tragedy of man. That we are doomed to perpetual conflict over the slight difference.[43]

"This theory of emotional gravitation, the coherence and attraction of like values, explains the history of peoples.[44] Different parts of the world have different geographic factors. One region may be hard and rugged and well defended from invaders. Its people would then naturally value neutrality and isolation. This would then become their group identity. Another region may overflow with food and wine, and its people would come to value hospitality, festivities, and family. This, too, would become their identity. Another region may be arid and a difficult place to live, but with wide-open vistas connecting it to many distant lands, its people would come to value authority, strong military leadership, and absolute dominion. This, too, is their identity.[45]

"And just as the individual protects her identity through beliefs, rationalizations, and biases, communities, tribes, and nations protect their identities the same way.[46] These cultures eventually solidify themselves into nations, which then expand, bringing more and more peoples into the umbrella of their value systems. Eventually, these nations will bump up against each other, and the contradictory values will collide.

"Most people do not value themselves above their cultural and group values. Therefore, many people are willing to die for their highest values—for their family, their loved ones, their nation, their god. And because of this willingness to die for their values, these collisions of culture will inevitably result in war.[47]

"War is but a terrestrial test of hope. The country or people who have adopted values that maximize the resources and hopes of its peoples the best will inevitably become the victor. The more a nation conquers neighboring peoples, the more the people of that conquering nation come to feel that they *deserve* to dominate their fellow men, and the more they will see their nation's values as the true guiding lights of humanity. The supremacy of those winning values then lives on, and the values are written up and lauded in our histories, and go on to be retold in stories, passed down to give future generations hope. Eventually, when those values cease to be effective, they will lose out to the values of another, newer nation, and history will continue on, a new era unfolding.

"This, I declare, is the form of human progress."

Newton finished writing. He placed his theory of emotional gravitation on the same stack with his three Laws of Emotion and then paused to reflect on his discoveries.

And in that quiet, dark moment, Isaac Newton looked at the circles on the page and had an upsetting realization: he had no orbit. Through years of trauma and social failure, he had voluntarily separated himself from everything and everyone, like a lone star flung on its own trajectory, unobstructed and uninfluenced by the gravitational pull of any system.

He realized that he valued no one—not even himself—and this brought him an overwhelming sense of loneliness and grief, because no amount of logic and calculation could ever compensate for the gnawing desperation of his Feeling Brain's never-ending struggle to find hope in this world.

I would love to tell you that Parallel Universe Newton, or Emo Newton, overcame his sadness and solitude. I would love to tell you that he learned to value himself and others. But like our universe's Isaac Newton, Parallel Universe Newton would spend the rest of his days alone, grumpy, and miserable.

The questions both Newtons answered that summer of 1666 had perplexed philosophers and scientists for generations. Yet, in a matter of a few months, this cantankerous, antisocial twenty-three-year-old had uncovered the mystery, had cracked the code. And there, on the frontiers of intellectual discovery, he tossed his findings aside to a musty and forgotten corner of a cramped study, in a remote backwater village a day's ride north of London.

And there, his discoveries would remain, hidden to the world, collecting dust.[48]

How to Make All Your Dreams Come True

Imagine this: it's 2:00 a.m. and you're still awake on the couch, staring bleary-eyed and foggy-brained at the television. Why? You don't know. Inertia simply makes it easier to sit there and keep watching than to get up and go to bed. So, you watch.

Perfect. This is how I get you: when you're feeling apathetic and lost and completely passive in the face of your fate. Nobody sits up staring at a TV at 2:00 a.m. if they have important shit to do the next day. Nobody struggles with the will to move their ass off the couch for hours on end unless they're having some sort of inner crisis of hope. And it's exactly this crisis that I want to speak to.

I appear on your TV screen. I'm a whirlwind of energy. There are loud, obnoxious colors, cheesy sound effects. I'm practically shouting. Yet, somehow, my smile is easy and relaxed. I'm comforting. It's as though I'm making eye contact with you and only you:

"What if I told you that I could solve all your problems?" I say.

Pfft, puh-lease, you think. *You don't know the half of my problems, buddy.*

"What if I told you I know how to make all your dreams come true?"

Riiiiight, and I'm the fucking tooth fairy.

"Look, I know how you feel," I say.

Nobody knows how I feel, you reflexively tell yourself, surprised at how automatic the response is.

"I, too, once felt lost," I say. "I felt alone, isolated, hopeless. I, too, used to lie awake at night for no particular reason, wondering if there was something wrong with me, wondering what was this invisible force standing between myself and my dreams. And I know that's what you're feeling, too. That you've somehow lost something. You just don't know what."

In truth, I say these things because they are experienced by everybody. They are a fact of the human condition. We all feel powerless to equalize with the inherent guilt that comes with our existence. We all suffer and are victimized to varying degrees, especially when we're young. And we all spend a lifetime trying to compensate for that suffering.

And in moments of our life when things aren't going so well, this makes us despair.

But like most people struggling, you've enveloped yourself so much in your pain that you've forgotten that pain is common, and that your strife is not uniquely yours—on the contrary, it's universal. And because you've forgotten this, you feel as if I'm speaking directly to you; as if, by some magical power, I'm peering into your soul and reading back to you the contents of your heart. For this, you sit up and at attention.

"Because," I repeat, "I have the solution to *all* your problems. I can make *all* your dreams come true." Now I'm pointing, and my finger looks gigantic on your TV screen. "I have all the answers. I have the secret of everlasting happiness and eternal life, and it's this . . ."

What I go on to say is so outlandish, so ridiculous, so absolutely perverse and cynical that you actually think it might be true. The problem is, you *want* to believe me. You *need* to believe me. I represent the hope and salvation your Feeling Brain desperately craves, that it needs. So, slowly, your Thinking Brain comes to the conclusion that my idea is so batshit crazy that it just might work.

As the infomercial drags on, that existential need to find meaning somewhere, *anywhere*, beats down your psychological defenses and lets me in. After all, I *have* demonstrated an uncanny knowledge of your pain, a backdoor entrance to your secret truth, a deep vein traveling through your heart. You then realize that in between all my big white teeth and shouty words, I've spoken to you: *I was once just as fucked as you . . . and I found my way out. Come with me.*

I keep going. I'm on a roll now. The camera angles are switching back and forth, grabbing me now from the side, now from the front. Suddenly, there's a studio audience in front of me. They're wrapped up in every word I say. A woman is crying. A man's jaw drops. And yours drops with it. I'm all up in your shit now. I will give you permanent fulfillment, motherfucker. I will fill any gap, plug any hole. Just sign up for one low price. What is happiness worth to you? What is hope worth to you? Act now, fucker.

Sign up. Today.

With that, you grab your phone. You go to the website. You put in the digits.

Truth and salvation and everlasting happiness. It's all yours. It's coming to you. Are you ready?

An Introduction to a Proven System That Will Help You Achieve Everlasting Bliss and Eternal Salvation!

(OR YOUR MONEY BACK)

Welcome, and congratulations on taking the first step to making all your dreams come true! By the end of this course you will have solved all your life's problems. You will live a life of abundance and freedom. You will be surrounded by adoring friends and loved ones. Guaranteed!*

It's so simple, anyone can do it. No education or certification required. All you need is an internet connection and a functioning keyboard, and you, too, can create your very own religion.

Yes, you heard me right. You, too, can start your very own religion—TODAY—and begin reaping the benefits of the thousands of mindlessly devoted followers who will lavish on you unconditional adoration, financial gifts, and more social media likes than you know what to do with.

In this so-simple-anyone-can-do-it six-step program, we will cover:

---

* Terms and conditions may apply.

Belief systems. Do you want your religion to be spiritual or secular? Past-focused or future-focused? Do you want it to be violent or nonviolent? These are all important questions, but don't worry, *only I* have the answers.

How to find your first followers. And more important: what do you want your followers to be? Rich? Poor? Male? Female? Vegan? I have the inside scoop!

Rituals, rituals, rituals! Eat this. Stand there. Recite that. Bow and kneel and clap your hands! Do the hokey pokey and turn yourself around! That's what it's all about! The most enjoyable part of religion is coming up with dumb stuff that you all agree somehow means something. I will provide you with a complete guide to developing the hippest, coolest rituals on the block. All the kids will be talking about it—mainly because they'll be forced to.

How to choose a scapegoat. No religion is complete without a common enemy upon which to project one's inner turmoil. Life is messy, but why deal with your problems when you can just blame somebody else for them? That's right, you'll discover the best way to choose an evil boogeyman (or boogeywoman!) and how to convince your followers to hate him/her. Nothing unites us like hating the same enemy. Get your assault rifles ready!

And finally, how to make money. Why start a religion if you don't profit from it? My guide will give you all the nitty-gritty details on how to milk the most out of your followers. Whether you're into money, fame, political power, or blood orgies, I've got you covered!

Look, we all need communities to build hope. And we all need hope to not go utterly fucking insane and start snorting bath salts. Religions are the basis for that communal hope. And we're going to learn how to build them from scratch.

Religions are a beautiful thing. When you get enough people together with the same values, they behave in ways they never would when alone. Their hope amplifies in a sort of network effect, and the social validation of being part of a group hijacks their Thinking Brains and lets their Feeling Brains run wild.[1]

Religions bring groups of people together to mutually validate one another and make one another feel important. It's a big silent agreement that if we all come together under some shared purpose, we will feel important and worthy, and the Uncomfortable Truth will be just that much farther away.[2]

This is *hugely* satisfying psychologically. People just lose their shit! And best of all, they become highly suggestible. Paradoxically, it's only in a group environment that the individual has no control, that he gains the perception of perfect self-control.

The danger of this immediate access to the Feeling Brain, though, is that large groups of people tend to do highly impulsive and irrational shit. So, on the one hand, people get to feel whole, like they're understood and loved. On the other hand, they sometimes transform into murderous, angry mobs.[3]

This guide will take you through the details of establishing your own religion so you can reap the benefits of thousands of suggestible followers. Let's get started.

Step One: Sell Hope to the Hopeless

I'll never forget the first time someone told me I had blood on my hands. I remember it as if it were yesterday.

It was 2005, a sunny, crisp morning in Boston, Massachusetts. I was a university student then and walking to class, minding my own business, when I saw a group of kids holding up pictures of the 9/11 terrorist attacks with captions that read, "America Deserved It."

Now, I don't consider myself the most patriotic person by any stretch of the imagination, but it seems to me that anyone holding such a sign in broad daylight immediately becomes a highly punchable person.

I stopped and engaged the kids, asking what they were doing. They had a little table set up with a smattering of pamphlets on top. One had Dick Cheney with devil's horns drawn on him and the words "Mass Murderer" written beneath. Another had George W. Bush with a Hitler mustache.

The students were part of the LaRouche Youth Movement, a group started by the far-left ideologue Lyndon LaRouche in New Hampshire. His acolytes would spend countless hours standing around college campuses in the Northeast, handing out flyers and pamphlets to susceptible college kids. And when I came upon them, it took me all of ten seconds to figure out what they actually were: a religion.

That's right. They were an ideological religion: an antigovernment, anticapitalist, anti–old people, antiestablishment religion. They argued that the international world order, from top to bottom, was corrupt. They argued that the Iraq War had been instigated for no other reason than that Bush's friends wanted more money. They argued that terrorism and mass shootings didn't exist, that such events were simply highly coordinated governmental efforts to control the population. Don't worry right-wing friends, years later, they would draw the same Hitler mustaches and make the same claims about Obama—if that makes you feel any better. (It shouldn't.)

What the LaRouche Youth Movement (LYM) does is pure genius. It finds disaffected and agitated college students (usually young men), kids who are both scared and angry (scared at the sudden responsibility they've been forced to take on and angry at how un-compromising and disappointing it is to be an adult) and then preach one simple message to them: "It's not your fault."

Yes, young one, you thought it was Mom and Dad's fault, but it's not their fault. Nope. And I know you thought it was your shitty professors and overpriced college's fault. Nope. Not theirs, either. You probably even thought it was the government's fault. Close, but still no.

See, it's the *system's* fault, that grand, vague entity you've always heard about.

This was the faith the LYM was selling: if we could just over-throw "the system," then *everything* would be okay. No more war. No more suffering. No more injustice.

Remember that in order to feel hope, we need to feel there's a better future out there (values); we need to feel as though we are capable of getting to that better future (self-control); and we need to find other people who share our values and support our efforts (community).

Young adulthood is a period when many people struggle with values, control, and community. For the first time in their lives, kids are allowed to decide who they want to be. Do they want to become a doctor? Study business? Take a psychology course? The options can be crippling.[4] And the inevitable frustration causes a lot of young people to question their values and lose hope.

In addition, young adults struggle with self-control.[5] For the first time in their lives, they don't have some authority figure watching over them 24/7. On the one hand, this can be liberating, exciting. On the other, they are now responsible for their own decisions. And if they kind of suck at getting themselves out of bed on time, going to their classes or a job, and studying enough, it's tough to admit that there's no one to blame but themselves.

And finally, young people are particularly preoccupied with finding and fitting into a community.[6] Not only is this important for their emotional development, but it also helps them find and solidify an identity for themselves.[7]

People like Lyndon LaRouche capitalize on lost and aimless young people. LaRouche gave them a convoluted political explanation to justify how disaffected they felt. He gave them a sense of control and empowerment by outlining a way (supposedly) to change the world. And finally, he gave them a community where they "fit in" and know who they are.

Therefore, he gave them hope.[8]

"Don't you think this is taking it a little too far?" I asked the LYM students that day, pointing to the pictures of the World Trade Center towers featured on their pamphlets.[9]

"No way, man. I say we're not taking it far enough!" one of the kids replied.

"Look, I didn't vote for Bush, and I don't agree with the Iraq War, either, but—"

"It doesn't matter who you vote for! A vote for anyone is a vote for the corrupt and oppressive system! You have blood on your hands!"

"Excuse me?"

I didn't even know *how* to punch someone, yet I found myself balling my hands into fists. Who the fuck did this guy think he was?

"By participating in the system, you are perpetuating it," the kid continued, "and therefore are complicit in the murder of millions of innocent civilians around the world. Here, read this." He shoved a pamphlet at me. I glanced at it, turned it over.

"That's fucking stupid," I said.

Our "discussion" went on like this for another few minutes. Back then, I didn't know any better. I still thought stuff like this was about reason and evidence, not feelings and values. And values cannot be changed through reason, only through experience.

Eventually, after I had gotten good and pissed off, I decided to leave. As I started walking off, the kid tried to get me to sign up for a free seminar. "You need to have an open mind, man," he said. "The truth is scary."

I looked back and replied with a Carl Sagan quote I had once read on an internet forum: "I think your mind is so open your brain fell out!"[10]

I felt smart and smug. He, presumably, felt smart and smug. No minds were changed that day.

We are the most impressionable when things are at their worst.[11] When our life is falling apart, it signifies that our values have failed us, and we're grasping in the dark for new values to replace them. One religion falls and opens up space for the next. People who lose faith in their spiritual God will look for a worldly God.

People who lose their family will give themselves away to their race, creed, or nation. People who lose faith in their government or country will look to extremist ideologies to give them hope.[12]

There's a reason that all the major religions in the world have a history of sending missionaries to the poorest and most destitute corners of the globe: starving people will believe anything if it will keep them fed. For your new religion, it's best to start preaching your message to people whose lives suck the most: the poor, the outcasts, the abused and forgotten. You know, people who sit on Facebook all day.[13]

Jim Jones built his following by recruiting the homeless and marginalized minorities with a socialist message minced with his own (demented) take on Christianity. Hell, what am I saying? Jesus Christ did the same damn thing.[14] Buddha, too. Moses—you get the idea. Religious leaders preach to the poor and downtrodden and enslaved, telling them that *they* deserve the kingdom of heaven—basically, an open "fuck you" to the corrupt elites of the day. It's a message that's easy to get behind.

Today, appealing to the hopeless is easier than ever before. All you need is a social media account: start posting extreme and crazy shit, and let the algorithm do the rest. The crazier and more extreme your posts, the more attention you'll garner, and the more the hopeless will flock to you like flies to cow shit. It's not hard at all.

But you can't just go online and say anything. No, you must have a (semi-)coherent message. You must have a vision. Because it's easy to get people riled up and angry about nothing—the news media have created a whole business model out of it. But to have hope, people need to feel that they are a part of some greater movement, that they are about to join the winning side of history.

And, for that, you must give them faith.

Step Two: Choose Your Faith

We all must have faith in something. Without faith, there is no hope.

Nonreligious people bristle at the word *faith*, but having faith is inevitable. Evidence and science are based on past experience. Hope is based on future experience. And you must always rely on some degree of faith that something will occur again in the future.[15] You pay your mortgage because you have faith that money is real, and credit is real, and a bank taking all your shit is real.[16] You tell your kids to do their homework because you have faith that their education is important, that it will lead them to their becoming happier, healthier adults. You have faith that happiness exists and is possible. You have faith that living longer is worth it, so you strive to stay safe and healthy. You have faith that love matters, that your job matters, that any of this matters.

So, there's no such thing as an atheist. Well, sorta. Depends what you mean by "atheist."[17] My point is that we must all believe, on faith, that *something is important*. Even if you're a nihilist, you are believing, on faith, that nothing is more important than anything else.

So, in the end, it's all faith.[18]

The important question, then, is: Faith in what? What do we choose to believe?

Whatever our Feeling Brain adopts as its highest value, this tippy top of our value hierarchy becomes the lens through which we interpret all other values. Let's call this highest value the "God Value."[19] Some people's God Value is money. These people view all other things (family, love, prestige, politics) through the prism of money. Their family will love them only if they make enough money. They will be respected only if they have money. All conflict, frustration, jealousy, anxiety—everything boils down to money.[20]

Other people's God Value is love. They view all other values through the prism of love—they're against conflict in all its forms, they're against anything that separates or divides others.

Obviously, many people adopt Jesus Christ, or Muhammad, or the Buddha, as their God Value. They then interpret everything they experience through the prism of that spiritual leader's teachings.

Some people's God Value is themselves—or, rather, their own pleasure and empowerment. This is narcissism: the religion of self-aggrandizement.[21] These people place their faith in their own superiority and deservedness.

Other people's God Value is another person. This is often called "codependence."[22] These people derive all hope from their connection with another individual and sacrifice themselves and their own interests for that individual. They then base all their behavior, decisions, and beliefs on what they think will please that other person—their own little personal God. This typically leads to really fucked-up relationships with—you guessed it—narcissists. After all, the narcissist's God Value is himself, and the codependent's God Value is fixing and saving the narcissist. So, it kind of works out in a really sick and fucked-up way. (But not really.)

All religions must start with a faith-based God Value. Doesn't matter what it is. Worshipping cats, believing in lower taxes, never letting your kids leave the house—whatever it is, it is a faith-based value that *this one thing* will produce the best future reality, and therefore gives the most hope. We then organize our lives, and all other values, around that value. We look for activities that enact that faith, ideas that support it, and most important, communities that share it.

It's around now that some of the more scientifically minded readers start raising their hands and pointing out that there are these things called *facts* and there is ample evidence to demonstrate that facts exist, and we don't need to have faith to know that some things are real.

Fair enough. But here's the thing about evidence: it changes nothing. Evidence belongs to the Thinking Brain, whereas values are decided by the Feeling Brain. You cannot verify values. They are, by definition, subjective and arbitrary. Therefore, you can argue about facts until you're blue in the face, but ultimately, it doesn't matter—people interpret the significance of their experiences through their *values*.[23]

If a meteorite hit a town and killed half the people, the über-traditional religious person would look at the event and say that it happened because the town was full of sinners. The atheist would look at it and say that it was proof there is no God (another faith-based belief, by the way), as how could a benevolent, all-powerful being let such an awful thing happen? A hedonist would look at it and decide that it was even more reason to party, since we could all die at any moment. And a capitalist would look at it and start thinking about how to invest in meteorite-defense technologies.

Evidence serves the interests of the God Value, not the other way around. The only loophole to this arrangement is when *evidence itself* becomes your God Value. The religion built around the worship of evidence is more commonly known as "science," and it's arguably the best thing we've ever done as a species. But we'll get to science and its ramifications in the next chapter.

My point is that all values are faith-based beliefs. Therefore, all hope (and therefore, all religions) are also based on faith, faith that something can be important and valuable and right despite the fact that there will never be a way to verify it beyond all doubt.

For our purposes, I've defined three types of religions, each type based on a different kind of God Value:

Spiritual religions. Spiritual religions draw hope from
supernatural beliefs, or belief in things that exist
outside the physical or material realm. These religions
look for a better future outside this world and this life.
Christianity, Islam, Judaism, animism, and Greek
mythology are examples of spiritual religions.

Ideological religions. Ideological religions draw hope
from the natural world. They look for salvation and
growth and develop faith-based beliefs regarding
this world and this life. Examples include capitalism,
communism, environmentalism, liberalism, fascism,
and libertarianism.

Interpersonal religions. Interpersonal religions draw hope
from other people in our lives. Examples of interpersonal
religions include romantic love, children, sports heroes,
political leaders, and celebrities.

Spiritual religions are high risk/high reward. They require, by far, the most skill and charisma to get going. But they also pay off the most in terms of follower loyalty and benefits. (I mean, have you *seen* the Vatican? Holy shit.) And if you build one really well, it'll last way after you die.

Ideological religions play the religion formation game on "Normal Difficulty." These religions take a lot of work and effort to create, but they're fairly common. But because they're so common, they run into a lot of competition for people's hopes. They are often described as cultural "trends," and indeed, few of them survive more than a few years or decades. Only the best last through multiple centuries.

Finally, interpersonal religions are playing the religion formation game on "Easy" mode. That's because interpersonal religions are as common as people themselves. Pretty much all of us, at some point in our lives, completely surrender ourselves and our self-worth to another individual. The interpersonal religion is sometimes experienced as an adolescent, naïve sort of love and it's the type of shit that you have to suffer through before you can ever grow out of it.

Let's start with spiritual religions, as they have the highest stakes and are arguably the most important religions in human history.

Spiritual Religions

From the pagan and animalistic rituals of early human cultures, to the pagan gods of antiquity, to the grandiose monotheistic religions that still exist today, the majority of human history has been dominated by a belief in supernatural forces and, most important, the hope that certain actions and beliefs in *this* life would lead to rewards and improvement in the *next* life.

This preoccupation with the next life developed because for most of human history, everything was completely fucked and 99 percent of the population had no hope of material or physical improvement in their lives. If you think things are bad today, just think about the plagues that wiped out a third of the population on an entire continent,[24] or the wars that involved selling tens of thousands of children into slavery.[25] In fact, things were so bad in the old days that the only way to keep everyone sane was by promising them hope in an afterlife. Old-school religion held the fabric of society together because it gave the masses a guarantee that their suffering was meaningful, that God was watching, and that they would be duly rewarded.

In case you haven't noticed, spiritual religions are incredibly resilient. They last hundreds, if not thousands, of years. This is because supernatural beliefs can never be proven or disproven. Therefore, once a supernatural belief gets lodged as someone's God Value, it's nearly impossible to dislodge it.

Spiritual religions are also powerful because they often encourage hope through death, which has the nice side effect of making a lot of people willing to die for their unverifiable beliefs. Hard to compete with that.

Ideological Religions

Ideological religions generate hope by constructing networks of beliefs that certain actions will produce better outcomes in *this* life only if they are adopted by the population at large. Ideologies are usually "isms": libertarianism, nationalism, materialism, racism, sexism, veganism, communism, capitalism, socialism, fascism, cynicism, skepticism, etc. Unlike spiritual religions, ideologies are verifiable to varying degrees. You can theoretically test to see whether a central bank makes a financial system more or less stable, whether democracy makes society fairer, whether education makes people hack one another to pieces less often, but at a certain point, most ideologies still rely on faith. There are two reasons for this. The first is that some things are just incredibly difficult, if not impossible, to test and verify. The other is that a lot of ideologies rely upon everyone in society having faith in the same thing.

For instance, you can't scientifically prove that money is intrinsically valuable. But we all believe it is, so it is.[26] You also can't prove that national citizenship is a real thing, or even that most ethnicities exist.[27] These are all socially constructed beliefs that we've all bought into, taken on faith.

The problem with evidence and ideologies is that humans have a tendency to take a little bit of evidence and run with it, generalizing a couple of simple ideas to entire populations and the planet.[28] This is our human narcissism at work—our need to invent our self-importance, our Feeling Brain run amok. So, even though ideologies are subject to evidence and verification, we're not exactly good at verifying them.[29] Humanity is so vast and complex that our brains have trouble taking it all in. There are too many variables. So, our Thinking Brains inevitably take short-cuts to maintain some otherwise shitty beliefs. Bad ideologies such as racism or sexism persist due to ignorance far more than malice. And people hold on to those bad ideologies because, sadly, they offer their adherents some degree of hope.

Ideological religions are difficult to start, but they are far more common than spiritual religions. All you have to do is find some reasonable-sounding explanation for why everything is fucked and then extrapolate that across wide populations in a way that gives people some hope, and voilà! You have yourself an ideological religion. If you've been alive for more than twenty years, surely you've seen this happen a few times by now. In my lifetime alone there have been movements in favor of LGBTQ rights, stem cell research, and decriminalizing drug use. In fact, a lot of what everyone is losing their shit about today is the fact that traditionalist, nationalist, and populist ideologies are winning political power across much of the world, and these ideologies are seeking to dismantle much of the work accomplished by the neoliberal, globalist, feminist, and environmentalist ideologies of the late twentieth century.

Interpersonal Religions

Every Sunday, millions of people come together to stare at an empty green field. The field has white lines painted on it. These millions of people have all agreed to believe (on faith) that these lines mean something important. Then, dozens of strong men (or women) plod onto the field, line up in seemingly arbitrary formations, and throw (or kick) around a piece of leather. Depending on where this piece of leather goes and when, one group of people cheers, and the other group of people gets really upset.

Sports are a form of religion. They are arbitrary value systems designed to give people hope. Hit the ball here, and you're a hero! Kick the ball there, and you're a loser! Sports deify some individuals and demonize others. Ted Williams is the best baseball hitter ever, and therefore, according to some, an American hero, an icon, a role model. Other athletes are demonized for coming up short, for wasting their talent, for betraying their followers.[30]

Yet, there is an even grander example of interpersonal religion than sports: politics. Across the world, we come together under a similar set of values and decide to bestow authority, leadership, and virtue onto a small number of people. Like the lines on a football field, political systems are entirely made up, the positions of power exist due only to the faith of the population. And whether it's a democracy or a dictatorship, the result is the same: a small group of leaders is idolized and exalted (or demonized) in the social consciousness.[31]

Interpersonal religions give us hope that another human being will bring us salvation and happiness, that one individual (or group of individuals) is superior to all others. Interpersonal religions are sometimes combined with supernatural beliefs and ideological beliefs, resulting in pariahs, martyrs, heroes, and saints. Many of our interpersonal religions develop around our leaders. A charismatic president or celebrity who seems to understand everything we go through can approach the level of a God Value in our eyes, and much of what we deem right or wrong is filtered through what is good or bad for our Dear Leader.

Fandom, in general, is a low-level kind of religion. Fans of Will Smith or Katy Perry or Elon Musk follow everything that person does, hang on every word he or she says, and come to see him or her as blessed or righteous in some way. The worship of that figure gives the fan hope of a better future, even if it's in the form of something as simple as future films, songs, or inventions.

But the most important interpersonal religions are our familial and romantic relationships. The beliefs and emotions involved in these relationships are evolutionary in nature, but they are faith-based all the same.[32] Each family is its own mini-church, a group of people who, on faith, believe that being part of the group will give their lives meaning, hope, and salvation. Romantic love, of course, can be a quasi-spiritual experience.[33] We seem to lose ourselves in someone we have fallen for, spinning all sorts of narratives about the cosmic significance of the relationship.

For better or worse, modern civilization has largely alienated us from these small, interpersonal religions and tribes and replaced them with large nationalist and internationalist ideological religions.[34] This is good news for you and me, fellow religion-builder, as we don't have as many intimate bonds to cut through to get our followers emotionally attached to us.

Because, as we'll see, religion is all about emotional attachment. And the best way to build those attachments is to get people to stop thinking critically.

Step Three: Preemptively Invalidate All Criticism or Outside Questioning

Now that your fledgling religion has its core tenets of faith, you need to find a way to protect that faith from the inevitable criticism that will be flung its way. The trick is to adopt a belief that creates a self-reinforcing us-versus-them dichotomy—that is, create a perception of "us" versus "them" in such a way that anyone who criticizes or questions "us" immediately becomes a "them."

This sounds difficult, but is actually quite easy. Here are some examples:

- If you don't support the war, then you support the terrorists.
- God created science to test our faith in God. Therefore, anything that contradicts the Bible is merely a test of our faith in God.
- Anyone who criticizes feminism is sexist.
- Anyone who criticizes capitalism is a Communist.
- Anyone who criticizes the president is a traitor.
- Anyone who thinks Kobe Bryant was better than Michael Jordan doesn't understand basketball; therefore, any opinion they hold about basketball is invalid.

The point of these false us-versus-them dichotomies is to cut off at the knees any reasoning or discussion before your followers start questioning their beliefs. These false us-versus-them dichotomies have the added benefit of always presenting the group with a common enemy.

Common enemies are hugely important. I know we all like to think we'd prefer to live in a world of perfect peace and harmony, but honestly, such a world wouldn't last for more than a few minutes. Common enemies create unity within our religion. Some sort of scapegoat, whether justified or not, is necessary to blame for our pain and maintain our hope.[35] Us-versus-them dichotomies give us the enemies we all desperately crave.

After all, you need to be able to paint a really simple picture for your followers. There are those who get "it" and those who do not get "it." Those who get it are going to save the world. Those who do not get it are going to destroy it. End of discussion. Whatever "it" is depends on whatever belief you're trying to sell—Jesus, Muhammad, libertarianism, gluten-free diets, intermittent fasting, sleeping in hyperbaric chambers and living off Popsicles. Also, it's not enough to tell your followers that nonbelievers are bad. You must demonize them. They are the downfall of everything that is good and holy. They ruin everything. They are fucking *evil*.

You must then convince your followers that it is of the utmost importance that everyone who does not get "it" be stopped, no matter what. People are either near the top of the value hierarchy or at the bottom; there are no in-betweeners in our religion.[36]

The more fear, the better. Lie a little bit if you have to—remember, people instinctually want to feel as though they're fighting a crusade, to believe that they are the holy warriors of justice and truth and salvation. So, say whatever you need to say. Get them to feel that self-righteousness to keep the religion going.

This is where conspiracy theories come in handy. It's not just that vaccines cause autism; it's that the medical and pharmaceutical industries are getting rich by destroying everyone's families. It's not just that pro-choicers have a different view on the biological status of a fetus; it's that they're soldiers sent by Satan to destroy good Christian families. It's not just that climate change is a hoax; it's that it's a hoax created by the Chinese government to slow the U.S. economy and take over the world.[37]

Step Four: Ritual Sacrifice for Dummies—So Easy, Anyone Can Do It!

Growing up in Texas, Jesus and football were the only gods that mattered. And while I learned to enjoy football despite being terrible at it, the whole Jesus thing never made a lot of sense to me. Jesus was alive, but then he died, but then he was alive again, then he died again. And he was a man, but he was also God, and now he's a kind of man-god-spirit-thing that loves everyone eternally (except maybe gay people, depending on whom you ask). It all struck me as kind of arbitrary, and I felt—how do I say this?—like people were just making shit up.

Don't get me wrong: I could get behind most of the moral teachings of Christ: be nice and love your neighbor and all that stuff. Youth groups were actually a ton of fun. (Jesus camp is maybe the most underrated summer activity of all time.) And the church usually had free cookies hiding somewhere, in some room, every Sunday morning, which, when you're a kid, is exciting.

But if I'm being totally honest, I didn't like being a Christian, and I didn't like it for a really dumb reason: my parents made me wear lame dress clothes. That's right. I questioned my family's faith and went atheist at age twelve over kiddie suspenders and bow ties.

I remember asking my dad, "If God already knows everything and loves me no matter what, why does he care what I wear on

Sundays?" Dad would shush me. "But Dad, if God will forgive us our sins no matter what, why not just lie and cheat and steal all the time?" Another shush. "But, Dad—"

The church thing never really panned out for me. I was sneaking Nine Inch Nails T-shirts into Sunday school before my balls had completely dropped, and a couple of years later, I struggled my way through my first Nietzsche book. From there, it was all downhill. I started acting out. I bailed on Sunday school to go smoke cigarettes in the adjoining parking lot. It was over; I was a little heathen.

The open questioning and skepticism eventually got so bad that my Sunday school teacher took me aside one morning and made me a deal: he'd give me perfect marks in our confirmation class and tell my parents I was a model student as long as I stopped questioning the logical inconsistencies of the Bible in front of all the other kids. I agreed.

This probably won't surprise you, but I'm not very spiritual—no supernatural beliefs for me, thank you. I get a sick pleasure from chaos and uncertainty. This, unfortunately, has condemned me to a life of struggle with the Uncomfortable Truth. But it's something I've come to accept about myself.

Now that I'm older, though, I get the whole dress-up-for-Jesus thing. Despite what I thought at the time, it wasn't about my parents (or God) torturing me. It was about respect. And not to God, but to the community, to the religion. Dressing up on Sunday is about virtue-signaling to the other churchgoers, "This Jesus stuff is *serious* business." It's part of the us-versus-them dynamic. It signals that you're an "us" and that you should be treated as such.

And then there are the robes . . . Ever notice that the most important moments in life are always accompanied by somebody in a robe? Weddings, graduations, funerals, court hearings, judicial committee hearings, open heart surgeries, baptisms, and yes, even church sermons.

I first noticed the robe thing when I graduated from college. I was hungover and on about three hours' sleep when I stumbled to my seat for commencement. I looked around and thought, holy shit, I haven't seen this many people wearing robes in one place since I went to church. Then I looked down and, to my horror, realized that I was one of them.

The robe, a visual cue signaling status and importance, is part of the ritual thing. And we need rituals because rituals make our values tangible. You can't think your way toward valuing something. You have to live it. You have to experience it. And one way of making it easier for others to live and experience a value is to make up cute outfits for them to wear and important-sounding words for them to say—in short, to give them rituals. Rituals are visual and experiential representations of what we deem important. That's why every good religion has them.

Remember, emotions *are* actions; the two are one and the same. Therefore, to modify (or reinforce) the Feeling Brain's value hierarchy, you need some easily repeatable yet totally unique and identifiable action for people to perform. That's where the rituals come in.

Rituals are designed to be repeated over a long period of time, which only lends them an even greater sense of importance— after all, it's not often you get to do the exact same thing that people five hundred years ago did. That's some heavy shit. Rituals are also symbolic. As values, they must also embody some story or narrative. Churches have guys in robes dipping bread in wine (or grape juice) and feeding it to a bunch of people to represent the body of Christ. The symbolism represents Christ's sacrifice (he didn't deserve it!) for our salvation (neither do we, but that's why it's powerful!).

Countries create rituals around their founding or around wars they've won (or lost). We march in parades and wave flags and shoot off fireworks and there's a shared sense that it all signifies something valuable and worthwhile. Married couples create their own little rituals and habits, their inside jokes, all to reaffirm their relationship's value, their own private interpersonal religion. Rituals connect us with the past. They connect us to our values. And they affirm who we are.

Rituals are usually about some sacrifice. Back in the old days, priests and chiefs would actually kill people on an altar, sometimes ripping out their still-beating hearts, and people would be screaming and banging on drums and doing all kinds of crazy shit.[38]

These sacrifices were made to appease an angry god, or ensure a good harvest, or bring about any number of other desired outcomes. But the real reason for ritual sacrifice was deeper than that.

Humans are actually horribly guilt-ridden creatures. Let's say you find a wallet with a hundred dollars in it but no ID or any other info about whom it belongs to. No one is around, and you have no clue how to find the owner, so you keep it. Newton's First Law of Emotion states that every action produces an equal and opposite emotional reaction. In this case, something good happens to you without your deserving it. Cue guilt.

Now think of it this way: You exist. You didn't do anything to deserve existing. You don't even know *why* you started existing; you just did. Boom—you have a life. And you have no idea where it came from or why. If you believe God gave it to you, then, holy shit! Do you owe Him big time! But even if you don't believe in God—damn, you're blessed with *life*! What did you ever do to deserve *that*? How can you live in such a way as to make your life worthwhile? This is the constant, yet unanswerable question of the human condition, and why the inherent guilt of consciousness is the cornerstone of almost every spiritual religion.

The sacrifices that pop up in ancient spiritual religions were enacted to give their adherents a feeling of repaying that debt, of living that worthwhile life. Though back in the day, they'd actually sacrifice human beings—a life for a life—eventually, people smartened up and realized that you could *symbolically* sacrifice a life (Jesus's, or whoever's) for the salvation of all mankind. That way, we didn't have to keep cleaning blood off the altar every other day. (And the flies—don't even get me started on the flies.)[39]

Most religious practices are developed for the alleviation of guilt. You could even say that that's really all prayer is: miniature episodes of guilt alleviation. You don't pray to God to say, "Fuck, yeah. I'm awesome!" No. Prayer is like a gratitude journal before there were gratitude journals: "Thanks, God, for letting me exist, even though it sucks to be me sometimes. I'm sorry I thought and did all those bad things." Boom! Sense of guilt absolved, at least for a while.

Ideological religions handle the guilt question far more efficiently than spiritual ones. Nations direct people's feelings of existential guilt toward service—"Our country gave you these opportunities, so put on a damn uniform and fight to protect them." Right-wing ideologies usually perceive necessary sacrifice in terms of protecting one's country and family. Left-wing ideologies usually see necessary sacrifice as giving up for the greater good of all society.

Finally, in interpersonal religions, sacrificing oneself generates a sense of romance and loyalty. (Think about marriage: I mean, you stand at an *altar* and promise to give your life to this other person.) We all struggle with the sense that we deserve to be loved. Even if your parents were awesome, you sometimes wonder, wow, why *me*? What did *I* do to deserve this? Interpersonal religions have all sorts of rituals and sacrifices designed to make people feel they deserve to be loved. Rings, gifts, anniversaries, wiping the piss off the floor when I miss the toilet—it's the little things that add up to one big thing. You're welcome, honey.

Step Five: Promise Heaven, Deliver Hell

If you've made it this far in starting your own religion it means you've assembled a nice group of hopeless people desperately avoiding the Uncomfortable Truth by studying a bunch of bullshit you've made up, ignoring their friends, and telling their families to fuck off.

Now it's time to get serious.

The beauty of a religion is that the more you promise your followers salvation, enlightenment, world peace, perfect happiness, or whatever, the more they will fail to live up to that promise. And the more they fail to live up to that promise, the more they'll blame themselves and feel guilty. And the more they blame themselves and feel guilty, the more they'll do whatever you tell them to do to make up for it.

Some people might call this the cycle of psychological abuse. But let's not allow such terms to ruin our fun.

Pyramid schemes do this really well. You give a scumbag some money for a bunch of products you don't want or need and then you spend the next three months desperately trying to get other people to sign up for the scheme under you and also buy and sell products nobody wants or needs.

And it doesn't work.

Then, instead of recognizing the obvious (the product is one big scam selling a scam to a scam to sell more scams), you blame yourself—because, look, the guy at the top of the pyramid has a *Ferrari*! And *you* want a Ferrari. So, clearly the problem must be *you*, right?

Fortunately, that guy with the Ferrari has graciously agreed to put on a seminar to help you sell more crap nobody wants to people who will then try to sell more crap nobody wants to more people who will sell it . . . and so on.

And at said seminar, most of the time is spent psyching you up with music and chants and creating an us-versus-them dichotomy ("Winners never give up! Losers believe it won't work for them!"), and you come away from the seminar really motivated and pumped, but still with no idea how to sell anything, especially crap nobody wants. And instead of getting pissed off at the money-based religion you've bought into, you get pissed off at yourself. You blame yourself for failing to live up to your God Value, regardless of how ill-advised that God Value is.

You can see this same cycle of desperation play out in all sorts of other areas. Fitness and diet plans, political activism, self-help seminars, financial planning, visiting your grandmother on a holiday—the message is always the same: the more you do it, the more you're told you need to do it to finally experience the satisfaction you've been promised. Yet that satisfaction never comes.

Look, time out for a second. Let me be the one to break the bad news to you: human pain is like a game of Whac-A-Mole. Every time you knock down one kind of pain, another one pops up. And the faster you whack them, the faster they come back.

The pain may get better, it may change shape, it may be less catastrophic each time. But it will always be there. It's part of us.[40]

It *is* us.

A lot of religious spokespeople out there make a lot of money claiming they can beat the pain of the Whac-A-Mole game for you, once and for all. But the truth is that there *is no end to the pain moles.* The faster you hit them, the faster they come back. And that's how all the douche canoes in the religion game stay in business so long: instead of admitting that the game is rigged, that our human nature is fundamentally designed to generate pain, they blame you for not winning the game. Or, worse, they blame some nebulous "them." If we could just get rid of "them," we'd all stop suffering. Pinky swear.[41] But that doesn't work, either. That just transfers the pain from one population to another, and amplifies it.

Because, seriously, if someone really could solve all your problems, they'd go out of business by next Tuesday (or get voted out of office next week). Leaders need their followers to be perpetually dissatisfied; it's good for the leadership business. If everything were perfect and great, there'd be no reason to follow anybody. No religion will ever make you feel blissful and peaceful all the time. No country will ever feel completely fair and safe. No political philosophy will solve everyone's problems all the time. True equality can never be achieved; someone somewhere will always be screwed over. True freedom doesn't really exist because we all must sacrifice some autonomy for stability. No one, no matter how much you love them or they love you, will ever absolve that internal guilt you feel simply for existing. It's all fucked. Everything is fucked. It always has been and always will be. There are no solutions, only stopgap measures, only incremental improvements, only slightly better forms of fuckedness than others. And it's time we stop running from that and, instead, embrace it.[42]

This is our fucked-up world. And we're the fucked-up ones in it.

Step Six: Prophet for Profit!

So, this is it. You've come to the end. You have your religion, and it's time to reap all its benefits. Now that you've got your little following giving you their money and cutting your grass, you can finally have everything you've ever wished for!

Want a dozen sex slaves? Just say the word. Make up scripture. Tell your followers that "Stage Six of Manatee Enlightenment" can only be found in the Prophet's orgasms.

Want a huge piece of land out in the middle of nowhere? Just tell your followers that only you can build paradise for them and it needs to be really far away—oh, and by the way, they need to pay for it.

Want power and prestige? Tell your followers to vote you into office or, even better, overthrow the government with violence. If you do your job well, they should be willing to give up their lives for you.

The opportunities really are endless.

No more loneliness. No more relationship problems. No more financial woes. You can fulfill your wildest dreams. You just have to trample on the hopes and dreams of thousands of other people to get there.

Yes, my friend, you've worked hard for this. Therefore, you deserve all the benefits without any meddlesome social concerns or pedantic arguments about ethics and whatnot. Because that's what you get to do when you start your own religion: *You* get to decide what is ethical. *You* get to decide what is right. And *you* get to decide who is righteous.

Maybe this whole "start a religion" thing makes you squirm. Well, I hate to break it to you, but you're already in one. Whether you realize or not, you've adopted some group's beliefs and values, you participate in the rituals and offer up the sacrifices, you draw the us-versus-them lines and intellectually isolate yourself. This is what we all do. Religious beliefs and their constituent tribal behaviors are a fundamental part of our nature.[43] It's impossible *not* to adopt them. If you think you're above religion, that you use logic and reason, I'm sorry to say, you're wrong: you are one of us.[44] If you think you're well informed and highly educated, you're not: you still suck.[45]

We all must have faith in something. We must find value somewhere. It's how we psychologically survive and thrive. It's how we find hope. And even if you have a vision for a better future, it's too hard to go it alone. To realize any dream, we need support networks, for both emotional and logistical reasons. It takes an army. Literally.

It's our value hierarchies—as expressed through the stories of religion, and shared among thousands or millions—that attract, organize, and propel human systems forward in a sort of Darwinian competition. Religions compete in the world for resources, and the religions that tend to win out are those whose value hierarchies make the most efficient use of labor and capital. And as it wins out, more and more people adopt the winning religion's value hierarchy, as it has demonstrated the most value to individuals in the population. These victorious religions then stabilize and become the foundation for culture.[46]

But here's the problem: Every time a religion succeeds, every time it spreads its message far and wide and comes to dominate a huge swath of human emotion and endeavor, its values change. The religion's God Value no longer comprises the principles that inspired the religion in the first place. Its God Value slowly shifts and becomes the preservation of the religion itself: not to lose what it has gained.

And this is where the corruption begins. When the original values that defined the religion, the movement, the revolution, get tossed aside for the sake of maintaining the status quo, this is narcissism at an organizational level. This is how you go from Jesus to the Crusades, from Marxism to the gulags, from a wedding chapel to divorce court. This corruption of the religion's original values rots away at the religion's following, thus leading to the rising up of newer, reactionary religions that eventually conquer the original one. Then the whole process begins again.

In this sense, success is in many ways far more precarious than failure. First, because the more you gain the more you have to lose, and second, because the more you have to lose, the harder it is to maintain hope. But more important, because by experiencing our hopes, we lose them. We see that our beautiful visions for a perfect future are not so perfect, that our dreams and aspirations are themselves riddled with unexpected flaws and unforeseen sacrifices.

Because the only thing that can ever truly destroy a dream is to have it come true.

CHAPTER 5

Hope Is Fucked

In the late nineteenth century, during a mild and glorious summer in the Swiss Alps, a hermetic philosopher, a self-anointed dynamite of mind and spirit, metaphorically came down off his mountaintop and, with his own money, published a book. The book was his gift to mankind, a gift that stood boldly upon the doorstep of the modern world and announced the words that would make the philosopher famous long after his death.

It announced, "God is dead!"—and more. It announced that the echoes of this death would be the harbinger of a new and dangerous age that would challenge us all.

The philosopher spoke these words as a warning. He spoke as a watchman. He spoke for us all.

Yet, the book sold fewer than forty copies.[1]

Meta von Salis woke before dawn to light the fire to boil water for the philosopher's tea. She fetched ice to cool the blankets for his achy joints. She gathered bones from yesterday's dinner to begin stewing a broth that would settle his stomach. She hand-washed his soiled linens. And soon, he would need his hair cropped and his mustache trimmed, and she realized she had forgotten to fetch a new razor.

This was Meta's third summer caring for Friedrich Nietzsche and probably, she figured, her last. She loved him—as a brother, that is. (When a mutual friend suggested they marry, they both laughed uproariously . . . and then became nauseated.) But Meta was approaching the limits of her charity.

She had met Nietzsche at a dinner party. She listened to him play piano and tell jokes and rambunctious stories of his antics with his old friend, composer Richard Wagner. Unlike in his writing, Nietzsche was polite and mild in person. He was an affectionate listener. He was a lover of poetry and could recite dozens of verses from memory. He'd sit and play word games for hours, sing songs and make puns.

Nietzsche was disarmingly brilliant. A mind so sharp he could slice a room open with only a few words. Aphorisms that would later become world famous seemed to spill out of him like fogged breath in cold air. "Talking too much about yourself can also be a means to conceal yourself," he would spontaneously add, quickly silencing the room.[2]

Meta often found herself speechless in his presence, not because of any overwhelmed emotion, but merely because her mind felt as though it were constantly a few paces behind his and needed a moment to catch up.

Yet, Meta was no intellectual slouch. In fact, she was a badass of her time. Meta was the first woman ever to earn a PhD in Switzerland. She was also one of the world's leading feminist writers and activists. She spoke four languages fluently and published articles all over Europe arguing for women's rights, a radical idea at the time. She was well traveled, brilliant, and headstrong.[3] And when she stumbled upon Nietzsche's work, she felt she had finally found someone whose ideas could push women's liberation out into the world.

Here was a man who argued for the empowerment of the individual, for radical personal responsibility. Here was a man who believed that individual aptitude mattered more than anything, that each human not only deserved expansion into his or her full potential but had the duty to exercise and push for that expansion. Nietzsche put into words, Meta believed, the core ideas and conceptual frameworks that would ultimately empower women and lead them out of their perpetual servitude.

But there was only one problem: Nietzsche wasn't a feminist. In fact, he found the whole idea of women's liberation ridiculous.

This didn't deter Meta. He was a man of reason; he could be persuaded. He simply needed to recognize his own prejudice and be freed from it. She began visiting him regularly, and soon they became close friends and intellectual companions. They spent summers in Switzerland, winters in France and Italy, forays into Venice, quick trips doubling back to Germany and then Switzerland again.

As the years wore on, Meta discovered that behind Nietzsche's penetrating eyes and gigantic mustache was a bundle of contradictions. He wrote obsessively of power while being himself frail and weak. He preached radical responsibility and self-reliance despite being wholly dependent on (mostly female) friends and family to take care of and support him. He cursed the fickle reviewers and academics who panned his work or refused to read it, while simultaneously boasting that his lack of popular success only proved his brilliance—as he once proclaimed, "My time has not come yet, some men are born posthumously."[4]

Nietzsche was, in fact, everything he claimed to loathe: weak, dependent, and wholly captivated and reliant on powerful, independent women. Yet, in his work, he preached individual strength and self-reliance, and was a woeful misogynist. His lifelong dependence on the care of women seemed to blur his ability to see them clearly. It would be the glaring blind spot in the vision of an otherwise prophetic man.

If there were a Hall of Fame for "most pain tolerated by a single individual," I would nominate Nietzsche as one of its first cornerstone inductees. He was continually sick as a child: Doctors applied leeches to his neck and ears and told him to spend hours without moving. He'd inherited a neurological disorder that brought about debilitating migraines throughout his life (and caused him to go mad in middle age). He was also incredibly sensitive to light, unable to go outside without thick blue-tinted glasses, and would be nearly blind by the age of thirty.

As a young man, he would join the military and serve briefly in the Franco-Prussian War. There, he would contract diphtheria and dysentery, which nearly killed him. The treatment at the time was acid enemas, which destroyed his digestive tract. For the rest of his life, he would struggle with acute digestive pain, was never able to eat large meals, and was incontinent for parts of his life. An injury from his cavalry days left parts of his body inflexible and, on his worst days, immovable. He often needed help standing up and would spend months at a time stuck alone in bed, unable to open his eyes due to the pain. In 1880, what he would later call "a bad year," he was bedridden 260 out of 365 days. He spent most of his life migrating between the French coast in the winter and the Swiss Alps in the summer, as he required mild temperatures to keep his bones and joints from aching.

Meta quickly discovered that she wasn't the only intellectual woman fascinated by this man. He had a parade of women coming by to take care of him for weeks or months at a time. Like Meta, these women were badasses of their time: They were professors and wealthy landowners and entrepreneurs. They were educated and multilingual and fiercely independent.

And they were feminists, the earliest feminists.

They, too, had seen the liberating message in Nietzsche's work. He wrote of social structures crippling the individual; feminists argued that the social structures of the age imprisoned them. He denounced the Church for rewarding the weak and mediocre; feminists, too, denounced the Church, for forcing women into marriage and subservience to men. And he dared recast the story of human history not as mankind's escape from and dominance over nature, but as mankind's growing ignorance to its own nature. He argued that the individual must empower himself and access ever-higher levels of freedom and consciousness. These women saw feminism as the next step to that higher liberation.

Nietzsche filled them all with hope, and they took turns caring for this deteriorating, broken man, hopeful that the next book, the next essay, the next polemic, would be the one that broke open the floodgates.

But for most of his life, his work was almost universally ignored.

Then Nietzsche announced the death of God, and he went from failing university professor to pariah. He was unemployable and basically homeless. No one wanted anything to do with him: no university, no publisher, not even many of his friends. He scrounged together money to publish his work himself, borrowing from his mother and sister to survive. He relied on friends to manage his life for him. And even then, his books hardly sold a copy.

Yet, despite it all, these women stuck with him. They cleaned him and fed him and carried him. They believed there was something in this decrepit man that could potentially change history. And so, they waited.

A Brief History of the World, According to Nietzsche

Let's say you drop a bunch of people onto a plot of land with limited resources and have them start a civilization from scratch. Here's what happens:

Some people are naturally more gifted than others. Some are smarter. Some are bigger and stronger. Some are more charismatic. Some are friendly and get along easily with others. Some work harder and come up with better ideas.

The people with natural advantages will accumulate more resources than others. And because they have more resources, they will have a disproportionate amount of power within this new society. They will be able to use that power to garner more resources and more advantages, and so on—you know, the whole "rich get richer" thing. Run this through enough generations, and pretty soon you have a social hierarchy with a small number of elites at the top and a large number of people getting completely hosed at the bottom. Since the advent of agriculture, all human societies have exhibited this stratification, and all societies must deal with the tension that emerges between the advantaged elite and the disadvantaged masses.[5]

Nietzsche called the elite the "masters" of society, as they have almost complete control over wealth, production, and political power. He called the working masses the "slaves" of society because he saw little difference between a laborer working his whole life for a small sum and slavery itself.[6]

Now, here's where it gets interesting. Nietzsche argued that the masters of society would come to see their privilege as well deserved. That is, they would craft value narratives to justify their elite status. Why shouldn't they be rewarded for it? It was *good* they were on top. They deserved it. They were the smartest and strongest and most talented. Therefore, they were the most righteous.

Nietzsche called this belief system, in which those who end up ahead do so because they deserve it, "master morality." Master morality is the moral belief that people get what they deserve. It's the moral belief that "might makes right," that if you earned something through hard work or ingenuity, you deserve it. No one can take that from you; nor should they. You are the best, and because you've demonstrated superiority, you should be rewarded for it.

Conversely, Nietzsche argued, the "slaves" of society would generate a moral code of their own. Whereas the masters believed they were righteous and virtuous because of their *strength*, the slaves of society came to believe that they were righteous and virtuous because of their *weakness*. Slave morality believes that people who have suffered the most, those who are the most disadvantaged and exploited, deserve the best treatment *because* of that suffering. Slave morality believes that it's the poorest and most unfortunate who deserve the most sympathy and the most respect.

Whereas master morality believes in the virtue of strength and dominance, slave morality believes in the virtue of sacrifice and submission. While master morality believes in the necessity of hierarchy, slave morality believes in the necessity of equality. While master morality is generally represented by right-wing political beliefs, slave morality is usually found in left-wing political beliefs.[7]

We all contain both these moralities within us. Imagine you're in a class at school and you study your ass off and get the highest test score. And because you got the highest test score, you're awarded benefits due to your success. You feel morally justified having those benefits; after all, you worked hard and earned them. You are a "good" student and a "good" person for being a good student. This is master morality.

Now imagine that you have a classmate. This classmate has eighteen siblings, all being raised by a single mother. This classmate works multiple part-time jobs and is never able to study because she is literally putting food on the table for her brothers and sisters. She fails the same exam that you passed with flying colors. Is that fair? No, it's not. You would probably feel that she deserves some sort of special exception due to her situation—maybe a chance to retake the test or to take it at a later date, when she has time to study for it. She deserves this because she is a "good" person for her sacrifices and disadvantages. This is slave morality.

In Newtonian terms, master morality is the intrinsic desire to create a moral separation between ourselves and the world around us. It is the desire to create moral gaps with us on top. Slave morality is, then, an intrinsic desire to equalize, to close the moral gap and alleviate suffering. Both are fundamental components of our Feeling Brain's operating system. Both generate and perpetuate strong emotions. And both give us hope.

Nietzsche argued that the cultures of the ancient world (Greek, Roman, Egyptian, Indian, and so on) were master morality cultures. They were structured to celebrate strength and excellence even at the expense of millions of slaves and subjects. They were warrior civilizations; they celebrated guts, glory, and bloodshed. Nietzsche also argued that the Judeo-Christian ethic of charity, pity, and compassion ushered slave morality to prominence, and continued to dominate Western civilization up through his own time. For Nietzsche, these two value hierarchies were in constant tension and opposition. They were, he believed, at the root of all political and social conflict throughout history.

And, he warned, that conflict was about to get much worse.

Each religion is a faith-based attempt to explain reality in such a way that it gives people a steady stream of hope. In a kind of Darwinian competition, those religions that mobilize, coordinate, and inspire their believers the most are those that win out and spread throughout the world.[8]

In the ancient world, pagan religions built on master morality justified the existence of emperors and warrior-kings who swept across the planet, expanding and consolidating territory and people. Then, about two thousand years ago, slave morality religions emerged and slowly began to take their place. These new religions were (usually) monotheistic and were not limited to one nation, race, or ethnic group. They preached their message to everyone because their message was one of equality: all people were either born good and later corrupted or were born sinners and had to be saved. Either way, the result was the same. *Everyone*, regardless of nation, race, or creed, had to be converted in the name of the One True God.[9]

Then, in the seventeenth century, a new religion began to emerge in Europe, a religion that would unleash forces more powerful than anything seen in human history.

Every religion runs into the sticky problem of evidence. You can tell people all this great stuff about God and spirits and angels and whatnot, but if the entire town burns down and your kid loses an arm in a fishing accident, well, then . . . oops. Where was God?

Throughout history, authorities have expended a lot of effort to hide the lack of evidence supporting their religion and/or to punish anyone who dared question the validity of their faith-based values. It's for this reason that, like most atheists, Nietzsche loathed spiritual religions.

Natural philosophers, as scientists were called in Isaac Newton's time, decided that the most reliable faith-based beliefs were those that had the most evidence supporting them. Evidence became the God Value, and any belief that was no longer supported by evidence had to be altered to account for the new observed reality. This produced a new religion: science.

Science is arguably the most effective religion because it is the first religion that is able to evolve and improve upon itself. It is open to anybody and everybody. It is not moored to a single book or creed. It is not beholden to some ancient land or people. It is not tethered to a supernatural spirit whose existence cannot be proven or disproven. It is an ongoing, ever-changing body of evidence-based beliefs, one that is free to mutate, grow, and shift as the evidence dictates.

The scientific revolution changed the world more than anything before or since.[10] It has reshaped the planet, lifted billions out of disease and poverty, and improved every aspect of life.[11] It is not an exaggeration to suggest that science may be the *only* demonstrably good thing humanity has ever done for itself. (Thank you, Francis Bacon, thank you, Isaac Newton, you fucking titans.) Science is singularly responsible for all the greatest inventions and advances in human history, from medicine and agriculture to education and commerce.

But science did something else even more spectacular: it introduced to the world the concept of growth. For most of human history, "growth" wasn't a thing. Change occurred so slowly that everyone died in pretty much the same economic condition they were born in. The average human from two thousand years ago experienced about as much economic growth in his lifetime as we experience in six months today.[12] People would live their entire lives, *and nothing changed*—no new developments, inventions, or technologies. People would live and die on the same land, among the same people, using the same tools, and nothing ever got better. In fact, things like plagues and famine and war and dickhead rulers with large armies often made everything worse. It was a slow, grueling, miserable existence.

And with no prospect for change or a better life in *this* lifetime, people drew their hope from spiritual promises of a better life in the *next* lifetime. Spiritual religions flourished, and dominated daily life. Everything revolved around the Church (or synagogue or temple or mosque or whatever). Priests and holy men were the arbiters of social life because they were the arbiters of hope. They were the only ones who could tell you what God wanted, and God was the only one who could promise any salvation or a better future. Therefore, these holy men dictated everything that was of value in society.

Then science happened, and shit got cray-cray. Microscopes and printing presses and internal combustion engines and cotton gins and thermometers and, finally, some goddamn medicine that actually worked. Suddenly, life got better. More important, you could *see* life getting better. People used better tools, had access to more food, were healthier, and made more money. Finally, you could look back ten years and say, "Whoa! Can you believe we used to live like that?"

And that ability to look back and see progress, see growth happen, changed how people viewed the future. It changed how they viewed themselves. Forever.

Now, you didn't have to wait until death to improve your lot.

You could improve it *here and now*. And this implied all sorts of wonderful things. Freedom, for one: How were you going to *choose* to grow today? But also responsibility: because you could now control your own destiny, you had to take responsibility for that destiny. And of course, equality: because if a big patriarchal God isn't dictating who deserves what, that must mean that either no one deserves anything or everyone deserves everything.

These were concepts that had never been voiced before. With the prospect of so much growth and change in *this* life, people no longer relied on spiritual beliefs about *the next* life to give them hope. Instead, they began to invent and rely upon the ideological religions of their time.

This changed everything. Church doctrines softened. People stayed home on Sundays. Monarchs conceded power to their subjects. Philosophers began to openly question God—and somehow weren't burned alive for doing so. It was a golden age for human thought and progress. And incredibly, the progress begun in that age has only accelerated and continues to accelerate to this day.

The scientific revolution eroded the dominance of spiritual religions and made way for the dominance of ideological religions. And this is what concerned Nietzsche. Because for all of the progress and wealth and tangible benefits that ideological religions produce, they lack something that spiritual religions do not: infallibility.

Once believed in, a supernatural deity is impervious to worldly affairs. Your town could burn down. Your mother could make a million dollars and then lose it all again. You could watch wars and diseases come and go. None of these experiences directly contradicts a belief in a deity, because supernatural entities are evidence-proof. And while atheists see this as a bug, it can also be a feature. The robustness of spiritual religions means that the shit could hit the proverbial fan, and your psychological stability would remain intact. Hope can be preserved because God is always preserved.[13]

Not so with ideologies. If you spend a decade of your life lobbying for certain governmental reform, and then that reform leads to the deaths of tens of thousands of people, that's on you. That piece of hope that sustained you for years is shattered. Your identity, destroyed. Hello darkness, my old friend.

Ideologies, because they're constantly challenged, changed, proven, and then disproven, offer scant psychological stability upon which to build one's hope. And when the ideological foundation of our belief systems and value hierarchies is shaken, it throws us into the maw of the Uncomfortable Truth.

Nietzsche was on top of this before anybody else. He warned of the coming existential malaise that technological growth would bring upon the world. In fact, this was the whole point of his "God is dead" proclamation.

"God is dead" was not some obnoxious atheistic gloating, as it is usually interpreted today. No. It was a lament, a warning, a cry for help. Who are *we* to determine the meaning and significance of our own existence? Who are *we* to decide what is good and right in the world? How can we bear this burden?

Nietzsche, understanding that existence is inherently chaotic and unknowable, believed that we were not psychologically equipped to handle the task of explaining our cosmic significance. He saw the spate of ideological religions that spewed forth in the Enlightenment's wake (democracy, nationalism, communism, socialism, colonialism, etc.) as merely postponing the inevitable existential crisis of mankind. And he hated them *all*. He found democracy to be naïve, nationalism stupid, communism appalling, colonialism offensive.[14]

Because, in a kind of backward Buddhist way, Nietzsche believed that any worldly attachment—to gender, race, ethnicity, nationality, or history—was a mirage, a make-believe faith-based construct designed to suspend us high over the chasm of the Uncomfortable Truth by a thin rope of meaning. And ultimately, he believed that all these constructs were destined to conflict with one another and cause far more violence than they solved.[15]

Nietzsche predicted coming conflicts between the ideologies built on master and slave moralities.[16] He believed that these conflicts would wreak greater destruction upon the world than anything else seen in human history. He predicted that this destruction would not be limited to national borders or different ethnic groups. It would transcend all borders; it would transcend country and people. Because these conflicts, these wars, would not be *for* God. They would be *between* gods.

And the gods would be us.

Pandora's Box

In Greek mythology, the world started out with only men.[17] Everyone drank a lot and didn't do any work. It was one big, everlasting frat party. The ancient Greeks called this "paradise." But if you ask me, it sounds like a special kind of hell.

The gods, recognizing that this was a fairly boring state of affairs, decided to spice up the situation a bit. They wanted to create a companion for mankind, someone who would command the men's attention, someone who would introduce complication and uncertainty to the easy life of shotgunning beer cans and playing foosball all night.

So, they decided to create the first woman.

For this project, every one of the major gods helped out. Aphrodite gave her beauty. Athena gave her wisdom. Hera gave her the ability to create a family. Hermes gave her charismatic speech. On and on, the gods installed gifts and talents and intrigues into woman like apps in a new iPhone.

The result was Pandora.

The gods sent Pandora to earth to introduce competition and sex and babies and arguments about the toilet seat. But the gods did something else, too: they sent her with a box. It was a beautiful box, embossed in gold and covered in intricate and delicate designs. The gods told Pandora to give the box to men, but also instructed her that it could never be opened.

Spoiler alert: people suck. Somebody opened Pandora's box— surprise, surprise, the men would all blame the woman for it— and out flew all the evils into the world: death, disease, hatred, envy, and Twitter. The bucolic sausage party was no more. Now men could kill each other. And, more important, now men had something to kill each other *for*: women, and the resources that attracted women. Thus, began the stupid dick-measuring contest also known as human history.

Wars started. Kingdoms and rivalries arose. Slavery happened. Emperors started conquering one another, leaving hundreds of thousands slaughtered in their wake. Entire cities were built and then destroyed. Meanwhile, women were treated as property, traded and bartered among the men like fancy goats or something.[18]

Basically, humans started being humans.

Everything appeared to be fucked. But in the bottom of that box there remained something shiny and beautiful.

There remained hope.

There are many interpretations of the Pandora's box myth, the most common being that while the gods punished us with all the evils of the world, they also equipped us with the one antidote to those evils: hope. Think of it as the yin and the yang of mankind's eternal struggle: everything is always fucked, but the more fucked things become, the more we must mobilize hope to sustain and overcome the world's fuckedness. This is why heroes such as Witold Pilecki inspire us: their ability to muster enough hope to resist evil reminds us that all of us are capable of resisting evil.

The sickness may spread, but so does the cure, because hope is contagious. Hope is what saves the world.

But here's another, less popular interpretation of the Pandora's box myth: What if hope is not the antidote to evil? What if hope is just another form of evil? What if hope just got left in the box?[19]

Because hope didn't just inspire Pilecki's heroics. Hope also inspired the Communist revolutions and the Nazi genocides. Hitler *hoped* to exterminate the Jews to bring about an evolutionarily superior human race. The Soviets *hoped* to instigate a global revolution to unite the world in true equality under communism. And let's be honest, most of the atrocities committed by the Western, capitalist societies over the past one hundred years were done in the name of hope: hope for greater global economic freedom and wealth.

Like a surgeon's scalpel, hope can save a life, and hope can take a life. It can uplift us, and it can destroy us. Just as there are healthy and damaging forms of confidence, and healthy and damaging forms of love, there are also healthy and damaging forms of hope. And the difference between the two is not always clear.

So far, I've argued that hope is fundamental to our psychology, that we need to (a) have something to look forward to, (b) believe ourselves in control of our fate enough to achieve that something, and (c) find a community to achieve it with us. When we lack one or all of these for too long, we lose hope and spiral into the void of the Uncomfortable Truth.

Experiences generate emotions. Emotions generate values. Values generate narratives of meaning. And people who share similar narratives of meaning come together to generate religions. The more effective (or affective) a religion, the more industrious and disciplined the adherents. And the more industrious and disciplined the adherents, the more likely the religion is to spread to other people, to give them a sense of self-control and a feeling of hope. These religions grow and expand and eventually define in-groups versus out-groups, create rituals and taboos, and spur conflict between groups with opposing values. *These conflicts must exist because they maintain the meaning and purpose for people within the group.*

Therefore, it is the conflict that maintains the hope.

So, we've got it backward: everything being fucked doesn't require hope; hope requires everything being fucked.

The sources of hope that give our lives a sense of meaning are the same sources of division and hate. The hope that brings the most joy to our lives is the same hope that brings the greatest danger. The hope that brings people closest together is often the same hope that tears them apart.

Hope is, therefore, destructive. Hope depends on the rejection of *what currently is.*

Because hope requires that something be broken. Hope requires that we renounce a part of ourselves and/or a part of the world. It requires us to be anti-*something.*

This paints an unbelievably bleak picture of the human condition. It means that our psychological makeup is such that our only choices in life are either perpetual conflict or nihilism—tribalism or isolation, religious war or the Uncomfortable Truth.

Nietzsche believed that none of the ideologies generated by the scientific revolution would hold up in the long run. He believed that, one by one, they would slowly kill each other off and/or collapse from within. Then, after a couple of centuries, the real existential crisis would begin. Master morality would have been corrupted. Slave morality would have imploded. We would have failed ourselves. For human frailties are such that everything we produce must be impermanent and unreliable.

Nietzsche instead believed that we must look beyond hope. We must look beyond values. We must evolve into something "beyond good and evil." For him, this morality of the future had to begin with something he called *amor fati*, or "love of one's fate": "My formula for greatness in a human being," he wrote, "is *amor fati*: that one wants nothing to be different, not forward, not backward, not in all eternity. Not merely bear what is necessary, still less conceal it—all idealism is mendacity in the face of what is necessary—but love it."[20]

Amor fati, for Nietzsche, meant the unconditional acceptance of all life and experience: the highs and the lows, the meaning and the meaninglessness. It meant loving one's pain, embracing one's suffering. It meant closing the separation between one's desires and reality not by striving for more desires, but by simply desiring reality.

It basically meant: hope for nothing. Hope for what *already* is—because hope is ultimately empty. Anything your mind can conceptualize is fundamentally flawed and limited and therefore damaging if worshipped unconditionally. Don't hope for more happiness. Don't hope for less suffering. Don't hope to improve your character. Don't hope to eliminate your flaws.

Hope for *this*. Hope for the infinite opportunity and oppression present in every single moment. Hope for the suffering that comes with freedom. For the pain that comes from happiness. For the wisdom that comes from ignorance. For the power that comes from surrender.

And then act *despite* it.

This is our challenge, our calling: To act without hope. To not hope for better. To *be* better. In this moment and the next. And the next. And the next.

Everything is fucked. And hope is both the cause and the effect of that fuckedness.

This is hard to swallow, because weaning ourselves off the sweet nectar of hope is like pulling a bottle away from a drunk. Without it, we believe we'll fall back into the void and be swallowed by the abyss. The Uncomfortable Truth frightens us, and so we spin stories and values and narratives and myths and legends about ourselves and the world to keep *that truth* at bay.

But the only thing that frees us *is* that truth: You and I and everyone we know will die, and little to nothing that we do will ever matter on a cosmic scale. And while some people fear that this truth will liberate them from all responsibility, that they'll go snort an eight ball of cocaine and play in traffic, the reality is that this truth scares them because it liberates them *to responsibility*. It means that there's no reason to *not* love ourselves and one another. That there's no reason to *not* treat ourselves and our planet with respect. That there's no reason to *not* live every moment of our lives as though it were to be lived in eternal recurrence.[21]

The second half of this book is an attempt to understand what a life without hope might look like. The first thing I'll say is that it's not as bad as you think. In fact, I believe it is better than the alternative.

The second half of this book is also an honest look at the

modern world and everything that is fucked with it. It's an evaluation done in the hope not of fixing it, but of coming to love it.

Because we must break out of our cycle of religious conflict. We must emerge from our ideological cocoons. We must let the Feeling Brain feel, but deny it the stories of meaning and value that it so desperately craves. We must stretch beyond our conception of good and evil. We must learn to love what *is*.

Amor Fati

It was Meta's last day in Sils Maria, Switzerland, and she planned to spend as much of it as she could outdoors.

Friedrich's favorite walk was around the east bank of Lake Silvaplana, half a kilometer from town. The lake was a shimmering, crystalline thing this time of year, wreathed by the mountains on a horizon pulverized by white peaks. It was on walks around this lake that he and Meta had first bonded four summers ago. This was how she wanted to spend her last day with him. This was how she wanted to remember him.

They left shortly after breakfast. The sun was perfect, and the air was silky. She led, and he hobbled along behind her with his walking stick. They passed barns and fields of cattle and a small sugar beet farm. Friedrich joked that the cows would be his most intellectual companions once Meta left. The two laughed and sang and picked walnuts as they went.

They stopped and ate around noon, beneath a larch tree. It was then that Meta began to worry. They had come far in their excitement. Much farther than she had anticipated. And now she could see that Friedrich was struggling, both physically and mentally, to keep it together.

The walk back was arduous for him. He dragged noticeably

now. And the reality of her leaving the next morning fell over them like an ominous moon, a pall upon their words.

He had grown grumpy, and achy. The stops were frequent. And he began muttering to himself.

Not like this, Meta thought. She didn't want to leave him like this, but she must.

It was late afternoon by the time they approached the village. The sun was waning, and the air was now a burden. Friedrich lagged by a good twenty meters, yet Meta knew the only way to get him all the way home was by *not* stopping for him.

They passed the same sugar beet farm, the same barn and the same cattle, his new companions.

"What was that?" Friedrich shouted. "Where has God gone, you say?"

Meta turned around and knew what she would find before she even saw it: Friedrich, walking stick waving in the air, shouting maniacally at a small group of cows chewing in front of him.

"I shall tell you," he said, breathing heavily. He raised his stick and gestured to the mountains around. "*We have killed him*—you and I! We are his murderers. But how have we done this?"

The cows chewed placidly. One swatted a fly with its tail.

"How were we able to drink up the seas? Who gave *us* the sponge to wipe away the horizon? What did we do when we unchained the earth from its sun? Are we not perpetually falling in all directions? Are we not straying as though through some Infinite nothing?"[22]

"Friedrich, this is silly," Meta said, trying to grab his sleeve and pull him along. But he yanked his arm away; there was madness in his eyes.[23]

"Where is God? *God is Dead*. God remains dead. And we have killed him," he declared.

"Please, stop this nonsense, Friedrich. Come on, let's go to the house."

"How shall we comfort ourselves, the murderers of all murderers? What was holiest and mightiest of all has bled to death under our knives: who will wipe this blood off us?"

Meta shook her head. It was no use. This was it. This was how it would end. She began to walk away.

"What water is there for us to clean ourselves? What festivals of atonement, what sacred games shall we have to invent? Is not the greatness of this deed too great for us? Must we ourselves not become gods simply to appear worthy of it?"

Silence. A moo rang out in the distance.

"Man is a rope, tied between beast and Superman—a rope over an abyss. What is great in man is that he is a bridge and not a goal: what can be loved in man is that he is an overture [to something greater.]"[24]

The words struck her. She turned and locked her gaze on his. It was this idea of man being an overture to something greater that had drawn her to Nietzsche so many years ago. It was this thought that had intellectually seduced her, because, for her, feminism and women's liberation (her ideological religion) were that "something greater." But, she realized, to Nietzsche, it was simply another construct, another conceit, another human failure, another dead god.

Meta would go on and do great things. In Germany and Austria, she would organize marches for women's suffrage—and achieve it. She would inspire thousands of women worldwide to stand up for their own god projects, for their own redemption, their own liberation. She would quietly, anonymously, change the world. She would liberate and free more human beings than Nietzsche and most other "great" men, yet she would do this from the shadows, from the backstage of history. Indeed, today, she is known mostly for being the friend of Friedrich Nietzsche—not as a star of women's liberation, but as a supporting character in a play about a man who correctly prophesized a hundred years of ideological destruction. Like a hidden thread, she would hold the world together, despite being barely seen and quickly forgotten.

She would go on, though. She knew she would. She must go on and attempt to cross the abyss, as we all must do; to live for others despite still not knowing how to live for herself.

"Meta," Nietzsche said.

"Yes?"

"I love those who do not know how to live," he said. "For they are the ones who cross over."

Part II:

EVERY
THING
IS
FUCKED

CHAPTER 6

The Formula of Humanity

Depending on your perspective, the philosopher Immanuel Kant was either the most boring person who ever lived or a productivity hacker's wet dream. For forty years he woke up every morning at five o'clock and wrote for exactly three hours. He would then lecture at the same university for exactly four hours, and then eat lunch at the same restaurant every day. Then, in the afternoon, he would go on an extended walk through the same park, on the same route, leaving and returning home at the exact same time. He did this for forty years. Every. Single. Day.[1]

Kant was efficiency personified. He was so mechanical in his habits, that his neighbors joked that they could set their clocks by when he left his apartment. He would depart for his daily walk at three thirty in the afternoon, have dinner with the same friend most evenings, and after working some more, would go to bed at exactly ten every night.

Despite sounding like a colossal bore, Kant was one of the most important and influential thinkers in world history. And from his single-room apartment in Königsberg, Prussia, he did more to steer the world than most kings, presidents, prime ministers, or generals before and since.

If you're living in a democratic society that protects individual freedoms, you have Kant partially to thank for that. He was one of the first to argue that *all* people have an inherent dignity that must be regarded and respected.[2] He was the first person ever to envision a global governing body that could guarantee peace across much of the world (an idea that would eventually inspire the formation of the United Nations).[3] His descriptions of how we perceive space and time would later help inspire Einstein's discovery of the theory of relativity.[4] He was one of the first to suggest the possibility of animal rights.[5] He reinvented the philosophy of aesthetics and beauty.[6] He resolved the two-hundred-year-old philosophical debate between rationalism and empiricism in the span of a couple of hundred pages.[7] And as if all that weren't enough, he reinvented moral philosophy, from top to bottom, overthrowing ideas that had been the basis of Western civilization since Aristotle.[8]

Kant was an intellectual powerhouse. If Thinking Brains had biceps, Kant's Thinking Brain was the Mr. Olympia of the intellectual universe.

As with his lifestyle, Kant was rigid and uncompromising in his view of the world. He believed that there was a clear right and wrong, a value system that transcended and operated outside any human emotions or Feeling Brain judgments.[9] Moreover, he lived what he preached. Kings tried to censor him; priests condemned him; academics envied him. Yet none of this slowed him down.

Kant didn't give a fuck. And I mean that in the truest and profoundest sense of the phrase.[10] He is the only thinker I have ever come across who eschewed hope and the flawed human values it relied upon; who confronted the Uncomfortable Truth and refused to accept its horrible implications; who gazed into the abyss with nothing but logic and pure reason; who, armed with only the brilliance of his mind, stood before the gods and challenged them . . .

. . . and somehow won.[11]

But to understand Kant's Herculean struggle, first we must take a detour, and learn about psychological development, maturity, and adulthood.[12]

How to Grow Up

When I was, like, four years old, despite my mother warning me not to, I put my finger on a hot stove. That day, I learned an important lesson: Really hot things suck. They burn you. And you want to avoid touching them ever again.

Around the same time, I made another important discovery: ice cream was stored in the freezer, on a shelf that could be easily accessed if I stood on my tippy toes. One day, while my mother was in the other room (poor Mom), I grabbed the ice cream, sat on the floor, and proceeded to gorge myself using my bare hands.

It was the closest I would come to an orgasm for another ten years. If there was a heaven in my little four-year-old mind, I had just found it: my own little Elysium in a bucket of congealed divinity. As the ice cream began to melt, I smeared an extra helping across my face, letting it dribble all over my shirt. This was all happening in slow motion, of course. I was practically bathing in that sweet, tasty goodness. *Oh yes, glorious sugary milk, share with me your secrets, for today I shall know greatness.*

Then Mom walked in—and all hell broke loose, which included but was not limited to a much-needed bath.

I learned a couple of lessons that day. One, stealing ice cream and then dumping it all over yourself and the kitchen floor makes your mother extremely angry. And two, angry mothers suck; they scold you and punish you. That day, much like the day with the hot stove, I learned what *not* to do.

But there was a third, meta-lesson being taught here, one of those lessons that are so obvious we don't even notice when they happen, a lesson that was far more important than the other lessons: eating ice cream is better than being burned.

This lesson was important because it was a value judgment. *Ice cream is better than hot stoves. I prefer sugary sweetness in my mouth than a bit of fire on my hand.* It was the discovery of preference and, therefore, prioritization. It was my Feeling Brain's decision that one thing in the world was better than another, the construction of my early value hierarchy.

A friend of mine once described parenthood as "basically just following around a kid for a couple decades and making sure he doesn't accidentally kill himself—and you'd be amazed how many ways a kid can find to accidentally kill himself."

Young children are always looking for new ways to accidentally kill themselves because the driving force behind their psychology is exploration. Early in life, we are driven to explore the world around us because our Feeling Brains are collecting information on what pleases and harms us, what feels good and bad, what is worth pursuing further and what is worth avoiding. We're building up our value hierarchy, figuring out what our first and primary values are, so that we can begin to know what to hope for.[13]

Eventually, the exploratory phase exhausts itself. And not because we run out of world to explore. Actually, it's the opposite: the exploratory phase wraps up because as we become older, we begin to recognize that there's *too much* world to explore. You can't touch and taste everything. You can't meet all the people. You can't see all the things. There's too much potential experience, and the sheer magnitude of our own existence overwhelms and intimidates us.

Therefore, our two brains begin to focus less on trying every-thing and more on developing some rules to help us navigate the endless complexity of the world before us. We adopt most of these rules from our parents and teachers, but many of them we figure out for ourselves. For instance, after fucking around near open flames enough, you develop a little mental rule that *all* flames are dangerous, not just the stove ones. And after seeing Mom get pissed off enough times, you begin to figure out that raiding the freezer and stealing dessert is *always* bad, not just when it's ice cream.[14]

As a result, some general principles begin to emerge in our minds: take care around dangerous things so you won't get hurt; be honest with your parents and they'll treat you well; share with your siblings and they'll share with you.

These new values are more sophisticated because they're ab-stract. You can't point to "fairness" or draw a picture of "prudence." The little kid thinks, ice cream is awesome; therefore, I want ice cream. But the adolescent thinks, ice cream is awesome, but steal-ing stuff pisses my parents off and I'll get punished; therefore, I'm *not* going to take the ice cream from the freezer. The adolescent applies if/then rules to her decision making, thinking through cause-and-effect chains in a way that a young child cannot.

As a result, an adolescent learns that strictly pursuing her own pleasure and avoiding pain often creates problems. Actions have consequences. You must negotiate your desires with the desires of those around you. You must play by the rules of society and authority, and then, more often than not, you'll be rewarded.

This is maturity in action: developing higher-level and more abstract values to enhance decision making in a wider range of contexts. This is how you adjust to the world, how you learn to handle the seemingly infinite permutations of experience. It is a

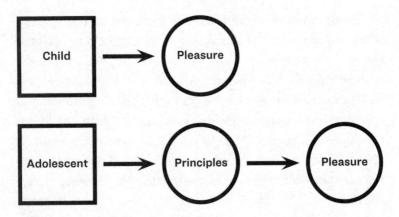

Figure 6.1: A child thinks only about his own pleasure, whereas an adolescent learns to navigate rules and principles to achieve her goals.

major cognitive leap for children and fundamental to growing up in a healthy, happy way.

Young children are like little tyrants.[15] They struggle to conceive of anything in life beyond what is immediately pleasurable or painful for them at any given moment. They cannot feel empathy. They cannot imagine what life is like in your shoes. All they know is that they want some fucking ice cream.[16]

A young child's identity is therefore very small and fragile. It is constituted by simply what gives pleasure and what avoids pain. Susie likes chocolate. She is afraid of dogs. She enjoys coloring. She is often mean to her brother. This is the extent of Susie's identity because her Thinking Brain has not yet developed enough meaning to create coherent stories for her. It's only when she's old enough to ask what the pleasure is *for*, what the pain is *for*, that she can develop some meaningful narratives for herself, and establish identity.

The knowledge of pleasure and pain is still there in adolescence. It's just that pleasure and pain no longer dictate most decision making.[17] They are no longer the basis of our values. Older children weigh their personal feelings against their understanding of rules, trade-offs, and the social order around them to plan and make decisions. This gives them larger, sturdier identities.[18]

The adolescent does the same stumbling around the young child does in learning what is pleasurable and what is painful, except the adolescent stumbles around by trying on different social rules and roles. If I wear this, will it make me cool? If I talk like that, will it make people like me? If I pretend to enjoy this music, will I be popular?[19]

This is an improvement, but there's still a weakness in this adolescent approach to life. Everything is seen as a trade-off. Adolescents approach life as an endless series of bargains: I will do what my boss says so I can get money. I will call my mother so I don't get yelled at. I will do my homework so I don't fuck up my future. I will lie and pretend to be nice so I don't have to deal with conflict.

Nothing is done for its own sake. Everything is a calculated transaction, usually made out of fear of the negative repercussions. Everything is a *means* to some pleasurable end.[20]

The problem with adolescent values is that if you hold them, you never actually stand for something outside yourself. You are still at heart a child, albeit a cleverer and much more sophisticated child. Everything still revolves around maximizing pleasure and minimizing pain, it's just that the adolescent is savvy enough to think a few moves ahead to get there.

In the end, adolescent values are self-defeating. You can't live your entire life this way, otherwise you're never actually living your own life. You're merely living out an aggregation of the desires of the people around you.

To become an emotionally healthy individual, you must break

out of this constant bargaining, endlessly treating everyone as a means to some pleasurable end, and come to understand even higher and more abstract guiding principles.

How to Be an Adult

When you google "how to be an adult," most of the results focus on preparing for job interviews, managing your finances, cleaning up after yourself, and not being a total asshole. These things are all great, and indeed, they are all things that adults are expected to do. But I would argue that, by themselves, they do not make you an adult. They simply prevent you from being a child, which is not the same thing.

That's because most people who do these things do them because they are rule- and transaction-based. They are a means to some superficial end. You prepare for a job interview because you want to get a good job. You learn how to clean your house because its level of cleanliness has direct consequences on what people think of you. You manage your finances because if you don't, you will be royally fucked one day down the road. Bargaining with rules and the social order allows us to be well-functioning human beings in the world.

Eventually, though, we realize that the most important things in life cannot be gained through bargaining. You don't want to bargain with your father for love, or your friends for companionship, or your boss for respect. Bargaining with people into loving or respecting you feels shitty. It undermines the whole project. If you have to convince someone to love you, then they don't love you. If you have to cajole someone into respecting you, then they will never respect you. If you have to convince someone to trust you, then they won't actually trust you.

The most precious and important things in life are, by definition, nontransactional. And to try to bargain for them is to immediately destroy them. You cannot conspire for happiness; it is impossible. But this is often what people try to do, especially when they seek out self-help and other personal development advice—they are essentially saying, "Show me the rules of the game I have to play, and I'll play it," not realizing that it's the very fact that they think there are rules to happiness that is preventing them from being happy.[21]

While people who navigate life through bargaining and rules can get far in the *material* world, they remain crippled and alone in their *emotional* world. This is because transactional values create relationships that are built upon manipulation.

Adulthood is the realization that sometimes an abstract principle is right and good for its own sake, that even if it hurts you today, even if it hurts others, being honest is still the right thing to do. In the same way that the adolescent realizes there's more to the world than the child's pleasure or pain, the adult realizes that there's more to the world than the adolescent's constant bargaining for validation, approval, and satisfaction. Becoming an adult is therefore developing the ability to do what is right for the simple reason that it is right.

An adolescent will say that she values honesty only because she has learned that saying so produces good results. But when confronted with difficult conversations, she will tell white lies, exaggerate the truth, and become passive-aggressive. An adult will be honest for the simple sake that honesty is more important than her own pleasure or pain. Honesty is more important than getting what you want or achieving a goal. Honesty is inherently good and valuable, in and of itself. Honesty is therefore an *end*, not a means to some other end.

An adolescent will say he loves you, but his conception of love is that he is getting something in return, that love is merely an emotional swap meet, where you each bring everything you have to offer and haggle with each other for the best deal. An adult will love freely without expecting anything in return because an adult understands that that is the only thing that can make love real. An adult will give without seeking anything in return, because to do so defeats the purpose of a gift in the first place.

The principled values of adulthood are unconditional—that is, they cannot be reached through any other means. They are ends in and of themselves.[22]

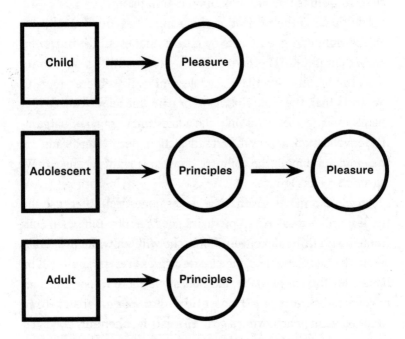

Figure 6.2: An adult is able to eschew his own pleasure for the sake of his principles.

There are plenty of grown-ass children in the world. And there are a lot of aging adolescents. Hell, there are even some young adults out there. That's because, past a certain point, maturity has nothing to do with age.[23] What matters are a person's *intentions*. The difference between a child, an adolescent, and an adult is not how old they are or what they do, but *why* they do something. The child steals the ice cream because it feels good, and he is oblivious or indifferent to the consequences. The adolescent doesn't steal because he knows it will create worse consequences in the future, but his decision is ultimately a bargain with his future self: I'll forgo some pleasure now to prevent greater future pain.[24]

But it's only the adult who doesn't steal for the simple principle that stealing is wrong. And to steal, even if she gets away with it, would make her feel worse about herself.[25]

Why We Don't Grow

When we are little kids, the way we learn to transcend the pleasure/pain values ("ice cream is good; hot stoves are bad") is by pursuing those values and seeing how they fail us. It's only by experiencing the pain of their failure that we learn to transcend them.[26] We steal the ice cream, Mom gets pissed off and punishes us. Suddenly, "ice cream is good" doesn't seem as straightforward as it used to—there are all sorts of other factors to consider. I like ice cream. And I like Mom. But taking the ice cream will upset Mom. What do I do? Eventually, the child is forced to reckon with the fact that there are trade-offs that must be negotiated.

This is essentially what good early parenting boils down to: implementing the correct consequences for a child's pleasure/pain-driven behavior. Punish them for stealing ice cream; reward them for sitting quietly in a restaurant. You are helping them understand that life is far more complicated than their own impulses or desires. Parents who fail to do this fail their children in an incredibly fundamental way because it won't take long for the child to have the shocking realization that the world does not cater to his whims. Learning this as an adult is incredibly painful—far more painful than it would have been had the child learned the lesson when he was younger. He will be socially punished by his peers and society for not understanding it. Nobody wants to be friends with a selfish brat. No one wants to work with someone who doesn't consider others' feelings or appreciate rules. No society accepts someone who metaphorically (or literally) steals the ice cream from the freezer. The untaught child will be shunned, ridiculed, and punished for his behavior in the adult world, which will result in even more pain and suffering.

Parents can fail their children in another way: they can abuse them.[27] An abused child also does not develop beyond his pain- and pleasure-driven values because his punishment follows no logical pattern and doesn't reinforce deeper, more abstract values. Instead of predictable failures, his experience is just random and cruel. Stealing ice cream sometimes results in overly harsh punishment. At other times, it results in no consequences at all. Therefore, no lesson is learned. No higher values are produced. No development takes place. The child never learns to control his own behavior and develops coping mechanisms to deal with the incessant pain. This is why children who are abused and children who are coddled often end up with the same issues when they become adults: they remain stuck in their childhood value system.[28]

Ultimately, graduating to adolescence requires trust. A child must trust that her behavior will produce predictable outcomes. Stealing always creates bad outcomes. Touching a hot stove also creates bad outcomes. Trusting in these outcomes is what allows the child to develop rules and principles around them. The same is true once the child grows older and enters society. A society without trustworthy institutions or leaders cannot develop rules and roles. Without trust, there are no reliable principles to dictate decisions, therefore everything devolves back into childish selfishness.[29]

People get stuck in the adolescent stage of values for similar reasons that they get stuck with childish values: trauma and/or neglect. Victims of bullying are a particularly notable example. A person who has been bullied in his younger years will move through the world with an assumed understanding that no one will ever like or respect him unconditionally, that all affection must be hard-won through a series of practiced conversation and canned actions. You must dress a certain way. You must speak a certain way. You must act a certain way—or else.[30]

Some people become incredibly good at playing the bargaining game. They tend to be charming and charismatic and are naturally able to sense what other people want of them and to fill that role. This manipulation rarely fails them in any meaningful way, so they come to believe that this is simply how the whole world operates. Life is one big high school gymnasium, and you must shove people into lockers lest ye be shoved first.

Adolescents need to be shown that bargaining is a never-ending treadmill, that the only things in life of real value and meaning are achieved without conditions, without transactions. It requires good parents and teachers not to succumb to the adolescent's bargaining. The best way to do this is by example, of course, by showing unconditionality by being unconditional yourself. The best way to teach an adolescent to trust is to trust him. The best way to teach an adolescent respect is to respect him. The best way to teach someone to love is by loving him. And you don't force the love or trust or respect on him—after all, that would make those things conditional—you simply give them, understanding that at some point, the adolescent's bargaining will fail and he'll understand the value of unconditionality when he's ready.[31]

When parents and teachers fail, it's usually because they themselves are stuck at an adolescent level of values. They, too, see the world in transactional terms. They, too, bargain love for sex, loyalty for affection, respect for obedience. In fact, they likely bargain with their kids for affection, love, or respect. They think this is normal, so the kid grows up thinking it's normal. And the shitty, shallow, transactional parent/child relationship is then replicated when the kid goes out and forms relationships in the world, because *he* then becomes a teacher or parent and imparts his adolescent values on children, causing the whole mess to continue for another generation.

Once older, adolescent-minded people will move through the world assuming that all human relationships are a never-ending trade agreement, that intimacy is no more than a feigned sense of knowing the other person for the mutual benefit of each one, that everyone is a means to some selfish end. And instead of recognizing that their problems are rooted in the transactional approach to the world itself, they will assume that the only problem is that it took them so long to do the transactions correctly.

It's difficult to act unconditionally. You love someone knowing you may not be loved in return, but you do it anyway. You trust someone even though you realize you might get hurt or screwed over. That's because to act unconditionally requires some degree of faith—faith that it's the right thing to do even if it results in more pain, even if it doesn't work out for you or the other person.

Making the leap of faith into a virtuous adulthood requires not just an ability to endure pain, but also the courage to abandon hope, to let go of the desire for things always to be better or more pleasant or a ton of fun. Your Thinking Brain will tell you that this is illogical, that your assumptions must inevitably be wrong in some way. Yet, you do it anyway. Your Feeling Brain will procrastinate and freak out about the pain of brutal honesty, the vulnerability that comes with loving someone, the fear that comes from humility. Yet, you do it anyway.

	CHILDHOOD	ADOLESCENCE	ADULTHOOD
VALUES	Pleasure/pain	Rules and roles	Virtues
SEES RELATIONSHIPS AS...	Power struggles	Performances	Vulnerability
SELF-WORTH	Narcissistic: wide swings between "I'm the best" and "I'm the worst"	Other-dependent: externally validated	Independent: largely internally validated
MOTIVATION	Self-aggrandizement	Self-acceptance	*Amor fati*
POLITICS	Extremist/nihilist	Pragmatic, ideological	Pragmatic, nonideological
IN ORDER TO GROW, HE/SHE NEEDS...	Trustworthy institutions and dependable people	Courage to let go of outcomes and faith in unconditional acts	Consistent self-awareness

Adult behaviors are ultimately seen as admirable and noteworthy. It's the boss who takes the fall for his employees' mistakes, the mother who gives up her own happiness for her child's, the friend who tells you what you need to hear even though it upsets you.

It's these people who hold the world together. Without them, we'd all likely be fucked.

It's no coincidence, then, that all the world's great religions push people toward these unconditional values, whether it's the unconditional forgiveness of Jesus Christ or the Noble Eightfold Path of the Buddha or the perfect justice of Muhammad. In their purest forms, the world's great religions leverage our human instinct for hope to try to pull people upward toward adult virtues.[32]

Or, at least, that's usually the original intention.

Unfortunately, as they grow, religions inevitably get co-opted by transactional adolescents and narcissist children, people who pervert the religious principles for their own personal gain. *Every* human religion succumbs to this failure of moral frailty at some point. No matter how beautiful and pure its doctrines, it ultimately becomes a human institution, and all human institutions eventually become corrupted.

Enlightenment philosophers, excited by the opportunities afforded the world by growth, decided to remove the spirituality from religion and get the job done with ideological religion. They jettisoned the idea of virtue and instead focused on measurable, concrete goals: creating greater happiness and less suffering; giving people greater personal liberties and freedoms; and promoting compassion, empathy, and equality.

And these ideological religions, like the spiritual religions before them, also caved to the flawed nature of all human institutions. When you attempt to barter for happiness, you destroy happiness. When you try to enforce freedom, you negate freedom. When you try to create equality, you undermine equality.

None of these ideological religions confronted the fundamental issue at hand: conditionality. They either didn't admit to or didn't deal with the fact that whatever you make your God Value, you will always be willing, at some point, to bargain away human life in order to get closer to it. Worshipping some supernatural God, some abstract principle, some bottomless desire, when pursued long enough, will always result in giving up your own humanity or the humanity of others in order to achieve the aims of that worship. And what was supposed to save you from suffering then plunges you back into suffering. The cycle of hope-destruction begins anew.

And this is where Kant comes in . . .

The One Rule for Life

Early in his life, Kant understood the Whac-A-Mole game of maintaining hope in the face of the Uncomfortable Truth. And like everyone who becomes aware of this cruel cosmic game, he despaired. But he refused to accept the game. He refused to believe that there was no inherent value in existence. He refused to believe that we are forever cursed to conjure stories to give our lives an arbitrary sense of meaning. So, he set out to use his big-biceped Thinking Brain to figure out what value without hope would look like.

Kant started with a simple observation. In all the universe, there is only one thing that, from what we can tell, is completely scarce and unique: consciousness. To Kant, the *only* thing that distinguishes us from the rest of the matter in the universe is our ability to reason—we're able to take the world around us and, through reasoning and will, improve upon it. This, to him, was special, exceedingly special—a miracle, almost—because for everything in the infinite span of existence, *we* are the only thing (that we know of) that can actually *direct existence.* In the known cosmos, *we* are the only sources of ingenuity and creativity. *We* are the only ones who can direct our own fate. *We* are the only ones who are self-aware. And for all we know, we are the only shot the universe has at intelligent self-organization.

Therefore, Kant cleverly deduced that, logically, the supreme value in the universe *is the thing that conceives of value itself.* The only true meaning in existence *is the ability to form meaning.* The only importance is the thing that decides importance.[33]

And this ability to choose meaning, to imagine importance, to invent purpose, is the only force in the known universe that can propagate itself, that can spread its intelligence and generate greater and greater levels of organization throughout the cosmos. Kant believed that without rationality, the universe would be a waste, in vain, and without purpose. Without intelligence, and the freedom to exercise that intelligence, we might as well all be a bunch of rocks. Rocks don't change. They don't conceive of values, systems, or organizations. They don't alter, improve, or create. They're just *there.*

But *consciousness*—consciousness can reorganize the universe, and that reorganization can add upon itself exponentially. Consciousness is able to take a problem, a system of a certain amount of complexity, and conceive and generate *greater complexity.* In a thousand years, we went from twiddling sticks in a small cave to designing entire digital realms connecting the minds of billions. In another thousand, we could easily be among the stars, reshaping the planets and space/time itself. Each individual action may not matter in the grand scheme of things, but the preservation and promotion of rational consciousness overall matters more than anything.

Kant argued that the most fundamental moral duty is the preservation and growth of consciousness, both in ourselves and in others. He called this principle of always putting consciousness first "the Formula of Humanity," and it kind of explains . . . well, like, everything, ever. It explains our basic moral intuitions. It explains the classic concept of virtue.[34] It explains how to act in our day-to-day lives without relying on some imagined vision of hope. It explains how to not be an asshole.

And, as if that weren't enough, it explains all of it in a single sentence. The Formula of Humanity states, "Act that you use humanity, whether in your own person or in the person of any other, always at the same time as an end, never merely as a means."[35]

That's it. The Formula of Humanity is the single principle that pulls people out of adolescent bargaining and into adult virtue.[36]

See, the problem with hope is that it is fundamentally transactional—it is a bargain between one's current actions for some imagined, pleasant future. Don't eat this, and you'll go to heaven. Don't kill that person, or you'll get in trouble. Work hard and save your money, because that will make you happy.

To transcend the transactional realm of hope, one must act *unconditionally*. You must love someone without expecting anything in return; otherwise it's not truly love. You must respect someone without expecting anything in return; otherwise you don't truly respect him. You must speak honestly without expecting a pat on the back or a high-five or a gold star next to your name; otherwise you aren't truly being honest.

Kant summed up these unconditional acts with one simple principle: you must treat humanity never merely as a means, but always as an end itself.[37]

But what does this look like in day-to-day life? Here's a simple example:

Let's pretend that I'm hungry and I want a burrito. I get in my car and drive to Chipotle and order my usual double-meat monster that makes me oh so happy. In this situation, eating the burrito is my "end" goal. It's ultimately why I'm doing everything else: getting in the car, driving, buying gas, and so on. All these things I do to get the burrito are the "means," i.e., the things I must do in order to achieve my "end."

Means are things that we do conditionally. They are what we bargain with. I don't want to get in my car and drive, and I don't want to pay for gas, but I do want a burrito. Therefore, I must do these other things to get that burrito.

An end is something that is desired for its own sake. It is the defining motivating factor of our decisions and behaviors. If I wanted to eat a burrito only because my wife wanted a burrito and I wanted to make her happy, then the burrito is no longer my end; it is now a means to an even greater end: making my wife happy. And if I only wanted to make my wife happy so I could get laid tonight, now my wife's happiness is a means to a greater end, which in this case is sex.

Likely that last example made you squirm a little bit, made you feel that I'm kind of a dirtbag.[38] That's *exactly* what Kant is talking about. His Formula of Humanity states that treating any human being (or any consciousness) *as a means to some other end* is the basis of all wrong behavior. So, treating a burrito as a means to my wife's end is fine. It's good to make your spouse happy sometimes! But if I treat my wife as a means to the end of sex, then I am now treating her merely as a means, and as Kant would argue, that is some shade of wrong.

Similarly, lying is wrong because you are misleading another person's conscious behavior in order to achieve your own goal. You are treating that person as a means to your own end. Cheating is unethical for a similar reason. You are violating the expectations of other rational and sentient beings for your own personal aims. You are treating everyone else who is taking the same test or following the same rules as a means to your own personal end. Violence, same deal: you are treating another person as a means to some greater political or personal end. Bad, reader. Bad!

Kant's Formula of Humanity doesn't only describe our moral intuition into what's wrong; it also explains the adult virtues, those actions and behaviors that are good for their own sake. Honesty is good in and of itself because it's the only form of communication that *doesn't* treat people merely as a means. Courage is good in and of itself because to fail to act is to treat either yourself or others as a means to the end of quelling your fear. Humility is good in and of itself because to fall into blind certainty is to treat others as a means to your own ends.

If there were ever to be a single rule to describe all desirable human behavior, the Formula of Humanity would probably be it. But here's the beautiful thing: unlike other moral systems or codes, the Formula of Humanity does not rely on hope. There's no great system to force onto the world, no faith-based supernatural beliefs to protect from doubt or lack of evidence.

The Formula of Humanity is merely a principle. It doesn't project some future utopia. It doesn't lament some hellish past. No one is better or worse or more righteous than anyone else. All that matters is that conscious will is respected and protected. End of story.

Because Kant understood that when you get into the business of deciding and dictating the future, you unleash the destructive potential of hope. You start worrying about converting people rather than honoring them, destroying evil in others rather than rooting it out in yourself.

Instead, he decided that the only logical way to improve the world is through improving ourselves—by growing up and becoming more virtuous—by making the simple decision, in each moment, to treat ourselves and others as ends, and never merely as means. Be honest. Don't distract or harm yourself. Don't shirk responsibility or succumb to fear. Love openly and fearlessly. Don't cave to tribal impulses or hopeful deceits. Because there is no heaven or hell in the future. There are only the choices you make in each and every moment.

Will you act conditionally or unconditionally? Will you treat others as merely means or as ends? Will you pursue adult virtue or childish narcissism?

Hope doesn't even have to enter into the equation. Don't hope for a better life. Simply *be* a better life.

Kant understood that there is a fundamental link between our respect for ourselves and our respect for the world. The values that define our identity are the templates that we apply to our interactions with others, and little progress can be made with others until we've made progress within ourselves.[39] When we pursue a life full of pleasure and simple satisfaction, we are treating *ourselves* as a means to our pleasurable ends. Therefore, self-improvement is not the cultivation of greater happiness but, rather, a cultivation of greater self-respect. Telling ourselves that we are worthless and shitty is just as wrong as telling others that they are worthless and shitty. Lying to ourselves is just as unethical as lying to others. Harming ourselves is just as repugnant as harming others. Self-love and self-care are therefore not something you learn about or practice. They are something you are ethically called to cultivate within yourself, even if they are all that you have left.

The Formula of Humanity has a ripple effect: your improved ability to be honest with yourself will increase how honest you are with others, and your honesty with others will influence them to be more honest with themselves, which will help *them* to grow and mature. Your ability not to treat yourself as a means to some other end will in turn allow you to better treat others as ends. Therefore, your cleaning up your relationship *with yourself* has the positive by-product of cleaning up your relationships with others, which then enables them to clean up their relationships with themselves, and so on.

This is how you change the world—not through some all-encompassing ideology or mass religious conversion or misplaced dreams of the future, but by achieving the maturation and dignity of each individual in the present, here and now. There will always be different religions and different value systems based on culture and experience; there will always be different ideas about where we're going and where we've come from. But, as Kant believed, the simple question of dignity and respect in each moment must be universal.

The Modern Maturity Crisis

Modern democracy was invented under the assumption that the average person is a selfish and delusional piece of shit, that the only way to protect us from ourselves is to create systems so interlocking and interdependent that no one person or group can completely hose the rest of the population.

Politics is a transactional and selfish game, and democracy is the best system of government thus far for the sole reason that it's the only system that openly admits that. It acknowledges that power attracts corrupt and childish people. Power, by its very nature, *forces* leaders to be transactional. Therefore, the only way to manage that is by enshrining adult virtues into the design of the system itself.

Freedom of speech, freedom of the press, guarantees of privacy and of the right to a fair trial—these are all implementations of the Formula of Humanity in social institutions, and they are implemented in such a way that they are incredibly difficult to threaten or change.

There's really only one way to threaten a democratic system: when one group decides that its values are more important than the system itself and it subverts the religion of democracy with some other, likely less virtuous, religion . . . and political extremism grows.

Political extremists, because they are intractable and impossible to bargain with, are, by definition, childish. They're a bunch of fucking babies. Extremists want the world to be a certain way, and they refuse to acknowledge any interests or values outside their own. They refuse to negotiate. They refuse to appeal to a higher virtue or principle above their own selfish desires. And they cannot be trusted to follow through on the expectations of others. They are also unabashedly authoritarian because, as children, they are desperate for an all-powerful parent to come and make everything "all right."[40]

The most dangerous extremists know how to dress up their childish values in the language of transaction or universal principle. A right-wing extremist will claim she desires "freedom" above all else and that she's willing to make sacrifices for that freedom. But what she really means is that she wants freedom from having to deal with any values that do not map onto her own. She wants freedom from having to deal with change or the marginalization of other people. Therefore, she's willing to limit and destroy the freedom of others in the name of her own freedom.[41]

Extremists on the left play the same game, the only thing that changes is the language. A leftie extremist will say that he wants "equality" for all, but what he really means is that he never wants anyone to feel pain, to feel harmed, or to feel inferior. He doesn't want anyone to have to face moral gaps, ever. And he's willing to *cause* pain and adversity to others in the name of eliminating those moral gaps.

Extremism, on both the right and the left, has become more politically prominent across the world in the past few decades.[42] Many smart people have suggested many complicated and overlapping explanations for this. And there likely *are* many complicated and overlapping reasons.[43]

But allow me to throw out another one: *that the maturity of our culture is deteriorating.*

Throughout the rich and developed world, we are not living through a crisis of wealth or material, but a crisis of character, a crisis of virtue, a crisis of means and ends. The fundamental political schism in the twenty-first century is no longer right versus left, but the impulsive childish values of the right *and* left versus the compromising adolescent/adult values of both the right and left. It's no longer a debate of communism versus capitalism or freedom versus equality but, rather, of maturity versus immaturity, of means versus ends.

CHAPTER 7

Pain Is the Universal Constant

One by one, the researchers shuttled the subjects down a hall and into a small room. Inside was a single beige computer console with a blank screen and two buttons, and nothing else.[1]

The instructions were simple: sit, stare at the screen, and if a blue dot flashes on it, press the button that reads, "Blue." If a purple dot flashes on the screen, press the button that reads, "Not Blue."

Sounds easy, right?

Well, each subject had to look at a thousand dots. Yes, a *thousand*. And when a subject finished, the researchers brought in another subject and repeated the process: beige console, blank screen, a thousand dots. Next! This went on with hundreds of subjects at multiple universities.

Were these psychologists researching a new form of psychological torture? Was this an experiment into the limitations of human boredom? No. Actually, the scope of the study was matched only by its inanity. It was a study with seismic implications, because more than any other academic study in recent memory, it explains much of what we see happening in the world today.

The psychologists were researching something they would call "prevalence-induced concept change." But because that's an absolutely awful name, for our purposes, I will refer to their discovery as the "Blue Dot Effect."[2]

Here's the deal with the dots: Most of them were blue. Some of them were purple. Some of them were some shade in between blue and purple.

The researchers discovered that when they showed mostly blue dots, everyone was pretty accurate in determining which dots were blue and which ones were not. But as soon as the researchers started limiting the number of blue dots, and showing more shades of purple, the subjects began to mistake purple dots for blue. It seemed that their eyes distorted the colors and continued to seek a certain number of blue dots, no matter how many were actually shown.

Okay, big deal, right? People mis-see stuff all the time. And besides, when you're staring at dots for hours on end, you might start to go cross-eyed and see all sorts of weird shit.

But the blue dots weren't the point; they were merely a way to measure how humans warp their perceptions to fit their expectations. Once the researchers had enough data on blue dots to put their lab assistants into a coma, they moved on to more important perceptions.

For example: next, the researchers showed the subjects pictures of faces that were some degree of threatening, friendly, or neutral. Initially, they showed them a large number of threatening faces. But as the experiment went on, as with the blue dots, they showed fewer and fewer—and the same effect occurred: the fewer threatening faces subjects were shown, the more the subjects began to misread friendly and neutral faces as being threatening. In the same way that the human mind seemed to have a "preset" number of blue dots it expected to see, it also had a preset number of threatening faces it expected to see.

Then the researchers went even further, because—fuck it, why not? It's one thing to see threats where there are none, but what about moral judgments? What about believing there's more evil in the world than there actually is?

This time, the researchers had the subjects read job proposals. Some of these proposals were unethical, involving some shady shit. Some proposals were totally innocuous and fine. Others were some gradation in between.

Once again, the researchers began by showing a mix of ethical and unethical proposals, and the subjects were told to keep an eye out for unethical proposals. Then, slowly, the researchers exposed people to fewer and fewer unethical proposals. As they did, the Blue Dot Effect kicked in. People began to interpret completely ethical proposals as being unethical. Rather than noticing that more proposals were showing up on the ethical side of the fence, people's minds *moved the fence* itself to maintain the perception that a certain number of proposals and requests were unethical. Basically, they redefined what was unethical without being consciously aware of doing so.

As the researchers noted, this bias has incredibly upsetting implications for . . . well, pretty much everything. Governmental committees designed to oversee regulations, when provided with a dearth of infractions, may start to perceive infractions where there are none. Task forces designed to check unethical practices within organizations will, when deprived of bad guys to accuse of wrongdoing, begin imagining bad guys where there are none.

The Blue Dot Effect suggests that, essentially, the more we look for threats, the more we will see them, regardless of how safe or comfortable our environment actually is. And we see this playing out in the world today.

It used to be that being the victim of violence meant somebody had physically harmed you. Today, many people have begun to use the word *violence* to describe words that made them feel uncomfortable, or even just the presence of a person they disliked.[3] *Trauma* used to mean specifically an experience so severe that the victim could not continue to function. Today, an unpleasant social encounter or a few offensive words are considered "trauma," and necessitate "safe spaces."[4] *Genocide* used to mean the physical mass murder of a certain ethnic or religious group. Today, the term *white genocide* is employed by some to lament the fact that the local diner now lists some of its menu items in Spanish.[5]

This is the Blue Dot Effect. The better things get, the more we perceive threats where there are none, and the more upset we become. And it is at the heart of the paradox of progress.

In the nineteenth century, Emile Durkheim, the founder of sociology and an early pioneer of the social sciences, ran a thought experiment in one of his books: What if there were no crime? What if there emerged a society where everyone was perfectly respectful and nonviolent and everyone was equal? What if no one lied or hurt each other? What if corruption did not exist? What would happen? Would conflict cease? Would stress evaporate? Would everyone frolic in fields picking daisies and singing the "Hallelujah" chorus from Handel's *Messiah*?[6]

Durkheim said no, that in fact the opposite would happen. He suggested that the more comfortable and ethical a society became, the more that small indiscretions would become magnified in our minds. If everyone stopped killing each other, we wouldn't necessarily feel good about it. We'd just get equally upset about the more minor stuff.

Developmental psychology has long argued something similar: that protecting people from problems or adversity doesn't make them happier or more secure; it makes them more easily insecure. A young person who has been sheltered from dealing with any challenges or injustices growing up will come to find the slightest inconveniences of adult life intolerable, and will have the childish public meltdown to prove it.[7]

What we find, then, is that our emotional reactions to our problems are not determined by the size of the problem. Rather, our minds simply amplify (or minimize) our problems to fit the degree of stress we expect to experience. Material progress and security do not necessarily relax us or make it easier to hope for the future. On the contrary, it appears that perhaps by removing healthy adversity and challenge, people struggle even more. They become more selfish and more childish. They fail to develop and mature out of adolescence. They remain further removed from any virtue. They see mountains where there are molehills. And they scream at each other as though the world were one endless stream of spilled milk.

Traveling at the Speed of Pain

Recently, I read a cool Albert Einstein quote on the internet: "A man should look for what is, and not what he thinks should be." It was great. There was a cute little picture with him looking all science-y and everything. The quote is poignant and smart-sounding, and it engaged me for all of a couple of seconds before I scrolled on my phone to the next thing.

Except there was one problem: Einstein didn't say it.

Here's another viral Einstein quote that gets passed around a lot: "Everyone is a genius. But if you judge a fish by its ability to climb a tree, it will live its whole life believing that it is stupid."

That's not Einstein, either.

Or how about "I fear the day when the technology overlaps with our humanity. The world will only have a generation of idiots"?[8]

Nope, not him.

Einstein might be the most ill-used historical figure on the internet. He's like our culture's "smart friend," the one we say agrees with us to make us sound smarter than we actually are. His poor mug has been plastered next to quotes about everything from God to mental illness to energy healing. None of which has anything to do with science. The poor man must be spinning in his grave.

People project shit onto Einstein to the point that he's become a kind of mythical figure. For example, the idea that Einstein was a poor student is bogus. He excelled at math and science from an early age, taught himself algebra and Euclidean geometry in a single summer at age twelve, and read Immanuel Kant's *Critique of Pure Reason* (a book that present-day graduate students struggle to finish) at age thirteen. I mean, the guy got a PhD in experimental physics earlier in life than some people get their first jobs, so clearly he was kind of into the school thing.

Albert Einstein didn't initially have big aspirations; he just wanted to teach. But being a young German immigrant in Switzerland, he couldn't get a position at the local universities. Eventually, with the help of a friend's father, he got a job at a patent office, a position mind-numbingly dull enough for him to sit around all day and imagine wacky theories about physics—theories that would soon flip the world on its head. In 1905 he published his theory of relativity, which launched him to worldwide fame. He left the patent office. Presidents and heads of state suddenly wanted to hang out with him. Everything was Gucci.

In his long life, Einstein would go on to revolutionize physics multiple times, escape the Nazis, warn the United States of the oncoming necessity (and danger) of nuclear weapons, and be the subject of a very famous photo in which he's sticking out his tongue.

But today, we also know him for the many excellent internet quotes that he never actually said.

Since the time of (real) Newton, physics had been based upon the idea that everything could be measured in terms of time and space. For example, my trash can is here next to me now. It has a particular position in space. If I pick it up and throw it across the room in a drunken rage, we could theoretically measure its location in space across time, determining all sorts of useful stuff like its velocity, trajectory, momentum, and how big a dent it will leave in the wall. These other variables are determined by measuring the trash can's movement across both time and space.

Time and space are what we call "universal constants." They are immutable. They are the metrics by which everything else is measured. If this sounds like common sense, it's because it is.

Then Einstein came along and said, "Fuck your common sense; you know nothing, Jon Snow," and changed the world. That's because Einstein proved that time and space are *not* universal constants. In fact, it turns out that our perceptions of time and space can change depending on the context of our observations. For example, what I experience as ten seconds, you could experience as five; and what I experience as a mile, you could theoretically experience as a few feet.

To anyone who has spent a significant amount of time on LSD, this conclusion might kind of make sense. But for the physics world at the time, it sounded like pure craziness.

Einstein demonstrated that space and time change depending on the observer—that is, they are *relative*. It is the *speed of light* that is the universal constant, the thing by which everything else must be measured. We are all moving, all the time, and the closer we get to the speed of light, the more time "slows down" and the more space contracts.

For example, let's say you have an identical twin. Being twins, obviously you are the same age. The two of you decide to go on a little intergalactic adventure, and each of you gets into a separate spaceship. Your spaceship travels at a pokey 50 kilometers per second, but your twin's travels at close to the speed of light—an insane 299,000 kilometers per second. You both agree to travel around space for a while and find a bunch of cool stuff and then meet back up after twenty earth years have passed.

When you get home, something shocking has happened. You have aged twenty years, but your twin has hardly aged at all. Your twin has been "gone" for twenty earth years, yet on his spaceship, he experienced only about one year.

Yeah, "What the fuck?" is what I said, too.

As Einstein once said, "Dude, that doesn't even make sense." Except it does (and Einstein never said that).

The Einstein example is important because it shows how our assumption of what is constant and stable in the universe can be wrong, and those incorrect assumptions can have massive implications on how we experience the world. We assume that space and time are universal constants because that explains how *we* perceive the world. But it turns out that they are not universal constants; they are variables to some other, inscrutable, nonobvious constant. And that changes everything.

I belabor this headache-inducing explanation of relativity because I believe a similar thing is going on within our own psychology: what we believe is the universal constant of our experience is, in fact, not constant at all. And, instead, much of what we assume to be true and real is relative to our own perception.

Psychologists didn't always study happiness. In fact, for most of the field's history, psychology focused not on the positive, but on what fucked people up, what caused mental illness and emotional breakdowns, and how people should cope with their greatest pains.

It wasn't until the 1980s that a few intrepid academics started asking themselves, "Wait a second, my job is kind of a downer. What about what makes people *happy*? Let's study that instead!" And there was much celebration, because soon dozens of "happiness" books would proliferate on bookshelves, selling in the millions to bored, angsty middle-class people suffering existential crises.

One of the first things psychologists did when they started to study happiness was to organize a simple survey.[9] They took large groups of people and gave them pagers—remember, this was the 1980s and '90s—and whenever the pager went off, each person was to stop and write down the answers to two questions:

1. On a scale of 1–10, how happy are you at this moment?

2. What has been going on in your life?

The researchers collected thousands of ratings from hundreds of people from all walks of life, and what they discovered was both surprising and incredibly boring: pretty much everybody wrote "7" all the time. At the grocery store buying milk? Seven. Attending my son's baseball game? Seven. Talking to my boss about making a big sale to a client? Seven.

Even when catastrophic stuff happened—Mom got cancer; I missed a mortgage payment on the house; Junior lost an arm in a freak bowling accident—happiness levels would dip to the two-to-five range for a short period, and then, after a while, would return to seven.[10]

This was true for extremely positive events as well. Getting a fat bonus at work, going on dream vacations, marriages—after the event, people's ratings would shoot up for a short period of time and then, predictably, settle back in at around seven.

This fascinated researchers. Nobody is fully happy all the time, but similarly, nobody is fully unhappy all the time, either. It seems that humans, regardless of our external circumstances, live in a constant state of mild-but-not-fully-satisfying happiness. Put another way, things are pretty much always fine, but they could also always be better.[11]

Life is apparently nothing but bobbing up and down and around our level-seven happiness. And this constant "seven" that we're always coming back to plays a little trick on us, a trick that we fall for over and over again.

The trick is that our brain tells us, "You know, if I could just have a little bit more, I'd finally get to ten and stay there."

Most of us live much of our lives this way, constantly chasing our imagined ten.

You think, hey, to be happier, I'm going to need to get a new job; so you get a new job. And then, a few months later, you feel you'd be happier if you had a new house; so you get a new house. And then, a few months later, it's an awesome beach vacation; so you go on an awesome beach vacation. And while you're on the awesome beach vacation, you're like, you know what I *fucking need*? A goddamn piña colada! *Can't a fucker get a piña colada around here*?! So, you stress about your piña colada, believing that just one piña colada will get you to your ten. But then it's a second piña colada, and then a third, and then . . . well, you know how this turns out: you wake up with a hangover and are at a three.

It's like Einstein once advised, "Never get wasted on cocktails with sugar-based mixers—if you need to go on a bender, may I recommend some seltzer, or if you're a particularly rich fuck, perhaps a fine champagne?"

Each of us implicitly assumes that *we* are the universal constant of our own experience, that *we* are unchanging, and our experiences come and go like the weather.[12] Some days are good and sunny; other days are cloudy and shitty. The skies change, but *we* remain the same.

But this is not true—in fact, this is backward. Pain is the universal constant of life. And human perception and expectations warp themselves to fit a predetermined amount of pain. In other words, no matter how sunny our skies get, our mind will always imagine just enough clouds to be slightly disappointed.

This constancy of pain results in what is known as "the hedonic treadmill," upon which you run and run and run, chasing your imagined ten. But, no matter what, you always end up with a seven. The pain is always there. What changes is your *perception* of it. And as soon as your life "improves," your expectations shift, and you're back to being mildly dissatisfied again.

But pain works in the other direction, too. I remember when I got my big tattoo, the first few minutes were excruciatingly painful. I couldn't believe I'd signed up for eight hours of this shit. But by the third hour, I'd actually dozed off while my tattoo artist worked.

Nothing had changed: same needle, same arm, same artist. But my perception had shifted: the pain became normal, and I returned to my own internal seven.

This is another permutation of the Blue Dot Effect.[13] This is Durkheim's "perfect" society. This is Einstein's relativity with a psychological remix. It's the concept creep of someone who has never actually experienced physical violence losing their mind and redefining a few uncomfortable sentences in a book as "violence." It's the exaggerated sense that one's culture is being invaded and destroyed because there are now movies about gay people.

The Blue Dot Effect is everywhere. It affects all perceptions and judgments. Everything adapts and shapes itself to our slight dissatisfaction.

And *that* is the problem with the pursuit of happiness.

Pursuing happiness is a value of the modern world. Do you think Zeus gave a shit if people were happy? Do you think the God of the Old Testament cared about making people feel good? No, they were too busy planning to send swarms of locusts to eat people's flesh.

In the old days, life was hard. Famines and plagues and floods were constant. The majority of populations were enslaved or enlisted in endless wars, while the rest were slitting each other's throats in the night for this or that tyrant. Death was ubiquitous. Most people didn't live past, like, age thirty. And this was how things were for the majority of human history: shit and shingles and starvation.

Suffering in the pre-science world was not only an accepted fact; it was often celebrated. The philosophers of antiquity didn't see happiness as a virtue. On the contrary, they saw humans' capacity for self-denial as a virtue, because feeling good was just as dangerous as it was desirable. And rightly so—all it took was one jackass getting carried away and the next thing you knew, half the village had burned down. As Einstein famously didn't say, "Don't fuck around with torches while drinking or that shit will ruin your day."

It wasn't until the age of science and technology that happiness became a "thing." Once humanity invented the means to improve life, the next logical question was "So what should we improve?" Several philosophers at the time decided that the ultimate aim of humanity should be to promote happiness—that is, to reduce pain.[14]

This sounded all nice and noble and everything on the surface. I mean, come on, who doesn't want to get rid of a little bit of pain? What sort of asshole would claim that *that* was a bad idea?

Well, *I* am that asshole, because it *is* a bad idea.

Because you can't get rid of pain—pain is the universal constant of the human condition. Therefore, the attempt to move away from pain, to protect oneself from *all* harm, can only backfire. Trying to eliminate pain only increases your sensitivity to suffering, rather than alleviating your suffering. It causes you to see dangerous ghosts in every nook, to see tyranny and oppression in every authority, to see hate and deceit behind every embrace.

No matter how much progress is made, no matter how peaceful and comfortable and happy our lives become, the Blue Dot Effect will snap us back to a perception of a certain amount of pain and dissatisfaction. Most people who win millions in the lottery don't end up happier in the long run. On average, they end up feeling the same. People who become paralyzed in freak accidents don't become unhappier in the long run. On average, they also end up feeling the same.[15]

This is because pain is the experience of life itself. Positive emotions are the temporary removal of pain; negative emotions the temporary augmentation of it. To numb one's pain is to numb all feeling, all emotion. It is to quietly remove oneself from living.

Or, as Einstein once brilliantly put it:

Just as a stream flows smoothly as long as it encounters no obstruction, so the nature of man and animal is such that we never

really notice or become conscious of what is agreeable to our will;
if we are to notice something, our will has to have been thwarted,
has to have experienced a shock of some kind. On the other
hand, all that opposes, frustrates and resists our will, that is to
say all that is unpleasant and painful, impresses itself upon us
instantly, directly and with great clarity. Just as we are conscious
not of the healthiness of our whole body but only the little place
where the shoe pinches, so we think not of the totality of our suc-
cessful activities but of some insignificant trifle or other which
continues to vex us.[16]

Okay, that wasn't Einstein. It was Schopenhauer, who was also German and also had funny-looking hair. But the point is, not only is there no escaping the experience of pain, but pain *is* the experience.

This is why hope is ultimately self-defeating *and* self-perpetuating: no matter what we achieve, no matter what peace and prosperity we find, our mind will quickly adjust its expectations to maintain a steady sense of adversity, thus forcing the formulation of a new hope, a new religion, a new conflict to keep us going. We will see threatening faces where there are no threatening faces. We will see unethical job proposals where there are no unethical job proposals. And no matter how sunny our day is, we'll always find that one cloud in the sky.

Therefore, the pursuit of happiness is not only self-defeating but also impossible. It's like trying to catch a carrot hanging by a string tied to a stick attached to your back. The more you move forward, the more you have to move forward. When you make the carrot your end goal, you inevitably turn yourself into the means to get there. And by pursuing happiness, you paradoxically make it less attainable.

The pursuit of happiness is a toxic value that has long defined our culture. It is self-defeating *and* misleading. Living well does not mean avoiding suffering; it means suffering for the right reasons. Because if we're going to be forced to suffer by simply existing, we might as well learn how to suffer well.

The Only Choice in Life

In 1954, after nearly seventy-five years of occupation and twenty years of war, the Vietnamese finally kicked the French out of their country. This should have been an unequivocally good thing. The problem was that that pesky Cold War was going on—a global religious war between the capitalist, liberal Western powers and the Communist Eastern Bloc. And when it turned out that Ho Chi Minh, the guy who gave the French the ass-kicking, was a Communist, well, everyone kind of freaked out and thought this could spark World War III.

Terrified of a major war, a bunch of heads of state sat down at a fancy table somewhere in Switzerland and agreed to skip the nuclear annihilation part and go straight to slicing Vietnam in half. Why a country that didn't do anything to anybody deserved to be cut in half, don't ask me.[17] But apparently everyone decided that North Vietnam would be Communist, South Vietnam would be capitalist, and that's that. Everyone would live happily ever after.

(Okay, maybe not.)

Here was the problem. The Western powers put a man named Ngo Dinh Diem in charge of South Vietnam until proper elections could be held. At first, everyone seemed to like this Diem guy. A devout Catholic, he was French educated, had spent a number of years in Italy, and was multilingual. Upon meeting him, U.S. vice president Lyndon Johnson called Diem "the Winston Churchill of Asia." He was practically one of us!

Diem was also charismatic and ambitious. He impressed himself not only on the Western leaders but also on the former Vietnamese emperor. Diem declared confidently that he would be the one to finally bring democracy to Southeast Asia. And everyone believed him.

Well, that's not what happened. Within a year of taking power, Diem outlawed every political party in South Vietnam other than his own. And when it came time for the country to have its referendum, he put his own brother in charge of managing all electoral sites. And you'll never believe this, but Diem won the election! With a mind-blowing 98.2 percent of the vote!

It turned out this Diem guy was a total piece of shit. Ho Chi Minh, the leader of North Vietnam, was a total piece of shit, too, of course. And if I learned anything in college, it's that the first rule of geopolitical theory is that when you have two total pieces of shit living next door to each other, millions of people die.[18]

And just like that, Vietnam spiraled back into civil war.

I'd love to tell you something surprising about Diem, but he kind of became your run-of-the-mill tyrant. He filled his administration with family members and corrupt cronies. He and his family lived in opulent luxury while famine swept across the countryside, causing hundreds of thousands to either defect or starve to death. He was so smug and incompetent that the United States would have to gradually start intervening to prevent South Vietnam from imploding, thus starting what Americans now know as the Vietnam War.

But despite how fucking awful Diem was, the Western powers stood by their man. After all, he was supposed to be one of them, a disciple of the liberal capitalist religion, standing strong against the Communist onslaught. It would take years and countless deaths for them to realize that Diem was not interested in their religion as much as his own.

As with many tyrants, one of Diem's favorite pastimes was oppressing and killing people he disagreed with. In this case, being a devout Catholic, Diem hated Buddhists. The problem was that Vietnam was roughly 80 percent Buddhist at the time, so that didn't exactly go over well with the population. Diem banned Buddhist-related banners and flags. He banned Buddhist holidays. He refused to provide governmental services to Buddhist communities. He raided and destroyed pagodas across the country, forcing hundreds of Buddhist monks into destitution.

The Buddhist monks organized and staged peaceful protests, but these were shut down of course. Then there were even bigger protests, so Diem made protesting illegal. When his police forces ordered the Buddhists to disperse, and the Buddhists refused, the police began to shoot protesters. At one peaceful march, they even hurled live grenades at groups of unarmed monks.

Western reporters knew this religious suppression was going on, but they were concerned primarily with the war with North Vietnam, so it wasn't really a priority. Few knew the extent of the problem, and fewer even bothered to cover the confrontations.

Then, on June 10, 1963, reporters received a cryptic message claiming that "something important" would occur the next day in Saigon, at a busy intersection just a few blocks from the presidential palace. The correspondents didn't think much of this, and most decided not to go. The next day, among a few journalists, only two photographers bothered to show up. One of them forgot his camera.

The other would win a Pulitzer Prize.

That day, a small turquoise car festooned with banners demanding religious freedom led a procession of a few hundred monks and nuns. The monks chanted. People stopped and watched the procession and then returned to their business. It was a busy street on a busy day. And by this point, Buddhist protests were nothing new.

The procession reached the intersection in front of the Cambodian embassy and stopped, blocking all cross traffic. The group of monks fanned out into a semi-circle around the turquoise car, silently staring and waiting.

Three monks got out of the car. One placed a cushion on the street, at the center of the intersection. The second monk, an older man named Thich Quang Duc, walked to the cushion, sat down in the lotus position, closed his eyes, and began to meditate.

The third monk from the car opened the trunk and took out a five-gallon canister of gasoline, carried it over to where Quang Duc was sitting, and dumped the gasoline over his head, covering the old man in fuel. People covered their mouths. Some covered their faces as their eyes began to water at the fumes. An eerie silence fell over the busy city intersection. Passersby stopped walking. Police forgot what they were doing. There was a thickness in the air. Something important was about to happen. Everyone waited.

With gasoline-soaked robes and an expressionless face, Quang Duc recited a short prayer, reached out, slowly picked up a match, and without breaking his lotus position or opening his eyes, struck it on the asphalt and set himself on fire.

Instantly, a wall of flames rose around him. His body became engulfed. His robe disintegrated. His skin turned black. A repulsive odor filled the air, a mixture of burnt flesh and fuel and smoke. Wails and screams erupted throughout the crowd. Many fell to their knees, or lost their balance entirely. Most were just stunned, shocked and immobilized by what was occurring.

(Copyright AP Photo/Malcolm Browne. Used with permission.)

Yet, as he burned, Quang Duc remained perfectly still.

David Halberstam, a correspondent for the *New York Times*, later described the scene: "I was too shocked to cry, too confused to take notes or ask questions, too bewildered to even think. . . . As he burned he never moved a muscle, never uttered a sound, his outward composure in sharp contrast to the wailing people around him."[19]

News of Quang Duc's self-immolation quickly spread, and angered millions all across the planet. That evening, Diem gave a radio address to the nation during which he was audibly shaken by the incident. He promised to reopen negotiations with the Buddhist leadership in the country and to find a peaceful resolution.

But it was too late. Diem would never recover. It's impossible to say exactly what changed or how, but the air was somehow different, the streets more alive. With the strike of a match and the click of a camera shutter, Diem's invisible grip on the country had been weakened, and everyone could sense it, including Diem.

Soon, thousands of people poured into the streets in open revolt against his administration. His military commanders began to disobey him. His advisers defied him. Eventually, even the United States could no longer justify supporting him. President Kennedy soon gave his nod of approval to a plan by Diem's top generals to overthrow him.

The image of the burning monk had broken the levee, and a flood ensued.

A few months later, Diem and his family were assassinated.

Photos of Quang Duc's death went viral before "going viral" was a thing. The image became a kind of human Rorschach test, in which everyone saw their own values and struggles reflected back at them. Communists in Russia and China published the photo to rally their supporters against the capitalist imperialists of the West. Postcards were sold across Europe railing against the atrocities being committed in the East. Antiwar protesters in the United States printed the photo to protest American involvement in the war. Conservatives used the photo as evidence of the need for U.S. intervention. Even President Kennedy had to admit that "no news picture in history has generated so much emotion around the world."[20]

The photo of Quang Duc's self-immolation triggered something primal and universal in people. It goes beyond politics or religion. It taps into a far more fundamental component of our lived experience: the ability to endure extraordinary amounts of pain.[21] I can't even sit up straight at dinner for more than a few minutes. Meanwhile, this guy was fucking *burning alive* and he didn't even move. He didn't flinch. He didn't scream. He didn't smile or wince or grimace or even open his eyes to take one last look at the world he had chosen to leave behind.

There was a purity to his act, not to mention an absolutely stunning display of resolve. It is the ultimate example of mind over matter, of will over instinct.[22]

And despite the horror of it all, it somehow remains . . . inspiring.

In 2011, Nassim Taleb wrote about a concept he dubbed "antifragility." Taleb argued that just as some systems become *weaker* under stress from external forces, other systems *gain strength* under stress from external forces.[23]

A vase is fragile: it shatters easily. The classic banking system is fragile, as unexpected shifts in politics or the economy can cause it to break down. Maybe your relationship with your mother-in-law is fragile, as any and every thing you say will cause her to explode in a fiery plume of insults and drama. Fragile systems are like beautiful little flowers or a teenager's feelings: they must be protected at all times.

Then you have robust systems. Robust systems resist change well. Whereas a vase is fragile and breaks when you sneeze on it, an oil drum—now that's fucking robust. You can throw that shit around for weeks, and nothing will happen to it. Still the same old oil drum.

As a society, we spend most of our time and money taking fragile systems and trying to make them more robust. You hire a good lawyer to make your business more robust. The government passes regulations to make the financial system more robust. We institute rules and laws like traffic lights and property rights to make our society more robust.

But, Taleb says, there is a third type of system, and that is the "antifragile" system. Whereas a fragile system breaks down and a robust system resists change, the antifragile system *gains* from stressors and external pressures.

Start-ups are antifragile businesses: they look for ways to fail quickly and gain from those failures. Drug dealers are also antifragile: the crazier shit gets, the more fucked up people want to get. A healthy love relationship is antifragile: misfortune and pain make the relationship stronger rather than weaker.[24] Veterans often talk about how the chaos of combat builds and reinforces life-changing bonds between soldiers, rather than disintegrating those bonds.

The human body can go either way, depending on how you use it. If you get off your ass and actively seek out pain, the body is antifragile, meaning it gets stronger the more stress and strain you put on it. The breaking down of your body through exercise and physical labor builds muscle and bone density, improves circulation, and gives you a really nice butt. But if you avoid stress and pain (i.e., if you sit on your damn couch all day watching Netflix), your muscles will atrophy, your bones will become brittle, and you will degenerate into weakness.

The human mind operates on the same principle. It can be fragile or antifragile depending on how you use it. When struck by chaos and disorder, our minds set to work making sense of it all, deducing principles and constructing mental models, predicting future events and evaluating the past. This is called "learning," and it makes us better; it allows us to gain from failure and disorder.

But when we avoid pain, when we avoid stress and chaos and tragedy and disorder, we become fragile. Our tolerance for day-to-day setbacks diminishes, and our life must shrink accordingly for us to engage only in the little bit of the world we can handle at one time.

Because pain is the universal constant. No matter how "good" or "bad" your life gets, the pain will be there. And it will eventually feel manageable. The question then, the *only* question, is: Will you engage it? Will you engage your pain or avoid your pain? Will you choose fragility or antifragility?

Everything you do, everything you are, everything you care about is a reflection of this choice: your relationships, your health, your results at work, your emotional stability, your integrity, your engagement with your community, the breadth of your life experiences, the depth of your self-confidence and courage, your ability to respect and trust and forgive and appreciate and listen and learn and have compassion.

If any of these things is fragile in your life, it is because you have chosen to avoid the pain. You have chosen childish values of chasing simple pleasures, desire, and self-satisfaction.

Our tolerance for pain, as a culture, is diminishing rapidly. And not only is this diminishment failing to bring us more happiness, but it's generating greater amounts of emotional fragility, which is why everything appears to be so fucked.

Which brings me back to Thich Quang Duc setting himself on fire and then just sitting there like a boss. Most modern Westerners know of meditation as a relaxation technique. You put on some yoga pants and sit in a warm, cushy room for ten minutes and close your eyes and listen to some soothing voice on your phone telling you that you're okay, everything's okay, everything's going to be fucking great, just follow your heart, blah, blah, blah.[25]

But actual Buddhist meditation is far more intense than simply de-stressing oneself with fancy apps. Rigorous meditation involves sitting quietly and mercilessly observing yourself. Every thought, every judgment, every inclination, every minute fidget and flake of emotion and trace of assumption that passes before your mind's eye is ideally captured, acknowledged, and then released back into the void. And worst of all, there's no end to it. People always lament that they're "not good" at meditation. There is no getting good. That's the whole point. You are supposed to suck at it. Just accept the suckage. Embrace the suckage. Love the suckage.

When one meditates for long periods of time, all sorts of wacky shit comes up: strange fantasies and decades-old regrets and odd sexual urges and unbearable boredom and often crushing feelings of isolation and loneliness. And these things, too, must simply be observed, acknowledged, and then let go. They, too, shall pass.

Meditation is, at its core, a practice of antifragility: training your mind to observe and sustain the never-ending ebb and flow of pain and not to let the "self" get sucked away by its riptide. This is why everyone is so bad at something seemingly so simple. After all, you just sit on a pillow and close your eyes. How hard can it be? Why is it so difficult to summon the courage to sit down and do it and then stay there? It should be easy, yet everyone seems to be terrible at getting themselves to do it.[26]

Most people avoid meditation the same way a kid avoids doing homework. It's because they know what meditation really is: it's confronting your pain, it's observing the interiors of your mind and heart, in all their horror and glory.

I usually tap out after meditating for around an hour, and the most I ever did was a two-day silent retreat. By the end of that, my mind was practically screaming for me to let it go outside and play. That length of sustained contemplation is a strange experience: a mix of agonizing boredom dotted with the horrifying realization that any control you thought you had over your own mind was merely a useful illusion. Throw in a dash of uncomfortable emotions and memories (maybe a childhood trauma or two), and shit can get pretty raw.

Now imagine doing that all day, every day, *for sixty years*. Imagine the steely focus and intense resolve of your inner flashlight. Imagine your pain threshold. Imagine your antifragility.

What's so remarkable about Thich Quang Duc is not that he chose to set himself on fire in political protest (although that is pretty damn remarkable). What's remarkable is the manner in which he did it: Motionless. Equanimous. At peace.

The Buddha said that suffering is like being shot by two arrows. The first arrow is the *physical* pain—it's the metal piercing the skin, the force colliding into the body. The second arrow is the *mental* pain, the meaning and emotion we attach to the being struck, the narratives that we spin in our minds about whether we deserved or didn't deserve what happened. In many cases, our mental pain is far worse than any physical pain. In most cases, it lasts far longer.

Through the practice of meditation, the Buddha said that if we could train ourselves to be struck only by the first arrow, we could essentially render ourselves invincible to any mental or emotional pain.

That, with enough practiced focus, with enough antifragility, the passing sensation of an insult or an object piercing our skin, or gallons of gasoline aflame over our body, would possess the same fleeting feeling as a fly buzzing across our face.

That while pain is inevitable, suffering is always a choice.

That there is always a separation between what we experience and how we interpret that experience.

That there's always a gap between what our Feeling Brain feels and what our Thinking Brain thinks. And in that gap, you can find the power to bear anything.

Children have a low tolerance for pain because the child's entire ethos revolves around the avoidance of pain. For the child, a failure to avoid pain is a failure to find meaning or purpose.

Therefore, even modest amounts of pain will cause the child to fall into fits of nihilism.

The adolescent has a higher pain threshold because the adolescent understands that pain is often a necessary trade-off to achieve his goals. The notion of enduring pain for some sort of future benefit thus allows the adolescent to incorporate some hardships and setbacks into his vision of hope: I will suffer through school so I can have a good career; I will deal with my obnoxious aunt so I can enjoy my holiday with the family; I will wake up at the ass-crack of dawn to work out because it will make me look sexy.

The problem arises when the adolescent feels that he got a bad bargain, when the pain exceeds his expectations and the rewards don't live up to the hype. This will cause the adolescent, like the child, to fall into a crisis of hope: I sacrificed so much and got so little back! What was the point? It will thrust the adolescent into the depths of nihilism and an unkindly visit with the Uncomfortable Truth.

The adult has an incredibly high threshold for pain because the adult understands that life, in order to be meaningful, requires pain, that nothing can or necessarily *should* be controlled or bargained for, that you can simply do the best you can do, regardless of the consequences.

Psychological growth is an escape from nihilism, a process of building more and more sophisticated and abstract value hierarchies in order to stomach whatever life throws our way.

Childish values are fragile. The moment the ice cream is gone, an existential crisis sets in—followed by a screaming shit fit. Adolescent values are more robust because they include the necessity of pain, but they are still susceptible to unexpected and/or tragic events. Adolescent values inevitably break down in extreme circumstances or over a long enough period of time.

Truly adult values are antifragile: they benefit from the unexpected. The more fucked up a relationship gets, the more useful honesty becomes. The more terrifying the world is, the more important it is to summon up the courage to face it. The more confusing life becomes, the more valuable it is to adopt humility.

These are the virtues of a post-hope existence, the values of true adulthood. They are the North Star of our minds and our hearts. No matter the turbulence or chaos taking place on earth, they stand above it all, untouched, always shining, always guiding us through the darkness.

Pain Is Value

Many scientists and techno enthusiasts believe that one day we will develop the capabilities to "cure" death. Our genetics will be modified and optimized. We will develop nanobots that monitor and eradicate anything that could medically threaten us. Biotechnology will enable us to replace and restore our bodies in perpetuity, thus allowing us to live forever.

It sounds like science fiction, but some even believe that we could achieve this technology in our lifetime.[27]

The idea of removing the possibility of death, of overcoming our biological fragility, of alleviating all pain, is incredibly exciting on the surface. But I think it could also be a psychological disaster in the making.

For one, if you remove death, you remove any scarcity from life. And if you remove scarcity, you remove the ability to determine value. Everything will seem equally good or bad, equally worthy or unworthy of your time and attention, because . . . well, you would have infinite time and attention. You could spend a hundred years watching the same TV show, and it wouldn't matter.

You could let your relationships deteriorate and fall away because, after all, those people are going to be around forever—so why bother? You could justify every indulgence, every diversion, with a simple "Well, it's not like it's going to kill me," and get on with it.

Death is psychologically necessary because it creates stakes in life. There is something to lose. You don't know what something is worth until you experience the potential to lose it. You don't know what you're willing to struggle for, what you're willing to give up or sacrifice.

Pain is the currency of our values. Without the pain of loss (or potential loss), it becomes impossible to determine the value of anything at all.

Pain is at the heart of all emotion. Negative emotions are caused by experiencing pain. Positive emotions are caused by alleviating pain. When we avoid pain and make ourselves more fragile, the result is our emotional reactions will be wildly disproportional to the importance of the event. We will flip our shit when our burger comes with too many leaves of lettuce. We will brim with self-importance after watching a bullshit YouTube video telling us how righteous we are. Life will become an ineffable roller coaster, sweeping our hearts up and down as we scroll up and down on our touchscreen.

The more antifragile we become, the more graceful our emotional responses are, the more control we exercise over ourselves, and the more principled our values. Antifragility is therefore synonymous with growth and maturity. Life is one never-ending stream of pain, and to grow is not to find a way to avoid that stream but, rather, to dive into it and successfully navigate its depths.

The pursuit of happiness is, then, an avoidance of growth, an avoidance of maturity, an avoidance of virtue. It is treating ourselves and our minds as a means to some emotionally giddy end.

It is sacrificing our consciousness for feeling good. It's giving up our dignity for more comfort.

The ancient philosophers knew this. Plato and Aristotle and the Stoics spoke of a life not of happiness, but of character, developing the ability to sustain pain and make the appropriate sacrifices—as that's really what life was in their time: one long, drawn-out sacrifice. The ancient virtues of bravery, honesty, and humility are all different forms of practicing antifragility: they are principles that gain from chaos and adversity.

It wasn't until the Enlightenment, the age of science and technology and the promise of never-ending economic growth, that thinkers and philosophers conceived of the idea summed up by Thomas Jefferson as "the pursuit of happiness." As the Enlightenment thinkers saw science and wealth alleviate poverty, starvation, and disease from the population, they mistook this *improvement* of pain to be the *elimination* of pain. Many public intellectuals and pundits continue to make this mistake today: they believe that growth has liberated us from suffering, rather than merely transmuting that suffering from a physical form to a psychological form.[28]

What the Enlightenment *did* get right is the idea that, on average, some pain is better than others. All else being equal, it is better to die at ninety than at twenty. It's better to be healthy than it is to be sick. It's better to be free to pursue your own goals than to be forced into servitude by others. In fact, you could define "wealth" in terms of how desirable your pain is.[29]

But we seem to have forgotten what the ancients knew: that no matter how much wealth is generated in the world, the quality of our lives is determined by the quality of our character, and the quality of our character is determined by our relationship to our pain.

The pursuit of happiness plunges us head-first toward nihilism and frivolity. It leads us toward childishness, an incessant and intolerant desire for something *more*, a hole that can never be filled, a thirst that can never be quenched. It is at the root of corruption and addiction, of self-pity and self-destruction.

When we pursue pain, we are able to *choose* what pain we bring into our lives. And this choice makes the pain meaningful—and therefore, it is what makes life feel meaningful.

Because pain is the universal constant of life, the opportunities to grow from that pain are constant in life. All that is required is that we don't numb it, that we don't look away. All that is required is that we engage it and find the value and meaning in it.

Pain is the source of all value. To numb ourselves to our pain is to numb ourselves to anything that matters in the world.[30] Pain opens up the moral gaps that eventually become our most deeply held values and beliefs.

When we deny ourselves the ability to feel pain for a purpose, we deny ourselves the ability to feel any purpose in our life at all.

CHAPTER 8

The Feelings Economy

In the 1920s, women didn't smoke—or, if they did, they were severely judged for it. It was taboo. Like graduating from college or getting elected to Congress, smoking, people believed back then, should be left to the men. "Honey, you might hurt yourself. Or worse, you might burn your beautiful hair."

This posed a problem for the tobacco industry. Here you had 50 percent of the population not smoking their cigarettes for no other reason than it was unfashionable or seen as impolite. This wouldn't do. As George Washington Hill, president of the American Tobacco Company, said at the time, "It's a gold mine right in our front yard." The industry tried multiple times to market cigarettes to women, but nothing ever seemed to work. The cultural prejudice against it was simply too ingrained, too deep.

Then, in 1928, the American Tobacco Company hired Edward Bernays, a young hotshot marketer with wild ideas and even wilder marketing campaigns.[1] Bernays's marketing tactics at the time were unlike anybody else's in the advertising industry.

Back in the early nineteenth century, marketing was seen simply as a means of communicating the tangible, real benefits of a product in the simplest and most concise form possible. It was believed at the time that people bought products based on facts and information. If someone wanted to buy cheese, then you had to communicate to them the facts of why your cheese was superior ("Freshest French goat milk, cured twelve days, shipped re-frigerated!"). People were seen as rational actors making rational purchasing decisions for themselves. It was the Classic Assumption: the Thinking Brain was in charge.

But Bernays was unconventional. He didn't believe that people made rational decisions most of the time. He believed the opposite. He believed that people were emotional and impulsive and just hid it really well. He believed the Feeling Brain was in charge and nobody had quite realized it.

Whereas the tobacco industry had been focused on persuading individual women to buy and smoke cigarettes through logical arguments, Bernays saw it as an emotional and cultural issue. If he wanted women to smoke, then he had to appeal not to their thoughts but to their values. He needed to appeal to women's *identities*.

To accomplish this, Bernays hired a group of women and got them into the Easter Sunday Parade in New York City. Today, big holiday parades are cheesy things you let drone on over the television while you fall asleep on the couch. But back in those days, parades were big social events, kind of like the Super Bowl or something.

As Bernays planned it, at the appropriate moment, these women would all stop and light up cigarettes at the same time. He hired photographers to take flattering photos of the smoking women, which he then passed out to all the major national newspapers. He told the reporters that these ladies were not just lighting cigarettes, they were lighting "torches of freedom," demonstrating their ability to assert their independence and be their own women.

It was all #FakeNews, of course, but Bernays staged it as a political protest. He knew this would trigger the appropriate emotions in women across the country. Feminists had won women the right to vote only nine years earlier. Women were now working outside the home and becoming more integral to the country's economic life. They were asserting themselves by cutting their hair short and wearing racier clothing. This generation of women saw themselves as the first generation that could behave independently of a man. And many of them felt very strongly about this. If Bernays could just hitch his "smoking equals freedom" message onto the women's liberation movement . . . well, tobacco sales would double and he'd be a rich man.

It worked. Women started smoking, and ever since, we've had equal-opportunity lung cancer.

Bernays went on to pull off these kinds of cultural coups regularly throughout the 1920s, '30s, and '40s. He completely revolutionized the marketing industry and invented the field of public relations in the process. Paying sexy celebrities to use your product? That was Bernays's idea. Creating fake news articles that are actually subtle advertisements for a company? All him. Staging controversial public events as a means to draw attention and notoriety for a client? Bernays. Pretty much every form of marketing and publicity we're subjected to today began with Bernays.

But here's something else interesting about Bernays: he was Sigmund Freud's nephew.

Freud was infamous because he was the first modern thinker to argue that it was the Feeling Brain that was really driving the Consciousness Car. Freud believed that people's insecurities and shame drove them to make bad decisions, to overindulge or to compensate for what they felt they lacked. Freud was the one who realized that we have cohesive identities, stories in our minds that we tell about ourselves, and that we are emotionally attached to those stories and will fight to maintain them.[2] Freud argued that, at the end of the day, we are animals: impulsive and selfish and emotional.

Freud spent most of his life broke. He was the quintessential European intellectual: isolated, erudite, deeply philosophical. But Bernays was an American. He was practical. He was driven. Fuck philosophy! He wanted to be rich. And boy, did Freud's ideas—translated through the lens of marketing—deliver in a big way.[3] Through Freud, Bernays understood something nobody else in business had understood before him: that if you can tap into people's insecurities, they will buy just about any damn thing you tell them to.

Trucks are marketed to men as ways to assert strength and reliability. Makeup is marketed to women as a way to be more loved and garner more attention. Beer is marketed as a way to have fun and be the center of attention at a party.

This is all Marketing 101, of course. And today it's celebrated as business as usual. One of the first things you learn when you study marketing is how to find customers' "pain points" . . . and then subtly make them feel worse. The idea is that you needle at people's shame and insecurity and then turn around and tell them your product will resolve that shame and rid them of that insecurity. Put another way, marketing specifically identifies or accentuates the customer's moral gaps and then offers a way to fill them.

On the one hand, this has helped produce all the economic diversity and wealth we experience today. On the other hand, when marketing messages designed to induce feelings of inadequacy are scaled up to thousands of advertising messages hitting every single person, every single day, there *have to be* psychological repercussions to that. And they can't be good.

Feelings Make the World Go 'Round

The world runs on one thing: feelings.

This is because people spend money on things that make them feel good. And where the money flows, power flows. So, the more you're able to influence the emotions of people in the world, the more money and power you'll accumulate.

Money is itself a form of exchange used to equalize moral gaps between people. Money is its own special, universal mini-religion that we all bought into because it makes our lives a little bit easier. It allows us to convert our values into something universal when we're dealing with one another. You love seashells and oysters. I love fertilizing soil with the blood of my sworn enemies. You fight in my army, and when we get home, I'll make you rich with seashells and oysters. Deal?

That's how human economies emerged.[4] No, really, they started because a bunch of angry kings and emperors wanted to slaughter their sworn enemies, but they needed to give their armies something in return, so they minted money as a form of debt (or moral gap) for the soldiers to "spend" (equalize) when (or if) they got back home.

Not much has changed, of course. The world ran on feelings then; it runs on feelings now. All that's changed is the gizmos we use to shit on each other. Technological progress is just one manifestation of the Feelings Economy. For instance, nobody ever tried to invent a talking waffle. Why? Because that'd be fucking creepy and weird, not to mention probably not very nutritious. Instead, technologies are researched and invented to—yep, you guessed it!—make people feel better (or prevent them from feeling worse). The ballpoint pen, a more comfortable seat heater, a better gasket for your house's plumbing—fortunes are made and lost around things that help people improve upon or avoid pain. These things make people feel good. People get excited. They spend money. Then it's boom times, baby.

There are two ways to create value in the marketplace:

1. **Innovations (upgrade pain).** The first way to create value is to replace one pain with a much more tolerable/desirable pain. The most drastic and obvious examples of this are medical and pharmaceutical innovations. Polio vaccines replaced a lifetime of debilitating pain and immobility with a few seconds of a needle prick. Heart surgeries replaced . . . well, death with having to recover from surgery for a week or two.

2. **Diversions (avoid pain).** The second way to create value in a marketplace is to help people *numb* their pain. Whereas upgrading people's pain gives them *better* pain, numbing pain just delays that pain, and often even makes it worse. Diversions are a weekend beach trip, a night out with friends, a movie with someone special, or snorting cocaine out of the crack of a hooker's ass. There's nothing necessarily wrong with diversions; we all need them from time to time. The problem is when they begin to dominate our lives and wrest control away from our will. Many diversions trip certain circuits in our brain, making them addictive. The more you numb pain, the worse that pain becomes, thus impelling you to numb it further. At a certain point, the icky ball of pain grows to such great proportions that your avoidance of that pain becomes compulsive. You lose control of yourself—your Feeling Brain has locked your Thinking Brain in the trunk and isn't letting it out until it gets its next hit of whatever. And the downward spiral ensues.

When the scientific revolution first got going, most economic progress was due to innovation. Back then, the vast majority of people lived in poverty: Everyone was sick, hungry, cold, and tired most of the time. Few could read. Most had bad teeth. It was no fun at all. Over the next few hundred years, with the invention of machines and cities and the division of labor and modern medicine and hygiene and representative government, a lot of poverty and hardship was alleviated. Vaccines and medicines have saved billions of lives. Machines have reduced backbreaking workloads and starvation around the world. The technological innovations that upgraded human suffering are undoubtedly a good thing.

But what happens when a large number of people are relatively healthy and wealthy? At that point, most economic progress switches from innovation to diversion, from upgrading pain to avoiding pain. One of the reasons for this is that true innovation is risky, difficult, and often unrewarding. Many of the most important innovations in history left their inventors broke and destitute.[5] If someone is going to start a company and take a risk, going the diversion route is a safer bet. As a result, we've built a culture in which most technological "innovation" is merely figuring out how to scale diversions in new, more efficient (and more intrusive) ways. As the venture capitalist Peter Thiel once said, "We wanted flying cars, instead we got Twitter."

Once an economy switches over primarily to diversions, the culture begins to shift. As a poor country develops and gains access to medicine, phones, and other innovative technologies, measurements of well-being track upward at a steady clip, as everyone's pain is being upgraded to better pain. But once the country hits First World level, that well-being flattens or, in some cases, drops off.[6] Meanwhile, mental illness, depression, and anxiety can proliferate.[7]

This happens because opening up a society and giving it modern innovations makes the people more robust and antifragile. They can survive more hardship, work more efficiently, communicate and function better within their communities.

But once those innovations are integrated and everyone has a cell phone and a McDonald's Happy Meal, the great modern diversions enter the marketplace. And as soon as the diversions show up, a psychological fragility is introduced, and everything begins to seem fucked.[8]

The commercial age commenced in the early twentieth century with Bernays's discovery that you could market to people's unconscious feelings and desires.[9] Bernays wasn't concerned with penicillin or heart surgery. He was hawking cigarettes and tabloid magazines and beauty products—shit people didn't need. And until then, nobody had figured out how to get people to spend copious amounts of money on stuff that wasn't necessary for their survival.

The invention of marketing brought a modern-day gold rush to satiate people's pursuit of happiness. Pop culture emerged, and celebrities and athletes got stupid rich. For the first time, luxury items started to be mass-produced and advertised to the middle classes. There was explosive growth in the technologies of convenience: microwavable dinners, fast food, La-Z-Boys, no-stick pans, and so on. Life became so easy and fast and efficient and effortless that within the short span of a hundred years, people were able to pick up a telephone and accomplish in two minutes what used to take two months.

Life in the commercial age, although more complex than before, was still relatively simple compared to today. A large, bustling middle class existed within a homogenous culture. We watched the same TV channels, listened to the same music, ate the same food, relaxed on the same types of sofas, and read the same newspapers and magazines. There was continuity and cohesion to this era, which brought a sense of security with it. We were all, for a time, both free and yet part of the same religion. And that was comforting. Despite the constant threat of nuclear annihilation, at least in the West, we tend to idealize this period. I believe that it's for this sense of social cohesion that many people today are so nostalgic.

Then, the internet happened.

The internet is a bona fide innovation. All else being equal, it fundamentally makes our lives better. Much better.

The problem is . . . well, the problem is *us*.

The internet's intentions were good: inventors and technologists in Silicon Valley and elsewhere had high hopes for a digital planet. They worked for decades toward a vision of seamlessly networking the world's people and information. They believed that the internet would liberate people, removing gatekeepers and hierarchies and giving everyone equal access to the same information and the same opportunities to express themselves. They believed that if everyone were given a voice and a simple, effective means of sharing that voice, the world would be a better, freer place.

A near-utopian level of optimism developed throughout the 1990s and 2000s. Technologists envisioned a highly educated global population that would tap into the infinite wisdom available at its fingertips. They saw the opportunity to engender greater empathy and understanding across nations, ethnicities, and lifestyles. They dreamed of a unified and connected global movement with a single shared interest in peace and prosperity.

But they forgot.

They were so caught up in their religious dreams and personal hopes that they forgot.

They forgot that the world doesn't run on information.

People don't make decisions based on truth or facts. They don't spend their money based on data. They don't connect with each other because of some higher philosophical truth.

The world runs on *feelings*.

And when you give the average person an infinite reservoir of human wisdom, they will not google for the information that contradicts their deepest held beliefs. They will not google for what is true yet unpleasant.

Instead, most of us will google for what is pleasant but untrue.

Having an errant racist thought? Well, there's a whole forum of racists two clicks away, with a lot of convincing-sounding arguments as to why you shouldn't be ashamed to have such leanings. The wife leaves you and you start thinking women are inherently selfish and evil? Doesn't take much of a Google search to find justifications for those misogynistic feelings.[10] Think Muslims are going to stalk from school to school, murdering your children? I'm sure there's a conspiracy theory somewhere out there that's already "proving" that.

Instead of stemming the free expression of our worst feelings and darkest inclinations, the start-ups and corporations dove right in to cash in on it. Thus, the greatest innovation of our lifetime has slowly transformed into our greatest diversion.

The internet, in the end, was not designed to give us what we need. Instead, it gives people what they want. And if you've learned anything about human psychology in this book, you already know that this is much more dangerous than it sounds.

#FakeFreedom

It must be an odd time to be a super-successful businessperson. On the one hand, business is better than ever. There's more wealth in the world than ever before, profits are breaking all-time highs, productivity and growth are doing great. Yet, meanwhile, income inequality is skyrocketing, political polarization is ruining everyone's family gatherings, and there seems to be a plague of corruption spreading across the world.

So, while there's exuberance in the business world, there's also a weird sort of defensiveness that sometimes comes out of nowhere. And this defensiveness, I've noticed, always takes the same form, no matter whom it comes from. It says: "We're just giving people what they want!"

Whether it's oil companies or creepy advertisers or Facebook stealing your damn data, every corporation that steps in some shit scrapes off their boot by frantically reminding everyone how they're just trying to give people what they want—faster download speeds, more comfortable air-conditioning, better gas mileage, a cheaper nose hair trimmer—and how wrong can that be?

And it is true. Technology gives people what they want faster and more efficiently than ever before. And while we all love to dogpile on the corporate overlords for their ethical faceplants, we forget that they're merely fulfilling the market's desires. They're supplying our demands. And if we got rid of Facebook or BP or whatever-giant-corporation-is-considered-evil-when-you-read-this, another would pop up to take its place.

So, maybe the problem isn't just a bunch of greedy executives tapping cigars and petting evil cats while laughing hysterically at how much money they're making.

Maybe what we want sucks.

For example, I *want* a life-size bag of marshmallows in my living room. I *want* to buy an eight-million-dollar mansion by borrowing money I can never pay back. I *want* to fly to a new beach every week for the next year and live off nothing but Wagyu steaks.

What I want is fucking terrible. That's because my Feeling Brain is in charge of what I want, and my Feeling Brain is like a goddamn chimpanzee who just drank a bottle of tequila and then proceeded to jerk off into it.

Therefore, I'd say that "give the people what they want" is a pretty low bar to clear, ethically speaking. "Give the people what they want" works only when you're giving them innovations, like a synthetic kidney or something to prevent their car from spontaneously catching on fire. Give *those* people what they want. But giving people too many of the diversions they want is a dangerous game to play. For one, many people want stuff that's awful. Two, many people are easily manipulated into wanting shit they don't actually want (see: Bernays). Three, encouraging people to avoid pain through more and more diversions makes us all weaker and more fragile. And four, I don't want your fucking Skynet ads following me around wherever I go and mining my fucking life for data. Look, I talked to my wife that one time about a trip to Peru—that doesn't mean you need to flood my phone with pictures of Machu Picchu for the next six weeks. And seriously, stop listening to my fucking conversations and selling my data to anyone and everyone who will pay you a buck.[II]

Anyway—where was I?

Strangely, Bernays saw all this coming. The creepy ads and the privacy invasion and the lulling of large populations into docile servitude through mindless consumerism—the dude was kind of a genius. Except, he was all in favor of it—so, make that an evil genius.

Bernays's political beliefs were appalling. He believed in what I suppose you could call "diet fascism": same evil authoritarian government but without the unnecessary genocidal calories. Bernays believed that the masses were dangerous and needed to be controlled by a strong centralized state. But he also recognized that bloody totalitarian regimes were not exactly ideal. For him, the new science of marketing offered a way for governments to influence and appease their citizens without the burden of having to maim and torture them left, right, and center.[12]

(The dude must have been a hit at parties.)

Bernays believed that freedom for most people was both impossible and dangerous. He was well aware, from reading Uncle Freud's writings, that the last thing a society should tolerate was everyone's Feeling Brains running the show. Societies needed order and hierarchy and authority, and freedom was antithetical to those things. He saw marketing as an incredible new tool that could give people the *feeling of having freedom* when, really, you're just giving them a few more flavors of toothpaste to choose from.

Thankfully, Western governments (for the most part) never sank so low as to directly manipulate their populations through ad campaigns. Instead, the opposite happened. The corporate world got so good at giving people what they wanted that they gradually gained more and more political power for themselves. Regulations were torn up. Bureaucratic oversight was ended. Privacy eroded. Money got more enmeshed with politics than ever before. And why did it all happen? You should know by now: they were just giving the people what they wanted!

But, fuck it, let's be real: "Give the people what they want" is just #FakeFreedom because what most of us want are diversions. And when we get flooded by diversions, a few things happen.

The first is that we become increasingly fragile. Our world shrinks to conform to the size of our ever-diminishing values. We become obsessed with comfort and pleasure. And any possible loss of that pleasure feels world-quaking and cosmically unfair to us. I would argue that a narrowing of our conceptual world is not freedom; it is the opposite.

The second thing that happens is that we become prone to a series of low-level addictive behaviors—compulsively checking our phone, our email, our Instagram; compulsively finishing Netflix series we don't like; sharing outrage-inducing articles we haven't read; accepting invitations to parties and events we don't enjoy; traveling not because we want to but because we want to be able to say we went. Compulsive behavior aimed at experiencing *more stuff* is not freedom—again, it's kind of the opposite.

Third thing: an inability to identify, tolerate, and seek out negative emotions is its own kind of confinement. If you feel okay only when life is happy and easy-breezy-beautiful-Cover-Girl, then guess what? You are not free. You are the opposite of free. You are the prisoner of your own indulgences, enslaved by your own intolerance, crippled by your own emotional weakness. You will constantly feel a need for some external comfort or validation that may or may not ever come.

Fourth—because, fuck it, I'm on a roll: the paradox of choice. The more options we're given (i.e., the more "freedom" we have), the less satisfied we are with whatever option we go with.[13] If Jane has to choose between two boxes of cereal, and Mike can choose from twenty boxes, Mike does not have more freedom than Jane. He has more *variety*. There's a difference. Variety is not freedom. Variety is just different permutations of the same meaningless shit. If, instead, Jane had a gun pointed to her head and a guy in an SS uniform screaming, "Eat ze fuckin' zereal!" in a really bad

Bavarian accent, *then* Jane would have less freedom than Mike. But call me up when *that* happens.

This is the problem with exalting freedom over human consciousness. More stuff doesn't make us freer, it imprisons us with anxiety over whether we chose or did the best thing. More stuff causes us to become more prone to treating ourselves and others as means rather than ends. It makes us more dependent on the endless cycles of hope.

If the pursuit of happiness pulls us all back into childishness, then fake freedom conspires to keep us there. Because freedom is not having more brands of cereal to choose from, or more beach vacations to take selfies on, or more satellite channels to fall asleep to.

That is variety. And in a vacuum, variety is meaningless. If you are trapped by insecurity, stymied by doubt, and hamstrung by intolerance, you can have all the variety in the world. But you are not free.

Real Freedom

The only true form of freedom, the only ethical form of freedom, is through self-*limitation*. It is not the privilege of choosing everything you want in your life, but rather, choosing what you will *give up* in your life.

This is not only real freedom, this is the *only* freedom. Diversions come and go. Pleasure never lasts. Variety loses its meaning. But you will always be able to choose what you are willing to sacrifice, what you are willing to give up.

This sort of self-denial is paradoxically the only thing that expands real freedom in life. The pain of regular physical exercise ultimately enhances your physical freedom—your strength, mobility, endurance, and stamina. The sacrifice of a strong work ethic gives you the freedom to pursue more job opportunities, to steer your own career trajectory, to earn more money and the benefits that come with it. The willingness to engage in conflict with others will free you to talk to anyone, to see if they share your values and beliefs, to discover what they can add to your life and what you can add to theirs.

You can become freer right now simply by choosing the limitations you want to impose on yourself. You can choose to wake up earlier each morning, to block your email until midafternoon each day, to delete social media apps from your phone. These limitations will free you because they will liberate your time, attention, and power of choice. They treat your consciousness as an end in itself.

If you struggle to go to the gym, then rent a locker and leave all your work clothes there so you *have to go* each morning. Limit yourself to two to three social events each week, so you are forced to spend time with the people you care about most. Write a check to a close friend or family member for three thousand dollars and tell them that if you ever smoke a cigarette again, they get to cash it.[14]

Ultimately, the most meaningful freedom in your life comes from your commitments, the things in life for which you have chosen to sacrifice. There is emotional freedom in my relationship with my wife that I would never be able to reproduce even if I dated a thousand other women. There is freedom in my having played guitar for twenty years—a deeply artistic expression—that I could not get if I just memorized dozens of songs. There is freedom in having lived in one place for fifty years—an intimacy and familiarity with the community and culture—that you cannot replicate no matter how much of the world you've seen.

Greater commitment allows for greater depth. A lack of commitment requires superficiality.

In the last ten years, there has been a trend toward "life hacking." People want to learn a language in a month, to visit fifteen countries in a month, to become a champion martial artist in a week, and they come up with all sorts of "hacks" to do it. You see it all the time on YouTube and social media these days: people undertaking ridiculous challenges just to show it can be done. This "hacking" of life, though, simply amounts to trying to reap the rewards of commitment without actually making a commitment. It's another sad form of fake freedom. It's empty calories for the soul.

I recently read about a guy who memorized moves from a chess program to prove he could "master" chess in a month. He didn't learn anything about chess, didn't engage with the strategy, develop a style, learn tactics. Nope, he approached it like a gigantic homework assignment: memorize the moves, win once against some highly ranked player, then declare mastery for yourself.[15]

This is not winning anything. This is merely the *appearance* of winning something. It is the appearance of commitment and sacrifice without the commitment and sacrifice. It is the appearance of meaning where there is none.

Fake freedom puts us on the treadmill toward chasing more, whereas real freedom is the conscious decision to live with less.

Fake freedom is addictive: no matter how much you have, you always feel as though it's not enough. Real freedom is repetitive, predictable, and sometimes dull.

Fake freedom has diminishing returns: it requires greater and greater amounts of energy to achieve the same joy and meaning. Real freedom has increasing returns: it requires less and less energy to achieve the same joy and meaning.

Fake freedom is seeing the world as an endless series of transactions and bargains which you feel you're winning. Real freedom is seeing the world unconditionally, with the only victory being over your own desires.

Fake freedom requires the world to conform to your will. Real freedom requires nothing of the world. It is only your will.

Ultimately, the overabundance of diversion and the fake freedom it produces limits our ability to experience real freedom. The more options we have, the more variety before us, the more difficult it becomes to choose, sacrifice, and focus. And we are seeing this conundrum play out across our culture today.

In 2000, the Harvard political scientist Robert Putnam published his seminal book *Bowling Alone: The Collapse and Revival of American Community*.[16] In it, he documents the decline of civic participation across the United States, arguing that people are joining and participating less in groups, instead preferring to do their activities alone, hence the title of the book: More people bowl today than before, yet bowling leagues are going extinct. People are bowling alone. Putnam wrote about the United States, but this not merely an American phenomenon.[17]

Throughout the book, Putnam shows that this is not limited to recreational groups but is affecting everything from labor unions to parent-teacher associations to Rotary clubs to churches to bridge clubs. This atomization of society has significant effects, he argues: social trust has declined, with people becoming more isolated, less politically engaged, and all-around more paranoid about their neighbors.[18]

Loneliness is also a growing issue. Last year, for the first time, a majority of Americans said they were lonely, and new research is suggesting that we're replacing a few high-quality relationships in our lives with a large number of superficial and temporary relationships.[19]

According to Putnam, the social connective tissue in the country is being destroyed by the overabundance of diversions. He argued that people were choosing to stay home and watch TV, surf the internet, or play video games rather than commit themselves to some local organization or group. He also predicts the situation will likely only get worse.[20]

Historically, when Westerners have looked at all the oppressed people throughout the world, we've lamented their lack of fake freedom, their lack of diversion. People in North Korea can't read the news or shop for clothes they like or listen to music that isn't state sponsored.

But this is not why North Koreans are not free. They lack freedom not because they are unable to choose their pleasures, but because they are not allowed to choose their pain. They are not allowed to choose their commitments freely. They are forced into sacrifices they would not otherwise want or do not deserve. Pleasure is beside the point—their lack of pleasure is a mere side effect of their real oppression: their enforced pain.[21]

Because, today, in most parts of the world, people are now able to choose their pleasures. They are able to choose what to read and what games to play and what to wear. Modern diversions are everywhere. But the tyranny of a new age is achieved not by depriving people of diversions and commitments. Today's tyranny is achieved by flooding people with so much diversion, so much bullshit information and frivolous distraction, that they are unable to make smart commitments. It's Bernays's prediction come true, just a few generations later than he expected. It took the breadth and power of the internet to make his vision of global propaganda campaigns, of governments and corporations silently steering the desires and wishes of the masses, a reality.[22]

But let's not give Bernays too much credit. After all, he did seem like kind of a douche balloon.

Besides, there was a man who saw all this coming way before Bernays, a man who saw the dangers of fake freedom, who saw the proliferation of diversions and the myopic effect they would have on people's values, how too much pleasure makes everyone childish and selfish and entitled and totally narcissistic and unbearable on Twitter. This man was far wiser and more influential than anyone you would ever see on a news channel or a TED Talk stage or a political soapbox, for that matter. This guy was the OG of political philosophy. Forget the "Godfather of Soul," this guy literally invented the idea of the soul. And he (arguably) saw this whole shitstorm brewing multiple millennia before anyone else did.

Plato's Prediction

English philosopher and mathematician Alfred North Whitehead famously said that all of Western philosophy was merely a "series of footnotes to Plato."[23] Any topic you can think of, from the nature of romantic love, to whether there's such a thing as "truth," to the meaning of virtue, Plato was likely the first great thinker to expound upon it. Plato was the first to suggest that there was an inherent separation between the Thinking Brain and the Feeling Brain.[24] He was the first to argue that one must build character through various forms of self-denial, rather than through self-indulgence.[25] Plato was such a badass, the word *idea* itself comes from him—so, you could say he invented the idea of an idea.[26]

Interestingly, despite being the godfather of Western civilization, Plato famously claimed that democracy was not the most desirable form of government.[27] He believed that democracy was inherently unstable and that it inevitably unleashed the worst aspects of our nature, driving society toward tyranny. He wrote, "Extreme freedom can't be expected to lead to anything but a change to extreme slavery."[28]

Democracies are designed to reflect the will of the people. We've learned that people, when left to their own devices, instinctively run away from pain and toward happiness. The problem then emerges when people achieve happiness: It's never enough. Due to the Blue Dot Effect, they never feel entirely safe or satisfied. Their desires grow in lockstep with the quality of their circumstances.

Eventually, the institutions won't be able to keep up with the desires of the people. And when the institutions fail to keep up with people's happiness, guess what happens.

People start blaming the institutions themselves.

Plato said that democracies inevitably lead to moral decay because as they indulge more in fake freedom, people's values deteriorate and become more childish and self-centered, resulting in the citizenry turning on the democratic system itself. Once childish values take over, people no longer want to negotiate for power, they don't want to bargain with other groups and other religions, they don't want to endure pain for the sake of greater freedom or prosperity. What they want instead is a strong leader to come make everything right at a moment's notice. They want a tyrant.[29]

There's a common saying in the United States that "freedom is not free." The saying is usually used in reference to the military and wars fought and won to protect the values of the country. It's a way of reminding people that, hey, this shit didn't just magically happen—thousands of people were killed and/or died for us to sit here and sip overpriced mocha Frappuccinos and say whatever the fuck we want. It's a reminder that the basic human rights we enjoy (free speech, freedom of religion, freedom of the press) were earned through a sacrifice against some external force.

But people forget that these rights are also earned through sacrifice against some *internal force*. Democracy can exist only when you are willing to tolerate views that oppose your own, when you're willing to give up some things you might want for the sake of a safe and healthy community, when you're willing to compromise and accept that sometimes things don't go your way.

Put another way: democracy requires a citizenry of strong maturity and character.

Over the last couple of decades, people seem to have confused their basic human rights with not experiencing any discomfort. People want freedom to express themselves, but they don't want to have to deal with views that may upset or offend them in some way. They want freedom of enterprise, but they don't want to pay taxes to support the legal machinery that makes that freedom possible. They want equality, but they don't want to accept that equality requires that everybody experience the same pain, not that everybody experience the same pleasure.

Freedom itself demands discomfort. It demands dissatisfaction. Because the freer a society becomes, the more each person will be forced to reckon and compromise with views and lifestyles and ideas that conflict with their own. The lower our tolerance for pain, the more we indulge in fake freedoms, the less we will be able to uphold the virtues necessary to allow a free, democratic society to function.

And that's scary. Because without democracy, we're *really* fucked. No, really—empirically, life just gets so much worse without democratic representation, in almost every way.[30] And it's not because democracy is so great. It's more that a functioning democracy fucks things up less often and less severely than any other form of government. Or, as Churchill famously once said, "Democracy is the worst form of government, except all the others."

The whole reason the world became civilized and everyone stopped slaughtering one another because of their funny hats is because modern social institutions effectively mitigated the destructive forces of hope. Democracy is one of the few religions that manages to allow other religions to live harmoniously alongside it and within it. But when those social institutions are corrupted by the constant need to please people's Feeling Brains, when people become distrustful and lose faith in the democratic system's ability to self-correct, then it's back to the shit show of religious warfare.[31] And with the ever-advancing march of technological innovations, each cycle of religious war potentially wreaks more destruction and devastates more human life.[32]

Plato believed societies were cyclical, bouncing back and forth between freedom and tyranny, relative equality and great inequality. It's pretty clear after the past twenty-five hundred years that this isn't exactly true. But there *are* patterns of political conflict throughout history, and you do see the same religious themes pop up again and again—the radical hierarchy of master morality versus the radical equality of slave morality, the emergence of tyrannical leaders versus the diffuse power of democratic institutions, the struggle of adult virtues against childish extremism. While the "isms" have changed throughout the centuries, the same hope-driven human impulses have been behind each movement. And while each subsequent religion believes *it* is the ultimate, capital *T* "Truth" to unite humanity under a single, harmonious banner, so far, each of them has only proven to be partial and incomplete.

CHAPTER 9

The Final Religion

In 1997, Deep Blue, a supercomputer developed by IBM, beat Garry Kasparov, the world's best chess player. It was a watershed moment in the history of computing, a seismic event that shook many people's understanding of technology, intelligence, and humanity. But today, it is but a quaint memory: of course a computer would beat the world champion at chess. Why wouldn't it?

Since the beginning of computing, chess has been a favorite means to test artificial intelligence.[1] That's because chess possesses a near-infinite number of permutations: there are more possible chess games than there are atoms in the observable universe. In any board position, if one looks only three or four moves ahead, there are already hundreds of millions of variations.

For a computer to match a human player, not only must it be capable of calculating an incredible number of possible outcomes, but it must also have solid algorithms to help it decide what's *worth* calculating. Put another way: to beat a human player, a computer's Thinking Brain, despite being vastly superior to a human's, must be programmed to evaluate more/less valuable board positions— that is, the computer must have a modestly powerful "Feeling Brain" programmed into it.[2]

Since that day in 1997, computers have continued to improve at chess at a staggering rate. Over the following fifteen years, the top human players regularly got pummeled by chess software, sometimes by embarrassing margins.[3] Today, it's not even close.

Kasparov himself recently joked that the chess app that comes installed on most smartphones "is far more powerful than Deep Blue was."[4] These days, chess software developers hold tournaments for their programs to see whose algorithms come out on top. Humans are not only excluded from these tournaments, but they'd likely not even place high enough for it to matter anyway.

The undisputed champion of the chess software world for the past few years has been an open-source program called Stockfish. Stockfish has either won or been the runner-up in almost every significant chess software tournament since 2014. A collaboration between half a dozen lifelong chess software developers, Stockfish today represents the pinnacle of chess logic. Not only is it a chess engine, but it can analyze any game, any position, giving grandmaster-level feedback within seconds of each move a player makes.

Stockfish was happily going along being the king of the computerized chess mountain, being the gold standard of all chess analysis worldwide, until 2018, when Google showed up to the party.

Then shit got weird.

Google has a program called AlphaZero. It's not chess software. It's artificial intelligence (AI) software. Instead of being programmed to play chess or another game, the software is programmed to *learn*—and not just chess, but any game.

Early in 2018, Stockfish faced off against Google's AlphaZero. On paper, it was not even close to a fair fight. AlphaZero can calculate "only" eighty thousand board positions per second. Stockfish? Seventy *million*. In terms of computational power, that's like me entering a footrace against a Formula One race car.

But it gets even weirder: the day of the match, AlphaZero *didn't even know how to play chess*. Yes, that's right—before its match with the best chess software in the world, AlphaZero had less than a day to learn chess from scratch. The software spent most of the day running simulations of chess games against itself, learning as it went. It developed strategies and principles the same way a human would: through trial and error.

Imagine the scenario. You've just learned the rules of chess, one of the most complex games on the planet. You're given less than a day to mess around with a board and figure out some strategies. And from there, your first game ever will be against the world champion.

Good luck.

Yet, somehow, AlphaZero won. Okay, it didn't just win. Alpha-Zero smashed Stockfish. Out of one hundred games, AlphaZero won or drew *every single game*.

Read that again: a mere *nine hours* after learning the rules to chess, AlphaZero played the best chess-playing entity in the world and did not drop a single game out of one hundred. It was a result so unprecedented that people still don't know what to make of it. Human grandmasters marveled at the creativity and ingenuity of AlphaZero. One, Peter Heine Nielsen, gushed, "I always wondered how it would be if a superior species landed on earth and showed us how they play chess. I feel now I know."[5]

When AlphaZero was done with Stockfish, it didn't take a break. *Pfft*, please! Breaks are for frail humans. Instead, as soon as it had finished with Stockfish, AlphaZero began teaching itself the strategy game Shogi.

Shogi is often referred to as Japanese chess, but many argue that it's more complex than chess.[6] Whereas Kasparov lost to a computer in 1997, top Shogi players didn't begin to lose to computers until 2013. Either way, AlphaZero destroyed the top Shogi software (called "Elmo"), and by a similarly astounding margin:

in one hundred games, it won ninety, lost eight, and drew two. Once again, AlphaZero's computational powers were far less than Elmo's. (In this case, it could calculate forty thousand moves per second compared to Elmo's thirty-five million.) And once again, AlphaZero hadn't even known how to play the game the previous day.

In the morning, it taught itself two infinitely complex games. And by sundown, it had dismantled the best-known competition on earth.

News flash: AI is coming. And while chess and Shogi are one thing, as soon as we take AI out of the board games and start putting it in the board rooms . . . well, you and I and everyone else will probably find ourselves out of a job.[7]

Already, AI programs have invented their own languages that humans can't decipher, become more effective than doctors at diagnosing pneumonia, and even written passable chapters of Harry Potter fan fiction.[8] At the time of this writing, we're on the cusp of having self-driving cars, automated legal advice, and even computer-generated art and music.[9]

Slowly but surely, AI will become better than we are at pretty much everything: medicine, engineering, construction, art, technological innovation. You'll watch movies created by AI, and discuss them on websites or mobile platforms built by AI, moderated by AI, and it might even turn out that the "person" you'll argue with will be an AI.

But as crazy as that sounds, it's just the beginning. Because here is where the bananas will really hit the fan: *the day an AI can write AI software better than we can.*

When *that* day comes, when an AI can essentially spawn better versions of itself, at will, then buckle your seatbelt, amigo, because it's going to be a wild ride and we will no longer have control over where we're going.

AI will reach a point where its intelligence outstrips ours by so much that we will no longer comprehend what it's doing. Cars will pick us up for reasons we don't understand and take us to locations we didn't know existed. We will unexpectedly receive medications for health issues we didn't know we suffered from. It's possible that our kids will switch schools, we will change jobs, economic policies will abruptly shift, governments will rewrite their constitutions—and none of us will comprehend the full reasons why. It will just happen. Our Thinking Brains will be too slow, and our Feeling Brains too erratic and dangerous. Like AlphaZero inventing chess strategies in mere hours that chess's greatest minds could not anticipate, advanced AI could reorganize society and all our places within it in ways we can't imagine.

Then, we will end up right back where we began: worshipping impossible and unknowable forces that seemingly control our fates. Just as primitive humans prayed to their gods for rain and flame—the same way they made sacrifices, offered gifts, devised rituals, and altered their behavior and appearance to curry favor with the naturalistic gods—so will we. But instead of the primitive gods, we will offer ourselves up to the AI gods.

We will develop superstitions about the algorithms. If you wear this, the algorithms will favor you. If you wake at a certain hour and say the right thing and show up at the right place, the machines will bless you with great fortune. If you are honest and you don't hurt others and you take care of yourself and your family, the AI gods will protect you.

The old gods will be replaced by the new gods: the algorithms. And in a twist of evolutionary irony, the same science that killed the gods of old will have built the gods of new. There will be a great return to religiosity among mankind. And our religions won't necessarily be so different from the religions of the ancient world—after all, our psychology is fundamentally evolved to deify what it doesn't understand, to exalt the forces that help or harm us, to construct systems of values around our experiences, to seek out conflict that generates hope.

Why would AI be any different?

Our AI gods will understand this, of course. And either they will find a way to "upgrade" our brains out of our primitive psychological need for continuous strife, or they will simply manufacture artificial strife for us. We will be like their pet dogs, convinced that we are protecting and fighting for our territory at all costs but, in reality, merely peeing on an endless series of digital fire hydrants.

This may frighten you. This may excite you. Either way, it is likely inevitable. Power emerges from the ability to manipulate and process information, and we always end up worshipping whatever has the most power over us.

So, allow me to say that I, for one, welcome our AI overlords.

I know, that's not the final religion you were hoping for. But that's where you went wrong: hoping.

Don't lament the loss of your own agency. If submitting to artificial algorithms sounds awful, understand this: you already do. And you *like* it.

The algorithms already run much of our lives. The route you took to work is based on an algorithm. Many of the friends you talked to this week? Those conversations were based on an algorithm. The gift you bought your kid, the amount of toilet paper that came in the deluxe pack, the fifty cents in savings you got for being a rewards member at the supermarket—all the result of algorithms.

We need these algorithms because they make our lives easier. And so will the algorithm gods of the near future. And as we did with the gods of the ancient world, we will rejoice in and give thanks to them. Indeed, it will be impossible to imagine life without them.[10] These algorithms make our lives better. They make our lives more efficient. They make *us* more efficient.

That's why, as soon as we cross over, there's no going back.

We Are Bad Algorithms

Here's one last way to look at the history of the world:

The difference between life and stuff is that life is stuff that self-replicates. Life is made out of cells and DNA that spawn more and more copies of themselves.

Over the course of hundreds of millions of years, some of these primordial life forms developed feedback mechanisms to better reproduce themselves. An early protozoon might evolve little sensors on its membrane to better detect amino acids by which to replicate more copies of itself, thus giving it an advantage over other single-cell organisms. But then maybe some other single-cell organism develops a way to "trick" other little amoeba-like things' sensors, thus interfering with their ability to find food, and giving *itself* an advantage.

Basically, there's been a biological arms race going on since the beginning of forever. This little single-cell thing develops a cool strategy to get more material to replicate itself than do other single-cell organisms, and therefore it wins the resources and reproduces more. Then another little single-cell thing evolves and has an *even better* strategy for getting food, and *it* proliferates. This continues, on and on, for billions of years, and pretty soon you have lizards that can camouflage their skin and monkeys that can fake animal sounds and awkward middle-aged divorced men spending all their money on bright red Chevy Camaros even though they can't really afford them—all because it promotes their survival and ability to reproduce.

This is the story of evolution—survival of the fittest and all that.

But you could also look at it a different way. You could call it "survival of the best information processing."

Okay, not as catchy, perhaps, but it actually might be more accurate.

See, that amoeba that evolves sensors on its membrane to better detect amino acids—that is, at its core, a form of information processing. It is better able than other organisms to detect the facts of its environment. And because it developed a better way to process information than other blobby cell-like things, it won the evolutionary game and spread its genes.

Similarly, the lizard that can camouflage its skin—that, too, has evolved a way to manipulate visual information to trick predators into ignoring it. Same story with the monkeys faking animal noises. Same deal with the desperate middle-aged dude and his Camaro (or maybe not).

Evolution rewards the most powerful creatures, and power is determined by the ability to access, harness, and manipulate information effectively. A lion can hear its prey over a mile away. A buzzard can see a rat from an altitude of three thousand feet. Whales develop their own personal songs and can communicate up to a hundred miles away from each other while underwater. These are all examples of exceptional information-processing capabilities, and that ability to receive and process information is linked to these creatures' ability to survive and reproduce.

Physically, humans are pretty unexceptional. We are weak, slow, and frail, and we tire easily.[11] But we are nature's ultimate information processors. We are the only species that can conceptualize the past and future, that can deduce long chains of cause and effect, that can plan and strategize in abstract terms, that can build and create and problem-solve in perpetuity.[12] Out of millions of years of evolution, the Thinking Brain (Kant's sacred conscious mind) is what has, in a few short millennia, dominated the entire planet and called into existence a vast, intricate web of production, technology, and networks.

That's because *we are algorithms.* Consciousness itself is a vast network of algorithms and decision trees—algorithms based on values and knowledge and hope.

Our algorithms worked pretty well for the first few hundred thousand years. They worked well on the savannah, when we were hunting bison and living in small nomadic communities and never met more than thirty people in our entire lives.

But in a globally networked economy of billions of people, stocked with thousands of nukes and Facebook privacy violations and holographic Michael Jackson concerts, our algorithms kind of suck. They break down and enter us into ever-escalating cycles of conflict that, by the nature of our algorithms, can produce no permanent satisfaction, no final peace.

It's like that brutal advice you sometimes hear, that the only thing all your fucked-up relationships have in common is you. Well, the only thing that all the biggest problems in the world have in common is us. Nukes wouldn't be a problem if there weren't some dumb fuck sitting there tempted to use them. Biochemical weapons, climate change, endangered species, genocide—you name it, none of it was an issue until we came along.[13] Domestic violence, rape, money laundering, fraud—it's all us.

Life is fundamentally built on algorithms. We just happen to be the most sophisticated and complex algorithms nature has yet produced, the zenith of about one billion years' worth of evolutionary forces. And now we are on the cusp of producing algorithms that are exponentially better than we are.

Despite all our accomplishments, the human mind is still incredibly flawed. Our ability to process information is hamstrung by our emotional need to validate ourselves. It is curved inward by our perceptual biases. Our Thinking Brain is regularly hijacked and kidnapped by our Feeling Brain's incessant desires—stuffed in the trunk of the Consciousness Car and often gagged or drugged into incapacitation.

And as we've seen, our moral compass too frequently gets swung off course by our inevitable need to generate hope through conflict. As the moral psychologist Jonathan Haidt put it, "morality binds and blinds."[14] Our Feeling Brains are antiquated, outdated software. And while our Thinking Brains are decent, they're too slow and clunky to be of much use anymore. Just ask Garry Kasparov.

We are a self-hating, self-destructive species.[15] That is not a moral statement; it's simply a fact. This internal tension we all feel, all the time? That's what got us here. It's what got us to this point. It's our arms race. And we're about to hand over the evolutionary baton to the defining information processors of the next epoch: the machines.

When Elon Musk was asked what the most imminent threats to humanity were, he quickly said there were three: first, wide-scale nuclear war; second, climate change—and then, before naming the third, he fell silent. His face became sullen. He looked down, deep in thought. When the interviewer asked him, "What is the third?" He smiled and said, "I just hope the computers decide to be nice to us."

There is a lot of fear out there that AI will wipe away humanity.

Some suspect this might happen in a dramatic *Terminator 2*–type conflagration. Others worry that some machine will kill us off by "accident," that an AI designed to innovate better ways to make toothpicks will somehow discover that harvesting human bodies is the best way.[16] Bill Gates, Stephen Hawking, and Elon Musk are just a few of the leading thinkers and scientists who have crapped their pants at how rapidly AI is developing and how underprepared we are as a species for its repercussions.

But I think this fear is a bit silly. For one, how do you prepare for something that is vastly more intelligent than you are? It's like training a dog to play chess against . . . well, Kasparov. No matter how much the dog thinks and prepares, it's not going to matter.

More important, the machines' understanding of good and evil will likely surpass our own. As I write this, five different genocides are taking place in the world.[17] Seven hundred ninety-five million people are starving or undernourished.[18] By the time you finish this chapter, more than a hundred people, just in the United States, will be beaten, abused, or killed by a family member, in their own home.[19]

Are there potential dangers with AI? Sure. But morally speaking, we're throwing rocks inside a glass house here. What do we know about ethics and the humane treatment of animals, the environment, and one another? That's right: pretty much nothing. When it comes to moral questions, humanity has historically flunked the test, over and over again. Superintelligent machines will likely come to understand life and death, creation and destruction, on a much higher level than we ever could on our own. And the idea that they will exterminate us for the simple fact that we aren't as productive as we used to be, or that sometimes we can be a nuisance, I think, is just projecting the worst aspects of *our own* psychology onto something we don't understand and never will.

Or, here's an idea: What if technology advances to such a degree that it renders individual human consciousness arbitrary? What if consciousness can be replicated, expanded, and contracted at will? What if removing all these clunky, inefficient biological prisons we call "bodies," or all these clunky, inefficient psychological prisons we call "individual identities," results in far more ethical and prosperous outcomes? What if the machines realize we'd be much happier being freed from our cognitive prisons and having our perception of our own identities expanded to include all perceivable reality? What if they think we're just a bunch of drooling idiots and keep us occupied with perfect virtual reality porn and amazing pizza until we all die off by our own mortality?

Who are we to know? And who are we to say?

Nietzsche wrote his books just a couple of decades after Darwin's *On the Origin of Species* was published in 1859. By the time Nietzsche came onto the scene, the world was reeling from Darwin's magnificent discoveries, trying to process and make sense of their implications.

And while the world was freaking out about whether humans *really* evolved from apes or not, Nietzsche, as usual, looked in the opposite direction of everyone else. He took it as obvious that we evolved from apes. After all, he said, why else would we be so horrible to one another?

Instead of asking what we evolved from, Nietzsche instead asked what we were evolving *toward*.

Nietzsche said that man was a transition, suspended precariously on a rope between two ledges, with beasts behind us and something greater in front of us. His life's work was dedicated to figuring out what that something greater might be and then pointing us toward it.

Nietzsche envisioned a humanity that transcended religious hopes, that extended itself "beyond good and evil," and rose above the petty quarrels of contradictory value systems. It is these value systems that fail us and hurt us and keep us down in the emotional holes of our own creation. The emotional algorithms that exalt life and make it soar in blistering joy are the same forces that unravel us and destroy us, from the inside out.

So far, our technology has exploited the flawed algorithms of our Feeling Brain. Technology has worked to make us less resilient and more addicted to frivolous diversions and pleasures, because these diversions are incredibly profitable. And while technology has liberated much of the planet from poverty and tyranny, it has produced a new kind of tyranny: a tyranny of empty, meaningless variety, a never-ending stream of unnecessary options.

It has also armed us with weapons so devastating that we could torpedo this whole "intelligent life" experiment ourselves if we're not careful.

I believe artificial intelligence is Nietzsche's "something greater." It is the Final Religion, the religion that lies beyond good and evil, the religion that will finally unite and bind us all, for better or worse.

It is, then, simply our job not to blow ourselves up before we get there.

And the only way to do that is to adapt our technology *for* our flawed psychology rather than to exploit it.

To create tools that promote greater character and maturity in our cultures rather than diverting us from growth.

To enshrine the virtues of autonomy, liberty, privacy, and dignity not just in our legal documents but also in our business models and our social lives.

To treat people not merely as means but also as ends, and more important, to do it at scale.

To encourage antifragility and self-imposed limitation in each of us, rather than protecting everyone's feelings.

To create tools to help our Thinking Brain better communicate and manage the Feeling Brain, and to bring them into alignment, producing the illusion of greater self-control.

Look, it may be that you came to this book looking for some sort of hope, an assurance that things will get better—do this, that, and the other thing, and everything will improve.

I am sorry. I don't have that kind of answer for you. Nobody does. Because even if all the problems of today get magically fixed, our minds will still perceive the inevitable fuckedness of tomorrow.

So, instead of looking for hope, try this:

Don't hope.

Don't despair, either.

In fact, don't deign to believe you know *anything*. It's that assumption of knowing with such blind, fervent, emotional certainty that gets us into these kinds of pickles in the first place.

Don't hope for better. Just *be* better.

Be something better. Be more compassionate, more resilient, more humble, more disciplined.

Many people would also throw in there "Be more human," but no—be a *better* human. And maybe, if we're lucky, one day we'll get to be *more* than human.

If I Dare . . .

I say to you today, my friends, that even though we face the difficulties of today and tomorrow, in this final moment, I will allow myself to dare to hope . . .

I dare to hope for a post-hope world, where people are never treated merely as means but always as ends, where no conscious-ness is sacrificed for some greater religious aim, where no identity is harmed out of malice or greed or negligence, where the ability to reason and act is held in the highest regard by all, and where this is reflected not only in our hearts but also in our social insti-tutions and business models.

I dare to hope that people will stop suppressing either their Thinking Brain or their Feeling Brain and marry the two in a holy matrimony of emotional stability and psychological maturity; that people will become aware of the pitfalls of their own desires, of the seduction of their comforts, of the destruction behind their whims, and will instead seek out the discomfort that will force them to grow.

I dare to hope that the fake freedom of variety will be rejected by people in favor of the deeper, more meaningful freedom of commitment; that people will opt in to self-limitation rather than the quixotic quest of self-indulgence; that people will demand something better of *themselves* first before demanding something better from the world.

That said, I dare to hope that one day the online advertising business model will die in a fucking dumpster fire; that the news media will no longer have incentives to optimize content for emo-tional impact but, rather, for informational utility; that technol-ogy will seek not to exploit our psychological fragility but, rather, to counterbalance it; that information will be worth something again; that *anything* will be worth something again.

I dare to hope that search engines and social media algorithms will be optimized for truth and social relevance rather than sim-ply showing people what they want to see; that there will be inde-pendent, third-party algorithms that rate the veracity of headlines, websites, and news stories in real time, allowing users to more quickly sift through the propaganda-laden garbage and get closer to evidence-based truth; that there will be actual respect for empirically tested data, because in an infinite sea of possible beliefs, evidence is the only life preserver we've got.

I dare to hope that one day we will have AI that will listen to all the dumb shit we write and say and will point out (just to us, maybe) our cognitive biases, uninformed assumptions, and prejudices—like a little notification that pops up on your phone letting you know that you just totally exaggerated the unemployment rate when arguing with your uncle, or that you were talking out of your ass the other night when you were doling out angry tweet after angry tweet.

I dare to hope that there will be tools to help people understand statistics, proportions, and probability in real time and realize that, no, a few people getting shot in the far corners of the globe does *not* have any bearing on you, no matter how scary it looks on TV; that most "crises" are statistically insignificant and/or just noise; and that most *real* crises are too slow-moving and unexciting to get the attention they deserve.

I dare to hope that education will get a much-needed facelift, incorporating not only therapeutic practices to help children with their emotional development, but also letting them run around and scrape their knees and get into all sorts of trouble. Children are the kings and queens of antifragility, the masters of pain. It is we who are afraid.

I dare to hope that the oncoming catastrophes of climate change and automation are mitigated, if not outright prevented, by the inevitable explosion of technology wrought by the impending AI revolution; that some dumb fuck with a nuke doesn't obliterate us all before that happens; and that a new, radical human religion doesn't emerge that convinces us to destroy our own humanity, as so many have done before.

I dare to hope that AI hurries along and develops some new virtual reality religion that is so enticing that none of us can tear ourselves away from it long enough to get back to fucking and killing each other. It will be a church in the cloud, except it will be experienced as one universal video game. There will be offerings and rites and sacraments just as there will points and rewards and progression systems for strict adherence. We will all log on, and stay on, because it will be our only conduit for influencing the AI gods and, therefore, the only wellspring that can quench our insatiable desire for meaning and hope.

Groups of people will rebel against the new AI gods, of course. But this will be by design, as humanity always needs factious groups of opposing religions, for this is the only way for us to prove our own significance. Bands of infidels and heretics will emerge in this virtual landscape, and we will spend most of our time battling and railing against these various factions. We will seek to destroy one another's moral standing and diminish each other's accomplishments, all the while not realizing that this was intended. The AI, realizing that the productive energies of humanity emerge only through conflict, will generate endless series of artificial crises in a safe virtual realm, where that productivity and ingenuity can then be cultivated and used for some greater purpose we won't ever know or understand. Human hope will be harvested like a resource, a never-ending reservoir of creative energy.

We will worship at AI's digitized altars. We will follow their arbitrary rules and play their games not because we're forced to, but because they will be designed so well that *we will want to*.

We need our lives to mean something, and while the startling

advance of technology has made finding that meaning more difficult, the ultimate innovation will be the day we can manufacture
significance without strife or conflict, find importance without the
necessity of death.

And then, maybe one day, we will become integrated with the
machines themselves. Our individual consciousnesses will be
subsumed. Our independent hopes will vanish. We will meet and
merge in the cloud, and our digitized souls will swirl and eddy
in the storms of data, a splay of bits and functions harmoniously
brought into some grand, unseen alignment.

We will have evolved into a great unknowable entity. We will
transcend the limitations of our own value-laden minds. We will
live beyond means and ends, for we will always be both, one and
the same. We will have crossed the evolutionary bridge into "something greater" and ceased to be human any longer.

Perhaps then, we will not only realize but finally embrace the
Uncomfortable Truth: that we imagined our own importance, we
invented our purpose, and we were, and still are, nothing.

All along, we were nothing.

And maybe then, only then, will the eternal cycle of hope and
destruction come to an end.

Or—?

Acknowledgments

This book, in many ways, lived up to its title while being written. There were many occasions when it seemed as though everything was irreparably fucked because I had fallen victim to my own overzealous hopes. Yet, somehow—often late at night, with me staring bleary-eyed at a mush of words on my screen—things came together. And now I am incredibly proud of the result.

I wouldn't have survived this ordeal without the help and support of a great number of people. My editor, Luke Dempsey, who lived with the same gun to his head for six months (or more) that I did—you really came through in stoppage time, mate. Thank you. Mollie Glick, who is more like a fairy godmother at this point than an agent—I wake up, and amazing shit just appears in my life out of nowhere. It's incredible. To my Web team, Philip Kemper and Drew Birnie, who continue to make me appear far more competent and knowledgeable than I actually am—I'm extremely proud of what the three of us have built online and I can't wait to see what you two are capable of in coming years.

And then there's the smattering of friends who showed up big when it counted: Nir Eyal—for getting me up and writing during many frigid New York mornings when I could easily have stayed in bed. Taylor Pearson, James Clear, and Ryan Holiday—for listening to me vent and ramble and freak out when I needed to (which was fairly often) and for patiently offering advice. Peter Shallard, Jon Krop, and Jodi Ettenberg—for dropping everything to read some maimed chapter and then sending me notes and feedback. Michael Covell—for being a top-shelf bro. And WS, who somehow managed to be both the cause and solution to this whole fucking mess—you were an unexpected inspiration without even trying to be. "The trick is you bite off more than you can chew . . . and then you chew it."

I'd be remiss if I did not give a shout out the NYC Chapter of the Gentleman's Literary Safari—how could I have known that a nerdy book club started in my kitchen last summer would regularly be the highlight of my month? Much of this book was born from those long philosophical meanderings with you guys. Thank you. And remember, lads: "Being is always the being of a being."

And finally, to my wonderful wife, Fernanda Neute. I could fill an entire page with superlatives about this woman and how much she means to me, and every single one of them would be true. But I will spare the ink and extra paper—just as she would want—and keep it short. Thank you for the gift of commitment and self-limitation. If I'm ever able to hope for nothing, it will be for the simple reason that I'm already with you.

Notes

Chapter 1: The Uncomfortable Truth

1. A. J. Zautra, *Emotions, Stress, and Health* (New York: Oxford University Press, 2003), pp. 15–22.

2. I don't use the word *hope* in this book in the way it is typically used academically. Most academics use "hope" to express a feeling of optimism: an expectation of or belief in the possibility of positive results. This definition is partial and limited. Optimism can feed hope, but it is not the same thing as hope. I can have no expectation for something better to happen, but I can still hope for it. And that hope can still give my life a sense of meaning and purpose despite all evidence to the contrary. No, by "hope," I am referring to a motivation toward something perceived as valuable, what is sometimes described as "purpose" or "meaning" in the academic literature. As a result, for my discussions of hope, I'll draw on research on motivation and value theory and, in many cases, try to fuse them together.

3. M. W. Gallagher and S. J. Lopez, "Positive Expectancies and Mental Health: Identifying the Unique Contributions of Hope and Optimism," *Journal of Positive Psychology* 4, no. 6 (2009): 548–56.

4. This is almost certainly an overstatement.

5. See Ernest Becker, *The Denial of Death* (New York: Free Press, 1973).

6. Am I allowed to cite myself? Fuck it, I'm going to cite myself. See Mark Manson, "7 Strange Questions That Help You Find Your Life Purpose," Mark Manson.net, September 18, 2014, https://markmanson.net/life-purpose.

7. For data on religiosity and suicide, see Kanita Dervic, MD, et al., "Religious Affiliation and Suicide Attempt," *American Journal of Psychiatry* 161, no. 12 (2004): 2303–8. For data on religiosity and depression, see Sasan Vasegh et al. "Religious and Spiritual Factors in Depression," *Depression Research and Treatment*, published online September 18, 2012, doi: 10.1155/2012/298056.

8. Studies done in more than 132 countries show that the wealthier a country becomes, the more its population struggles with feelings of meaning and purpose. See Shigehiro Oishi and Ed Diener, "Residents of Poor Nations Have a Greater Sense of Meaning in Life than Residents of Wealthy Nations," *Psychological Science* 25, no. 2 (2014): 422–30.

9.   Pessimism is widespread in the wealthy, developed world. When the public opinion data company YouGov surveyed people in seventeen countries in 2015 on whether they believed the world was getting better, worse, or staying the same, fewer than 10 percent of people in the richest countries believed it was getting better. In the United States, only 6 percent said it was getting better. In Australia and France, that figure was only 3 percent. See Max Roser, "Good News: The World Is Getting Better. Bad News: You Were Wrong About How Things Have Changed," World Economic Forum, August 15, 2018, https://www.weforum.org/agenda/2018/08/good-news-the-world-is-getting-better-bad-news-you-were-wrong-about-how-things-have-changed.

10.   The books I refer to are Steven Pinker's *Enlightenment Now: The Case for Reason, Science, Humanism, and Progress* (New York: Viking, 2018), and Hans Rosling's *Factfulness: Ten Reasons We're Wrong About the World—And Why Things Are Better Than You Think* (New York: Flatiron Books, 2018). I needle the authors a bit here, but these are two excellent and important books.

11.   This "corner to corner" phrase is a riff on Andrew Sullivan's excellent piece on this same topic. See Andrew Sullivan, "The World Is Better Than Ever. Why Are We Miserable?" *Intelligencer*, March 9, 2018.

12.   Max Roser and Esteban Ortiz-Ospina, "Global Rise of Education," published online at OurWorldInData.org, 2018, https://ourworldindata.org/global-rise-of-education.

13.   For an exhaustive treatment of the historical reduction in violence, Pinker's book is indispensable. See Steven Pinker, *The Better Angels of Our Nature: Why Violence Has Declined* (New York: Penguin Books, 2012).

14.   Pinker, *Enlightenment Now*, pp. 214–32.

15.   Ibid., pp. 199–213.

16.   "Internet Users in the World by Regions, June 30, 2018," pie chart, InternetWorldStats.com, https://www.internetworldstats.com/stats.htm.

17.   Diana Beltekian and Esteban Ortiz-Ospina, "Extreme Poverty Is Falling: How Is Poverty Changing for Higher Poverty Lines?" March 5, 2018, Our WorldInData.org, https://ourworldindata.org/poverty-at-higher-poverty-lines.

18.   Pinker, *The Better Angels of Our Nature*, pp. 249–67.

19.   Pinker, *Enlightenment Now*, pp. 53–61.

20.   Ibid., pp. 79–96.

21.   Vaccinations are probably the single greatest advancement of human well-being in the past one hundred years. One study found that the WHO's global vaccination campaign in the 1980s likely prevented more than twenty

million cases of dangerous diseases worldwide and saved \$1.53 trillion in health care costs. The only diseases ever eradicated entirely were eradicated due to vaccines. This is part of why the antivaccination movement is so infuriating. See Walter A. Orenstein and Rafi Ahmed, "Simply Put: Vaccinations Save Lives," *PNAS* 114, no. 16 (2017): 4031–33.

22. G. L. Klerman and M. M. Weissman, "Increasing Rates of Depression," *Journal of the American Medical Association* 261 (1989): 2229–35. See also J. M. Twenge, "Time Period and Birth Cohort Differences in Depressive Symptoms in the U.S., 1982–2013," *Social Indicators Research* 121 (2015): 437–54.

23. Myrna M. Weissman, PhD, Priya Wickramaratne, PhD, Steven Greenwald, MA, et al., "The Changing Rates of Major Depression," *JAMA Psychiatry* 268, no. 21 (1992): 3098–105.

24. C. M. Herbst, "'Paradoxical' Decline? Another Look at the Relative Reduction in Female Happiness," *Journal of Economic Psychology* 32 (2011): 773–88.

25. S. Cohen and D. Janicki-Deverts, "Who's Stressed? Distributions of Psychological Stress in the United States in Probability Samples from 1983, 2006, and 2009," *Journal of Applied Social Psychology* 42 (2012): 1320–34.

26. For a harrowing and impassioned analysis of the opioid crisis ripping through North America, see Andrew Sullivan, "The Poison We Pick," *New York Magazine*, February 2018, http://nymag.com/intelligencer/2018/02/americas-opioid-epidemic.html.

27. "New Cigna Study Reveals Loneliness at Epidemic Levels in America," Cigna's Loneliness Index, May 1, 2018, https://www.multivu.com/players/English/8294451-cigna-us-loneliness-survey/.

28. The Edelman Trust Index finds a continued decline in social trust across most of the developed world. See "The 2018 World Trust Barometer: World Report," https://www.edelman.com/sites/g/files/aatuss191/files/2018-10/2018_Edelman_Trust_Barometer_Global_Report_FEB.pdf.

29. Miller McPherson, Lynn Smith-Lovin, and Matthew E. Brashears, "Social Isolation in America: Changes in Core Discussion Networks over Two Decades," *American Sociological Review* 71, no. 3 (2006): 353–75.

30. Wealthier countries, on average, have higher suicide rates than poorer countries. Data can be found from the World Health Organization, "Suicide Rates Data by Country," http://apps.who.int/gho/data/node.main.MHSUICIDEASDR?lang=en. Suicide is also more prevalent in wealthier neighborhoods compared with poorer neighborhoods. See Josh Sanburn, "Why Suicides Are More Common in Richer Neighborhoods," *Time*, November 8, 2012, http://business.time.com/2012/11/08/why-suicides-are-more-common-in-richer-neighborhoods/.

31.   Each of these is true, by the way.

32.   My three-part definition of hope is a merging of theories on motivation, value, and meaning. As a result, I've kind of combined a few different academic models to suit my purposes.

The first is self-determination theory, which states that we require three things to feel motivated and satisfied in our lives: autonomy, competence, and relatedness. I've merged autonomy and competence under the umbrella of "self-control" and, for reasons that will become clear in chapter 4, restyled relatedness as "community." What I believe is missing in self-determination theory—or, rather, what is implied but never stated—is that there is something *worth being motivated for*, that there is something valuable in the world that exists and deserves to be pursued. That's where the third component of hope comes in: values.

For a sense of value or purpose, I've pulled from Roy Baumeister's model of "meaningfulness." In this model, we need four things to feel that our life is meaningful: purpose, values, efficacy, and self-worth. Again, I've lumped "efficacy" under the "self-control" umbrella. The other three, I've put under the umbrella of "values," things we believe to be worthwhile and important and that make us feel good about ourselves. Chapter 3 will dissect at length my understanding of values. To learn more about self-determination theory, see R. M. Ryan and E. L. Deci, "Self-Determination Theory and the Facilitation of Intrinsic Motivation, Social Development, and Well-being," *American Psychologist* 55 (2000): 68–78. For Baumeister's model, see Roy Baumeister, *Meanings of Life* (New York: Guilford Press, 1991), pp. 29–56.

Chapter 2: Self-Control Is an Illusion

1.   Elliot's case is adapted from Antonio Damasio, *Descartes' Error: Emotion, Reason, and the Human Brain* (New York: Penguin Books, 2005), pp. 34–51. Elliot is the pseudonym given to the patient by Damasio.

2.   This and many of the examples from his family life (Little League games, *Family Feud*, etc.) are fictionalized simply to illustrate the point. They are not from Damasio's account and probably didn't happen.

3.   Ibid., p. 38. Damasio uses the term *free will*, whereas I use the term *self-control*. Both can be thought of in self-determination theory as the need for autonomy (see Damasio, *Descartes' Error*, chap. 1, note 32).

4.   Waits muttered the joke on Norman Lear's television show *Fernwood 2 Night* in 1977, but he didn't come up with it. Nobody knows where the joke originated, and if you try to find out online, you'll lose yourself down a rabbit hole of theories. Some have credited the joke to the writer Dorothy Parker, others to comedian Steve Allen. Waits himself claimed he didn't remember where he first heard it. He also admitted that the joke wasn't his.

5.   Some early frontal lobotomies actually used icepicks. Walter Freeman, the biggest proponent of the procedure in the United States, used icepicks exclusively before moving away from them because too many were breaking off and getting stuck inside patients' heads. See Hernish J. Acharya, "The Rise and Fall of Frontal Leucotomy," in W. A. Whitelaw, ed., *The Proceedings of the 13th Annual History of Medicine Days* (Calgary: University of Calgary, Faculty of Medicine, 2004), pp. 32–41.

6.   Yes, every neuroscientist in this book is named Antonio.

7.   Gretchen Diefenbach, Donald Diefenbach, Alan Baumeister, and Mark West, "Portrayal of Lobotomy in the Popular Press: 1935–1960," *Journal of the History of the Neurosciences* 8, no. 1 (1999): 60–69.

8.   There was an odd conspiracy theory among music journalists in the 1970s that Tom Waits faked his alcoholism. Articles and even entire books were written about this. While it's highly likely Waits exaggerated his "hobo poet" persona for performance value, he has openly commented on his alcoholism for years now. A recent example was in a 2006 interview with the *Guardian*, where he said, "I had a problem—an alcohol problem, which a lot of people consider an occupational hazard. My wife saved my life." See Sean O'Hagan, "Off Beat," *Guardian*, October 28, 2006, https://www.theguardian.com/music/2006/oct/29/popandrock1.

9.   Xenophon, *Memorabilia*, trans. Amy L. Bonnette (Ithaca, NY: Cornell University Press, 2014), book 3, chap. 9, p. 5.

10.   René Descartes, *The Philosophical Works of Descartes*, trans. Elizabeth S. Haldane and G. R. T. Ross (1637; repr. New York: Cambridge University Press, 1970), 1:101.

11.   Kant actually argued that reason was the root of morality and that the passions were more or less irrelevant. To Kant, it didn't matter how you felt, as long as you did the right thing. But we'll get to Kant in chapter 6. See Immanuel Kant, *Groundwork to the Metaphysics of Morals*, trans. James W. Ellington (1785; repr. Indianapolis, IN: Hackett Publishing Company, Inc., 1993).

12.   See Sigmund Freud, *Civilization and Its Discontents*, trans. James Strachey (1930; repr. New York: W. W. Norton and Company, 2010).

13.   I know this because I'm unfortunately part of this industry. I often joke that I'm a "self-hating self-help guru." The fact is, I think most of the industry is bullshit and that the only way really to improve your life is not by feeling good but, rather, by getting better at feeling bad.

14.   Great thinkers have cut the human mind into two or three pieces since forever. My "two brains" construct is just a summary of the concepts of these earlier thinkers. Plato said that the soul has three parts: reason

(Thinking Brain), appetites, and spirit (Feeling Brain). David Hume said that all experiences are either impressions (Feeling Brain) or ideas (Thinking Brain). Freud had the ego (Thinking Brain) and the id (Feeling Brain). Most recently, Daniel Kahneman and Amon Tversky had their two systems, System 1 (Feeling Brain) and System 2 (Thinking Brain), or, as Kahneman calls them in his book *Thinking: Fast and Slow* (New York: Farrar, Straus and Giroux, 2011), the "fast" brain and the "slow" brain.

15.   The "willpower as a muscle" theory of willpower, also known as "ego depletion," is in hot water in the academic world at the moment. A number of large studies have failed to replicate ego depletion. Some meta-analyses have found significant results for it while others have not.

16.   Damasio, *Descartes' Error*, pp. 128–30.

17.   Kahneman, *Thinking: Fast and Slow*, p. 31.

18.   Jonathan Haidt, *The Happiness Hypothesis: Finding Modern Truth in Ancient Wisdom* (New York: Penguin Books, 2006), pp. 2–5. Haidt says he got the elephant metaphor from the Buddha.

19.   This silly Clown Car analogy actually works well for describing how toxic relationships between selfish narcissists form. Anyone who is psychologically healthy, whose mind is not a Clown Car, will be able to hear a Clown Car coming from a mile away and avoid contact with it as much as possible. But if you are a Clown Car yourself, your circus music will prevent you from hearing the circus music of other Clown Cars. They will look and sound normal to you, and you will engage with them, thinking that all the healthy Consciousness Cars are boring and uninteresting, thus entering toxic relationship after toxic relationship.

20.   Some scholars believe that Plato wrote *The Republic* as a response to the political turbulence and violence that had recently erupted in Athens. See *The Republic of Plato*, trans. Allan Bloom (New York: Basic Books, 1968), p. xi.

21.   Christendom borrowed a lot of its moral philosophy from Plato and, unlike many ancient philosophers such as Epicurus and Lucretius, preserved his works. According to Stephen Greenblatt, in *The Swerve: How the World Became Modern* (New York: W. W. Norton and Company, 2012), early Christians held on to the ideas of Plato and Aristotle because the two believed in a soul that was separate from the body. This idea of a separate soul gibed with Christian belief in an afterlife. It's also the idea that spawned the Classic Assumption.

22.   Pinker, *The Better Angels of Our Nature*, pp. 4–18. The comment about chopping off someone's nuts is my own flourish, of course.

23.   Ibid., pp. 482–88.

24. The oft-repeated motto of Woodstock and much of the free-love movement of the 1960s was "If it feels good, do it!" This sentiment is the basis for a lot of New Age and countercultural movements today.

25. An excellent example of this self-indulgence in the name of spirituality is depicted in the Netflix original documentary *Wild Wild Country* (2018), about the spiritual guru Bhagwan Shree Rajneesh (aka Osho) and his followers.

26. The best analysis I've seen of this tendency among twentieth-century spiritual movements to mistake indulging one's emotions for some greater spiritual awakening came from the brilliant author Ken Wilber. He called it the Pre/Trans Fallacy and argued that because emotions are pre-rational, and spiritual awakenings are post-rational, people often mistake one for the other—because they're both nonrational. See Ken Wilber, *Eye to Eye: The Quest for a New Paradigm* (Boston, MA: Shambhala, Inc., 1983), pp. 180–221.

27. A. Aldao, S. Nolen-Hoeksema, and S. Schweizer, "Emotion-Regulation Strategies Across Psychopathology: A Meta-analytic Review," *Clinical Psychology Review* 30 (2010): 217–37.

28. Olga M. Slavin-Spenny, Jay L. Cohen, Lindsay M. Oberleitner, and Mark A. Lumley, "The Effects of Different Methods of Emotional Disclosure: Differentiating Post-traumatic Growth from Stress Symptoms," *Journal of Clinical Psychology* 67, no. 10 (2011): 993–1007.

29. This technique is known as the Premack principle, after psychologist David Premack, to describe the use of preferred behaviors as rewards. See Jon E. Roeckelein, *Dictionary of Theories, Laws, and Concepts in Psychology* (Westport, CT: Greenwood Press, 1998), p. 384.

30. For more about "starting small" with behavioral changes, see "The Do Something Principle," from my previous book, *The Subtle Art of Not Giving a Fuck: A Counterintuitive Approach to Living a Good Life* (New York: HarperOne, 2016), pp. 158–63.

31. One way to think about "guardrails" for your Consciousness Car is to develop implementation intentions, little if/then habits that can unconsciously direct your behavior. See P. M. Gollwitzer and V. Brandstaetter, "Implementation Intentions and Effective Goal Pursuit," *Journal of Personality and Social Psychology* 73 (1997): 186–99.

32. Damasio, *Descartes' Error*, pp. 173–200.

33. In philosophy, this is known as Hume's guillotine: you cannot derive an "ought" from an "is." You cannot derive values from facts. You cannot derive Feeling Brain knowledge from Thinking Brain knowledge. Hume's guillotine has had philosophers and scientists spinning in circles for centuries now. Some thinkers such as Sam Harris try to rebut it by pointing out

that you can have factual knowledge *about* values—e.g., if a hundred people believe suffering is wrong, then there is factual evidence of their physical brain state about their beliefs about suffering being wrong. But the decision to take that physical representation as a serious proxy for philosophical value, *is itself a value* that cannot be factually proven. Thus, the circle continues.

Chapter 3: Newton's Laws of Emotion

1.   Some of the biographical portions of this chapter are fictionalized.

2.   Newton actually wrote this in a journal as a teen. See James Gleick, *Isaac Newton* (New York: Vintage Books, 2003), p. 13.

3.   Nina Mazar and Dan Ariely, "Dishonesty in Everyday Life and Its Policy Implications," *Journal of Public Policy and Marketing* 25, no. 1 (Spring 2006): 117–26.

4.   Nina Mazar, On Amir, and Dan Ariely, "The Dishonesty of Honest People: A Theory of Self-Concept Maintenance," *Journal of Marketing Research* 45, no. 6 (December 2008): 633–44.

5.   So, if you're unfamiliar with Newton or don't remember your high school science, Newton is the godfather of modern physics. In terms of the impact of his discoveries, he is arguably the most influential thinker in world history. Among his many discoveries, his core ideas about physics (inertia, conserved force, etc.) were described in his Three Laws of Motion. Here, I present Newton's Three Laws of *Emotion*, a play on his original discoveries.

6.   See Michael Tomasello, *A Natural History of Human Morality* (Cambridge, MA: Harvard University Press, 2016), pp. 78–81.

7.   Damasio, *Descartes' Error*, pp. 172–89.

8.   This is why passive aggression is unhealthy for relationships: It doesn't explicitly state where a person perceives a moral gap. Instead, it simply opens up another gap. You could say the root of interpersonal conflict comes from differing perceptions of moral gaps. You thought I was being an asshole. I thought I was being nice. Therefore, we have a conflict. But unless we openly state our values and what we each perceived, we will never be able to equalize or restore hope to the relationship.

9.   This is an example of "intrinsic motivation," when the simple pleasure of doing an activity well, rather than for an external reward, motivates you to continue doing that activity. See Edward L. Deci and Richard M. Ryan, *Intrinsic Motivation and Self-Determination in Human Behavior* (New York: Plenum Press, 1985), pp. 5–9.

10.   You could say that negative emotions are rooted in a sense of losing control, while positive emotions are rooted in a sense of having control.

11.   Tomasello, *A Natural History of Human Morality*, pp. 13–14.

12.   Robert Axelrod, *The Evolution of Cooperation* (New York: Basic Books, 1984), pp. 27–54.

13.   This also comes from David Hume, "Of the Association of Ideas," section 3 in *An Enquiry Concerning Human Understanding*, ed. Eric Steinberg, 2nd ed. (1748; repr. Indianapolis, IN: Hackett Classics, 1993); and Hume, *A Treatise of Human Nature*, Book 2: *Of the Passions*, parts 1 and 2 (Mineola, NY: Dover Philosophical Classics, 2003).

14.   He didn't invent the term, but I have to give credit to the psychologist Jordan Peterson's interviews and lectures, as he has greatly popularized the term *value hierarchy* in recent years.

15.   Manson, *The Subtle Art of Not Giving a Fuck*, pp. 81–89.

16.   See Martin E. P. Seligman, *Helplessness: On Depression, Development, and Death* (New York: Times Books, 1975).

17.   There is a third alternative: you can refuse to recognize the existence of a moral gap at all. But this is incredibly difficult to do and requires a high degree of self-awareness, not to mention willingness to forgive others.

18.   What's interesting is that narcissists will even *justify* their pain with claims of their superiority. Ever hear the phrase "They hate me because they're envious"? Or "They attack me because they're afraid of me"? Or "They just don't want to admit that I'm better than they are"? The Feeling Brain merely flips its self-worth on its head: we're not being harmed because we suck; we're being harmed because we're great! So, the narcissist goes from feeling that the self deserves nothing to feeling that the self deserves everything.

19.   Ironically, he was kind of right. The Treaty of Versailles decimated Germany economically and was responsible for many of the internal struggles that allowed Hitler to rise to power. His "they hate us because we're so great" style of messaging clearly resonated with the beleaguered German population.

20.   I am referring to Elliot Rodger, who uploaded his creepy YouTube video "Elliot Rodger's Retribution" just before driving to the sorority house.

21.   Self-worth is an illusion because all values are illusory and based on faith (see chapter 4 for further discussion) and because the self is itself an illusion. For a discussion of this second idea, see Sam Harris, *Waking Up: A Guide to Spirituality Without Religion* (New York: Simon and Schuster, 2014), pp. 81–116.

22.   David Foster Wallace talked about this "default setting" of consciousness in his wonderful speech "This Is Water." See David F. Wallace, *This Is Water: Some Thoughts, Delivered on a Significant Occasion, About Living*

a Compassionate Life (New York: Little, Brown and Company, 2009), pp. 44–45.

23. This is popularly known as the Dunning-Kruger effect, named for the researchers who discovered it. See Justin Kruger and David Dunning, "Unskilled and Unaware of It: How Difficulties in Recognizing One's Own Incompetence Lead to Inflated Self-Assessments," *Journal of Personality and Social Psychology* 77, no. 6 (1999): 1121–34.

24. Max H. Bazerman and Ann E. Tenbrunsel, *Blind Spots: Why We Fail to Do What's Right and What to Do About It* (Princeton, NJ: Princeton University Press, 2011).

25. This is known as the false consensus effect. See Thomas Gilovich, "Differential Construal and the False Consensus Effect," *Journal of Personality and Social Psychology* 59, no. 4 (1990): 623–34.

26. Shout out to the late TV painter Bob Ross (RIP), who used to say, "There's no such thing as mistakes, just happy accidents."

27. This is known as the actor-observer bias, and it explains why everyone is an asshole. See Edward Jones and Richard Nisbett, *The Actor and the Observer: Divergent Perceptions of the Causes of Behavior* (New York: General Learning Press, 1971).

28. Basically, the more pain we experience, the larger the moral gap. And the larger the moral gap, the more we dehumanize ourselves and/or others. And the more we dehumanize ourselves and/or others, the more easily we justify causing suffering to ourselves or others.

29. The healthy response here would be (c), "some boys are shit," but when we experience extreme pain, our Feeling Brains generate intense feelings about entire categories of experience and are not able to make those distinctions.

30. Obviously, there are a lot of variables at work here: the girl's previously held values, her self-worth, the nature of the breakup, her ability to achieve intimacy, her age, ethnic and cultural values, and so on.

31. A 2016 computer model study found that there are six types of stories: rise (rags to riches), fall (riches to rags), rise and then fall (Icarus), fall and then rise (man in a hole), rise and then fall and then rise (Cinderella), fall and then rise and then fall (Oedipus). These are all essentially permutations of the same good/bad experience, plus good/bad deserving. See Adrienne LaFrance, "The Six Main Arcs in Storytelling, as Identified by an A.I.," *The Atlantic*, July 12, 2016, https://www.theatlantic.com/technology/archive/2016/07/the-six-main-arcs-in-storytelling-identified-by-a-computer/490733/.

32. The field of psychology is in the midst of a "replicability crisis," that is, a large percentage of its major findings are failing to be replicated in further

experiments. See Ed Yong, "Psychology's Replication Crisis Is Running Out of Excuses," *The Atlantic*, November 18, 2018, https://www.theatlantic.com /science/archive/2018/11/psychologys-replication-crisis-real/576223/.

33. Division of Violence Prevention, "The Adverse Childhood Experiences (ACE) Study," National Center for Injury Prevention and Control, Centers for Disease Control and Prevention, Atlanta, GA, May 2014, https://www .cdc.gov/violenceprevention/acestudy/index.html.

34. Real-life Newton was actually a raging, vindictive asshole. And yes, he was a loner, too. He apparently died a virgin. And records suggest that he was probably quite proud of that fact.

35. This is what Freud incorrectly identified as repression. He believed that we spend our lives repressing our painful childhood memories, and by bringing them back into consciousness, we liberate the negative emotions bundled up inside ourselves. In fact, it turns out that remembering past traumas doesn't provide much benefit. Indeed, the most effective therapies today focus not so much on the past as on learning to manage future emotions.

36. People often mistake our core values for our personality, and vice versa. Personality is a fairly immutable thing. According to the "Big Five" personality model, one's personality consists of five basic traits: extraversion, conscientiousness, agreeableness, neuroticism, and openness to new experience. Our core values are judgments made early in life, based partly on personality. For instance, I might be highly open to new experiences, which thus inspires me to value exploration and curiosity from an early age. This early value will then play out in later experiences and create values related to it. Core values are difficult to dig up and change. Personality cannot be changed much, if at all. For more on the "Big Five" personality model, see Thomas A. Widiger, ed., *The Oxford Handbook of the Five Factor Model* (New York: Oxford University Press, 2017).

37. William Swann, Peter Rentfrow, and Jennifer Sellers, "Self-verification: The Search for Coherence," *Handbook of Self and Identity* (New York: Guilford Press, 2003), pp. 367–83.

38. This is the law-of-attraction bullshit that's been around in the self-help industry for ages. For a thorough takedown of this type of nonsense, see Mark Manson, "The Staggering Bullshit of 'The Secret,'" MarkManson.net, February 26, 2015, https://markmanson.net/the-secret.

39. The ability to remember past experiences and project future experiences occurs only with the development of the prefrontal cortex (the neurological name for the Thinking Brain). See Y. Yang and A. Raine, "Prefrontal Structural and Functional Brain Imaging Findings in Antisocial, Violent, and Psychopathic Individuals: A Meta-analysis," *Psychiatry Research* 174, no. 2 (November 2009): 81–88.

40. Jocko Willink, *Discipline Equals Freedom: Field Manual* (New York: St. Martin's Press, 2017), pp. 4–6.

41. Martin Lea and Steve Duck, "A Model for the Role of Similarity of Values in Friendship Development," *British Journal of Social Psychology* 21, no. 4 (November 1982): 301–10.

42. This metaphor essentially says that the more we value something, the more unwilling we are to question or change that value, and therefore the more painful it is when that value fails us. It's like if you think about the different degrees of pain between the death of a parent versus the death of an acquaintance, or how emotional you get when someone insults or questions one of your favorite music groups from when you were a kid versus when you're an adult.

43. Freud called this the "narcissism of the slight difference," and observed that it is usually groups of people with the most in common who feel the most hatred for one another. See Sigmund Freud, *Civilization and Its Discontents*, trans. David McLintock (1941; repr. New York: Penguin Books, 2002), pp. 50–51.

44. Tomasello, *A Natural History of Human Morality*, pp. 85–93.

45. This idea is known as "cultural geography." For a fascinating discussion, see Jared Diamond, *Guns, Germs and Steel: The Fates of Human Societies* (New York: W. W. Norton and Company, 1997).

46. Tomasello, *A Natural History of Human Morality*, pp. 114–15.

47. Or, as military theorist Carl von Clausewitz famously put it, "War is the continuation of politics by other means."

48. Real Isaac Newton's Laws of Motion also sat collecting dust for about twenty years before he dug them out and showed them to anyone.

Chapter 4: How to Make All Your Dreams Come True

1. Gustave Le Bon, *The Crowd: A Study of the Popular Mind* (1896; repr. New York: Dover Publications, 2002), p. 14.

2. Jonathan Haidt calls this phenomenon the "hive hypothesis." See Jonathan Haidt, *The Righteous Mind: Why Good People Are Divided by Politics and Religion* (New York: Vintage Books, 2012), pp. 261–70.

3. Le Bon, *The Crowd*, pp. 24–29.

4. Barry Schwartz and Andrew Ward, "Doing Better but Feeling Worse: The Paradox of Choice," in P. Alex Linley and Stephen Joseph, *Positive Psychology in Practice* (Hoboken, NJ: John Wiley and Sons, 2004), pp. 86–103.

5. Adolescent brains continue to develop well into their twenties, particularly the parts of the brain responsible for executive functioning. See S. B. Johnson, R. W. Blum, and J. N. Giedd, "Adolescent Maturity and the Brain:

The Promise and Pitfalls of Neuroscience Research in Adolescent Health Policy," *Journal of Adolescent Health: Official Publication of the Society for Adolescent Medicine* 45, no. 3 (2009): 216–21.

6. S. Choudhury, S. J. Blakemore, and T. Charman, "Social Cognitive Development During Adolescence," *Social Cognitive and Affective Neuroscience* 1, no. 3 (2006): 165–74.

7. This work in identity definition is the most important project of adolescents and young adults. See Erik H. Erikson, *Childhood and Society* (New York: W. W. Norton and Company, 1963), pp. 261–65.

8. My guess is that people like LaRouche aren't consciously exploitative. It's more likely that LaRouche himself was psychologically stuck at an adolescent level of maturity and therefore pursued adolescent causes and appealed to other lost adolescents. See chapter 6.

9. The dialogue here is approximate based on my recollection. It was fifteen years ago, so obviously I don't remember exactly what was said.

10. I decided to look up where Sagan said this, and it turns out that, like most quotes found on the internet, someone else had said it, and fifty years before Sagan. Professor Walter Kotschnig was apparently the first one to be published saying it, in 1940. See https://quoteinvestigator.com/2014/04/13/open-mind/.

11. Eric Hoffer, *The True Believer: Thoughts on the Nature of Mass Movements* (New York: Harper Perennial, 1951), pp. 3–11.

12. Ibid., pp. 16–21.

13. Ibid., pp. 26–45.

14. What's interesting about Jesus is that the historical record implies that he likely began as a political extremist, attempting to lead an uprising against the Roman Empire's occupation of Israel. It was after his death that his ideological religion was transmuted into a more spiritual religion. See Reza Aslan, *Zealot: The Life and Times of Jesus of Nazareth* (New York: Random House Books, 2013).

15. This notion comes from Karl Popper's ideas about falsifiability. Popper, building on the work of David Hume, basically said that no matter how many times something has happened in the past, it can never logically be *proven* that it will happen again in the future. Even though the sun has risen in the east and set in the west every day for thousands of years and no one has ever had a contrary experience, this does not *prove* that the sun will rise in the east tomorrow. All it does is tell us the overwhelming probability of the sun rising in the east.

Popper argued that the only empirical truth we can ever know is not via experimentation but, rather, falsifiability. Nothing can ever be proven. Things can only be *disproven*. Therefore, even something as mundane and obvious as the sun rising in the east and setting in the west is still believed on some degree of faith, even though it is almost entirely certain always to happen.

Popper's ideas are important because they logically demonstrate that even scientific facts rely on some modicum of faith. You can do an experiment a million times and get the same result every time, but that does not prove it will happen the million and first time. At some point, we choose to rely on the belief that it will continue to happen once its results are so statistically significant that it'd be insane not to believe them.

For more on Popper's ideas about falsification, see Karl Popper, *The Logic of Scientific Discovery* (1959; repr. New York: Routledge Classics, 1992). What I find interesting is that mental illnesses that induce delusions, hallucinations, and such may, fundamentally, be dysfunctions of faith. Most of us take it for granted that the sun will rise in the east and that things fall to the ground at a certain rate and that we're not just going to float away because gravity decided to take a coffee break. But a mind that struggles to build and maintain faith in anything would potentially be tortured by these possibilities all the time, thus making it go mad.

16. Faith also assumes that your shit is real and that you aren't just a brain in a vat merely imagining all your sense perceptions—a favorite trope of philosophers. For a fun dive into whether you can ever actually know if anything exists, check out René Descartes's *Meditations on First Philosophy*.

17. The word *atheist* can signify a number of things. Here, I'm simply making the point that we all must buy into beliefs and values based on faith, even if they're not supernatural beliefs and values. See John Gray, *Seven Types of Atheism* (New York: Farrar, Straus and Giroux, 2018).

18. David Hume, *A Treatise of Human Nature*. Hume writes that "all knowledge degenerates into probability; and this probability is greater or less, according to our experience of the veracity or deceitfulness of our understanding, and according to the simplicity or intricacy of the question" (1739, part 4, section 1).

19. A God Value is not the same thing as Blaise Pascal's "God-shaped hole." Pascal believed that because man's desires were insatiable, only something infinite could ever satiate him—that infinite thing being God. A God Value is different in that it is simply the top of one's value hierarchy. You might feel miserable and empty and still have a God Value. In fact, the cause of your misery and emptiness is likely your chosen God Value.

20. For further discussion on how superficial God Values such as money affect your life, see Mark Manson, "How We Judge Others Is How We Judge Ourselves," MarkManson.net, January 9, 2014, https://markmanson.net/how-we-judge-others.

21. Like money or government or ethnicity, the "self" is also an arbitrary mental construct based on faith. There is no proof that your experience of "you" actually exists. It is merely the nexus of conscious experience, an interconnection of sense and sensibility. See Derek Parfit, *Reasons and Persons* (Cambridge, UK: Cambridge University Press, 1984), pp. 199–280.

22. There are a number of ways to describe unhealthy forms of attachment to another person, but I went with the term *codependence* because of its widespread mainstream usage. The word comes from Alcoholics Anonymous (AA).

Alcoholics noticed that in the same way that they were addicted to the bottle, their friends and family were seemingly addicted to supporting and caring for them in their addiction. The alcoholics were dependent on alcohol to feel good and normal, and these friends and family members who were "codependent," as they used the alcoholics' addiction to feel good and normal as well. *Codependency* has since found more widespread use—basically, anyone who becomes "addicted" to supporting or receiving validation from another person can be described as codependent.

Codependence is a strange form of worship, where you put a person on a pedestal and make him the center of your world, the basis of your thoughts and feelings, and the root of your self-esteem. In other words, you make the other person your God Value. This, unfortunately, leads to extremely destructive relationships. See Melody Beattie, *Codependent No More: How to Stop Controlling Others and Care for Yourself* (Center City, MN: Hazelden Publishing, 1986); and Timmen L. Cermak, MD, *Diagnosing and Treating Co-Dependence: A Guide for Professionals Who Work with Chemical Dependents, Their Spouses, and Children* (Center City, MN: Hazelden Publishing, 1998).

23. See discussion of "Hume's guillotine," from note 33 in chapter 2.

24. The Black Death killed one hundred million to two hundred million people in Europe in the fourteenth century, reducing the population by anywhere from 30 to 60 percent.

25. This refers to the infamous Children's Crusade of 1212. After multiple failed Crusades by Christians to retake the Holy Land from the Muslims, tens of thousands of children journeyed to Italy to volunteer to go to the Holy Land and convert Muslims peacefully. A charismatic leader promised the children that the sea would part once they reached the Mediterranean, allowing them to walk to Jerusalem on foot. Spoiler alert: it didn't. Instead, merchant ships gathered up the children and took them across the sea to Tunisia, where most of them were sold into slavery.

26. Interestingly, you could say that money was invented as a way to tally and track moral gaps between people. We invented the concept of debt to justify our moral gaps—I did you this favor, so now you owe me something in return—and money was invented as a way of tracking and managing

debt across a society. This is known as the "credit theory" of money, and it was first proposed by Alfred Mitchell Innes back in 1913, in a journal article titled "What Is Money?" For a nice overview of Mitchell Innes and the credit theory of money, see David Graeber, *Debt: The First 5,000 Years, Updated and Expanded Edition* (2011; repr. Brooklyn, NY: Melville House Publishing, 2014), pp. 46–52. For an interesting discussion of the importance of debt in human society, see Margaret Atwood, *Payback: Debt and the Shadow Side of Wealth* (Berkeley, CA: House of Anansi Press, 2007).

27. Okay, the ethnicities thing is a bit controversial. There *are* minor biological differences between populations with different ancestries, but differentiating among people based on those differences is also an arbitrary, faith-based construct. For instance, who is to say that all green-eyed people aren't their own ethnicity? That's right. Nobody. Yet, if some king had decided hundreds of years ago that green-eyed people were a different race that deserved to be treated terribly, we'd likely be mired in political issues around "eye-ism" today.

28. You know, like what I'm doing with this book.

29. It's probably worth noting again that there's a replicability crisis going on in the social sciences. Many of the major "findings" in psychology, economics, and even medicine are not able to be replicated consistently. So, even if we could easily handle the complexity of measuring human populations, it would still be incredibly difficult to find consistent, empirical evidence that one variable had an outweighed influence over another. See Yong, "Psychology's Replication Crisis Is Running Out of Excuses."

30. All my life, I've been fascinated by how athletes go from heroes to villains and back to heroes again. Tiger Woods, Kobe Bryant, Michael Jordan, and Andre Agassi have all been demigods in people's minds. Then, one unseemly revelation caused each to become a pariah. This relates back to what I said in chapter 3 about how the superiority/inferiority of the person can flip-flop easily because what remains the same is the magnitude of the moral gap. With someone like Kobe Bryant, whether he's a hero or a villain, what remains the same is the intensity of our emotional reaction to him. And that intensity is caused by the size of the moral gap that is felt.

31. I have to give a shout-out to Yuval Noah Harari and his brilliant book *Sapiens: A Brief History of Humankind* (New York: HarperCollins, 2015) for the description of governments, financial institutions, and other social structures as mythic systems that exist thanks only to the shared beliefs of a population. Harari synthesized many of these ideas first, and I'm just riffing on him. The whole book is worth a read.

32. Pair bonding and reciprocal altruism are two evolutionary strategies that emerge in consciousness as emotional attachment.

33.   The definition of "spiritual experience" I'm most fond of is that it's a trans-egoic experience—meaning, your identity or sense of "self" transcends your body and consciousness and expands to include all perceived reality. Trans-egoic experiences can be achieved in a variety of ways: psychedelic drugs, intense meditation for long periods, and moments of extreme love and passion. In these heightened states, you can "meld" into your partner, feeling as though you are the same being, thus temporarily achieving a trans-egoic state. This "melding" with someone else (or the universe) is why spiritual experiences are often perceived as "love," as they are both a surrendering of one's ego-identity and unconditional acceptance of some greater entity. For a cool explanation of this kind of stuff based on Jungian psychology, see Ken Wilber, *No Boundary: Eastern and Western Approaches to Personal Growth* (1979; repr. Boston, MA: Shambhala, 2001).

34.   As countries industrialize, their religiosity drops precipitously. See Pippa Norris and Ronald Inglehart, *Sacred and Secular: Religion and Politics Worldwide*, 2nd ed. (2004; repr. New York: Cambridge University Press, 2011), pp. 53–82.

35.   René Girard, *Things Hidden Since the Foundation of the World*, trans. Stephen Bann and Michael Metteer (repr. 1978; Stanford, CA: Stanford University Press, 1987), pp. 23–30.

36.   Similar to science being a religion in which we worship evidence, humanism could be seen as worshipping the "in-betweenism" of all people—that there are no inherently good or evil people. As Aleksandr Solzhenitsyn put it, "The line dividing good and evil cuts through the heart of every human being."

37.   Sadly, these conspiracy theories are prominent in the United States today.

38.   I'm being a bit dramatic, but human sacrifice did occur in pretty much every major ancient and prehistoric civilization we know of. See Nigel Davies, *Human Sacrifice in History and Today* (New York: Hippocrene Books, 1988).

39.   For an interesting discussion of innate guilt and the role of human sacrifice, see Ernest Becker, *Escape from Evil* (New York: Freedom Press, 1985).

40.   Freud, *Civilization and Its Discontents*, pp. 14–15.

41.   Ibid., p. 18.

42.   Manson, *The Subtle Art of Not Giving a Fuck*, pp. 23–29.

43.   E. O. Wilson, *On Human Nature* (1978; repr. Cambridge, MA: Harvard University Press, 2004), pp. 169–92.

44.   Reasoning skills break down when one is confronted with emotionally charged issues (i.e., issues that touch our highest values). See Vladimíra

Čavojová, Jakub Šrol, and Magdalena Adamus, "My Point Is Valid; Yours Is Not: My-Side Bias in Reasoning About Abortion," *Journal of Cognitive Psychology* 30, no. 7 (2018): 656–69.

45. Actually, you may suck even more. Research shows that the more well informed and educated someone is, the more politically polarized his opinions. See T. Palfrey and K. Poole, "The Relationship Between Information, Ideology, and Voting Behavior," *American Journal of Political Science* 31, no. 3 (1987): 511–30.

46. This idea was first published in F. T. Cloak Jr., "Is a Cultural Ethology Possible?" *Human Ecology* 3, no. 3 (1975): 161–82. For a less academic discussion, see Aaron Lynch, *Thought Contagion: How Beliefs Spread Through Society* (New York: Basic Books, 1996), pp. 97–134.

Chapter 5: Hope Is Fucked

1. Nietzsche first announced the death of God in 1882, in his book *The Gay Science*, but the quote is most famously associated with *Thus Spoke Zarathustra*, which was released in four parts from 1883 to 1885. After the third part, all publishers refused to have anything to do with the project, and Nietzsche therefore had to scrape together the money to publish the fourth part himself. That's the book that sold fewer than forty copies. See Sue Prideaux, *I Am Dynamite!: A Life of Nietzsche* (New York: Tim Duggan Books, 2018), pp. 256–60.

2. Everything spoken by Nietzsche in this chapter is an actual line lifted from his work. This one comes from F. Nietzsche, *Beyond Good and Evil*, trans. Walter Kaufmann (1887; repr. New York: Vintage Books, 1963), p. 92.

3. The story of Nietzsche with Meta in this chapter is loosely adapted from his summers with a handful of women (the others being Helen Zimmern and Resa von Schirnhofer) over 1886–87. See Julian Young, *Friedrich Nietzsche: A Philosophical Biography* (Cambridge, UK: Cambridge University Press, 2010), pp. 388–400.

4. Friedrich Nietzsche, *Ecce Homo*, trans. by R. J. Hollingdale (1890; repr. New York: Penguin Classics, 1979), p. 39.

5. Some anthropologists have gone so far as to call agriculture, because of its inevitable tendency to create inequality and social stratification, "the worst mistake in the history of the human race." See Jared Diamond's famous essay "The Worst Mistake in the History of the Human Race," *Discover*, May 1987, http://discovermagazine.com/1987/may/02-the-worst-mistake-in-the-history-of-the-human-race.

6. Nietzsche's initial description of master and slave moralities comes from *Beyond Good and Evil*, pp. 204–37. He expounds on each morality fur-

ther in *The Genealogy of Morality* (1887). The second essay in *The Genealogy of Morality* (New York: Penguin Classics, 2014) is where I was first exposed to the concept of "the moral gap" discussed in chapter 3. In that essay, Nietzsche argues that each of our individual moralities is based on our sense of debt.

7.   Haidt, *The Righteous Mind*, pp. 182–89.

8.   Richard Dawkins, *The Selfish Gene: 30th Anniversary Edition* (Oxford, UK: Oxford University Press, 2006), pp. 189–200.

9.   It's interesting that most polytheistic religions haven't had this obsession with conversion that the monotheistic religions have had. The Greeks and Romans were more than happy to let the indigenous cultures follow their own beliefs. It wasn't until slave morality that the religious Crusades began. This is probably because a slave morality religion cannot abide cultures that hold different beliefs. Slave moralities require the world to be equal—and to be equal, you cannot be different. Therefore, those other cultures had to be converted. This is the paradoxical tyranny of any extremist left-wing belief system. When equality becomes one's God Value, differences in belief cannot be abided. And the only way to destroy difference in belief is through totalitarianism.

10.   See Pinker, *Enlightenment Now*, pp. 7–28.

11.   My biggest qualm with Pinker's book is that he conflates the scientific revolution with the philosophical Enlightenment. The scientific revolution predates the Enlightenment and is independent of the latter's humanistic beliefs. This is why I make a point of stressing that *science*, and not necessarily Enlightenment ideologies, is the best thing to have happened in human history.

12.   Estimates of GDP per capita growth done by author with data from Angus Maddison, *The World Economy: A Millennial Perspective*, Organisation for Economic Co-operation and Development (OECD), 2006, p. 30.

13.   There is evidence suggesting that populations become more religious immediately after natural disasters. See Jeanet Sinding Bentzen, "Acts of God? Religiosity and Natural Disasters Across Subnational World Districts," University of Copenhagen Department of Economics Discussion Paper No. 15-06, 2015, http://web.econ.ku.dk/bentzen/ActsofGodBentzen.pdf.

14.   There's no written record of Nietzsche's thoughts on communism, but he surely must have been aware of it. And given his disgust for slave morality in general, he almost certainly loathed it. His beliefs in this regard have long been mistaken for being a precursor to Nazism. But Nietzsche hated the German nationalism burgeoning during his lifetime and had a falling out with a number of friends and family (most notably Wagner) because of it.

Nietzsche's own sister and brother-in-law were ardent nationalists and anti-Semites. He found both beliefs to be stupid and offensive, and said as much to them. In fact, his globalist view of the world was rare and radical at the time. He strictly believed in the value of a person's deeds, nothing else— no system, no race, no nationality. When his sister told him that she and her husband were moving to Paraguay to start a New Germania, where people could breed a society from pure German blood, he is said to have laughed in her face so hard that she didn't speak to him again for years.

It's tragic, then (and ironic), that his work would be co-opted and warped by Nazi ideology after his death. Sue Prideaux gives a stirring account of how his philosophy came to be corrupted, and the slow, fifty-year rehabilitation it went through to get the reading it deserves. See Prideaux, *I Am Dynamite!*, pp. 346–81.

15. Buddhist philosophy would describe these cycles of hope creation and destruction as *samsara*, which is generated and perpetuated due to our attachments to worldly, impermanent values. The Buddha taught that the fundamental nature of our psychology is *dukkha*, a concept loosely translated as "craving." He warned that human cravings can never be satiated, and that we generate suffering in our constant quest to fulfill those cravings. The idea of relinquishing hope is very much in line with the Buddhist idea of reaching *nirvana*, or letting go of all psychological attachments or cravings.

16. Nietzsche, *Ecce Homo*, pp. 96–104.

17. The Pandora's Box myth, as told in this section, comes from Hesiod's *Work and Days*, lines 560–612.

18. This is kind of a joke, but also kind of not. For the horrific origins of matrimony in the ancient world, see Stephanie Coontz, *Marriage, a History: How Love Conquered Marriage* (New York: Penguin Books, 2006), pp. 70–86.

19. Apparently, the Greek word Hesiod used for "hope" could also be translated as "deceptive expectation." Thus, there has always been a less popular, pessimistic interpretation of the myth based on the idea that hope can also lead to destruction. See Franco Montanari, Antonios Rengakos, and Christos Tsagalis, *Brill's Companion to Hesiod* (Leiden, Netherlands: Brill Publishers, 2009), p. 77.

20. Nietzsche, *Ecce Homo*, pp. 37–38.

21. Friedrich Nietzsche, *The Gay Science*, trans. Walter Kaufmann (1882; repr. New York: Vintage Books, 1974), §341: 273–74.

22. The beginning of his rant about God being dead comes from the "Madman" section of ibid., §125: 181–82.

23. This "impassioned and lengthy" speech to cows near Lake Silvaplana actually happened, according to Meta von Salis. It was possibly one of Nietz-

sche's first episodes of psychosis, which began to surface around this time. See Young, *Friedrich Nietzsche*, p. 432.

24. The rest of Nietzsche's lines in this chapter come from Friedrich Nietzsche, *Thus Spoke Zarathustra*, trans. R. J. Hollingdale (1883; repr. New York: Penguin Classics, 2003), p. 43. "[H]e is an overture to something greater" is my own interpretation of Nietzsche's idea of the *Übermensch*, or "superman." The original text reads, "[H]e is a going-across," where there "going-across" is a metaphor for man's evolution into becoming the *Übermensch*—that is, into something greater.

Chapter 6: The Formula of Humanity

1. M. Currey, *Daily Routines: How Artists Work* (New York: Alfred A. Knopf, 2013), pp. 81–82.

2. Immanuel Kant, *The Metaphysics of Morals*, ed. Lara Denis, trans. Mary Gregor (1797; repr. Cambridge, UK: Cambridge University Press. 2017), p. 34.

3. In his 1795 essay "Towards Perpetual Peace," Kant proposed a world governing body. See Immanuel Kant, *Perpetual Peace and Other Essays*, trans. Ted Humphrey (1795; repr. Indianapolis, IN: Hackett Publishing Company, 1983), pp. 107–44.

4. S. Palmquist, "The Kantian Grounding of Einstein's Worldview: (I) The Early Influence of Kant's System of Perspectives," *Polish Journal of Philosophy* 4, no. 1 (2010): 45–64.

5. Granted, he suggested it hypothetically. Kant didn't believe that animals had will or reason, but he did say that if animals were capable of will and reason, they should be afforded the same rights as humans. Today, there's a strong argument that many animals are capable of will and reason. For a discussion of this, see Christine M. Korsgaard, "A Kantian Case for Animal Rights," in *Animal Law: Developments and Perspectives in the 21st Century*, ed. Margot Michael, Daniela Kühne, and Julia Hänni (Zurich: Dike Verlag, 2012), pp. 3–27.

6. Hannah Ginsborg, "Kant's Aesthetics and Teleology," *The Stanford Encyclopedia of Philosophy*, ed. Edward N. Zalta, 2014, https://plato.stanford.edu/archives/fall2014/entries/kant-aesthetics.

7. The dispute was between "rationalists" and "empiricists," and the book was Kant's most famous work, *Critique of Pure Reason*.

8. Kant sought to establish an entire ethical system with rationality as its God Value. I won't get into the intricacies of Kantian ethics here, as there are many flaws in Kant's system. For this chapter, I have merely plucked what I believe to be the most useful principle and conclusion from Kant's ethics: the Formula of Humanity.

9.   There's a subtle contradiction here. Kant sought to develop a value system that existed outside the subjective judgments of the Feeling Brain. Yet
the desire to build a value system on reason alone *is itself a subjective judgment made by the Feeling Brain.* Put another way, couldn't you say that Kant's
desire to create a value system that transcended the confines of religion was
itself a religion? This was Nietzsche's criticism of Kant. He thought Kant
was a fucking joke. He found Kant's ethical system absurd and his belief
that he had transcended faith-based subjectivity naïve at best and outright
narcissistic at worst. Therefore, it will strike readers with a background in
philosophy as strange that I'm relying on the two of them so much for my
book's argument. But I don't see this as much of an issue. I think that each
man got something right that the other missed. Nietzsche got it right that
all human beliefs are inherently imprisoned by our own perspectives and
are, therefore, faith-based. Kant got it right that some value systems produce
better and more logical results than others due to their potentially universal
desirability. So, technically, yes, Kant's ethical system is another form of
faith-based religion. But I also think that in the same way that science, and
its belief in putting one's faith in what has the most evidence, produces the
best belief systems, Kant stumbled upon the best basis for creating value
systems—that is, one should value that which perceives value above all else:
consciousness.

10.   In terms of minimizing fucks given, Kant's lifestyle choices would
probably make him the world champion. See Manson, *The Subtle Art of Not
Giving a Fuck,* pp. 15–19.

11.   This statement could be interpreted in a number of ways. The first
interpretation is that Kant managed to step outside the subjective space
of Feeling Brain value judgments to create a universally applicable value
system. Philosophers two hundred fifty years later are still arguing about
whether he accomplished this—most say he didn't. (See note 9 in this chapter for my take.)
    The second interpretation is that Kant ushered in an age of nonsuper-
natural views of morality—the belief that morality could be deduced *outside*
spiritual religions. This is absolutely true. Kant set the stage for a scientifically pursued moral philosophy that continues today.
    The third interpretation of this statement is that I'm hyping the fuck
out of Kant to keep people interested in the chapter. This is also absolutely
true.

12.   It is important to point out that I will be applying Kant's ideas in this
chapter in ways he never applied them himself. The chapter is a strange
three-way marriage of Kantian ethics, developmental psychology, and virtue
theory. If that doesn't get your nipples hard, I don't know what will.

13. The developmental framework in this chapter is derived from (and simplifies) the work of Jean Piaget, Lawrence Kohlberg, Robert Kegan, Erik Erikson, Søren Kierkegaard, and others. In Kegan's model, my definition of "childhood" maps his Stages 1 and 2 (Impulsive and Imperial), my definition of "adolescence" maps his Stages 3 and 4 (Interpersonal and Institutional), and my "adulthood" maps his Stage 5 (Interindividual). For more on Kegan's model, see R. Kegan, *The Evolving Self: Problem and Process in Human Development* (Cambridge, MA: Harvard University Press, 1982). In Kohlberg's model, my "childhood" maps his Preconventional stage of moral development (Obedience and Punishment orientation and Instrumental orientations), my "adolescence" maps his Conventional stage of moral development (Good Boy/Nice Girl and Law-and-Order orientations), and my "adulthood" maps his Postconventional stage of moral development (Social Contract and Universal-Ethical-Principle orientations). For more on Kohlberg's model, see L. Kohlberg, "Stages of Moral Development," *Moral Education* 1, no. 51 (1971): 23–92. In Piaget's model, my "childhood" maps his Sensorimotor and Preoperational stages, my "adolescence" maps his Concrete Operational stage, and my "adulthood" loosely maps his later Formal Operational stage. For more about Piaget's theory of psychological development, see J. Piaget, "Piaget's Theory," *Piaget and His School* (Berlin and Heidelberg: Springer, 1976), pp. 11–23.

14. The development of rules and roles occurs in Piaget's Concrete Operational stage and Kegan's Interpersonal stage. See note 13.

15. Kegan, *The Evolving Self*, pp. 133–60.

16. Children do not develop what is called the "theory of mind" until ages three to five. Theory of mind is said to be present when someone is able to understand that other people have conscious thoughts and behaviors independent of them. Theory of mind is necessary for empathy and most social interactions—it's how you understand someone else's perspective and thinking process. Children who struggle to develop theory of mind are often diagnosed as being on the autism spectrum or having schizophrenia, ADHD, or some other problem. See B. Korkmaz, "Theory of Mind and Neurodevelopmental Disorders in Childhood," *Pediatric Research* 69 (2011): 101R–8R.

17. The philosopher Ken Wilber has a wonderful phrase to describe this process of psychological development. He says that later developmental stages "transcend and include" previous stages. So, an adolescent still has his pleasure- and pain-based values, but higher-level values based on rules and roles supersede the lower, childish values. We all still like ice cream, even once we're adults. The difference is the adult is able to prioritize higher, abstract values such as honesty or prudence over his love of ice cream; a

child is not. See K. Wilber, *Sex, Ecology, Spirituality: The Spirit of Evolution* (Boston, MA: Shambhala, 2000), pp. 59–61.

18.   Recall from Emo Newton's Second and Third Laws that stronger, sturdier identities grant us more emotional stability in the face of adversity. One reason that children are so emotionally volatile is because their understanding of themselves is flimsy and superficial, so unexpected or painful events affect them that much more.

19.   Teenagers are obsessively focused on what their peers think of them because they are cobbling together identities for themselves based on social rules and roles. See Erikson, *Childhood and Society*, pp. 260–66; and Kegan, *The Evolving Self*, pp. 184–220.

20.   This is where I first begin to merge Kant's moral system with developmental theory. Treating people as means rather than ends is representative of Stages 2–4 in Kohlberg's theory of moral development.

21.   Albert Camus put it well when he said, "You will never be happy if you continue to search for what happiness consists of."

22.   Again, fusing Kohlberg's Stages 5 and 6 with Kant's "thing in itself" requirement for moral universalization.

23.   According to Kohlberg's model of moral development, by age thirty-six, 89 percent of the population has achieved the adolescent stage of moral reasoning; only 13 percent ever achieve the adult stage. See L. Kohlberg, *The Measurement of Moral Judgment* (Cambridge, MA: Cambridge University Press, 1987).

24.   Just as the adolescent bargains with other people, she bargains with future (or past) selves in a similar manner. This idea that our future and past selves are independent individuals separate from our present-moment perceptions is put forth by Derek Parfit in *Reasons and Persons*, pp. 199–244.

25.   Remember, we derive our self-esteem from how well we live up to our values (or how well we reinforce the narratives of our identity). An adult develops values based on abstract principles (virtues) and will derive his self-esteem from how well he adheres to those principles.

26.   We all require a "Goldilocks" amount of pain to mature and develop. Too much pain traumatizes us—our Feeling Brain becomes unrealistically fearful of the world, preventing any further growth or experience. Too little pain, and we become entitled narcissists, falsely believing the world can (and should!) revolve around our desires. But if we get the pain just right, then we learn that (a) our current values are failing us, and (b) we have the power and ability to transcend those values and create newer, higher-level, more-encompassing values. We learn that it's better to have compassion for everyone rather than just our friends, that it's better to be honest in all sit-

uations rather than simply the situations that help us, and that it's better to maintain humility, even when we're confident in our own rightness.

27. In chapter 3, we learned that abuse and trauma generate low self-esteem, narcissism, and a self-loathing identity. These inhibit our ability to develop higher-level, abstract values because the pain of failure is constant and too intense—the child must spend all her time and energy escaping it. Growth requires engaging the pain, as we'll see in chapter 7.

28. See J. Haidt and G. Lukianoff, *The Coddling of the American Mind: How Good Intentions and Bad Ideas Are Setting Up a Generation for Failure* (New York: Penguin Press, 2018), pp. 150–65.

29. See F. Fukuyama, *Trust: The Social Virtues and the Creation of Prosperity* (New York: Free Press Books, 1995), pp. 43–48.

30. A great example of this phenomenon was the Pickup Artist (PUA) community in the mid-2000s, a group of socially isolated, maladapted males who congregated to study social behaviors in order to be liked by women. The movement didn't last for more than a few years because, ultimately, these were childish and/or adolescent men who desired adult relationships, and no amount of studying of or practice in social behaviors can produce a nontransactional, unconditional loving relationship with a partner. See Mark Manson, *Models: Attract Women Through Honesty* (self-published, 2011).

31. Another way to think about this is the popular concept of "tough love." You allow the child to experience pain because it is by recognizing what still matters in the face of the pain that she achieves higher values and grows.

32. So far I've been ambiguous as to what I mean by "virtues." This is partly because different philosophers and religions embraced different virtues.

33. Kant, *Groundwork to the Metaphysics of Morals*, pp. 9–20.

34. It's important to note that Kant's derivation of the Formula of Humanity was not based on moral intuition, nor on the ancient concept of virtue—these are connections I am making.

35. Kant, *Groundwork of the Metaphysics of Morals*, pp. 40–42.

36. And here is where all three come together. The Formula of Humanity is the underlying principle of the virtues of honesty, humility, bravery, and so on. These virtues define the highest stages of moral development (Kohlberg's Stage 6; Kegan's Stage 5).

37. The key word here is *merely*. Kant admits that it's impossible never to use anyone as a means. If you treated everyone unconditionally, you would be forced to treat yourself conditionally, and vice versa. But our actions toward ourselves and others are multilayered. I can treat you as a means *and* an end at the same time. Maybe we're working on a project together, and I

encourage you to work longer hours both because I think it will help you and because I believe it will help me. Kant says this is fine. It's only when I'm manipulating you purely for selfish reasons that I veer into being unethical.

38. Kant's Formula of Humanity perfectly describes the principle of consent in sex and relationships. Not to seek explicit consent, either from the other person or from yourself, is to treat one or both of you merely as a means in the pursuit of pleasure. Explicit consent means actively treating the other person as an end and the sex as a means.

39. In other words, people who treat themselves as means will treat others as means. People who don't respect themselves won't respect others. People who use and destroy themselves will use and destroy others.

40. Ideological extremists usually look to some great leader. Spiritual extremists tend to think that the apocalypse is coming and that their savior will descend from heaven and pour them a coffee or something.

41. It is possible that all God Values that do not adhere to the Formula of Humanity end in paradox. If you are willing to treat humanity as a means to gain greater freedom or equality, then you will inevitably destroy freedom and equality. More on this in chapters 7 and 8.

42. By political extremism, I mean any political movement or party that is inherently antidemocratic and willing to subvert democracy in favor of some ideological (or theological) religious agenda. For a discussion of these developments around the world, see F. Fukuyama, *Identity: The Demand for Dignity and the Politics of Resentment* (New York: Farrar, Straus and Giroux, 2018).

43. Globalization, automation, and income inequality are also popular explanations with a lot of merit.

Chapter 7: Pain Is the Universal Constant

1. The study this section describes is David Levari et al., "Prevalence-Induced Concept Change in Human Judgment," *Science* 29 (June 29, 2018): 1465–67.

2. Prevalence-induced concept change measures how our perceptions are altered by the prevalence of an expected experience. I will be using "Blue Dot Effect" in this chapter a bit more widely to describe *all* shifting of perception based on expectations, not just prevalence-induced expectations.

3. Whenever I see a news story about college kids freaking out over a campus speaker they don't like and equating offensive speech with trauma, I wonder what Witold Pilecki would have thought.

4. Haidt and Lukianoff, *The Coddling of the American Mind*, pp. 23–24.

5.   Andrew Fergus Wilson, "#whitegenocide, the Alt-right and Conspiracy Theory: How Secrecy and Suspicion Contributed to the Mainstreaming of Hate," *Secrecy and Society*, February 16, 2018.

6.   Emile Durkheim, *The Rules of Sociological Method and Selected Texts on Sociology and Its Method* (New York: Free Press, 1982), p. 100.

7.   Hara Estroff Marano, "A Nation of Wimps," *Psychology Today*, November 1, 2004, https://www.psychologytoday.com/us/articles/200411/nation-wimps.

8.   These three false Einstein quotes were gathered from M. Novak, "9 Albert Einstein Quotes That Are Totally Fake," *Gizmodo*, March 14, 2014, https://paleofuture.gizmodo.com/9-albert-einstein-quotes-that-are-totally -fake-1543806477.

9.   P. D. Brickman and D. T. Campbell, "Hedonic Relativism and Planning the Good Society," in M. H. Appley, ed. *Adaptation Level Theory: A Symposium* (New York: Academic Press, 1971).

10.   Recent research has challenged this and found that extremely traumatic events (the death of a child, for instance) can permanently alter our "default level" of happiness. But the "baseline" happiness remains true through the vast majority of our experiences. See B. Headey, "The Set Point Theory of Well-Being Has Serious Flaws: On the Eve of a Scientific Revolution?" *Social Indicators Research* 97, no. 1 (2010): 7–21.

11.   Harvard psychologist Daniel Gilbert refers to this as our "psychological immune system": no matter what happens to us, our emotions, memories, and beliefs acclimate and alter themselves to keep us at mostly-but-not-completely happy. See D. Gilbert, *Stumbling on Happiness* (New York: Alfred A. Knopf, 2006), pp. 174–77.

12.   By "we," I am referring to our perceived experience. Basically, we don't question our perceptions; we question the world—when, in fact, it's our perceptions that have altered themselves and the world has remained the same.

13.   Throughout this chapter, I don't use the Blue Dot Effect in the exact scientific way that the researchers studied prevalence-induced concept change. I'm essentially using it as an analogy for and example of a larger psychological phenomenon that takes place: our perceptions adapt to our preset emotional tendencies and expectations, not the other way around.

14.   See J. S. Mill, *Utilitarianism*, 2nd ed. (1863; repr. Indianapolis, IN: Hackett Classics, 2001).

15.   P. Brickman, D. Coates, and R. Janoff-Bulman, "Lottery Winners and Accident Victims: Is Happiness Relative?" *Journal of Personality and Social Psychology* 36, no. 8 (1978): 917–27.

16.   A. Schopenhauer, *Essays and Aphorisms*, trans. R. J. Hollingdale (New York: Penguin Classics, 1970), p. 41.

17.   In case you ask me anyway, they did it because splitting the country in two is what produced a resolution to the Korean War the previous decade. The communists got the north. The capitalists got the south. And everyone could go home and be happy. They figured they could just skip the fighting part in Vietnam and go straight to the resolution. Spoiler alert: it didn't work.

18.   Shout out to Boston University's International Relations department. That one's for you.

19.   David Halberstam, *The Making of a Quagmire* (New York: Random House, 1965), p. 211.

20.   Zi Jun Toong, "Overthrown by the Press: The US Media's Role in the Fall of Diem," *Australasian Journal of American Studies* 27 (July 2008): 56–72.

21.   Malcolm Browne, the photographer who took the photo, later said, "I just kept shooting and shooting and shooting and that protected me from the horror of the thing."

22.   In chapter 2, we talked about the Classic Assumption, and how it fails because it tries to suppress the Feeling Brain rather than trying to align with it. Another way to think of the practice of antifragility is like the practice of aligning your Thinking Brain with your Feeling Brain. By engaging with your pain, you can harness the Feeling Brain's impulses and channel them into some productive action or behavior. It's no wonder that meditation has been scientifically shown to increase attention span and self-awareness and reduce addiction, anxiety, and stress. Meditation is essentially a practice for managing the pain of life. See Matthew Thorpe, "12 Science-Based Benefits of Meditation." *Healthline*, July 15, 2017, https://www.healthline.com/nutrition/12-benefits-of-meditation.

23.   N. N. Taleb, *Antifragile: Things That Gain from Disorder* (New York: Random House, 2011).

24.   This is actually an excellent litmus test for figuring out if you should be with someone: Do *external* stressors bring you closer together or not? If not, then you have a problem.

25.   While I'm ripping on meditation apps here, I do want to say that they're good introductions to the practice. They're just . . . introductory.

26.   I am the world's biggest proponent of meditation who seemingly can never actually get himself to sit down and fucking meditate. One good technique a friend of mine, who teaches meditation, taught me: when you're struggling to get yourself to meditate, simply find the number of minutes that's not intimidating for you. Most people try to do ten or fifteen minutes. If that seems daunting, agree with yourself to do five. If *that* seems daunting, lower it to three. If that seems daunting, lower it to one. (Everyone can do one minute!) Basically, keep lowering the number of minutes in your

"agreement" with your Feeling Brain until it doesn't *feel* scary anymore. Once again, this is simply your Thinking Brain negotiating with your Feeling Brain until you're able to align them and do something productive. This technique works wonders with other activities, by the way. Working out, reading a book, cleaning the house, *writing a book* (*cough*)—in every case, just lower the expectation until it stops feeling scary.

27. See Ray Kurzweil, *The Singularity Is Near: When Humans Transcend Biology* (New York: Penguin Books, 2006).

28. Pinker makes the argument that the gains in physical health and safety more than compensate for any increases in anxiety and stress. He also makes the argument that adulthood requires greater degrees of anxiety and stress due to increased responsibilities. That's probably true, but that doesn't mean our anxiety and stress aren't serious problems. See Pinker, *Enlightenment Now*, pp. 288–89.

29. In my previous book, this is how I define a "good life." Problems are inevitable. A good life is a life with good problems. See M. Manson, *The Subtle Art of Not Giving a Fuck*, pp. 26–36.

30. This is why addiction produces a downward spiral: numbing ourselves to pain numbs us to meaning and an ability to find value in anything, thus generating greater pain, and thus inducing greater numbing. This continues until one reaches "rock bottom," a place of such immense pain that you can't numb it anymore. The only way to relieve it is by engaging it and growing.

Chapter 8: The Feelings Economy

1. The story of Edward Bernays in this chapter comes from Adam Curtis's wonderful documentary *The Century of Self*, BBC Four, United Kingdom, 2002.

2. This is *actually* what the ego is, in the Freudian sense: our conscious stories about ourselves and our never-ending battle to maintain and protect those stories. Having a strong ego is actually psychologically healthy. It makes you resilient and confident. The term *ego* has since been butchered in self-help literature to essentially mean narcissism.

3. In the 1930s, I guess Bernays started to feel bad because he was actually the one who made Freud a global phenomenon. Freud was broke, living in Switzerland, worried about the Nazis, and Bernays not only got Freud's ideas published in the US, but popularized them by having major magazines write articles about them. The fact that he is a household name today is largely due to Bernays's marketing tactics, which coincidentally, were based on his theories.

4.   See chapter 4, note 26.

5.   Examples include Johannes Gutenberg, Alan Turing, and Nikola Tesla, et al.

6.   A. T. Jebb et al., "Happiness, Income Satiation and Turning Points Around the World," *Nature Human Behaviour* 2, no. 1 (2018): 33.

7.   M. McMillen, "Richer Countries Have Higher Depression Rates," WebMD, July 26, 2011, https://www.webmd.com/depression/news/20110726/richer-countries-have-higher-depression-rates.

8.   Here's a fun theory about war and peace I came up with: the common assumption about war is that it starts because a group of people are in such a painful situation that they have no option but to fight for their survival. Let's call it the "Nothing to Lose" theory of war. The Nothing to Lose theory of war is often framed in religious terms: the little guy fighting the corrupt powers for his fair share, or the mighty free world uniting to vanquish the tyranny of communism. These narratives make for great action movies. That's because they're easily digestible, value-laden stories that help unite the Feeling Brains of the masses. But, of course, reality isn't that simple.

   People don't just start revolutions because they are subjugated and oppressed. Every tyrant knows this. People who are kept in perpetual pain come to accept the pain and see it as natural. Like an abused dog, they become placid and detached. It's why North Korea has continued as long as it has. It's why the slaves in the United States rarely rose up in violent revolt.

   Instead, allow me to suggest that people start revolutions because of pleasure. When life becomes comfortable, people's tolerance of discomfort and inconvenience lessens to the point where they see even the slightest of slights as unforgivable travesties, and as a result, they lose their shit.

   Political revolution is a privilege. When you're starving and destitute, you're focused on surviving. You don't have the energy or will to worry about the government. You're just trying to make it to next week.

   And if that sounds bananas, rest assured that I didn't just make that part up. Political theorists call these "revolutions of rising expectations." In fact, it was the famed historian Alexis de Tocqueville who pointed out that most of the people who instigated the French Revolution were not the poor masses "storming the Bastille," but rather, people from wealthy counties and neighborhoods. Similarly, the American Revolution was not instigated by downtrodden colonists, but the wealthy landowning elites who believed it a violation of their liberty and dignity to see their taxes go up. (Some things never change.)

   World War I, a war that involved thirty-two countries and killed seventeen million people, started because a rich Austrian dude got shot in Serbia. At the time, the world was more globalized and economically prosperous than at any other time in history. World leaders believed a massive global conflict to be impossible. No one would risk such a crazy venture when there was so much to be lost.

But that's exactly why they risked it.

Throughout the twentieth century, revolutionary wars sprung up across the world, from East Asia to the Middle East and Africa to Latin America, not because people were oppressed or starving, but because their economies were growing. And with their introduction to economic growth, people found that their desires outpaced the ability of the institutions to supply those desires.

Here's another way to look at it: when there's way too much pain in a society (people are starving and dying and getting diseases and stuff), people get desperate, have nothing to lose, say "Fuck it," and start lobbing Molotov cocktails at old men in suits. But when there's not enough pain in a society, people start getting more and more upset by tinier and tinier infractions, to the point where they're willing to become violent over something as stupid as a quasi-offensive Halloween costume.

Just as an individual needs a Goldilocks amount of pain (not too much, but not too little, either) to grow and mature and become an adult with a strong character, societies also need a Goldilocks amount of pain (too much, and you become Somalia; too little, and you become that asshole who loaded up a bunch of trucks with automatic weapons and occupied a national park because . . . freedom).

Let's not forget the whole reason that deadly conflict exists in the first place: it gives us hope. Having a sworn mortal enemy out there trying to kill you is the quickest way to find purpose and be present in your life. It drives us together into communities like nothing else. It gives our religions a cosmic sense of meaning that cannot be acquired any other way.

It's prosperity that causes crises in hope. It's having six hundred channels and nothing to watch. It's having fifteen matches on Tinder but no one good to date. It's having two thousand restaurants to choose from but feeling sick of all the same old food. Prosperity makes meaning more difficult. It makes pain more acute. And ultimately, we need meaning way more than we need prosperity, lest we come face-to-face with that wily Uncomfortable Truth again.

Financial markets spend most of their time expanding as more economic value is produced. But eventually, when investments and valuations outrun actual output, when enough money gets caught up in pyramid schemes of diversion rather than innovation, the financial market contracts, washing out all the "weak money," knocking out the many businesses that were overvalued and not actually adding value to society. Once the washout is complete, economic innovation and growth, now course-corrected, can continue.

In the "Feelings Economy," a similar expansion-contraction pattern happens. The long-term trend is toward pain reduction through innovation. But in times of prosperity, people indulge more and more in diversions, demand fake freedoms, and become more fragile. Eventually, they begin to become feverishly upset over things that merely a generation or two before would have seemed frivolous. Pickets and protests erupt. People start sewing badges on their sleeves and wearing funny hats and adopting the ideological religion du jour to justify their rage. Hope becomes more difficult to find amid the twinkling array of diversions. And eventually, things escalate to the point where someone does something stupid and extreme, like shoot an archduke or ram a 747 into a building, and war erupts, killing thousands, if not millions.

And as the war rages, the real pain and deprivation set in. Economies collapse. People go hungry. Anarchy ensues. And the worse the conditions get, the more antifragile people become. Before, with their satellite cable TV package and a dead-end job, they didn't know what to hope for. Now they know exactly what to hope for: peace, solace, respite. And their hope ends up uniting what used to be a fractured, disparate population under the banner of one religion.

Once the war is over, with the immense destruction etched in their recent memory, people learn to hope for simpler things: a stable family, a steady job, a child who is safe—like actually safe. Not this "Don't let them play outside by themselves" safe.

Hope is reset throughout society. And a period of peace and prosperity resumes. (Sort of.)

There's one last component to this harebrained theory that I still haven't spoken about: inequality. During periods of prosperity, more and more economic growth is driven by diversions. And because diversions scale so easily—after all, who doesn't want to post selfies on Instagram?—wealth becomes extremely concentrated in fewer hands. This growing wealth disparity then feeds the "revolution of rising expectations." Everyone feels that their life is supposed to be better, yet it's not what they expected; it's not as pain-free as they had hoped. Therefore, they line up on their ideological sides—master moralists over here, slave moralists over there—and they fight.

And during the fighting and destruction, no one has time for diversions. In fact, diversions can get you killed.

No, in war, everything is about gaining an advantage. And to gain an advantage, you must invest in innovations. Military research has driven most of the greatest innovation in human history. War not only restores balance to people's hope and fragility, but it is, sadly, also the only thing that dependably resets wealth inequality. It's another boom/bust cycle. Although, this time, instead of it being financial markets or a population's fragility, it's political power.

The sad fact is that war is not only an inherent part of human existence; it's likely a necessary by-product of our existence as well. It's not an evolutionary bug; it's a feature. Of the past 3,400 years, humans have been at peace for a total of 268 of them. That's not even 8 percent of recorded history.

War is the natural fallout from our erroneous hopes. It's where our religions get tested for their solidarity and usefulness. It's what promotes innovation and motivates us to work and evolve.

And it is the only thing that is consistently able to get people to get over their own happiness, to develop true virtue of character, to develop an ability to withstand pain, and to fight and live for something other than themselves.

This is likely why the ancient Greeks and Romans believed virtue necessitated war. There was an inherent humility and bravery required not just to succeed in war, but also to be a good person. The strife brings out the best in us. And, in a sense, virtue and death always go hand in hand.

9.   The "commercial age" is just something I made up, if I'm being honest. Really, what it refers to, I suppose, is the postindustrial age, the age when commerce began to expand into producing unnecessary goods. I think of it as similar to what Ron Davison calls the "Third Economy." See R. Davison, *The Fourth Economy: Inventing Western Civilization*, self-published ebook, 2011.

10.   This is a well-documented issue. See Carol Cadwalladr, "Google, Democracy, and the Truth About Internet Search," *Guardian*, December 4, 2016, https://www.theguardian.com/technology/2016/dec/04/google-democracy -truth-internet-search-facebook.

11.   Not only is this sort of surveillance creepy, but it's a perfect illustration of a tech company treating its customers as mere means rather than ends. In fact, I would argue that the feeling of creepiness is itself the sensation of being treated as merely a means. Even though we "opt in" to these services that harvest our data, we're not fully knowledgeable and/or aware of this; therefore, it feels as though we haven't consented. This feeling of nonconsent is what makes us feel disrespected and treated as a means, and is therefore why we get upset. See K. Tiffany, "The Perennial Debate About Whether Your Phone Is Secretly Listening to You, Explained," *Vox*, December 28, 2018, https://www.vox.com/the-goods/2018/12/28/18158968/facebook-micro phone-tapping-recording-instagram-ads.

12.   You know, because torture doesn't scale well.

13.   Barry Schwartz, *The Paradox of Choice: Why More is Less* (New York: Ecco, 2004).

14.   There's a lot of data that shows that this is incredibly effective. It's another example of working *with* your Feeling Brain (in this case, scaring it

into doing the right thing) rather than against it. This is so effective that the researchers who originally studied it created a website called stickk.com that allows people to set up these agreements with their friends. I actually used it to hit a deadline with my last book (and it worked!).

15. He ended up losing to the chess grandmaster because, as it turns out, chess has hundreds of millions of potential moves, and it's impossible to map out an entire game from beginning to end. I'm citing no source because this hack job doesn't deserve more attention.

16. Robert Putnam, *Bowling Alone: The Collapse and Revival of American Community* (New York: Simon and Schuster, 2001).

17. F. Sarracino, "Social Capital and Subjective Well-being Trends: Comparing 11 Western European Countries," *Journal of Socio-Economics* 39 (2010): 482–517.

18. Putnam, *Bowling Alone*, pp. 134–43.

19. Ibid., pp. 189–246.

20. Ibid., pp. 402–14.

21. This is a more ethical and effective way at looking at liberty. Take, for instance, the controversies in Europe over whether Muslim women can wear hijabs. A fake-freedom perspective would say that women should be liberated *not* to wear a hijab—i.e., they should be given more opportunity for pleasure. This is treating the women as a means to some ideological end. It is saying that they don't have the right to choose their own sacrifices and commitments, that they must subsume their beliefs and decisions to some broader ideological religion about freedom. This is a perfect example of how treating people as a means to the end of freedom undermines freedom. Real freedom means you allow the women to choose what they wish to sacrifice in their lives, thus allowing them to wear the hijabs. For a summary of the controversy, see "The Islamic Veil Across Europe," *BBC News*, May 31, 2018, https://www.bbc.com/news/world-europe-13038095.

22. Unfortunately, with cyber warfare, fake news, and election meddling possible through global social media platforms, this is truer than ever before. The "soft power" of the internet has allowed savvy governments (Russia, China) to effectively influence the populations of rival countries rather than having to infiltrate the countries physically. It only makes sense that in the information age, the world's greatest struggles would be over information.

23. Alfred N. Whitehead, *Process and Reality: Corrected Edition*, ed. David Ray Griffin and Donald W. Sherburne (New York: The Free Press, 1978), p. 39.

24. Plato, *Phaedrus*, 253d.

25. Plato, *The Republic*, 427e and 435b.

26. Plato's "theory of forms" appears in a number of dialogues, but the most famous example is his cave metaphor, which occurs in *The Republic*, 514a–20a.

27. It's worth noting that the ancient definition of *democracy* differs from the modern one. In ancient times, *democracy* meant that the population voted on everything and there were few to no representatives. What we refer to today as democracy is technically a "republic," because we have elected representatives who make decisions and determine policy. That being said, I don't think this distinction changes the validity of the arguments of this section at all. A decline in maturity in the population will be reflected in worse elected representatives, who were Plato's "demagogues," politicians who promise everything and deliver nothing. These demagogues then dismantle the democratic system while the people cheer its dismantling, as they come to see the system itself, rather than the poorly selected leadership, as the problem.

28. Plato, *The Republic*, 564a–66a.

29. Ibid., 566d–69c.

30. Democracies go to war less often than autocracies, affirming Kant's "perpetual peace" hypothesis. See J. Oneal and B. Russett, "The Kantian Peace: The Pacific Benefits of Democracy, Interdependence, and International Organizations, 1885–1992," *World Politics* 52, no. 1 (1999): 1–37. Democracies promote economic growth. See Jose Tavares and Romain Wacziarg, "How Democracy Affects Growth," *European Economic Review* 45, no. 8 (2000): 1341–78. People in democracies live longer. See Timothy Besley and Kudamatsu Masayuki, "Health and Democracy," *American Economic Review* 96, no. 2 (2006): 313–18.

31. Interestingly, low-trust societies rely more on "family values" than do other cultures. One way to look at it is that the less hope people derive from their national religions, the more they look for hope in their familial religions, and vice versa. See Fukuyama, *Trust*, pp. 61–68.

32. This is an explanation of the paradox of progress that I haven't really dived into: that with every improvement of life, we have more to lose and less to gain than before. Because hope relies on the perception of future value, the better things become in the present, the more difficult it can be to envision that future and the easier to envision greater losses in the future. In other words, the internet is great, but it also introduces all sorts of new ways for society to collapse and everything to go to hell. So, paradoxically, each technological improvement also introduces novel ways for us to all kill one another, and ourselves.

Chapter 9: The Final Religion

1.   In 1950, Alan Turing, the father of computer science, created the first chess algorithm.

2.   It turns out that it is unbelievably difficult to program "Feeling Brain" functionality into a computer, while Thinking Brain functionality has long surpassed human capacity. That's because our Feeling Brains operate using our entire neural networks, whereas our Thinking Brains just do raw computations. I'm probably butchering this explanation, but it's an interesting twist on the development of AI—just as we perpetually struggle to understand our own Feeling Brains, we also struggle to create them in machines.

3.   In the years that followed Kasparov's initial defeat, both he and Vladimir Kramnik battled a number of top chess programs to draws. But by 2005, chess programs Fritz, Hydra, and Junior shellacked top grandmasters in matches, sometimes not even dropping a single game. By 2007, human grandmasters were given move advantages, pawn advantages, and choices of openings—and still lost. By 2009, everybody just stopped trying. No point.

4.   This is true, although not literally. In 2009, the mobile chess software Pocket Fritz beat Deep Blue in a ten-game match. Fritz won despite having less computing—meaning it's superior software, not that it's more powerful.

5.   Michael Klein, "Google's AlphaZero Destroys Stockfish in 100-game Match," Chess.com, December 7, 2017, https://www.chess.com/news/view/google-s-alphazero-destroys-stockfish-in-100-game-match.

6.   Shogi is considered more complex because you are able to take control of your opponent's pieces, leading to far more variations than even with chess.

7.   For a discussion of the potential mass unemployment caused by AI and machine automation, check out the excellent E. Brynjolfsson and A. McAfee, *Race Against the Machine: How the Digital Revolution Is Accelerating Innovation, Driving Productivity, and Irreversibly Transforming Employment and the Economy* (Lexington, MA: Digital Frontier Press, 2011).

8.   K. Beck, "A Bot Wrote a New Harry Potter Chapter and It's Delightfully Hilarious," *Mashable*, December 17, 2017, https://mashable.com/2017/12/12/harry-potter-predictive-chapter.

9.   J. Miley, "11 Times AI Beat Humans at Games, Art, Law, and Everything in Between," *Interesting Engineering*, March 12, 2018, https://interestingengineering.com/11-times-ai-beat-humans-at-games-art-law-and-everything-in-between.

10.   Much in the same way that today it's almost impossible to imagine life without Google, email, or cell phones.

11.   Evolutionarily speaking, humans gave up a lot to make their big brains possible. Compared to other apes, and especially mammals, we're slow, weak, and fragile and have poor sensory perceptions. But most of what we lack in physical capabilities was given up to allow for the brain's greater use of energy and longer gestation period. So, really, things worked out in the end.

12.   See D. Deutsch, *The Beginning of Infinity: Explanations that Transform the World* (New York: Penguin Books, 2011).

13.   Well, technically, most of these didn't exist until we came along, but I suppose that's partly the point.

14.   Haidt, *The Righteous Mind*, pp. 32–34.

15.   The self-hatred is a reference to the inherent guilt that comes with existence, discussed in chapter 4. The self-destruction is, well, self-evident.

16.   Such outlandish scenarios are actually quite serious and covered well in Nick Bostrom's *Superintelligence: Paths, Dangers, Strategies* (New York: Oxford University Press, 2014).

17.   Michal Kranz, "5 Genocides That Are Still Going on Today," *Business Insider*, November 22, 2017, https://www.businessinsider.com/genocides -still-going-on-today-bosnia-2017-11.

18.   "Hunger Statistics," Food Aid Foundation, https://www.foodaidfoun dation.org/world-hunger-statistics.html.

19.   Calculated by author based on statistics from National Coalition Against Domestic Violence, https://ncadv.org/statistics.

About the Author

MARK MANSON is the *New York Times* and international bestselling author of *The Subtle Art of Not Giving a Fuck* (with over five million in sales in the United States alone). His blog, MarkManson.net, attracts more than two million readers per month. Manson lives in New York City.